Claudia

Claudia

A Path Well Traveled

The Autobiography of
Claudia Gilligan
1947 - 2022

Cover Art by Claudia Gilligan
Poems: The Calf-Path by Sam Walter Foss
And: High Flight by John Gillespie Magee
Are in the public domain.

*First Edition

ISBN: 978-1-958328-02-6

DEDICATION

This book is dedicated to my daughter,
Tami Mel-lene (Chilcoat) Anderson,
and my son, Andy Martin Chilcoat,
with sincere apologies for all I did not
know when you were growing up.

It is also dedicated to all my grandchildren,
great-grandchildren, nieces, nephews
and all those who will come in the future.

Remember: It's about the journey,
not the destination.

Other books
by Claudia Gilligan

Claudia's Poems Along The Way

And

Claudia's I'm Too Lazy To Be A Vegan: But Why We All Should Be!

Acknowledgments

This book has been a very interesting endeavor as I was working to piece together years of memories and get it in the right order. Before my sister, Teri, passed, she was one of my sources for getting the chronology straight. It would have been a much more difficult task had she not been there for me.

My husband Tom has been a great help in editing, and his ability to remember dates and details from the past thirty-five years is better than anyone I know. He has always been there to encourage me when I felt exhausted from reliving some of the emotions from the past.

I would also like to acknowledge my Kinesiologist, who deals in Neuro-Emotional Technique (as well as many other techniques), Dr. Marvin R. Terry, DC, of Orlando, Florida, for keeping my arm working and my emotions in check throughout this difficult process. He is truly a miracle worker.

And, of course, special acknowledgment is in order for my niece, Sandie Kirwin, for her heroic efforts to do the final editing, to find those last few errors that I could read a dozen times, but could never see. She further wrote the foreword for this book which is embarrassingly complimentary.

Thank you, one and all.

Table of Contents

Foreword i

1. Indianapolis, Indiana 1

2. Foster Care 21

3. Salina, Kansas 31

4. Inglewood, California 35

5. Hawthorne, California 41

6. School and Church 55

7. A Kid's Life 73

8. Pack and Go 81

9. Tempe, Arizona 95

10. Life Changes Again 99

11. Out of the Frying Pan, Into the Fire 103

12. Perris, California 111

13. The Dentist 117

14. A New Life 119

15. Second Marriage 131

16. Modeling and More 143

17. Strange Stuff....157
18. The End of Marriage Two....169
19. Getting Another Divorce....179
20. Starting Over....183
21. Husband Number Three....193
22. Phoenix, Arizona....201
23. Husband Number Four....209
24. Another New Beginning....219
25. My Search Continues....237
26. The Lessons I Learned....253
27. Moving On....263
28. Marriage Number Five....275
29. I Want My Black Belt....285
30. Europe and Weird Fun....293
31. Thirty-Four and Counting....307
32. Simi Valley and Treasure....327
33. Moving Right Along....345
34. Next!....351
35. A Rusty Motorcycle....363
36. A High IQ Man....371

37. A Moment in Time....................385
38. Another Generation....................399
39. Your Alligator Mouth....................411
40. 911 Attack and More....................429
41. All New Things....................433
42. You Get a Stent and You Get a Stent....................441
43. Retirement at Last....................451
44. No More Cheese!....................465
45. Change, Change, Change....................475
46. The Bucket List....................503
47. The Covid-19 Pandemic....................507
48. Seventy-Five and Counting....................519
Filmography....................531

Foreword

It is difficult for me to remember that I know the details of my Aunt's early life because her sister is my mother. It's difficult because it does not match her, there is no victim here, or an emotionally trashed human, like she should be. Is it because of her spirit? Another spirit? LOL, or maybe from Gramps.

Yes, my Aunt Claudia, so powerful, mesmerizing, genius, hilarious, addicting, who can do anything, and is attractive to everyone. You adore her or are jealous as hell of her.

I am so lucky to have lived parallel to her, learning things so incredible about life. I'm talking about self-help seeking. I've watched as she has lived a life of searching, wondering, wanting to know self, God, and everything in between and I've been fortunate to have been in the classroom! WOW!

Her story is so powerful. This story gives you a gut-wrenching firsthand feeling of what it was like to be a woman during a time when women were just second class, there to serve, nothing more. Well, not her! She rose above every situation that tried to bring her down, every single one.... I watched. In this book, she tells you exactly how she did it.

I don't know a stronger person, a stronger woman. She IS the result of keeping her agreements. The kind of agreements you make with yourself, and others, what is more important?

There aren't enough hours for me to tell you how great she is and besides, this is her book.

Although I do want to tell you my very favorite memory of my Aunt.

She went out with me a few times to my usual Hollywood hangs, way back in the nineteen-hundreds, kids! (haha). ALL my famous rocker friends were always asking me, "WHO IS THAT?"! She was so stunning, like a movie star dripping in diamonds and fur, so classy and SO, SO BEAUTIFUL!

I'm glad she wrote this book, even the parts that make me cry. You just can't believe someone is going thru this bullshit in life.

It's a book with history about my family as well, I cherish this information and hope the next generations will as well. I cherish my Aunt Claudia too, she's one of the best humans I've ever known! This is her story, but it is a story we can all learn from.

Sandie Kirwin
Las Vegas, Nevada
May 11, 2022

Chapter 1
Indianapolis, Indiana

The only place I can think to start is before I, Claudia Marlene Gilligan was born, which was in 1947, just two years after World War II had ended.

My parents met and married during World War II. My dad, James Emmett Gilligan, was a Second Lieutenant and a pilot in the United States Air Force, and I'm sure he cut a handsome figure in his flyboy uniform. My dad was born in Indianapolis, Indiana, on July 4, 1920, so he would be a little over 22 1/2 years old when my parents married on February 7, 1943.

My father enlisted, in the Air Force, on August 2, 1941, when he was 21 years old. Documentation shows he was 5' 7 1/2" tall and weighed 140 pounds. He is white, with black hair, grey eyes and a scar on his right cheek. He looked a bit like Clark Gable with a thin black mustache.

My mother, Pearl Helen Bodfield, was a simple farm girl from Nebraska. She was only about four foot six inches tall, weighed about 90 pounds and wore a size four shoe. She had beautiful, curly, dark, reddish-brown hair and was very exotic looking with strikingly blue eyes and a tiny button nose. Mother was born on August 5, 1919, so she would have been 23 years old when they married.

Mother had been married previously at age 18 to a man named William O. Cochran, aged 21, in Kenton, Oklahoma, on January 23, 1937, and they had a child who died of "SIDS" (Sudden Infant Death). The baby's name was Delores Agnes Cochran, born October 27, 1937. She died on February 22, 1938. She was three months twenty-six days old. Mother never talked much about her ex-husband, but as I understand it, they broke up because of the baby's death. All Mother would say was that she found the baby dead in her crib.

My parents met in the USO club, and I think my father's description of my mother was accurate throughout her entire life: "She was just a cute little girl that wanted to dance."

My parents were just two ordinary people. I don't think their story was so much different than many who lived through the war. I would ponder who they were and what their "back story" was for many years of my life.

My dad's parents were pretty wealthy for the time. They were Irish and English Catholics.

Grandpa Gilligan was a second-generation American. His father, John Martin Gilligan, was born in 1835 in Loughrea, Ireland, and came to America during the potato famine. He and his brother, Patrick Gilligan, came to America in about 1848, at about age 13, with their cousin, Mary Gilligan, who was charged with their safety for the passage to the new world.

Born on January 1, 1888, my Grandpa Gilligan started as a "blacksmith." He owned two blacksmith shops in the Indianapolis area that later became automobile garages. He later became a bootlegger during prohibition, and which is where I think his money came from. When I was young, he owned a company that delivered coal.

On my father's side, my grandmother, Agnes Adora Worland, was born June 6, 1897, and was the daughter of William Edward Worland, born in 1873, and Nadie Adella Thompson, born in 1877 who died in 1902 at age 25. My grandmother was raised by a stepmother, Anna Marie

Will, who my dad knew as "Grandma Worland."

My Grandparents lived in a big old three-story mansion in Indiana, with a winding staircase and a giant stained-glass window above it. They had paid servants. My grandma Gilligan was of English extraction. She was stoic, proud, and did not talk a lot, but it was usually worth listening to when she did. She put up with my grandfather, who she must have loved deeply or was just stuck with since she was Catholic and, in those days, one just did not divorce…

Grandpa Gilligan was Irish, hot-tempered, and pretty much a no-nonsense man. He was also a drunk. He seldom spoke unless he was drinking, and then he was loud, belligerent, and obnoxious. I was afraid of him and steered clear as much as possible.

My dad had worked for his father, and I guess my grandfather was a pretty harsh taskmaster. My dad tells the story of a time when he was 17 years old, and was fixing an engine in the automobile garage my granddad owned, and the engine fell on my dad's arm breaking it. It made grandpa so mad that he wouldn't take dad to the doctor until he finished fixing the engine. Whether this is true or not, I do not know, but after all that I've gone through in life, I would believe people are capable of anything.

Dad had the advantage of his parent's money. He was well-educated, had some college, and should have had a bright future. Alas, the war changed so much for so many.

Having enlisted in 1941, my father became a pilot in the Air Force. He graduated from flying school with a second lieutenants' commission. He received "advanced training" at the flying school at Williams Field, Chandler, Arizona, and then went on to teach other pilots to fly bombers. I have seen a newspaper article where he blew out a tire on takeoff but safely landed the airplane. I know he had missions in Italy and Africa because he had pictures of himself in those countries.

One of his favorite stories, in later life, was of one student who became airsick and vomited into a bag. Green in the face, the young man, thinking to dispose of the bag, went to a small camera chute and dropped the bag into it. Of course, the air pressure pushed the bag back up into the cockpit, and there were "strings of puke" flying everywhere. My dad told this story so colorfully that it nearly made one sick to hear it.

The family my mother came from is a confusing mix of genetics. Trying to track their family tree has been a real challenge. She said she was mostly Irish, with a bit of French, Canadian, German, and English, and just a bit of "savage" that Mother said was Cherokee.

I have had my DNA analyzed, and I am 99.7% Northwestern European, which translates to: 47.5% French & German, 46.4% British & Irish, 0.4% Scandinavian, 5.4% Broadly Northwestern European. Then there is trace ancestry which is 0.2% Angolan & Congolese and 0.1% Indigenous American. My grandparents were primarily Irish and English on my father's side, so I guess the rest comes from my mother. The DNA report also states that I have more "Neanderthal" DNA than 64% of those tested. Well, maybe that explains a lot!

I never met my mother's parents, that I recall. My grandfather on my mother's side was, Loran Andy Bodfield, who's WW1 draft card (1917) shows that he worked for Claude Smith French, who was my great-grandfather on my mother's side, so that is where he met and married Claude's daughter, Verda Lolita French, my grandmother.

Though Mother always professed that we were Cherokee, I have, along with having my DNA tested, I have researched on Ancestry.com and have found no Cherokee anywhere in our tree.

Mother was not very sophisticated. Not to say she was not smart, just not sophisticated. She had lived the first eighteen years, of her life, on a farm. She only went two years to high school, but she did educate herself, and she was very intelligent. She had four brothers and one sister. I don't remember ever seeing her parents and only once met one of her brothers. Her family was not very close. It explains a lot of how my mother was toward us kids. I never remember her hugging me or any close contact with her.

My parents had four children together. Teresa (Teri) Verda was born August 13, 1945, I was born March 21, 1947, James Patrick (Pat) was born December 28, 1949, and Dennis Edward was born October 2, 1951. All of us were born in Indianapolis, Indiana, just after the end of World War 1l. There was no birth control other than the "Rhythm Method" in those days. I don't think my mother wanted so many kids, but about every eighteen months, she popped one out.

My parent's marriage wasn't a good marriage; it was a war marriage. So many people clung to each other out of fright and loneliness, not knowing how long they would live. Tomorrow was no longer a promise. The men went off to war, and the women stayed home and waited. And when the war ended, many married couples didn't know who each other was.

My parents fought, it seems like, every night. We would lie in our beds, terrified of the noise and physical fighting. All kids of dysfunctional marriages think it is their fault, and I was no exception.

Many things were going on in the world at that time. In 1947 Harry S. Truman was President of the United States. There was no Vice President because Truman had taken over when Franklin D. Roosevelt died of a cerebral hemorrhage, on April 12, 1945.

Bacterial infections such as pneumonia and diarrhea were, up until the mid-1940s, the number one cause of human death in the developing world. Folk medicine had used some type of antibiotic medicine for many millennia. The ancient Egyptians applied a piece of moldy bread to infected wounds. But real understanding of infection and bacteria didn't come until the 20th century. The first "antibiotics" were made widely available in about 1945.

I was one of the lucky ones who survived my childhood because of the new antibiotics. My very first memory was when I was about two years old, and I had "Measles, Whooping Cough, Pneumonia, and dehydration." I only know what I had because later in life, my mother told me and showed me where she had written it in my "baby book." I just remember being in a bed with bars and my mother walking away. I stood with my arms out, begging her to come back. When she didn't, I flopped down in the bed and cried myself to sleep. That would become the story of my life.

I know my mother did not get along with her mother-in-law. I remember a time when all four of us kids were put in a taxicab and sent to my grandmother's house. I vividly remember the taxicab driver's chest was sunk in, deformed, and he had a wheezing breath. Naturally, we thought he was some kind of a monster, and we were scared to death.

My mother had sent us to my grandmother's house, unexpectedly, and my grandmother wasn't having any of it. My grandmother put us right back in the cab and sent us back. Of course, she didn't know how frightened we were of the cab driver, and in the battle between my mother and her mother-in-law, they just never noticed what our experience was.

Other memories I have from that time are of dad, his brothers, and his father, drunk, angry, and fighting in the front yard of one of their houses. They weren't just yelling. They were physically hitting each other, and all of them were bleeding. I can tell you that this is a very frightening thing for children, and it changes who they are. I was quiet, shy, and did not want to disturb anyone lest they start fighting. I felt like a ghost, observing the world from the shadows.

Despite my grandfather and the "men" in the family fighting and drinking, I have some good memories of my grandmother's house.

I remember sitting in a hole in the middle of the table, eating. My mind's eye thought I was in the middle of a big dining table, but many years later, I figured out what that must have been when I bought a high chair for my daughter. The highchair was about three feet square, and the chair was at the back so that it appeared to be a table all around. Funny how little eyes interpret what they "think" they see.

Grandma Gilligan's house was a three-story mansion with large, mahogany crown molding. There was a curved staircase with a gold, upholstered bench halfway up where you could sit beneath the stained-glass window. I sometimes fell asleep on that bench looking at the beautiful window.

There was a big grand piano in the front room and two television sets, side by side. My grandfather would watch both TV sets at one time. I don't know what he watched because there were only a couple of channels in those early days of TV. In the days when television was so new, I remember an airplane writing in the sky, "Gilligan's buy Muntz TV," when we got our first one. We couldn't afford a refrigerator, but we had a TV. I will explain that later.

Today kids have huge flat-screen color TVs that hang on the wall and weigh very little. They don't realize that it was only a short time ago that television became a household item. Televisions had been produced in small quantities before World War II, but they had only been about seven inches wide, and you had to have a magnifying glass in front of them to even see the black and white picture. To change channels or turn the volume up, you had to use the "knobs" on the front of the set. There were no remote controls until the 1960s.

In 1947 (the year I was born), televisions were very small, and only about 0.5 % of households owned one. A 12-inch black and white TV costs about $445 ($5,661 in 2022). What we take for granted today and what fills so much of our day was not an item when I was little. But, by the mid-1950s, it would start to be a regularly used item.

I remember being put down for a nap, at my grandmother's house, in a big bed, in a big room, with blue lights in the chandelier. My sister, Teri, didn't have to take a nap, and I fought it. She would wait until she thought I was asleep and then close the door. The doors of grandma's house were big mahogany doors that you could lock with a "skeleton key." I would get up and look through the keyhole and see her having a "tea party" with her dolls in the next room. I was furious! To this day, it is very hard to close a door on me when I am sleeping, without waking me. I guess I'm still a little afraid of "missing out on something!"

Teri and I had a doll whose wig had come off. I guess I have to explain that one a bit. In those days, dolls with "rooted" hair had not yet been invented. Dolls had a glued-on wig if they had hair at all. Most dolls only had painted-on hair. We had a doll with a "real" synthetic hair wig. At any rate, the doll's wig had come off, and we used to play "hide the doll wig" with it. Children can make a game of anything.

One time, one of us must have hidden the wig and then we were called to go home because we couldn't remember where the doll's wig was hidden. Each time, after that, when we went to grandma's house, we would look for the wig, but we never found it again. Our poor doll had globs of hard glue sticking up on her head, which would have been pretty frightening looking when you think about it.

I think Grandma's house is the most prevalent in my memory of that time because it was relatively happy despite the drunken fights. Kids don't know what "normal" is. Whatever their life is about is "normal "to them.

I remember, at a very young age, going fishing with my mom and dad to a place called, Fall Creek" in Indiana. Whenever they caught a "sunfish," they put it in a bucket. When they had several fish in the bucket, they told Teri and me to take it upstream and dump the fish back into the water.

I know it took both of us to carry the bucket, and I have no idea how far "upstream" was. We took the bucket, but when we went to dump it, I went in too. I panicked and was thrashing around. I felt like I was drowning. Then dad pulled me out by one arm. That is about all I remember, but it was enough to give me a fear of water.

At my mother's house, a few of the memories from that time are of being very hungry and afraid.

This was back in the days when many people still had an icebox instead of a refrigerator. An icebox was a little cabinet made of wood with two (or more) compartments. It was lined with steel and painted white. It had a compartment in the top for a block of ice and the rest for your food. The "Iceman" came around daily and if you needed ice, you would put a sign in the window. The iceman would knock on the door, and if you didn't answer right away, he just came in and yelled out, "Iceman." He would then put the ice in the icebox and leave.

I'm sure kids these days have no clue what it was like before everyone had these big refrigerators. There was no need for a freezer because there were no frozen foods to speak of. The first frozen dinner wasn't invented until 1953. If you ate meat, you bought it fresh, and there were seldom leftovers.

Milk was delivered to the home in the 1940s and early 1950s. The milkman delivered milk in glass bottles and left it on the doorstep in a little rack that could accommodate several bottles. You left the empty bottles in the rack for him to take back to be reused. Most people had a "standing" order of what they wanted. If you wanted something different or extra, you would usually put a note in one of the bottles or the rack for the milkman. The milkman came around once a week to collect the money for the amount of product you had ordered.

The milk in those days was not "homogenized." Milk settled to the bottom and the cream came to the top, which most people poured off for their coffee. There were no flavored creamers like we have today. To me, the cream was the best-tasting milk in the world. I remember climbing up onto the kitchen table and getting a bottle of that milk. I couldn't have been more than four years old. I pulled the cardboard stopper out of the top, and with shaky hands, tipped it up and drank that cream right off the top. Oh, that was good. I don't know if I was shaking from hunger or the weight of the bottle. That's all I remember of that incident, and I think I only remember it because I was very hungry, and my mother was furious with me when she discovered what I had done. I don't know where my mother was when I did this, but then, I have very little recollection of her unless something was wrong.

The late 1940s and early 1950s were so different than today. I don't know if there was as much crime as there seems to be today, because we never heard of crime. Newspapers, radio, or gossip over the back fence was, the only way anyone found out about anything. Newspapers had mostly "Local" news. There were only 10 minutes of TV news, no internet, and not many people had phones which were a whole different thing from what they are today. At any rate, no one locked their doors and everyone felt safe, at least from burglars.

This was just after World War ll had ended. All the soldiers came home and started families. Every neighbor was just like your parent and you minded what they said. Coming out of the war, it seems like neighbors were closer and friendlier to each other.

Cameras at the time were boxy kind of thing that used "film." You held it to your eye and looked through the "view finder" to take a picture. After taking the picture, you turned a knob which pulled the film forward for the next "shot." Most pictures were taken outside in the daytime, because most people did not own a "flash attachment." A flash attachment was a round, aluminum bowl kind of thing that a bulb was placed in. When you took the picture, the bulb flashed simultaneously, creating enough light for the "exposure." The bulb was disposable and was only good for one "flash" shot. The film had about twelve "exposures" on it. It was called "exposures" because the "shutter" would open for a fraction of a second and the film would be "exposed."

The film had to be taken to a store for "processing." You had to pay for "development" and the number of pictures you wanted. People usually only took pictures on special occasions like birthdays, Christenings, Easter, and Christmas. Most people did not take many pictures because it was a costly luxury.

If you could not afford to get your pictures developed right away, you put the roll of film in a drawer until you had the money. I have often come across old rolls of film in a box stored somewhere. Having one developed could be a delight to find pictures of Christmas past or some other holiday, or it could be a costly disappointment to find that whatever had been on it was lost forever. For this reason, there are very few pictures of my childhood.

I remember a cousin named "Pierre." Pierre was the son of my grandmother's sister, Ada. He was a few years older than us kids. We spent the night at his house, and Pierre told us that unless we slept with our legs curled up, and our feet tucked in, the rats would bite off our toes. I slept in that fetal position for much of my life, and it still is the most comfortable position for me. I'm very fond of my toes.

I have a memory of being in a house, though I couldn't tell you what it looked like. Someone came to the door, and I remember my mother telling us to hide and not make any noise. We all crouched down behind the sofa. We didn't know why we were hiding, but I knew my mother's voice was very serious. I later figured out that it was a bill collector she was dodging.

My mother was an upholsterer and seamstress by trade, and she owned an upholstery shop. It was called "Peggy's Upholstery." I recollect that it was a big shop. There were lots of sofas and chairs that we, sometimes, got to rip off the old fabric so my mother could replace it. We must have spent a lot of time there because most memories of my mother are in that shop.

One day, a man with a big belly came into the shop. He wanted to look around at what Mother had for sale. She went back to work and he looked around. I guess I was following him. He carried a newspaper held in front of him, and at some point, he moved the paper and his penis was sticking out of his pants. He looked me right in the eye and smiled. I ran and told my mother. Mother was furious with him and I guess she ran him off. I remember I was scared to death because I did not know what an adult penis was. I just knew it was ugly. It is funny how ideas change with age!

Another memory of the upholstery shop is my mother's booze. She kept it on a table behind some furniture. Teri and I found it and drank some. It was like fire in my mouth. We must have drunk a bit of it because my mother noticed that some was missing and lined us up to smell our breath. I don't remember the outcome of the "sniff test," but I don't remember getting beaten for it. Maybe that was my first drunk. It was certainly not my last.

At times, I went with my mother to a fabric warehouse to buy upholstery fabric. She would leave me in the car. She told me that if I got out of the car, one of the big trucks with hoses on the back would "suck" me up and she would never see me again. I laugh now when I see a big semi-truck because the hoses are so small, but to my little mind, back then, it was possible. I would hide on the floor in the back seat until she came out. I was terrified.

And lastly, from that time, I remember my mother's friend, Joann. who babysat us. We went to her house one day, and while playing outside, I wandered off and met a little black girl down the street. I didn't think anything of it because my grandmother had a black woman who worked for her, and she was very nice, and while I may have noticed her color was different, I didn't make a distinction.

We were playing on the sidewalk in front of the little girl's house with our dolls and having a great time when suddenly, someone grabbed me by my hair and pulled me up and shook me. At first, I didn't know what had grabbed me. I just tried to hold onto my hair as I was dragged down the street. It was Joann, and she was screaming at me.

"What are you doing playing with that dirty little N...!"

I think I was in shock because I had no idea what she was screaming about. She dragged me back to her house and whipped me.

My great grandfather who came over from Ireland.
John Martin Gilligan Born: May 10, 1835
Died: February 17, 1904 Died at age 68
Married: Mary L. Buhmiller October 18, 1877

My grandmother on my dad's side.
Agnes Adora Worland (Gilligan) Picture Circa 1910 - age 13.
Born: June 16, 1897
Died: July 2, 1989 Died at age 92

Left:
My grandfather, Albert Martin Gilligan And grandmother Agnes Adora Gilligan.

My dad's parents 1965

I am age 18

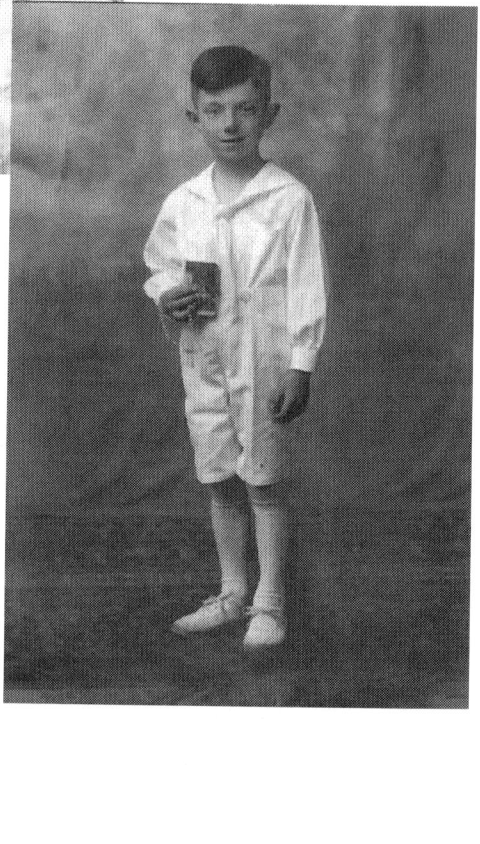

Right: My dad
James Emmitt Gilligan
About 1927
Communion
Age about 7 years

My grandmother on
my mother's side.
Verda Lolita French.

As a young woman

Verda Lolita French
(Rudolph)
As a senior

Born:
December 18, 1899

Died:
February 11, 1977
Died at age 77

Left: My parent's wedding picture February 7, 1943

Pearl Helen (Peggy) Bodfield age 23
James Emmett Gilligan age 22

Mother: Born August 5, 1919
Died: July 5, 1983
Died at age 64

Father: Born July 4, 1920
Died April 21, 1992
Died at age 72

Right: Claudia 1947
Age 6 months

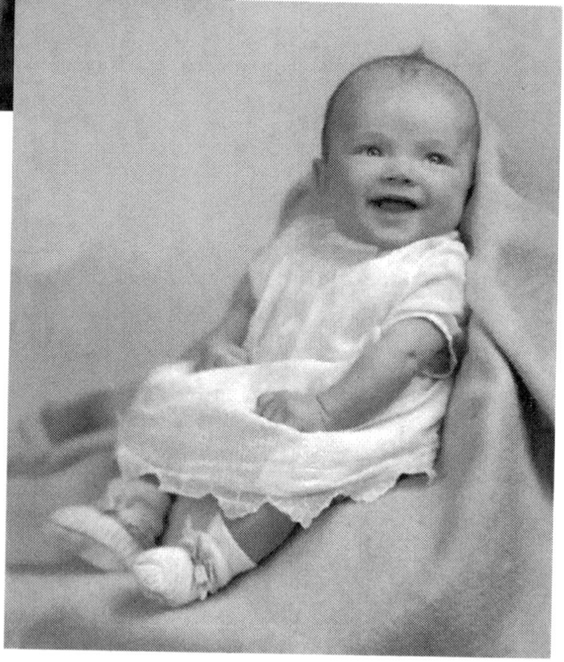

Left:
Claudia 1948
Age 1 year

Right:
Teri age 3
Claudia age 1

Claudia Gilligan

Left: 1949
Claudia 2 years 6 months old
Teri 4 years old

Right: 1951

Pat: 2
Claudia: 3 1/2
Teri: 5

Chapter 2
Foster Care

From court documents, I know that my parents split up on February 15, 1952. At that time, our ages were: Teri, six and a half, Me, four years 10 months, Pat was two years and Dennis was four months old. My father started divorce proceedings against my mother sighting, "Cruel and Inhumane Treatment." The definitions for these grounds are: 1. Physical attacks upon a spouse. 2. Constant screaming, profanity or other verbal abuse. 3. Publicly flaunting a relationship with another man or woman. 4. Intentional refusal by a spouse to have sexual relations that physically affect the other spouse.

Records also show that my father had been discharged from the Air Force on October 21, 1945, but re-enlisted on March 15, 1953.

After that, I remember being in foster care homes. These were homes we stayed in, day and night. My mother was supposed to pay the people, from the support money my father paid to her, but she usually kept the money for herself. That is probably why I remember several different homes.

I have seen the records of my father's payments to the Juvenile Court, so I know he upheld his responsibilities, paying $30 per week or about $120 a month (about $1,265 per month in 2022 money). That was not a lot for four kids. From what I have found on the internet, my father's pay would have been about $250 to $289 per month, so that would have been a little less than half of his pay. I also have letters my father kept from different places we stayed, stating that they had not been paid by my mother.

In December of 1953, we went to stay with a woman named "Madge." She was big, what today would be considered obese, and smelled a bit "rancid." Her husband, who worked in a toilet paper factory, was short and bald, but he wasn't around much. Madge had a big "razor strop" and wasn't afraid to use to whip us. A razor strop was a soft piece of leather about eighteen inches long with harder leather pieces at each end. It was used to straighten and polish the blade of a straight razor, which many men used to shave with, in those days.

I went to school, as I was over five years old. I remember going to the school bus stop, and the reason I remember that is because it was snowing and bone cold. I don't think I noticed it on the way because we played around in the snow. I just remember standing at the bus stop and Teri saying we had missed the bus. She didn't want to go home because we would get a whipping. I was so cold my bones hurt. I cried and begged until Teri finally took us back home, and we got whipped with the razor strop, and that was that. To this day, I hate, hate, hate, the cold.

I'm not sure if it was that same house or a different one, but I remember being locked in a basement. I don't remember Teri or Dennis being there though they must have been. I remember Pat and two little boys that I recall were German. I don't remember why I thought they were German, but that is my recall. The basement was dank and smelled musty. There was only one bare, dim, little light bulb hanging down from the ceiling. I was scared and hungry.

We didn't get much to eat, and one of the little German boys kept pointing to a barrel of apples and saying, "Pol-tink." We couldn't reach them. I have never found the word in any translation and have no idea if it meant apple or if the boys were even German. I just remember that we weren't allowed to eat the apples, and the little boy was crying.

Pat, who was almost four years old, and I crept up the wooden staircase, looked through a crack in the door, and saw the family sitting at a table eating what looked like a big turkey dinner. We could smell the food through the crack. It made our mouths water and our little bellies rumble. We hugged each other and crept back down the stairs. I don't know the circumstances; I just know it was a very cruel thing to do to little kids, and it would affect me for many years. I think that it instilled, in me, that I wasn't worth much.

Records show that we were there from December 9, 1953, to March 1954, about three months. I think the dinner Pat and I observed was probably Christmas dinner.

A letter from a juvenile court judge and dated December 9, 1953, to my father, who was stationed at F.E. Warren A.F.B. Wyoming states:

Dear Lt. Gilligan:

We wish to inform you that Mrs. Gilligan has placed the children in the home of Mrs. Masden at 320 E. 31st Street. The arrangements are that Mrs. Masden will be caring for the children full-time.

On November 19, 1953 the Court Order of October 8, 1953 was modified and the support money is now sent to Mrs. Pearl Gilligan at 1126 Eugene Street.

From the time the children were moved from Mrs. Wilson's home until they were placed with Mrs. Masden, we had several complaints that the children were neglected.

Since you are planning to be home in the near future, it is suggested that you make some permanent placement for your children through either the Marion County Department of Public Welfare or Catholic Charities Bureau in order to prevent any other complaints about the children being neglected.

If we can be of service to you in the future, please feel free to get in touch with us.

Yours Very Truly,
Harold N. Fields - Judge

The next place, we were taken to, was Fred and Mary Potter's house. It was a potato farm, and it was out in the rural Indiana countryside near Danville, Indiana. I remember my mother taking us there with a man I can only assume was Leroy Ostby, her third husband. (They were never really married) At any rate, we went to "the farm" around the first of March, 1954

The Potter's farm consisted of a very old rundown white house surrounded by potato fields. The house was dirty, and the furnishings were old and dilapidated. There was also a long, dark, dank barn that hadn't been used in years. I have looked it up on the internet and I have located what I think is the house and find that it was built in 1915.

The Potters had two daughters who were about my and Teri's age. I have little memory of them except for one time that my mother came to the farm and brought us big Easter baskets. Easter was on April 18th in 1954. It was the first Easter basket I can ever remember having. We were so excited.

That was the only time that I remember my mother coming back to the farm, and it was the last time I saw her until I was about ten years old. At any rate, when my mother left, the baskets were taken away from us and given to the Potter's daughters, Jeannie and Juney. I don't remember if we got anything from the basket or not; I just remember being very disappointed, angry, and thinking it wasn't fair.

My grandmother Gilligan came to the farm once. She brought us some toys and costume jewelry. I don't remember if we were allowed to keep the items or not; I just remember grandma coming to the farm.

On the farm, my sister, Teri, went to school, but I was not allowed to. I don't know why because the records show that I was over six years old.

I spent my days chasing wild cats and kittens in the old barn. I would dress them in doll clothes. I don't know that I had a doll, but I had a doll buggy, and I remember a little bonnet that I put on the cats. Once I caught them, I swaddled them in a dirty little blanket so tight they couldn't move. It was a tussle, but that was the only way I could keep them from scratching me. Then, I would tie the little bonnet on them. I wheeled them around the farm until they would finally wiggle out of the blanket and run away with the bonnet still on. Later, I would find the bonnet somewhere on the farm, and I would go hunt for another wild cat. They scratched the hell out of me, but even at that age, I was very determined.

One day Fred came into the barn and talked very nice to me. He was interested in what I was doing and talked to me about the wild cats I was chasing. The next thing I knew, he had me by the neck, pinned against the wall. I was facing the wall and could see through the boards to the potato field outside. He held me by the neck, got very close to my ear, and whispered, "You just hold still and you won't get hurt. Do you understand?" I nodded, yes. God, I remember his hot, wet, stinky breath even now. I stood still and faced the wall looking out through the cracks in the boards at the potato field. The leaves of the potato plants swayed gently in the breeze. I guess he jacked off while fingering me with the other hand. It is not that it hurt, but his hot breath and his threats were what was traumatic. When he was finished, he whispered, "If you tell anyone about this, I will kill you and bury your body in the field where no one will ever find you." I was left terrified, shaken, and confused.

After that, I tried to hide from Fred, but sometimes he seemed to show up out of nowhere. I had stopped going into the barn for the cats and tried to stay close to Mary, but she was not having it and would "shoo" me out of the house.

The farm had electricity but did not have plumbing. We had an outhouse. For those who don't know what an outhouse is, it is a place to go to the toilet, which consists of a hole dug in the ground with a little house built above it. The house is about four feet by four feet, and the hole is about four or five feet deep. There is a seat built over the hole in the back portion, which consists of about a 12 to 18-inch piece of wood with one or two big holes cut into it for your butt. Ours was a two-seater. There were no toilet seats, just the holes. Looking down from the top, it seemed like a long way to the bottom and it smelled bad.

Fred followed me to the outhouse. He said he would stuff me down the hole if I made any noise. I think he was afraid Mary might find us. After that, I was afraid to go in there alone, so I would always try to wait until Teri came home from school and get her to go with me. Sometimes, I would squat in the field and pee, terrified that Fred would pop out of one of those potato plants.

At night, you never went outside to go to the toilet. Instead, you had an empty "coffee can" that we called the "honey pot," in our bedroom. Rich people had "chamber pots," but poor people had "honey pots." I still remember the smell. I always tried to sneak up to our room to use the coffee can so Fred wouldn't catch me in the outhouse.

I remember holding my brother, Pat, over the hole in the outhouse so that he could go potty. His little arms clung desperately to my neck. "Don't let me fall, sister, please don't let me fall." I don't think people who have never been in a "real" outhouse can fathom how much trauma it can put upon a little child when they have to use one. Pat was so afraid of the outhouse that he sometimes wet his pants. Then he was really in trouble, but if he couldn't find me or Teri, to help him, it was better than the terror of the outhouse alone.

As I said, we had no indoor plumbing to speak of on the farm. We did have a pump handle in the kitchen. At least you didn't have to go outside for water, but you still had to pump it up into a bucket.

I don't know how often we bathed, but I remember we had a big aluminum tub that was brought in and put on the kitchen floor that Mary filled with bucket after bucket of water. She also heated some water on the stove to make the water, not warm, but a little better than cold. The oldest kids bathed first. Then down in age. Probably because the little ones did not know dirty water from clean. The last kid had the coldest, dirtiest water, which is where the phrase, "don't throw the baby out with the bathwater," comes from. With six kids on the farm, it was probably some pretty dirty water for the littlest kid, which was my baby brother, Dennis.

One day, Teri and I did something "bad." I have no recall of what it might have been. For punishment, we had to go and pick a switch off a bush and switch ourselves on the legs with it until we cried. It had to be a particular size switch. Mary had to approve of it. Mary and Fred could truthfully say that THEY had never hit us. This is kind of torture for a kid. Teri, however, had no problem. A couple of whacks and she was crying for real. At that time, I had stopped crying, at least, I had stopped crying in front of people. I kept hitting myself and I would pretend to cry, but I had no tears left. My legs were bleeding before the punishment was finished. Maybe I was born stubborn, which, I have been accused of for most of my life.

Teri and I weren't the only ones who went through trauma. I remember my brother, Pat, who could only have been about four years old. I guess he was a little messy when eating and it pissed them off, so they put his food on the floor and made him lick it up like a dog. Oh, the memory of my poor little brother on his hands and knees eating off the floor. I don't know how often it happened or if it was only once, but it is still just a very sad and emotional memory for me.

Next, I remember the day they killed the chicken. That's what you do on a farm. If you are going to eat chicken, you kill a chicken! I don't know why we kids witnessed this, but we did. Fred picked up a chicken by the head and swung it in a circle and its body popped off. The chicken fell to the ground, but it wasn't dead. It ran, aimlessly, because it had no eyes without its head. Blood pumped out its neck. The chicken ran right for my brother, Pat. It seemed that no matter which way Pat ran, the chicken followed. Pat was screaming and so terrified. I grabbed him and tried to pick him up. Pat climbed up me in a blind panic. The chicken, finally, fell over dead. Fred and Mary thought it was so funny. How much terror and trauma can a child handle, and how unthinking are adults?

In later years, my brother, Pat, who became a Vietnam veteran, would be diagnosed with Post Traumatic Stress Disorder (PTSD) by the Veteran's Hospital, but they denied it was from the war and laid it to what happened in his childhood.

My baby brother Dennis suffered the most. He was about two years and four months old. I remember him sitting on a little wooden potty chair and Mary smacking him in the face because he wouldn't go potty. He cried and cried and finally couldn't catch his breath. His little face turned blue, and his eyes were big and scared. "Stop it, stop it" I yelled. "You're killing my brother!" The only thing I could think to do was attack her, and the only thing I could reach was her leg. I grabbed Mary by the leg and bit her as hard as I could. She tasted like dirt, blood, and salt. She grabbed me and threw me off of her onto the floor, but she stopped hitting Dennis. Dennis had no breath left and fell forward onto the floor. He laid there on the linoleum floor with a big red ring around his butt from sitting on the pot for so long. Mary picked him up by one arm, shook him, and then threw him at me. "You take care of him," she yelled. He was OK, but not OK. How could he ever be OK? How could any of us ever be OK? We were like animals in a violent jungle that just did not stop.

When I was in my thirties, my dad showed me letters from Mary Potter saying that my mother had not paid her in months. That might have been why they seemed to hate us so much, but it does not excuse the abuse we suffered.

Having read letters about our stay at the Potter's, I can see that no one knew what was going on there. My dad was thoroughly fooled by what they said. In one letter, my father said he wanted to make permanent arrangements for us to stay with them. I write this here because I want people to know how fooled they can be. Maybe there are good people in this world, I wouldn't trust many of them with my children.

While I held resentment for Fred and Mary for many years afterward and often had fantasies of how I would call them to account, it never happened. One day, I realized that they had probably been dead for many years.

I don't know how long we were on "the farm" I think I was so traumatized that I just tuned out, turned off, and endured.

One of my last memories was of me hiding under the aluminum

washtub in the backyard. I was curled up and shaking because Fred was looking for me. I was praying to God to get us out of that place. "Please, Please, Please," I pled. "I promise I'll be good the rest of my life." And God heard my prayers, and they were answered.

1952 Claudia 4, Pat 2 1/2, Teri 5 1/2, Dennis 1
Before going to foster care

Chapter 3
Salina, Kansas

One day, a blue 1953 Ford car pulled into the farm's driveway. A man and a woman got out. I didn't recognize either of them. It turned out that he was my father. I hadn't seen him in a couple of years, probably since I was about three, and I just did not remember him. The woman was his girlfriend, Docia Biley, (Dodie). They had come to get us.

Oh, thank you God, you answered my prayers. I was determined to be as good a child as anyone could want.

We moved to Salina, Kansas. My dad was stationed at Smoky Hill Air Force Base. We lived in a big white house, and my stepmother was wonderful. She brushed my hair, and we always had clean clothes, and she took good care of us. Best of all, I went to school.

We were so happy. I remember my little brother, Dennis, dancing around and around to Jim Reeves's song "Bimbo."

Bimbo, Bimbo, where ya gonna go-e-o
Bimbo, Bimbo, whatcha gonna do-e-o
Bimbo, Bimbo, does your mommy know-ooo
That you're goin' down the road to see a little girleo.

Dennis would clap his hands and dance in a circle wiggling his butt, and giggling. He was precious.

And then one day, I came home from school, and Dodie was in the kitchen making coffee and crying.

"Mommy, what's wrong?" I asked.

"Oh, Claudia," she said, "Dennis died."

Dennis had a cancerous tumor on his kidney. That's why he could never be potty trained. There wasn't a lot they could do back in 1954. They had removed one of his kidneys, but he still died. I think the poor little guy died from all the stress and trauma he had lived through. I think he was just done with this life. In a way, he died alone. He didn't know his father or Dodie. His sisters and brother, the only ones he knew, were not allowed to be with him. He only had sterile doctors and nurses. His mother did not even know he had died and would not for years. How very tragic and very, very sad.

And the world shifted!

We went to my brother's funeral. I'm not sure if I truly understood the death of a human at age seven. I certainly don't think it is good for little kids to go to a funeral and view a dead body at that age, especially if it is a sibling. That was probably the worst trauma I have ever experienced.

Walking up to the little casket with Teri and Pat, hand in hand, we stopped and stared at Dennis, who was always so animated. He was eerily still. I reached up and put my hand on his chest. All I felt was cold, cold, again the freezing cold. The cold from his little body crept up my arm and into my heart. I will never forget that day. Dennis was about two years and ten months old and had known little more than misery his entire life.

That was the day I became angry at God and myself. I remembered the pleading and bargaining I had done under that tub in the backyard on the Potter's farm, and God had betrayed me!

I also felt guilty because somehow, I decided that we had left the farm because Dennis had gotten sick; otherwise, dad would not have come for us. In my twisted, traumatized world, I felt I had caused his cancer. That was how God had answered my prayers.

Being a good Catholic, my dad tried getting a "Mass" for my brother, but the church refused because my dad had not attended church recently, and neither had Dennis. This was the end of the church in my dad's mind. He said he would never set foot in a church again. To the best of my knowledge, he never did.

I had gone to Catholic school at some point. I started out being left-handed. The nuns would hit my hand with a ruler if I tried to write with my left hand. This would be unheard of today, but it was very serious back then. Left-handed people were thought to be possessed by the devil. That seems ridiculous today, but it wasn't questioned then. I didn't know if I was possessed by the devil or not, but I knew I had gone through hell. My little brain couldn't accept this. I started my own rebellion against religion.

I remember we had to pray for Sister Mary Agnes' knees (or whatever her name was). I guess she had arthritis very badly and could barely walk. Every day we prayed for Sister's knees. I started asking impertinent questions. Like, "why doesn't God fix Sister's knees, aren't they supposed to be married and can't he perform miracles?"

Nothing made sense to me after Dennis' death. I was seven years old, and I was just left with a lot of sadness, anger, loneliness, and guilt. People were mean and couldn't be trusted, and all I thought was that "When I grow up, things will be different."

That is the kind of thing a child tells them self so that they can keep going. I would always go to a fantasy place where everything was different and pretty and new and fun. Without hope of something better, how can one endure? Had I known what my future would be at that time, I think I might have just given up. I lived in a fantasy world and became a hopeless optimist in life, because without that, I had nothing.

Salina, Kansas. After dad rescued us from the farm.
The last days of Dennis' life. Teri 9, Dennis 3, Pat 5, Claudia 7

Chapter 4
Inglewood, California

On August 6, 1954, my dad received an honorable discharge from the Air Force. He had only served one year and four months on a four-year contract, but I think he got out because of Dennis' death and because Dodie was pregnant.

My dad bought a 50-foot trailer, loaded us all in the car, and moved us to Inglewood, California. We lived in the "Hollywood Park Trailer Lodge" on Century Boulevard.

My dad's court papers show that his divorce was not final until April 29, 1955, but he and Dodie were married on November 17, 1954.

Shortly after that, Dodie gave birth to a little girl, Jeananne (Ja-nee-nee), on December 30, 1954. We called her "Nini" (nee-nee) for short. She was so adorable. I, of course, wanted to put her in my doll buggy and put a bonnet on her, but Dodie was too protective for that.

Life was good for a while on Century Blvd. We no longer went to Catholic School. Walking to Whelan Elementary School, that we now went to, we met a man named Ray McGavin. Ray owned the "Shady Acres" trailer park down the street from us. We met him on the way home from school. I know he was up there in years, probably in his 70s when we met him. He had no children, and we basically had no supervision, so we were an instant match. At first, I was very leery of him. I did not trust men …. Or women for that matter. I hung back behind Teri. He was never pushy and allowed me to be in the background, and over time I came to trust him. He gave us more attention than anyone else ever had. My dad never seemed to be around, and Dodie now had Nini to occupy her.

Ray taught us our numbers; Addition, subtraction, and multiplication. Each day we stopped on our way home from school and he would get out the "flashcards" he had made from his business cards. The problem was on one side; the answer on the other. If you got the answer right, you got a penny. If you got the answer wrong, you lost two pennies. I loved it. I don't remember much about school, but I do remember learning math from Ray.

It seems strange that we would be allowed to go to a stranger's house at the ages; of 8, 7, and 5, but that's what we did. I can't even imagine letting kids that age walk home by themselves, but times were different back then. I think my dad did go and talk to Ray when he found out what we were doing, but I guess he decided Ray was OK because we continued to go.

In school, we always started our day off by standing, with our right hand over our hearts, and reciting the "Pledge of Allegiance" to our flag. We were taught to love our country because it was so special, and I think we believed it. There was a certain pride that we took in our flag.

Dodie was a Jehovah's Witness and did not believe in celebrating Christmas or any other day. Dad, on the other hand, did believe in Christmas. I guess Dad insisted that Dodie give us presents for Christmas, but they were mostly underwear, sox or something we needed anyway. I remember one year we did get a big box of 24 games for the three of us. I know we had a little Christmas tree, but Christmas just wasn't ever what I thought it should be. My friends at school got a load of stuff, and I always got disappointed. Dodie would tell me I was a greedy little urchin.

Come on; I was seven! I vowed that when I grew up, Christmas would be wonderful!

Ray was a great friend to us kids and always saw that we had a real Christmas gift.

After what I had gone through as a child, I didn't let on to wanting much. Dodie derided me if I did, and I had learned that people could hurt you if they knew what you liked. But I remember the year Ray got me a beautiful, Ballerina doll. I think that was the best gift I ever had. I thought she was the most beautiful doll I had ever seen. I could not hide the joy and guarded my doll jealously, because I was afraid someone would take it from me as they did the Easter baskets.

One other Christmas, I remember getting a coat. What was great about the coat was that there was a $5.00 bill in the pocket when I put it on. When I discovered it, my dad winked at me because he had put it there. That was a huge amount of money in those days. (About $52 in 2022 money) I went to the "Thrifty Drug Store" and bought a crystal teardrop necklace and some toys. The crystal sparkled in pastel hues, and I was mesmerized by its beauty. I'm sure I still have it in my treasures, somewhere.

July 17, 1955 Disneyland opened, and we had heard so much advertising on TV about it, but we could never afford to go. Sometime in the summer of 1956, Ray came to our rescue and took me, Teri, Pat, and a couple of our friends to the park. At that time, it cost $1.00 each to get into the park, and then it cost $2.50 each for a ticket booklet for about eight rides. The tickets were labeled A, B, C, D, and E. The "E" ticket was for the best rides. Ray paid to have a picture taken to commemorate the day and then bought souvenirs and food.

I know we would never have made it to Disneyland if it weren't for

Ray. He put out a lot of money for us, and I am grateful that this kind man cared enough to take under his wing three little kids that desperately needed someone to care.

Disneyland was another world to me. I remember how happy and amazed I was. It was such a beautiful place. My whole life was an E-ticket ride that day. The one thing that I really, really wanted was pair of Mickey Mouse ears with my name embroidered on them, but I was too shy, embarrassed, and ashamed to ask for them. I didn't want to seem like the ungrateful urchin that Dodie always accused me of being.

I know I thanked Ray for what he did for us or gave me, but somehow, I don't think I was ever grateful enough or told him enough how important he was in my life. I carry, in my heart, so much love and gratitude for him to this day. Without him in our life, I genuinely think we would have been much different. He somehow, at least temporarily, restored some of our faith in people. After Ray passed away a few years later, my life certainly had an empty spot. Thank You, Ray, for all your kindness. It truly made a difference. I can only hope you got as much joy out of our relationship as I did.

One year, the Shriners Club took us to a grand Christmas celebration. I think one of our neighbors must have turned our name in as being poor. The Shriners gave us food, candy, and a Christmas present. I was delighted. They made that Christmas a very happy one. The celebration was held at the Shrine auditorium and it was packed with kids. Somehow, I never realized that all those other kids were poor just like us.

Today, at Christmas, whenever I see a Shriners Club member collecting money for children, I give them everything I have in my wallet. I never know when I will see them, but that first member I see gets everything in my purse. That is just my way of saying Thank you!

Left:
1955 Claudia age 8

Right:
1956 Claudia age 9

1955
Dad with kids.

Teri 10
Nini 4 months
Pat 6
Claudia 8

Ray McGavin with kids at Disneyland 1956

Ray, Linda, Teri 11, Marty, Pat 7, Claudia 9

Chapter 5
Hawthorne, California

We only lived in the trailer for about a year or so, and then Dad and Dodie bought a house at 526 S. Ramona Avenue in Hawthorne, California, when I was in the third grade. It was a small white house with two bedrooms and one bath, but Dodie and dad made the dining room into a bedroom for themselves. Teri and I shared one tiny bedroom that had bunk beds. Nini and Pat had the other bedroom. I think Dodie spent most nights in Nini's room because I seldom remember her being in the dining room bed with dad.

Dodie worked as a typist, and dad was an insurance claims adjuster. They had not gotten along since just after Nini was born. Dad was drunk a lot of the time, and I think Dodie carried most of the burden. I didn't realize it at the time, of course, but looking back, I can see it. I can only imagine what it was like for her to be saddled with three heathen kids when she just wanted to spend time with her only daughter.

I guess I was "self-centered." I worried about things related to me. I worried about a lot of things. Like, "what would happen to us if they got a divorce? Would we be sent to another foster home?"

About this time, I remember seeing a movie about a little boy that couldn't speak but could sing a song. "I'm a happy merry butterfly, with a flit flut flut as the flutter flies, tra la la la la, tra la la la la, la la." For some reason, that song made me happy, and, after that, whenever something bad happened, instead of being in the experience, I would sing that in my head. "I'm a happy merry butterfly".... and I would skip away, happy.

I tuned out as best I could, but under my shy, introverted exterior, I worried a lot and I never felt worthy. I never felt wanted.... Well, for the most part, I wasn't.

The kids in school thought I was Japanese because of the shape of my eyes. They would walk on the back of my shoes and shove me, calling me a dirty "Jap." I have absolutely no Japanese in me. My DNA has established that. I would eventually grow into my eyes, and men would think I looked exotic, but for now, I was just an outcast.

The school further terrorized kids. In 1945 the USA dropped the first Nuclear Bombs on Hiroshima and Nagasaki, Japan killing more than three hundred and fifty thousand people. Because of this, we were afraid someone would bomb us. The USA devised a "Duck and Cover" drill for the schools. This was some serious stuff. What made them think that lying crouched on your knees with your head down under your desk and your hands over your neck could possibly do anything in the event of a nuclear blast? Did anyone see those films on what a nuclear blast does? There was so much stuff in our young environment to be fearful of that underneath everything we might present to the public, there was a whole lot of fear. I would have rather that they did not tell us about the "bomb" that might take us out. Let it just surprise us because we would all die anyway.

We ran the streets when not in school, playing out until the street lights came on as most kids did. We rode skateboards made out of old skates nailed to a 2 x 4 x 12-inch piece of wood. We jumped rope, played Red Rover, and hopscotch.

The street we lived on was a hill with about a six percent grade. We would ride the skateboard from the top of the hill down to the bottom.

About halfway down was a fence of our neighbor's yard and opposite the fence, next to the street was a telephone pole. There was about a two-foot clearance between them. If you didn't quite clear the pole, you took a nasty fall and usually skinned both knees. No, we didn't wear helmets and knee pads because they hadn't been invented yet, as far as I know.

Another place we rode our skateboards was on the school roof. Pat and I would climb up a fence and somehow get on top of the school. The roof was a big flat area. I have no idea why we decided that was a good idea, but we did. I don't know how we survived!

I remember the day I lost my hopscotch lager. It was a round, rubber disk called a "Hoppy Taw." It devastated my eight-year-old world. Toys weren't easy to come by, and I cherished my Hoppy Taw. I was sitting on the porch all deflated when my dad came home from work and found me.

"What's wrong, Claudi?" he asked, mocking my sad face.

Pouting, I said, "I lost my Hoppy Taw."

Now, I'm sure he had not a clue of what a Hoppy Taw was, but when my dad was sober, he was one of the kindest people in my world, and that day he was sober.

"Well," he said, "I guess you'll have to buy a new one."

"I can't," I replied, "I don't have any money!"

"Well," he said, "let's see if we can fix that. And with that, he upended and walked on his hands up and down the walkway letting the change fall out of his pockets. When he got to the steps, he stood up and said, "Will that fix it?"

"Oh yes," I squealed as I grabbed up the coins.

That is one of my favorite memories of my dad. Most days, he was mean, but that day he was "super dad." A few years ago, I came across a "Hoppy Taw" in a retro toy store, and I had to buy it because it reminded me of the good times and that day with my dad.

One day, a salesman came to our door. My dad was drunk. The salesman was selling "hard plastic dinnerware." The man gave his pitch about how unbreakable the dishes were. Dad grinned and said, "So, my kids can't break them?"

"Nope!" he assured my dad.

Dad took three of his plates and handed one to each of us kids. "Break that," my dad commanded. No problem, we hit them on the porch rail and the plates snapped in two. If my dad told you to do something, you did it ... especially if he was drinking. Dad took the broken plates, handed them back to the salesman, and laughed.

"Unbreakable .... Right!" my dad said and walked back into the house. The poor man went off shaking his head.

Television had now become an evening thing. There was now a load of Western shows like: Cheyenne, The Restless Gun, Tales of the Wells Fargo, Legends of Wyatt Earp, and Wagon Train. There were kids' shows like: Lassie, Rin Tin Tin, Howdy Doody Time, Sheriff John, and Chucko the Clown. There were also the "Sitcoms" (situation comedy) like: I Love Lucy, December Bride, and The Phil Silver Show. In 1955 through 1958 was my favorite, Mickey Mouse Club. I so wanted to be like Annette Funicello and sing and dance.

TV was not on all night, but signed off at midnight and came back on at 6:00 a.m. I remember the sign-off poem that was recited called "High Flight" written by John Gillespie Magee Jr.

High Flight

Oh! I have slipped the surly bonds of earth
And danced the skies on laughter-silvered wings;
Sunward I've climbed and joined the tumbling mirth
Of sun-split clouds - and done a hundred things
You have not dreamed of
- wheeled and soaring and swung
High in the sunlit silence. Hov'ring there
I've chased the shouting wind along and flung

My eager craft through footless halls of air.
Up, up the long delirious, burning blue,
I've topped the windswept heights with easy grace
Where never lark or even eagle flew -
And while with silent lifting mind I've trod
The high interspaced sanctity of space,
Put out my hand and touched the face of God.

Behind the reading of the poem flew the grand old flag of the United States of America with soft music accompanying in a whisper.

I can remember hearing the poem narrated and getting goosebumps. It was strong, patriotic, and magical. Sadly, the writer of the poem, John Gillespie Magee, an American, who had joined the Royal Canadian Air Force (before the U.S. had joined the war) as a fighter pilot in 1940 was killed in a mid-air collision over England on December 11, 1941.

Somehow this poem touched me and gave me a lasting love of poetry.

After the poem finished, a "test pattern" came on with a picture of an Indian in full headdress. The entire test pattern was used for adjusting cameras and your TV set when needed. Until TV stations started broadcasting twenty-four hours a day, (sometime in the early 1980s) the test pattern was used all over the world.

Telephones were a bit different in those days also. Of course, this was before computers, cell phones, and the like.

Being "On the phone" was a luxury to most ordinary people. There was, usually, only one phone in a house, and it was attached to the wall by a short wire cord. You didn't pick it up and walk around with it.

The telephone consisted of two parts hooked together: the "base unit" and the "handset." The base unit was like a square black box with four points sticking up that was called "the cradle." The cradle was what you put the "headset" on when it was not in use. The headset looked like it was half of a dumbbell with a wire attaching it to the base unit, and then the base unit was attached to the wall with another wire. You put one end of the headset to your ear and spoke into the other end of it. The front of the base unit had a circular plate called a "dial" with holes around the edge for your fingers. The dial had a circle of paper behind it, and in each hole of the dial, there was a number and three letters, except for the first and last hole. Starting on the top right and going around counter clockwise were the numbers 1 through 9 and the last one on the bottom right was zero (for the operator). Letters two through nine also had three letters above the numbers. To "dial" a number, you put your finger in the hole of the corresponding number (or letter) and pulled (rotated) the dial to the right until it hit a "stop," which was a small curved piece of metal.

Telephone numbers were different then as well. While "area codes" were invented in 1947, you did not need them for local calls. If you had to make a long-distance call, you usually had to call an "operator" by dialing zero, and she would dial it for you with the area code.

To make a "local" call, you picked up the headset, listened for a "dial tone," and then dialed the number you wanted. Most phones were on a "party line," which means that some of your neighbors used the same line as you. If someone was on your line when you picked up the phone, you could hear their conversation. Politeness dictated that you hung up and tried again later. If it was an emergency call you needed to make and someone was on the line, you let them know and asked them to hang up. There always seemed to be a very talkative person who was always on the line.

You had to dial a seven-digit number for the police or fire department in an emergency. In 1968 in the United States, the first (speed dial) 911 call was made in Haleyville, Alabama by Alabama Speaker of the House Rankin Fite and answered by U.S. Rep. Tom Bevill. It took a while for the 911 emergency number to catch on.

In the 1950s, phone numbers were assigned to an "exchange," and each exchange had a name and serviced about 10,000 people. So, part of your "number" was the exchange name, which is why phones had letters and numbers on them. As I recall, our phone number was "Orchard" 19492 or OR19492. Today it would be 671-9492.

For the most part, kids did not use the phone. However, occasionally we would call a random number and say things like, "Is your refrigerator running?" And when they said, "Yes," we would say, "Then you better go and catch it!" and we would hang up. I recently saw that used in the movie, "The Grinch," and it brought back fun memories of childhood days.

Another prank we played was "Ding Dong Ditch." That is where you collect all the dog poo or snails you could find and scoop them into a brown lunch sack. Then you put it on a neighbor's porch, lit the bag on fire, rang the bell, and then ran like hell. When the person opened the door, they tried to stomp the fire out, and of course, out came the poo or slimy snails.

At the back of our backyard was a small area between two of our neighbors' fences, out of which we made a "clubhouse." It was about three feet between the fences and ran about fifteen feet long. We spent many hours between those two fences. We were sometimes hiding from dad when he was on the rampage, sometimes hiding from Dodie and chores, and sometimes we met there just because it was fun.

I remember collecting chicken bones from one of our neighbors' yards and lining them up on the backboard of the fence. Lots of people had chickens in their yard back then. The neck bones of the chickens look like Tiny little skulls. I pretended that the sculls were little fairy skulls. Sometimes when I was very mad or sad, that was who I talked to. There's just nothing like ranting at a chicken bone to make you feel better.

One thing we kept in the "Clubhouse" was our marbles. We played marbles in the backyard. We dug holes under the big old olive tree. We played "Poison," a game where if you got your "shooter" in the hole, you got to collect all the marbles within a hands distance around the hole. Teri was the best, but then, she was the oldest and had the biggest (longest) hands. We spent hours, in the dirt, playing with our marbles.

We also, sometimes, slept out in the backyard. If dad was drunk and likely to get violent, we would stuff our blankets and pillows out the bathroom window, and then we followed. We slept under the olive tree where we couldn't be seen from the house. Sometimes we would lie in the grass and look at the stars. There were a lot more stars, that could be seen in those days than today. The city lights now block them out.

The lady who lived on our backyard's left side was "Old Lady Simms." We must have driven her nuts. We were not quiet, we were rude, and we got into her backyard and chased her chickens. Not only that, but we threw food over the fence for the chickens to eat. It was our way of getting rid of food that we didn't want. Let me explain.

My stepmother decided, all of a sudden, that black pepper was good for you. She put a ton of black pepper in everything. My mouth felt like it was on fire, and try as I may, I just couldn't eat it, and neither could Pat or Teri. We complained to Dodie, who could only tell us we were lucky to even have food and we should be grateful that she buys it for us. She could have put it only on her food, but she refused to budge.

So, at mealtime, when she prepared a dish that had a load of pepper on it, we would dawdle at the table until she left the kitchen. It those days you had to eat everything on your plate because kids were starving in the world. (Whatever that means) Once Dodie left the room we would scrape all our plates onto one plate one of us would sneak it out the back door and dump it over the fence to Mrs. Simms' chickens. Needless to say, we were all very skinny.

The food over the fence trick worked well until Mrs. Simms knocked on our door and informed my stepmother to keep her kids from dumping food over the fence, it was killing her chickens! To my young mind, this proved that Dodie was, in fact, trying to kill us.

Of course, we were called and questioned and reiterated that we couldn't eat the pepper. She was furious, but somehow, she stopped putting so much pepper on our food.

I don't think Dodie was a bad person; she had her own story to tell. I can't tell my story from anyone's point of view but my own. So, please understand that this is not about stepmother bashing, it is what I "perceived as my experience."

I have to say a bit about food back then. Food was different. We were on the poor side, but even wealthier people didn't eat much different than we did. I know because I ate at some friends' houses that were better off than we were. They just had desserts, which we seldom had.

People almost always ate starch as the "main" part of their meal. Potatoes were our usual, but sometimes we had spaghetti, pasta, rice or beans. You usually had another vegetable like peas, carrots, or corn and maybe some salad consisting of lettuce, tomato and onions. And, sometimes, but not always, we had a very small portion of meat.

In those days, the only oil/fat I knew about was Crisco, bacon drippings, butter, and margarine. Margarine, as we know it today, has only been around since about 1950. At first, it was dyed pink, in several states, because the "dairy industry" was at war with the "margarine industry." Today there is a long aisle in every supermarket devoted solely to "oils. This contributes hugely to our health issues today. "Added oil has never been in the human diet"! No, not even olive oil in the amounts we use today.

Speaking of health, in those days, there was no "well-baby" care. You only went to the doctor if you were dying. (Well, almost). For everything else, there were "home remedies." I can't tell you how many times I had to have a "mustard plaster" on my chest for a cold.

A mustard plaster is made of ¼ cup ground mustard seed, ½ cup flour, and 2 Tablespoons warm water. Spread the mixture on a large piece of cheesecloth or cotton, fold it in half, and put it on the chest for about half an hour. I hated it, but the alternative was "Vick's VapoRub smeared on your chest. I hated Vick's! My sister loved "Vick's" and would even eat it .... yuck!

A small cut or skinned knee was taken care of with Mercurochrome. That is banned today because it contains mercury. (We used to break thermometers and play with the mercury.) If you got cut badly or stepped on a nail, broken glass, or anything like that, you soaked your body part in hot Epsom Salts water for about 20 minutes a couple of times a day if it got red and infected.

For pain, there was an Aspirin. If you had a sore throat, you had to gargle hot saltwater. Constipation was prunes or prune juice. For a cold, you were given a hot toddy consisting of hot tea with lemon and a teaspoon of whiskey. And that was about all that happened to you.

Although …… One time, I was home alone and I wanted something off the top of the refrigerator that Dodie had hidden there. It was probably a banana because Dodie always bought bananas for Nini, and we weren't allowed to eat them. That just made them more enticing; the forbidden fruit. Anyway, I got a kitchen chair and then tried to stand on the refrigerator handle to crawl up and get the treat. The handle was in the shape of a square but wider at the top than the bottom. Just as I reached for my ill-gotten goods, my foot slipped and I fell, hitting my thigh on the pointed corner of the handle. It tore about a half inch triangle shaped chunk of meat out of my right thigh, and it was hanging on by a thread of a piece of skin. I started crying. There was no one to help me, and the blood was running down my leg. Through the tears, I put the chunk of meat back in the hole and decided I would go to my friend's house down the street and get help.

I only got a short distance down the street when the leg gave out. So, I crawled the rest of the way while dragging my leg. My friend's grandmother put peroxide in the hole and on the piece of meat, then put Mercurochrome on it, stuck the chunk back in, and then taped it shut. It healed, but I still have a scar to remind me not to steal. I didn't need a doctor, and I didn't tell dad or Dodie what happened because I would have gotten a spanking for trying to take Nini's bananas in the first place.

My sister, Teri, got tonsillitis that couldn't be cured with hot saltwater. She had to go to a doctor to have her tonsils out when she was about twelve. She also had a broken arm at some point. Other than that, and the brief memory of when I was two and had Whooping Cough, etcetera, I can't ever remember going to a doctor until I was about 15 years old when I got a sinus infection and my eyes were almost swollen shut.

People seldom went to the doctor. Now they scare the hell out of you that you will get some dread disease and die if you don't show up for a "checkup" several times a year. Now kids have "Well Baby" visits to the doctor and get about 50 vaccinations before they are school age. Each shot requires a doctor's visit. No wonder we need medical insurance today.

The three of us were no longer innocent children, and we caused all kinds of hell for Dodie. One of the things we did was to see how fast we could get a babysitter to quit. Poor Dodie had so much to contend with that we never considered at the time.

It was tough enough to find a babysitter at a reasonable price, but to have them quit in the first week was even tougher. We had to put up with our parents, but we resented being pushed around by someone else.

Getting rid of babysitters started with one who insisted on putting salt on Nini's oatmeal instead of sugar. Nini hated it and would cry. I tasted it, and it was loaded with salt and was nasty. The oatmeal went over the fence to Mrs. Simms' chickens.

Teri, Pat, and I went into the garden, collected all the snails we could find and put them in a box. We had Geranium flowers that snails love.

There must have been about a hundred snails in the box. We put a bow on it and gave it to the sitter. She opened it and screamed. She threw the box on the floor and ran out the door. She never even came back for her pay, as far as I know.

We got rid of several babysitters for one reason or another. Pretty soon, we didn't need a reason; it just became the thing to do.

The last babysitter we had was Mrs. Picquelle. She was a little, plump Polish woman who wore sensible shoes with little raised heels. As soon as she showed up, we started with the pranks, jokes, and teasing. We would tell her a tree had fallen across the street. She went to look and we would start laughing. We pulled all kinds of things on her, like hiding the potato peeler or unplugging a lamp. We did anything to get a rise. Mrs. Picquelle took it all in stride and went about her business. The box of snails didn't scare her; she said she was going to cook them up for our lunch!

One day the tree across the street did fall over. We tried to tell her, but she would not look. She would grin and say, "No, no, no, you children aren't going to fool me." And she would laugh. She went the whole day deliberately averting her eyes from the front window. When she went out the door to go home that evening, she saw that the tree had, indeed, fallen over. She was so surprised. The three of us gathered around her to say, "See, we tried to tell you."

We could find no fault with Mrs. Picquelle. She was a wonderful, loving, happy, efficient woman, and we were very lucky to have her for many years. She was an important and wonderful part of our lives.

1957 Claudia 10 years old

Chapter 6
School and Church

At first, other than my time in Catholic School, when the Nuns hit my hand for being a lefty, I loved school. It was a chance to get away from everything I hated at home. The schoolwork was easy. But that love didn't last long.

After moving to Hawthorne, California, I went to Ramona Grade School. I was in the third grade. Up to this point, kids were nice to me and I enjoyed playing with them. I don't remember any bad incidents in first or second grade. But third grade was different. I think that is about the age at which kids start seeing differences in each other. This was when the kids started calling me a dirty Jap and shoved me around.

I did not have nice clothes. My stepmother bought our clothes at the thrift store. I'm sure this was out of necessity, which, of course, I did not understand at the time.

At school, we had "snack time." For a nickel, each kid got a small carton of milk and a Graham Cracker. I didn't have a nickel. Dodie couldn't afford such a luxury. I was the only kid in my class that didn't have that quarter each week for my snack. My teacher found a way so that I didn't feel left out. Each day, I went to the cafeteria and got a tray with the milk and crackers for the Kindergarten kids. I would take it to their classroom and thus earn my milk and cracker.

My father had lost his job. Well, he had lost his driver's license because of a 502 (Drunk Driving Charge), and he only had a bicycle to get to work …. more often to the bar. So, Dodie had to cloth and feed four kids on a typist's salary. I don’t know if dad made any money, but if he did, he spent it on alcohol. They often fought about money, and he would hit her, and she would scream and cry. Eventually, he would take her purse and take what money she had. Listening to the fighting was horrible. “I’m a happy merry butterfly…….”

I’ve looked it up, and a typist in 1955 made about $60 per week BEFORE taxes (about $625 in 2022 money). The minimum wage was $0.75 an hour or about $30 a week. Here are some other prices from 1955.

Average Yearly income: $4,137 (Dodie made about $3,000)
Average House: $9,100
Ford car: $1606-$2944
Milk: $.92 (gal)
Bread $.18
Eggs, doz.: $.61
Potatoes, 10 lb. bag: $.53
Gas: $.23 per gallon
Sirloin chops: $ .69 lb.
Pot Roast: $.43 lb.
Coffee: $.93 lb.
Postage stamp: $.03
Starkist Tuna, 6 ½ oz. can: $.25
<u>*Clothes*</u>
Girls dress $1.99 to $5.00
Girls shoes $3.50 to $5.00
Baby Sitter: $15.00 per week

You can see from this that her little salary would not cover it all. But an eight-year-old does not have this understanding. It wasn't that I was greedy or extravagant. I only wanted to fit in. I rebelled against my hand-me-down clothes. The kids at school laughed at me.

I remember one time during the "May Day" celebration at school. My class was supposed to dance around a pole with streamers hanging down. I was having so much fun. It seemed like everyone's parents were there except mine, but that was alright, I was having fun anyway. While I was dancing, the sole came off my shoe, and the top turned around backward. I tripped and the kids laughed. I was so humiliated! I ran away. I ran out of the school and just kept going. I did not get home until dark and I was barefoot. Dodie was angry with me because I didn't have my shoes. I tried to tell her what happened, but she didn't understand, or it seemed to me, she didn't care either. I'm sure all she was thinking about was putting out more money, which she didn't have, for shoes.

One little girl at school picked on me pretty often (today, we call it "bullying"). She was one of the best-dressed girls in my class, and she was very cute and very popular. She looked down her nose at me and made remarks that made other kids snigger. One day, I lost it and caught her outside of school when we were walking home. I ripped the belts off her pretty little dress and punched her. She ran off crying, which I thought was OK because she caused me so much pain.

About this time in my life, I started developing twitches. I twitched my nose and my ring fingers. My bicep muscle would tighten for a second for no reason. I was compelled to do it. It wasn't a choice. I hated it because it made me stand out as more different. Dodie couldn't stand to be around me when it happened. She would yell, "Stop that damn twitching or get out of here." Today, most people would notice it as "anxiety twitching." Life was piling up on me. To cover my discomfort in life, I often became the "class clown." I loved to make people laugh; that was the only way I could survive because of how shy I was.

In 1957 the movie "Blood of Dracula" came out. I was ten years old. It was playing at "The Plaza" Movie Theater, which was a mile away from where we lived. My sister, Teri, wanted to see it. In those days, it cost a quarter to get into the movies. We knew the son of the man who owned the theater so that we could get in for free occasionally. Sometimes, Dodie or dad would give us the quarter for admission, and then if we got in free, we would buy candy with the extra money.

Teri talked me into seeing the movie "Dracula." It scared the crap out of me. I watched most of the movie through my fingers or looking down at the floor. I remember walking home in the dark or near dark, and I just knew a vampire was lurking behind every bush. I walked with my hands on my neck to protect myself. Teri laughed at me. The movie didn't scare her, or she wasn't letting on if it did. I think I was just at that vulnerable age in life where most things scared you. At any rate, I can tell you that I never became a fan of "horror movies."

Not long after seeing the movie, Dodie, Nini, and I were going down to the supermarket for groceries, which was a once-a-week trip. I have no idea where Teri and Pat were. The market was two very long blocks away from us, and we would walk there, and then Dodie would push a shopping cart home with the groceries.

It was a cold winter day, and I had forgotten my sweater. When we got outside, Dodie told me to go back in and get my sweater. I looked at the house, which looked dark, silent, and spooky, and I wouldn't go back in. This became a fight. Dodie didn't want me to catch a cold. I didn't want Dracula to get me. Somehow the more she insisted, the more scared I became. I was too afraid to go in by myself. She got mad and insisted. Crying, I finally ran in and grabbed the sweater and, in a panic, ran back out. Fortunately, Dracula wasn't in my house that day.

My dad often told us about his friend, "Strother Martin." He was an actor. Dad and Strother had been on the swim team in school in Indiana. Dad had telephoned Strother, and he had invited all of us to his house for a barbecue.

We drove a long way into the hills, but we finally got to his house. I was surprised to see that Strother was shorter than my dad. He was only about 5' 5" tall.

They hugged each other and reminisced about the "old days." He talked about his movie roles and said he almost always died at the end.

Strother got a phone call while we were there and walked around his house carrying the phone. He had a very, very long cord on the phone. I had never seen a phone being walked around a house like that.

While Strother and dad talked, we swam in his pool and had a great time. Then Pat dove in and hit his mouth on the bottom of the pool, knocking out his front tooth and cutting his mouth. Even with Pat getting hurt, it was a really fun day for us.

After that, we always looked for Strother Martin in the credits of the TV shows. He played a lot of parts in cowboy movies, and as he said, he usually wound up dead!

That was the only time we went to see Strother Martin. We seldom went anywhere as a family. Sometimes we visited Dodie's brother, Vern, in Green Valley, California, but not very often.

We used to perform plays on our front porch. We would write the play, make costumes, put out chairs for the neighbors, and perform the plays. We would charge a nickel for our performance. We sometimes got a few kids to watch, but usually, we just did our play for the squirrels.

One thing that Teri and I did was sing for a dime! Two old women, who lived around the corner from us, and who would sit on their porch and watch people go by, motioned to us that they wanted to talk. So, we stopped and spoke to them. They asked us if we could sing the song "Que Sera, Sera" (whatever will be will be). We did not know the song. They told us that if we learned it, they would give us each a dime if we sang it for them. We learned the song and often went around to sing for our dime! They always giggled and applauded and gave us our dime.

In those days, you could buy music on a 45 RPM record (revolutions per minute). Dodie had a few "records" and a little "record player" on which to play them.

One day, my teacher asked us, students, to bring a record for "show and tell" to school. I asked Dodie if I could bring a record, but she refused. I must have caught her on a very bad day because she said, "Keep your grubby little meat hooks off my stuff." Her manner hurt my feelings, so I stole one of her records and took it to school.

Somehow, I forgot to bring the record home. I intended to put it back, and Dodie would never miss it. That never happened. When I finally remembered the record, the teacher couldn't find it.

Every time Mickey Mouse Club came on TV, they had a commercial for records. Whenever the commercial came on, I would become hyper, make noise, and jump around the front room. I was trying to keep Dodie distracted least she see the commercial and think to go check her records. Dumb, I know. But to a kid, a distinct possibility! It was just fear and panic for me, and it served me right for stealing the record in the first place. You would have thought I had learned something from the refrigerator accident.

One day in school, we had a history lesson about life in the 1850s, and we were given an assignment to write a poem about something to do with that time. Here is the poem I wrote.

The Doom of Death That Day
by Claudia Gilligan 1955

Ma was sick and pa was down,
And I was on my way to town.
A doctor there I was to seek,
So he could come and take a peek.
Maybe he could save the life,
Of my poor pa and his dear wife.

It was dark, I could hardly see,
But I knew God was guiding me.
I got there quick and got the Doc.
T'was half past three so said the clock.
We got back soon and ma was saved,
But, my poor pa, he died next day.

A funeral we did have for him,
In a light that was so dim.
Ma and I will live on,
Until our dying day,
Remembering that dark night,
And the doom of death that day.

It was a bit morose for a third-grader, but I was proud of it. I had no idea I could write poetry. We each had to read our poem to the class. When I was done, the teacher looked at me and asked if I had written it or did someone help me. The class laughed. I was embarrassed and humiliated.

I think the teacher could have at least taken me in private to ask that question. I had written that poem, and I never had anyone help me with anything. I was furious. After that, I continued to write poetry for much of my life, but I seldom shared it with anyone till much later.

I further lost interest in school. I had a hard time doing homework because I was developing OCD (Obsessive, Compulsive Disorder). I did not know what it was then, but if I made one mistake on a homework paper, I threw it away and started over. For those who don't know, this was way before computers. You couldn't backspace and correct. We wrote everything out with a pencil, by hand on lined paper. If you made a mistake, you had to erase it. An erasure mark usually showed up on your paper, and I just could not accept that. "They" don't know what causes OCD, but I believe that it is about controlling something when the rest of your life is out of your control.

Some kind of perfectionism was setting in. I couldn't deal with anything in odd numbers unless it was "one." I remember stealing one of Nini's little plastic plates, from her tea set, because she had an odd number of them. I wasn't trying to be mean. I was just somehow compelled. Nini was a very smart little girl, and she noticed that one, of her plates, was missing. One day, after doing the dishes, I threw away a fork because the numbers were odd. This kind of thing would plague me for many years.

The only subject I was interested in was reading. My teacher would read to us every day and I was so mesmerized. While she read, I created pictures in my head. The first book ever read to me was "Charlotte's Web" by E.B. White. Books took me away. I could go anywhere in a book. I fell in love with reading and have been a voracious reader ever since. And I also have to admit that I still have a copy of Charlotte's Web in my library.

I got in trouble for not paying attention in class and not turning in my homework. Somehow, I came to the attention of Mrs. Bodes, our school principal. She was a very short and very plump woman who always had a big wad of keys dangling from her wrist. She called me into her office and talked with me. At some point, I unloaded. I told her how I hated my stepmother, how my dad was mean when he drank, how the kids laughed at my clothes and how I didn't cheat and how unfair life was. Whew!

Mrs. Bodes was a very kind soul. She arranged to take my sister, Teri, and me to her house. She had a couple of daughters who were close to my and Teri's sizes. Mrs. Bodes went through her daughters' closets and had us try on clothes and anything that fit, even slightly, she gave to us. What a sweet, sweet woman. I did not mind wearing those clothes because they were very nice. After that, whenever I got the chance, I would walk with Mrs. Bodes in the schoolyard. I was like a needy little dog begging for affection.

I think I was in fourth grade when we had a school play at Christmas. I was supposed to play the part of a little girl who was afraid of Santa. I practiced and practiced my lines. On the night of the play, I looked out at all of the parents. It seemed like everyone had someone come to see them except me. I stood looking out at the audience and just started crying. I guess the audience thought that was what I was supposed to do because they clapped. I ran off the stage and out the door. I cried all the way home.

In the summertime, we would go swimming at Hawthorne High swimming pool. They had two swimming pools. One was for "swimming," and the other was “diving.” One year, Teri and our friend, Marty, talked me into jumping off the platform into the diving pool. This was a bit crazy because I did not know how to swim very well and had a fear of drowning from an incident when I was about three or four.

The lifeguard made me get into the water and swim the length of the pool before he would let me jump from the platform. I guess I was able to swim well enough to do it because there I was up on the platform with Teri and Marty.

Looking down, it seemed like a looooong way. I started to panic and changed my mind. I wanted to go back down the ladder and forget it. Teri and Marty had a different idea! They each grabbed one of my arms, dragged me to the edge, and jumped in the water. It felt like I went down a hundred feet. I bobbed to the top but was too scared to swim. Instead, I kept grabbing people, trying to hold my head above water. Eventually, it took all the lifeguards to get us all out, and I had lost the top of my bathing suit. Not that I had anything to show, but I was humiliated, scared, and angry. My sister had a mean streak and it was often turned on me.

Another bad memory, from Ramona School, was joining the Brownies. I never got a uniform, but I "flew up" to the Girl Scouts within a few weeks. Dodie didn’t want to buy me the Girl Scout uniform. I pleaded with her, but she said she couldn’t afford it. The troop leader said she would try to find one for me.

In Girl Scouts, the girls took turns taking home the "snack box." They would bring cupcakes, candy bars, or something their mothers would bake for snack time. When it was my turn, Dodie would only give me some little ten-for-a-penny suckers to bring. I was so embarrassed. I took the suckers in and handed the box to the leader telling her I had to drop out of Girl Scouts because we were moving.... which was a lie. I just couldn't stand any more humiliation. That was the end of my Girl Scout experience. Of course, I was later asked why I hadn't moved. I fluffed it off with, "my parents changed their mind," but I never went back to girl scouts.

There were a few boys at school that I thought were cute, but I would never even look at them. I was a shy, twitching, perfectionist who did not pay attention in class.

I seldom got valentines on Valentine's Day at school and then only from some girl who gave them to everyone. I was rarely able to give valentines because we didn't have the money for them. Small things make the difference in whether a kid fits in.

I did have a couple of friends in childhood. Marty lived down the street from us and was between Teri and my age. She was tall, like, at least a foot taller than we were. And she was a bit wild. She had four older brothers, and they all lived with her father and grandmother. Marty was as poor as we were, but it didn't seem to bother her. She taught us how to shoplift to get what we wanted. Although she was more of Teri's friend, she and I remained friends for many years until a man came between us.

My other friend was Robbin, who was my age and went to my school. She had a pretty bad life. Robbin turned hurt into violence, kicking the shit out of people who got in her way. Robbin taught me how to fight. She is the one who instigated me into getting that little girl after school and ripping up her pretty little dress. She got me into several fights and then her and I got into a fight, and I got the better of her. I guess she was a good teacher.

We went to church on Sundays. Dad never went, and Dodie was Jehovah's Witness, but they dutifully sent us to St. Joseph's Catholic Church every Sunday.

We walked about a mile and a half by ourselves. Service was in Latin in those days, and I didn't understand a bit of it, nor did I care to. I just stood when everyone stood and kneeled when everyone kneeled. Mostly, I just chewed on the pew in front of me. I guess I liked the taste of the oil they used on the wood.

I suspect that Dodie sent us to get rid of us for a few hours. She had to wash and iron all our clothes for the week on her days off. Permanent press fabric had not been invented yet.

Clothes washing was different then. Many people still had a "wringer" washing machine. A wringer washing machine had a barrel-style basin and an apparatus on the top with two rollers which you ran the clothes through to squeeze out the water. Machines had improved by 1950, but not everyone could afford the closed box "free spin" model. I can't remember which kind we had, but it seems like we still had the wringer-style washer.

Clothes dryers were around in the 1950s, but most people couldn't afford them, and most women preferred to hang their clothes outside on a "clothesline" because the clothes smelled better and clothes dryers, like any "new-fangled" invention, weren't trusted for many years after they came out. Unfortunately, clothes required ironing if they were hung outside.

The first "Steam and Dry" iron was out in the 1950s, but that was a luxury. The iron we had was only an iron. To prepare clothes for ironing, you had to "sprinkle" the clothes with water and then roll them up for a bit, so that the water would dampen the whole fabric. Sometimes you put a rolled-up piece of clothing in the freezer so it would better distribute the moisture.

Another thing that took a lot of time was "washing hair." If you had long hair, it could be a hassle. Most kids washed their hair in the bathtub and then let it dry naturally.

Home "Hair dryers" did not come out until the late 1960s. It was a plastic-covered motor with a three-foot hose attached and that had a plastic "bonnet" attached to it. It took over an hour to dry if you had thick hair as I did.

I remember Dodie combing out the snarls in my wet hair and me "faunching," as she called it. I was "faunching" because she was brutal.

Getting back to my story. One day, while we were walking by the Bank of America, on the way home from church, Teri stopped to adjust her slip. Pat snuck in behind her and stuck his hand down the "night deposit" slot and pulled out an envelope. Teri yelled at him to put it back, but then she decided to see what was in it first. There was cash! I don't even remember how much it was, but it was cold hard cash. It was more money than we had ever seen. We headed to the "Thrifty Drug Store" and bought Mickey Mouse watches, little bracelets, some toys, and candy. Boy, we felt rich! We, of course, hid our "loot" from our parents, not that they paid much attention to us anyway.

You understand, of course, that this was before the ATM (Automated Teller Machine) was invented, which was 1968. ATMs did not become part of mainstream banking until late in the 1980s. Today, we can't imagine how we did without them. I think that, in the near future, we will do away with paper money and every transaction will be done with our cell phones. Banks and ATMs will be a thing of the past.

We became very willing churchgoers. On the way to church, we would stop at the bank. Teri would hide Pat behind her and pretend she was adjusting her slip. In those days we wore wide "poodle" skirts and big crinoline slips, kind of like a square-dancing outfit. It was easy to hide little, skinny, Pat behind her. I was the lookout. We would get a couple envelopes. Some had money, some had checks, and some had both. We usually tore up the checks and trashed them and the envelopes somewhere down the street. Then we walked on to church. We always put a few dollars into the offering basket as a kind of penitence.

This went on for quite some time. I felt some guilt, but not guilty enough to stop. After all, so much had been taken from us. We never thought about those people whose money we were stealing. It might have been the difference in food on the table or paying their rent. It just never occurred to us.

Then one day we came home and Dodie was there with two men in suits. It was the FBI. Dodie had found our stash and some bank envelopes and had read in the newspaper about money missing from the bank. Somehow, she had put it together and had called the bank and announced to them, "I think my kids are robbing your bank."

The FBI agents were very friendly to us. They didn't yell and they weren't mad. They only wanted to know how we did it. We told them and they measured Pat's height and his arm and just shook their heads. You could almost see the smile behind their stern looks. They put all of us in their car and drove us to the bank and asked Pat to take out an envelope, which he did quite easily. They were satisfied that we had indeed robbed the bank.

They took us back home and thanked Dodie. When they left, she took a stick to our backside and that was the end of our "rich" days.

The bank changed out the slot with one that was skinnier and had sharp metal teeth in it. Many people don't know why those slots changed, but we had changed the banking industry worldwide.

I want to mention something about "spanking." In the 1950s and 60s, children were routinely spanked. Even teachers were allowed to hit children. Men spanked their wives, and even in the 1960s and 1970s, it was glorified in movies such as the 1963 blockbuster "McClintock." Set in the 1850s, it shows everyone laughing as John Wayne spanks Marlene O'Hara with a coal shovel.

In 1871 in the Alabama case of Fulgham V. State, the state court ruled as follows concerning the physical discipline of a husband toward his wife:

"A rod which may be drawn through the wedding ring is not now deemed necessary to teach the wife her duty and subjection to the husband. The husband is therefore not justified or allowed by law to use such weapon, or any other, for her moderate correction. The wife is not to be considered as the husband's slave. And the privilege, ancient though it be, to beat her with a stick, to pull her hair, choke her, spit in her face or kick her about the floor, or to inflict upon her indignities, is not now acknowledged by our law."

Because men had, historically, been the money maker and women were, in fact, not allowed to own anything, it was believed that he was the absolute ruler of his wife. Reading the history of women's rights is an enlightening experience. A child's rights were far below a woman's.

Even though the law forbids it, a man could spank (or beat) his wife and the police would just look the other way. It wasn't until the 1970s that women activists started a movement to get "domestic violence" stopped, and it has only been in very recent history that the laws have been enforced.

This is a bit of a sidetrack, but I think it is important to understand how the world was during my upbringing. Much of what happened to us was not unusual for the times. Most children were spanked at one time or another. Lots of people were poor, and I'm sure other kids might have had shabby clothes or drunken parents, but I did not know about their plight. I've heard lots of people say. "We were poor, but I didn't know it." Well, it didn't happen that way for me. We were poor and I knew it. I only knew my story and I felt very sorry for myself. Shows on TV showed much different homes and parents than what I had, which was about all I had to compare to.

I think, somehow, the brain keeps track of the bad you perceive in your life and often forgets the good times. The brain is set up to help you survive. It doesn't need to remember the good times because that IS surviving. The bad times are times of danger, and your brain needs to remember those times to steer you away from like situations.

In the waning days of my childhood, I met Jimmy Kane. My sister remembers that we met him and his brother at Pacific Ocean Park (POP) in Santa Monica, California. He was the love of my ten or eleven-year-old world. My sister, who was about twelve or thirteen, was dating his brother, Johnny. What two young girls were doing in Santa Monica or how we got there is beyond me. We probably hitchhiked, as we did many times, and, no, hitchhiking was not unusual for the times.

I know Jimmy and Johnny lived in Culver City, which was at least 10 miles away from us, which was a considerable distance for young girls to travel. At any rate, I loved Jimmy and he loved me. We didn't see each other often, but it was great when we did. When Jimmy wasn't around I just dreamed of him. I remember kissing him once. An awkward ten-year-old, don't know what you are doing, kind of kiss.

I remember the four of us spending the day at Pacific Ocean Park. What a great day. Jimmy bought me a "Lord's Prayer" cup and saucer. I treasured that gift and as a matter of fact, it is sitting in my china cabinet today. It was the first gift a boy gave me and it is cherished.

I don't know how Jimmy and I drifted apart. I think it might have been because I moved with my mother at some point.

At any rate, Jimmy Kane was my first love. It was the most innocent and pure love of a child.

1958 Claudia age 11 Japanese ?

Chapter 7
A Kid's Life

Sometime in about 1957, Dodie went on vacation to visit her mother in South Dakota. I was about ten, Teri was twelve, and Pat was about eight years old. Dodie took Nini with her and left Teri, Pat, and me with dad. She was not wasting money on a babysitter when Nini wasn't there, and she figured we did not need a babysitter since dad was not working. It was on about the second day that dad disappeared.

I remember the woman next door asking me if I was hungry, and she fixed me a peanut butter and jelly sandwich and brought it out to me.

My sister recalls that we blew a fuse trying to vacuum and all the lights went out. We didn't have circuit breakers in our house like in today's homes. We had a "fuse box." Breakers and fuse boxes are meant to prevent fires. When a wire gets too "hot," the fuse or circuit breaker shuts the power down. A fuse box has holes into which you screw a one-inch round fuse. If you blow a fuse, you could put a penny between the box and the fuse, and it would run until the wire melts and your house catches fire. Not having replacement fuses and not knowing how to use a penny, fortunately, we could not turn the power back on.

Somehow the man next door, who was a policeman, found out that our dad was not home, no one was watching us, and we had no lights. After investigating, he took us to the police station.

I think because we were rowdy and wild, we were eventually put into a jail cell. It wasn't locked until Pat became so disruptive, that finally, they did lock the door. I just remember my brother crawling up the bars and acting like a monkey. They tried to locate dad, but when they couldn't, they sent us to "Lathrop Hall," which was a Juvenile court facility. They did a very invasive (in my opinion) "medical exam" on us. I guess it was to determine if we had been sexually molested, but because I did not understand it and it was much like what Fred Potter had done to me, I fought them. Trust me when I say, it took a lot of staff to hold this wild cat down. I did not like Lathrop Hall and fought with other kids in the daytime and cried myself to sleep at night.

My dad had to go to court to get us back. I don't know how long that took, but I have a sense it was several weeks.

I had a cat that I named "Puff" after the cat in the book we had in school called "Fun with Dick & Jane." I usually took the cat to bed with me at night and put it under the covers. I guess the cat liked it because it would sleep all night right next to me and purr. My sister would tease me, saying I would rub all the hair off the cat, but I didn't care. A cat's purr is very soothing when you are a lonely little kid.

My brother, Pat, had a dog. It was supposed to be the family dog, but it became Pat's dog. We named it "Rascal," but then had to rename it "Rascal Ann" after we found out it was a girl. It is interesting to note that Dodie, as poor as we were, allowed us to have pets, and she bought food for them.

Kids in those days had "chores" to do every day, and you didn't expect to get paid to do them. One of mine was washing dishes and I hated it.

Just as an aside, houses in those days were far different from today. There were no "dishwashers" in most homes. Though dishwashers in some fashion had been around since the 1930s, they were only for rich people. My grandmother had one, of course, but dishwashers didn't become "affordable" until the mid-1970s.

There were no "Microwave Ovens." It wouldn't be until the 1970s before they too would be affordable. Leftovers were heated on the stovetop or in the stove's oven. Since there were no microwave ovens and food was cooked on the stove, by the time the whole family got to the table the food was usually cold.

There were no affordable "Electric Coffee Makers" until the mid-1960s. The same was true for "Electric Can Openers." There were no Toaster Ovens, Electric Slow Cooker, Rice Cooker, or Electric Skillet." Our kitchen had an electric toaster, but that was about the only thing electric.

Today, everything is electric, and most kids have only to "load and unload" the "dishwasher," which I'm sure they hate to do as much as I hated washing dishes by hand.

One time I remember Teri tied the belts of my dress to the kitchen drawers so I couldn't get away and would have to do the dishes. Like that was going to stop me! I just ripped the belts off my dress and got away. It is so strange the things one remembers.

There were no "garbage disposals" in most houses. Everything went into the trash and would be burned.

In those days there was no "trash pick-up." Almost every house in California had an "Incinerator," which was made of concrete blocks. It was about two feet square with a small smokestack on the back of it. Ours was underneath the big Pomegranate tree on the side of the backyard. Leaves, trash, and anything else needing to be disposed of were all burned in the incinerator.

I wish we had that Pomegranate tree today. We ate many Pomegranates and gave them out as treats on Halloween.

Halloween was one of our favorite times. Kids made their costumes in those days. I don't know if you could buy costumes in the stores, but most people would not have wasted their money buying a costume when part of the fun was making one. Pirate, ghost or hobo were favorites.

We didn't have fancy "Trick or Treat" bags. We used pillowcases! We would go "Trick or Treating" until way after dark. Sometimes we would go out the day before and tell people we were leaving town the next day and wouldn't get to Trick or Treat. Most people believed us and gave us candy. Then the next night, we would have a little different costume and go again. This was a bonanza for poor kids who, more often than not, didn't have a penny to buy a piece of candy, which is what many candies cost in those days.

I have a vivid memory of Teri stripping Pat's clothes off him, putting him in a dress, and locking him outside. This happened several times until Pat got back in and beat the poo out of her one day. Trying to get away from him, I remember her running through the kitchen and out the back door. Pat grabbed a sharp kitchen knife and threw it at her. She just made it out as the knife stuck in the door. Twang! She was lucky the door closed or the knife would have been in her back!

When Pat got mad, he was dangerous, and he gave no thought to anyone's safety, including his own. I recall him getting mad and butting his head into our bedroom wall. It made a big hole in the wallboard, which became a hidey-hole for our "treasures." We just taped a picture over it and no one was the wiser.

Our bedroom was right next to the dining room that had been

converted to a bedroom for dad and supposedly, Dodie. When dad came home, he would hang his pants on the doorknob on his side of the door that separated the two rooms. Sometimes, one of us would quietly open the door, reach around and put our hand in his pocket and take some coins. One day Pat was doing it, but instead of just taking whatever his hand landed on, he was fishing around to find the "biggest" coins. The sound of the change being jostled around woke my dad. He looked up and saw Pat. "What are you doing with your hand in my pocket, boy?" he asked. Pat, being the honest kid that he was, replied, "Stealing your money!"

Pat had a thing for saving money. He used to bury his change in a jar in the backyard. Teri and I had planted some potatoes in a flower bed and when we went to dig up our potatoes, we came across one of his jars. Of course, we took the money. His habits never changed and later in life we called him Scrooge because of his thrifty habits. I think he got most of the Scottish DNA.

Dodie used to crochet little doilies with a tiny little hook and thin, brightly colored string. She made beautiful doilies with ruffles and different designs. She usually did it in the morning while she drank her coffee before she went to work, which was probably the most peaceful time of her day.

I, of course, had to disturb that time for her because I was so fascinated that you could make anything out of a ball of string and a hooked piece of metal. I begged her to teach me. At first, she would not. I was the kid that seldom sat still. But, eventually, she showed me and gave me my own thread and hook to practice with. And practice I did. When I was crocheting was probably the quietest I ever was. It took a lot of my concentration. Eventually, I got pretty good and I would sneak into

Dodie's crocheting and I would do some on the one she was making. She could tell the difference, of course. She called me on it but laughed and stripped out the part I had done. Then one day she didn't catch it, and I knew I had finally conquered crocheting. I felt very proud of myself.

One day my dad, being drunk, decided I needed to learn how to fix an alarm clock. There is no accounting for what gets into a drunk's mind.

It was a little wind-up clock. He gave it to me in a shoebox in hundreds of pieces and said, "Fix this."

"What was wrong with it before you took it apart?" I asked.

"Nothing," he replied, "and there better not be anything wrong with it when you're finished!"

There was, of course, no internet to go to. In those days we used a "Dictionary" or an "Encyclopedia" as our reference sources. You would be surprised to find out how much information was in an encyclopedia.

Our encyclopedia was a set of about 20 books divided into the alphabet. Letters that had a lot of entries had their own book and letters with fewer entries were combined into a book. You could get an entire set of encyclopedias at the grocery store. You could buy one book each week for about $0.99 if you bought a certain amount of groceries.

I looked up the "alarm clock" in the encyclopedia, but it only said what it was. This caused me to panic. I had no idea what my dad might do to me. The longer it took, the more concerned I got. Every day, I thought it might be the day he would ask about the clock. Eventually, I got our friend Marty's brother to help me.

When I eventually took the clock back to my dad all fixed, he didn't even remember giving it to me. I had suffered in fear for months and he didn't even remember it!

It was around this age when my dad showed me some pictures of his private parts with an erection. Of course, he was drunk. "Here," he said, shoving about four or five Polaroid pictures at me. "This is what a real man looks like!" When I saw what they were, I threw them down on the floor and ran out the front door. "I'm a happy merry butterfly…."

My sister, Nini, said he showed her some pictures like that some years later. I don't know if they were the same pictures that he had saved or if it was new ones. It was certainly inappropriate to show that kind of thing to your nine or ten-year-old daughter. The subject was never brought up again. I don't know if he even remembered the incident, but I certainly did.

The world is not a safe place for young girls. In later life, my granddaughters would think I was overprotective when I wouldn't even let them go to a restroom by themselves, but things that happened to me are why I was so overprotective.

My dad, having been in the service, sometimes took to teaching us how to make our bed. If he walked in our room and it was a mess, he would go on a rampage. The covers on the bed had to be tucked in tight so a quarter would bounce off of the mattress. If you failed the test, you had to stand with your arms straight out like a cross. After a short time, your arms started burning. It only got worse the longer you stood. If you let your arms down you got knocked across the room and kicked in the butt. Teri and Pat didn't do so well and sometimes just dropped their arms right away. After all, if you are eventually going to drop them and get further punishment, why go through all the torture of trying to keep your arms up in the first place. I devised a way that I could go a long time without the pain and eventually shared it with Pat and Teri. I didn't know it, but I was learning hypnosis. I just envisioned my arms resting on an invisible wall. My arms felt light as a feather….. and, "I'm a happy merry butterfly…

Kimball Leroy (Kim) and Peggy Lee (Peppy)

Kimball born: February 2, 1955
Peggy Lee born: April 4, 1956

Chapter 8
Pack and Go

Somewhere around the age of ten, my mother came back into our lives. We were told she was coming, but I had some very mixed feelings about it. At that point, I couldn't remember what she looked like. I had been about five or six when I had last seen her. I resented what she had done to us. I was really angry about Dennis. So much was coming up for me that I was just a mass of twitching.

I wasn't sure what to call her. I called Dodie, "Mommy." Should I call her Mother? Would a "Mother" dump her kids with hateful people like the Potters? My little brain was having a hard time coping. By the time she arrived, I ended up saying, "Hi Peggy," with just a little contempt in my voice. Of course, I wanted her to hug me and say she was sorry, but she never did, not that day and not any other day.

I don't remember much more from that day. I'm sure there is more I should remember, but I think I was so stressed out that I was just in survival mode.

She said she married Leroy Ostby and they had two more children, Kimball Leroy and Peggy Lee. So that was seven children she had had. I think I resented her for that. How could she just dump the four kids she had and run off with a boyfriend and have two more children?

Eventually, we became reacquainted with "Mother." She and her family had moved to Lancaster, California. The three of us went there to visit her and meet her kids. They were very young. Kimball Leroy was born February 2, 1955, and Peggy Lee, "Peppy" was born April 4, 1956. "Kimmy" was about seven years ten months younger than me, while Peggy Lee (Peppy) was about nine years younger.

It wasn't good. We were jealous of her kids and they were taking up all her time. It wasn't that we wanted her to neglect them; we just really, really needed her too.

She showed me my baby book that she still had. It had some things filled out, but not much. I wrote in my baby book that I loved to sing. I was interested in nursing. I wanted to be a writer. My milestone in life is to "make something of myself forgetting the past and living for the future. I wrote that my "hobby" was, "Getting the most out of life when life is so ruff and mixed up!" My favorite Actors were; Elvis Presley, Bing Crosby, Ricky Nelson, Debby Reynolds. My favorite song was "Scarlet Ribbons." My "ambitions" were to be: Singer, writer, poet, and millionaire or to be in some field of entertainment.

The next few years seem to blend in a confusing sort of a jumble. Both sets of parents moved several times and the three of us played, what I call, "pack and go, to and fro."

My dad and Dodie moved to Redondo Beach and my mother moved to La Puente.

Dad was as violent as ever. Beating Dodie and knocking us kids around was a pretty regular occurrence. One of his favorite things was to bang our heads together; man, that really hurt and you saw stars. The other thing was to "cuff our ears." That is where he took one cupped hand on each side of your head and hit you in the ears. The air pressure from the cupped hand is what hurt so bad. It felt like an ice pick being stuck in your ear. As a result, my sister, Teri, became nearly deaf though we didn't realize it for many years. Pat's hearing was affected, but not as bad as

Teri's, until he was about fifty years old. I wound up with acute hearing. I can hear a pin drop in the next room. I have ringing in the ears that is constant. Loud noises are very painful. I have to concentrate when in a crowd because I can hear everything all at once and therefore I can't hear the person in front of me. It seems like the first word hurts my ears and so they shut down. I usually miss the first part of a sentence, so I have to read lips.

The other trick dad had was to backhand you and knock you down and then literally kick you in the ass. All three of us have chronic back problems as a result of this.

I was in about the fourth or fifth grade when my mother became pregnant again. She was only about four foot six and had this cute little belly sticking out. She did not stop drinking. She wasn't a mean drunk like dad. Mother was a fun, party girl. She loved to dance and sing.

This baby would be named Denise if a girl and Darren if a boy. This was way before ultrasound could determine the gender of a baby, as that technology was not developed until the late into the 1970s in the United States. I don't recall how far along she was, but I just remember she fell off a barstool and miscarried. In all, Mother had had three children die. All of them were born in October and all of their names started with the letter D. What a strange and ironic thing to happen.

This was sometime in the 1960s, as best I can recall, and "fetal alcohol syndrome" wasn't discovered until 1973. Up until that time, doctors never cautioned about pregnant women drinking.

I recall going to a boy's house after school. His name was Ray. His parents and his brother were deaf and they talked "sign language." I was fascinated with it, and I had a crush on Ray. He was Teri's friend though.

At his house, there was a room (could have been the garage) that we went in and played records. In those days, you played vinyl 45 rpm records on a record player. There were several boys and girls and we just danced and had fun. That is one of the good memories of that time. It was because of those days that I later learned the ABCs of sign and some hand sign as well.

It was about this time that I went out with a young man that I knew as Zeke, from our neighborhood. He was very nice and polite, but he was as shy as I was, so it wasn't much of a date. He later became a popular singing star named, "Chris Montez." I don't think we had much of a chance because, at that time, we moved from Hawthorne to Redondo Beach.

I went to the seventh grade in Redondo Beach. I think the name of the school was Adams Middle School. I was about thirteen years old. As most parents can attest, little girls become monsters at about thirteen and I was no exception. My shyness had turned to sullenness. I was more into kicking the shit out of the world than putting up with its crap. I didn't pay much attention in class. I was more into friends, music, and smoking.

It was unfortunate that we had no supervision or anyone to teach us not to smoke. In those days everyone smoked. Doctors on TV even smoked. Famous actors smoked on TV. Even Lucille Ball smoked. All four of our parents smoked. We would all pay a price for smoking.

Teri, Pat, and I had tried smoking at a very young age and by the time I was in the seventh grade, I was pretty much hooked. Cigarettes were pretty easy to come by. You could steal them from a drunken parent or buy them in a machine. Cigarette machines were everywhere. You could buy a pack from a machine for $0.23 when I first started smoking. You put in a quarter, pulled the handle out for the brand of choice and you got two pennies back, sealed in the pack. We liked "Marlboro." Later in life, I switched to "Winston."

I wore my hair in a "Beehive." A Beehive was long hair teased or backcombed and then wound around and around and stacked about a foot high on your head. It took a ton of hair spray to get it to hold. It looked like a beehive. My friends and I wore a couple of razor blades hidden in ours. That was only in case someone grabbed your hair in a fight. At night you took the razor blades out and wrapped your hair in a scarf to keep it from coming undone.

A beehive hairdo was the rage in the late fifties and sixties. At some point, a rumor went around that a girl died because a "black Widow" spider got in her hair and stung her to death. It was later proved to be false. I'm not sure when that rumor came around, but I suspect it was started by someone on the school board that was trying to institute some rules that had been taken away.

For some time, the schools were able to enforce a "dress code." They had all kinds of rules about how long your gym shorts had to be, how long your skirts were, and all kinds of other rules. The parents of some girl sued the school board over a beehive hairdo. The girl's mother said she had paid good money to have her daughter's hair done and she had a right to wear it to school. Apparently, she won and that started the decline in "dress codes" and probably the decline in a lot of other rules in the schools.

Next, I wore my hair in a "Chicano" style because most of my friends were Mexican. We used "Bobby pins" and curled a small tress of hair around our finger and then put two pins crossways on it right up close to the scalp. When you undid it, you had a mass of tight curls that you teased a bit. The front was smoothed back in a high bump and pinned in the back.

I also wore dark, black eyeliner, so my eyes looked like two piss holes in a snowbank. To finish off my outfit, I wore a long, black coat that served to cover my shabby clothes, which didn't matter at that point because if anyone teased me, I just kicked the shit out of them. I was a four foot seven, 90-pound wildcat with a chip on my shoulder. I would later mellow out, but the seventh grade was a hard year for me.

One night my friend, Rena, and I were at one of our favorite haunts when a girl said something I didn't like and I just started fighting with her. Of course, a crowd gathered and everyone was yelling for one or the other of us. All of a sudden, a huge arm grabbed me around the waist and pulled me off her. She was held by someone else.

The person who had me, I would later find out was named, "Fats." And, that was because he weighed about three hundred pounds. He took me and sat me on the back of his motorcycle and we rode off. He stopped a few blocks away, got off his bike, and just looked at me. He offered me a cigarette and lit one for himself. "How old are you?" He asked. "I'm 16," I replied. I wasn't. "You're lying," he said. He put the cigarette in his mouth and climbed back on the bike and went back to where he had gotten me.

He knew Rena and her older sister, Olga. He belonged to a well-known biker gang. Fats became my guardian. We would party in what we referred to as the "tules." It was just a place out in the sticks with a bond fire and some old car seats to sit on. There would be maybe thirty or so people. There was plenty of beer and marijuana for everyone. That is everyone but me. Fats had let it be known that I was his. I wasn't like his deb but more like his little sister. He would sit me on a seat and give me one beer. He pointed to some weed someone was smoking and said,

"Leave that shit alone."

No one messed with me and I was too afraid of him to buck what he said. People drank, smoked, played music, and danced, but no one got violent like my dad. If anyone had a beef, Fats figured out who was right and who was wrong. No one argued with Fats. Fats never tried to molest me and neither did anyone else. He explained the rules to everyone and that was that.

Today, looking at my 13-year-old granddaughter, I just cringe to think of what might have happened to me. All my granddaughters wonder why I am so protective of them. Well, my life is why.

Not long after that, my mother moved to Inglewood, California. She lived at 123 Cedar Avenue, right across the street from the Inglewood High football field. Teri and I went to live with her. Pat stayed with Dad and Dodie, who had moved to Normandy Avenue in Los Angeles.

Mother worked at "Curly's Tavern" a few blocks away. Leroy worked as a "break operator" at a machine shop. They both drank and partied. Mother cooked sometimes but mostly she didn't. This was before there was a fast-food restaurant on every corner. I think there was a McDonald's, but it was a long way away. Sometimes you just settled for a can of soup for dinner. Kimmy and Peppy learned to fend for themselves at a very young age. I think they ate a lot of cereal.

Sometimes we got bread or donuts off the "Helm's Bakery" truck that came around every day.

I remember going to school and my mom shoving a piece of white bread spread with butter and sugar in my hand on my way out the door. I would be head down on my school desk by ten o'clock when the sugar wore off.

Mother's sense of humor was one of her better features. No wonder men were attracted to her. I remember Christmas of about 1960 when Mother got a "record & talk" doll for Peppy. You pulled a string to record something and when you pulled the string again, that was what the doll said. She took the doll to work and of course, it was passed around the bar and everyone had something funny that they thought the doll should say. Somehow, Mother forgot to erase the doll and when Peppy opened it and pulled the string for the first time, it said something like, “Hey, bitch, get me another beer!”

This was in the day when the "I Love Lucy" show was not allowed to show Ricky and Lucy in the same bed together. They had twin beds. Women were not said to be “pregnant,” they were "in the family way." Men did not cuss in public and if a damn or hell slipped out in front of a woman, they immediately apologized. God forbid anything stronger was uttered. It was an uptight society with a long list of rules and what this doll said was just so far out of line …. And so funny!

I want to throw in a couple of other things about that era. People were all over free items. Cottage cheese came in beautifully colored aluminum tumblers. We had a big collection of them. We got our dish towels out of Breeze detergent. Around this time, the gas stations and food stores gave out “Blue Chip Stamps” or “S&H Green Stamps.” When you bought something, they gave you stamps which you pasted into a book. You could take the books to a “redemption center” and exchange them for an array of items. Many a Christmas gift came from the Blue-Chip Redemption center.

That same year, Teri and I got our first transistor radio. It was made by Sony and came with earphones. Before this time, radios had "vacuum tubes" which made them big and heavy. This new radio technology made it easy to take with you. No wires and no tubes.

Pack and Go

I must have had OK grades even though I didn't turn in much homework and sometimes fell asleep in class. At any rate, I was going to graduate from the eighth grade and I needed a dress. Not that we had the money for dresses. My parents had to have money for drinking, smoking, and partying.

One night when Mother came home from the bar, she brought me the most hideous red and white strapless dress. That was supposed to be my "eighth-grade" graduation dress. I had no boobs, what was I going to hold that dress up with? It would have been a great dress for a hooker! The entire dress was row after row of alternating, one-inch, red and white chiffon netting. It went down past my knees. I knew she was gauche and unsophisticated, but I didn't think she was stupid. I was pissed and determined that I was NOT going to my graduation. Interestingly enough, Dodie came through for me and bought me the most beautiful little, appropriate, pink satin and chiffon dress. I did participate in the graduation even though no family showed up for it; I felt beautiful. Thank You, Dodie!

Moving on to high school was a treat. I say that sarcastically. By now, my top teeth all had cavities between them, so I never smiled and covered my mouth with my hand. I still had twitches, OCD, no boobs yet and I dressed poorly. Well, you can bet I was "Miss Popularity."

Puberty is hell! It was an agonizing time when you cry or get mad at nothing and never know why. God knows I had enough to contend with. Now I had pimples!

My strong suit was anger. Sometimes it was like a switch was thrown and I would get so angry I could just bite myself. Other times I was docile and would lay or sit and read.

I loved to read. I would read almost anything. My mother read "Earl Stanley Gardner" mysteries. She got the books delivered to her through the mail. As soon as she was finished with a book, I glommed onto it.

For some reason, we had a set of "Stoddard's Lectures" that had been published in 1897. John Lawson Stoddard was a world traveler and he wrote books about all his travels. I could lose myself in them for days on end. I particularly remember his essay on "The Blue Grotto" in Italy. Even though the pictures in the book were black and white, in my mind's eye, I could see what that grotto would look like. I was determined that someday I would get to Italy and The Blue Grotto. When I grew up, life would be different and I would show everyone!

Reading is probably what kept me sane for most of my life. I could leave this world for a better one and be back by dinner time.

My sister, Teri had a dog. It was a nasty little mutt that liked to bite people (including me). One day, I was home alone and the police came to the door. They said that Teri's dog had bit a neighbor kid the day before, and they needed to quarantine the dog to see if it had rabies. I didn't know what to do, so I let them take the dog. They gave me a receipt for the dog, which I laid on the coffee table.

I went back to my room and must have been playing dress up, or something, because I fell asleep, on the bed, wearing a pair of stiletto high heels.

The next thing I know, Teri was hitting me and screaming about me giving her dog away. For some reason, she thought I just called and gave her dog to the animal shelter.

Being woken from a sound sleep by someone hitting you is shocking and you automatically defend yourself. I guess I tried to kick her away and the heel of one of the shoes cut a big gash across her stomach. She grabbed the shoe and started hitting me with the stiletto heel. I had several deep holes, in my legs from this, but could hardly defend myself because of having the other heel on, which made me off balance. I finally got the other shoe off and then I beat the crap out of her. Of course, she later found out what had really happened with the dog, but she was still mad at me for letting them take it. What did she think I was supposed to do?

As I said, I did not enjoy school and often got in trouble for fighting. If someone messed with me or my sister, I attacked. It was that switch that flipped.

One day I was in my typing class, which was in a big two-story building, and I had a bit of trouble. There was no air conditioning in those days and it was hot and sticky, so the windows were all open. We had a few of the new, modern, electric typewriters, but mostly we had the old Underwood mechanical typewriters. The old mechanical typewriters were hard for me to use. Unlike computers of today, typewriters had a ribbon impregnated with ink that ran across the front and it had "keys," like little hammers with the letters on them. When you pressed on a key, the hammer came up, hit the ribbon onto the paper, and left a print of the letter. The "electric" typewriters were much easier to use because you barely had to hit the keys for them to print. I have small hands and my little fingers could not press down hard enough on the "a, s and p, etc." to make it print on the mechanical typewriter.

We were having a typing test and the teacher assigned me to the old-style mechanical typewriter, and of course, I failed the test. I asked if I could redo it on one of the electric typewriters, but she said, "No. You won't have those if you get a job so you have to learn with what you will be using." Well, wasn't she thoroughly modern Millie? I thought that was absurd. Of course, people would be switching to the new ones. They were FASTER! Hello? It became a screaming match. She was a dried-up, very old lady (younger than I am now) and I was done. I picked up the old, Underwood typewriter, which weighed about 30 pounds, walked to the window, and threw it out. It smashed into a million pieces, luckily it didn't anyone on the steps below. She just stood with her mouth open.

She couldn't even speak. She just pointed at the door.

"Office," she croaked.

I was suspended for a week and when I came back, she said she would pass me if I didn't show up in her class …. Ever again. OK!

I moved back in with dad for a brief stint, but he was getting crazier by the day. He said he was from the planet Quintomoso and his name was, actually, Captain Cormorant. He had an implant in the back of his head, which was how he took over my dad's body. Implant or not, he was the same crazy bastard I always knew.

One of the things he loved to do was to come into my bedroom at night and turn the mattress over and dump me onto the floor. He was sitting by himself and drinking and decided he wanted some company. He usually chose me. I think Pat was his only son since Dennis died, Teri would cry too much and Nini was too young. I was in the middle and hence the "expendable" child.

He had been taking a correspondence course to become a lawyer. He loved to dump me out of bed and make me help with his homework or argue with him. He would tell me the circumstances of a case and then tell me which side to take and I would have to make the argument for my side. That is how I, eventually, became an argumentative bitch that could take any position and argue it well. I didn't have to be right, I only had to be convincing. At any point, he might backhand me off the chair because I wasn't making sense. Then he called me stupid. In my mind, I would scream at him, "I'm not stupid, I'm smart, smarter than you, old man!"

Sometimes, he would ask me what a word meant and if I didn't know he would throw a "Black's Law" dictionary at me and say something like, "look it up, you ignorant bitch." So, I would look it up and read the definition, but it would have more words that I didn't know, and so I would have to look those words up, and on and on it would go until morning .... If I was lucky. Sometimes he would get frustrated with me and backhand me and knock me off the chair.

Sometimes he got so mad he got his gun and held it to my head. Standing behind me, he put his left hand on the left side of my head and put the gun to my right temple, and press on both sides. I was scared shitless. I would just shake and my stomach would do a flip and I would have to swallow down the puke because I was afraid to move.

When I was about fourteen, something snapped in me. The fear went away. I had had enough. "Pull the trigger you son of a bitch because I am tired of being afraid!" I said with gritted teeth. I thought he would pull the trigger. Dead silence and then he started laughing. He put the gun down and said, "Well, finally you have some moxie." He never pulled a gun on me again.

Later in life, I would become grateful for his teaching. Not the method, but I did learn language and law which would serve me later on in life.

I guess, I wondered why Dodie never tried to save me from my dad's abuse, but I guess, it was her, and perhaps Nini, or me. Again, I'm the expendable child.

Claudia Gilligan

Left:1959 Claudia 12

Right: 1960 Claudia 13

Above: 1961 Claudia

Claudia's Beehive Hairdo age 14

Chapter 9
Tempe, Arizona

Shortly after that, my aunt, Dorothea (Gilligan) Lockhart, came to town, and somehow it was arranged for me to move to Tempe, Arizona with her. She was divorced and had two grown kids. She lived alone. So, off to Arizona I went. By that time, I was failing school. I had switched schools a couple of times. I was sullen and got in a lot of fights. I think they thought I would change in a new environment.

Arizona was going to be kind of a new start for me. Aunt Dorothea was very attentive to me. She made me beautiful dresses and bought other things for me. I never had so much attention.

I went to Coronado High School the first year it opened so the year was 1964 and I was fourteen and a half years old. I still had bad teeth and twitches, although they did calm down a bit. My acne cleared up. That probably had something to do with a change in diet. I made a mental note of that.

I did OK in school and made a friend, Pam Strem. Pam was taller than me, very pretty, and carried big purses. I very much enjoyed her friendship. She kept me on an even keel. I didn't want to be the angry person I had been in California and I tried very hard to change and fit in.

I had one teacher at school that I loved. He was my geography teacher and I think he had been all over the world. In class, he wouldn't teach from a book exactly, but he would tell stories of places he had been. He told the stories so well that you felt like you were there. He was my new Stoddard.

At Christmas time, my cousin, Dorothea's son, Douglas, came home from the Air Force for an extended visit. Doug and I hung out and ….. We fell in love. He was so funny and amazing. We went out on rides and got something to eat. One time we were in Dorothea's car and he was showing off his driving skills with me, and sideswiped another car. We told Dorothea some bullshit story, which she bought, and that was all that happened with that.

Dorothea thought we were just friends at first, but pretty soon she started to get the idea that there was more going on. It was easy for me to think I was in love, no one, other than Jimmy Kane, had ever treated me so good.

At Christmas, Doug bought me some blue mascara and said he got it because I had beautiful blue eyes. Oh, be still my beating heart.

Doug went back to base after Christmas, but we wrote to each other and continued the relationship whenever he came home for a visit.

By trade, Dorothea was an accountant, but she was also a very good artist and her friends were artists. They often gathered for a "salon" at our house and it was very interesting meeting all these strange people.

One artist, Pieter Prins, who I think was a portrait artist, also painted beautiful cowboy scenes where the campfire looked like it would be hot to the touch, it looked so real. He was from Holland and spoke Dutch and English. It seemed like most of her friends were from different countries.

Ted DeGrazia was another of the artist that I remember. He was the most popular and his paintings were sold in a gallery in Scottsdale. He was kind of the interpreter for the group. I don't remember the names of all the people. They were just artists who gathered to drink as far as I was concerned. And drink they did. It was a fun group of people.

Ted DeGrazia spoke many languages. Others would speak and he would tell us what they said and answer back. Dorothea laughed a lot and everyone got drunker and drunker which was when I would sneak out.

I started my art career in Arizona. Dorothea gave me my first easel and paints and I had loads of advice from all the artists who came through Dorothea's house. It became a bit confusing because I tried to do everything that everyone told me. The only thing they all seemed to agree on was that I had a natural eye and talent.

Dorothea confided in me to: "Ignore them all and just let your natural talent emerge." She said that she felt she had had too many teachers and was always trying to change to please this or that teacher to the point that she lost "her" art. I have always remembered that.

At some point, Dorothea met a man named John Wicke. It didn't take long for a romance to blossom. John was a strange man with a very funny laugh, kind of like a donkey braying, but Dorothea was in love, and at that point, I was out. I think it was partly because she wanted to separate Doug and me and partly because she wanted to be alone with John.

I was sent back to California and moved back in with my mother in Inglewood, California.

Aunt Dorothea (Gilligan) Wicke when she was young.

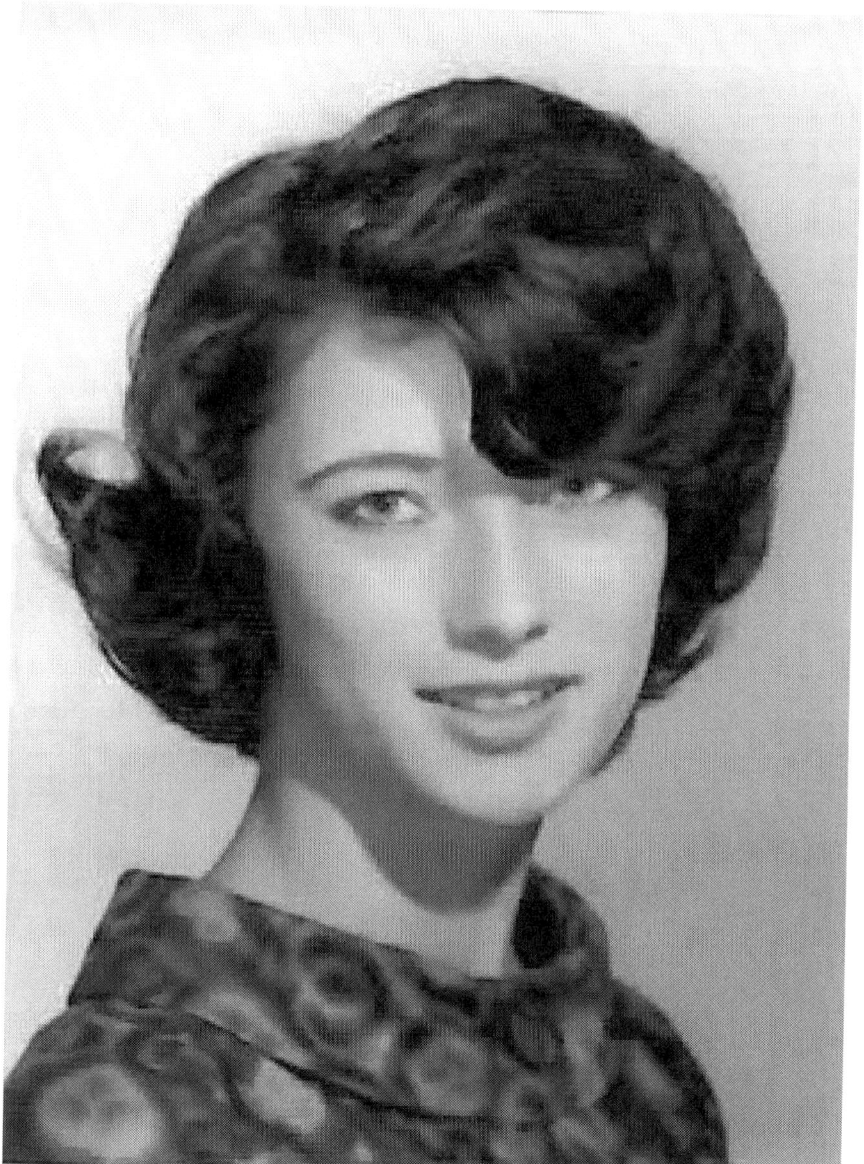

1962 Claudia age 15

Chapter 10
Life Changes Again

Moving back to Inglewood was not a good move for me. It put me right back into all the crap that was going on there. I think it was summertime because I can't remember going back to school. I was probably fifteen or so years old.

Mother still worked at the bar. She would come home drunk and would sit on the toilet and Teri and I would sit on the claw foot bathtub and she would tell us all the jokes she had heard at work that day. Ah, what better way to bond with your daughters that to take a shit and tell them all the dirty jokes you heard at work?

Mother often brought home groups of men and had poker games (among other things). Teri and I learned that we could con money from some of these men with a little smile and little coaxing. They would let us play a hand or two of poker and we usually won. We would wind up with $20 or $30, enough to buy the makeup and clothes we wanted.

Teri had a boyfriend, Sam, who had a car. We would often go to his house. Anywhere was better than where we were. Teri finally moved in with Sam's parents at some point, which left me alone at Mother's.

I was fortunate enough to get a part-time job at a restaurant by the high school. That gave me, at least, a little money for clothes.

I met a man named Jim, at the bar in which Mother worked. He was older than me. I was fifteen and he was twenty-four. He was a machinist. Of course, I fell in love. He was so kind and sweet. Even though I was only 15, he wanted to have sex, and believe it or not, I was still a virgin.

He was OK not having sex until one night he wasn't. We had a big fight and he hit me and knocked me down on the sidewalk. I literally saw stars when my head hit the concrete.

He cried and begged me to forgive him and I bought into it. He was so remorseful. My dad was never remorseful so this was something new to me. I felt he must really be sorry. He never hit me again until after I married him!

Mother and Leroy weren't getting along. It might have had something to do with all the men Mother brought home.

I remember one night, Mother accused me of "being with" her husband, Leroy. It wasn't true, but you couldn't convince her of that. She was blind drunk and chased me out of the house with a butcher knife. Mother was usually a happy drunk so this was very scary for me. I remember hiding in the bushes. I was barefoot and freezing. I sat there for hours waiting for her to pass out or go to bed so I could sneak through the bedroom window. She didn't remember it the next day.

I think the real truth was that she was trying to pin something on Leroy because she had a boyfriend, Forrest Webster, "Tex." It wasn't long before she moved in with Tex and left me with my step-dad and their two kids, Kimmy and Peppy.

I didn't know what to do. I had no place to go except to my dad's house and that wasn't an option I cared for.

Leroy and I talked it out. He needed someone to take care of the kids and I needed a place to stay. He would pay me $15.00 a week to take care of the kids and keep house.

The house was a pigsty. My mother was never into housework though she could clean when she wanted to. I went to work cleaning the house. It took about a week. Peppy was pretty happy, but Kimmy was not, because I threw away some bottle caps he had under his bed. I did not know it was a "collection." I thought they were trash.

The last thing I was going to clean was the oven. I opened the door and there was a big roaster pan in it. I opened the lid and there was a half-eaten chicken FULL of maggots. My stomach almost came up. I slammed the lid down and put it back in the oven. I told Leroy when he came home from work that I couldn't clean it and he took care of it. It was a long time before I could bring myself to bake anything in that oven or that pan or to eat chicken. I knew how to cook spaghetti and very few other dishes, but somehow, we got along.

I continued to date Jim and take care of the kids. I dressed them for school every morning, made sure they had clean clothes, and cooked as best I could for them. I cuddled them and tried to make it OK that their mother had run away. I knew what that was like.

One day, the kids did not come home from school on time. I was concerned. I walked to the school thinking they might be dawdling somewhere, but they were nowhere. Yes, in those days, five and six-year-old children walked to school and back by themselves.

I called Leroy at work and he came home and we both looked for them. We finally called the police. I have to tell you, we were both afraid. I didn't usually experience fear, but I was afraid for them. I had too much experience in what could happen to children that age.

It turned out that mother had picked them up when they were walking home from school. No word to me or Leroy. She didn't consider anyone but herself. I was furious. So was Leroy. She didn't return the kids for several weeks. What she wanted was money from Leroy.

It was now only me and Leroy which didn't look good. My mother also threatened to bring charges against him if I stayed. Leroy was one of the few men in my life that had never been inappropriate with me. And she was trying to paint him the bad guy. To show you what I mean, one time, Teri had a bottle of whiskey and we were trying to get out of the house with it. We were going to a party. Teri wrapped the bottle in a sweater. We went for the door. Somehow the bottle slipped, hit the floor, and rolled under the couch. Teri said, "Oh shit, I dropped my perfume bottle." She pretended to search under the couch for the bottle but it had rolled too far back to reach it. Our mission became to get Leroy to leave the front room so we could get the bottle.

We sat on the couch and started talking about anything that we thought would embarrass him enough to get him to leave. We talked about boys. Teri talked about her period. Leroy just sat reading his newspaper. We finally had to give up and leave. The bottle of whisky stayed under the couch and we did not recover it until the next day. I don't think Leroy even heard us. He supported us financially, but other than that, I don't think he paid any attention to us at all.

When I turned sixteen, Jim asked me to marry him and it seemed like the perfect solution. That made me more in love with him than ever. He was my "Prince Charming," just like in Cinderella. I knew my life was going to be better and I was excited to get it started.

I think the "Cinderella Complex" was rather appropriate here. Having seen the movie as a young girl, I always thought "Prince Charming" would show up and save me from the reality of life. He would fix all my problems and I would never be alone again. Did I mention that I have always been an optimist? Because of this, my new husband would take on a God-like persona to me and I would look up to him for everything.

Chapter 11

Out of the Frying Pan, Into the Fire

On November 23, 1963, I married Jim. Of course, I had a second-hand dress, but nothing mattered. Prince Charming had rescued me from my wicked stepmother and hateful life and I was getting out.

We didn't have a honeymoon. We moved into a little house behind a house that one of my mother's drinking buddies rented. Jim worked five days a week and I played house. I was looking forward to a great future. For the first time in my life, I was happy. Sex was awkward for me because I knew nothing about it. Jim was a bit disappointed, but he had married a sixteen-year-old virgin, what did he expect?

I scrupulously cleaned my home and did the best I could at cooking. I walked to the little corner store to buy groceries. The butcher would tell me how to cook whatever I bought and he never led me wrong. Back then you didn't buy pieces of chicken; you bought a whole chicken and had to cut it up yourself. I became pretty good at fried chicken and Jim often complimented me on my cooking. Life was good for a few months.

Then one day, I had taken care of Kim and Peppy for Leroy. They were a bit wild but you have to understand that they had had a tough life too. My sister, Teri, compared all of our upbringings as; "Like being raised by a pack of wolves." It wasn't much different for Kim and Peppy.

At any rate, that night while Jim and I were in bed, he said, "If they were my kids I would beat the shit out of them!"

I was very protective of them and without thinking, I said, "Over my dead body!" Without a word, Jim balled up his fist and hit me full force, right in the mouth and nose. It broke my nose and knocked out two of my front teeth. That was the end of my "Prince Charming" fantasy and the start of a lot of shit. Of course, he begged me to forgive him and he explained how the whole thing was, actually, my fault.

From about that time on, Jim referred to me as a whore, bitch, and stupid. He often beat me and I never knew what would set him off. He was like a Jekyll and Hyde. It wasn't that he was drunk. Unlike my father, he did it sober. Then he always cried and told me how much he loved me and begged me to forgive him. And I did. Little by little, I became isolated from my family and friends. I was damaged and desperate and he intended on owning a wife and raising her the way he wanted.

I told people that my teeth had just fallen out. Like I said, my teeth had big cavities between them so it was easy to sell. Jim said we would get them fixed, but whenever I brought it up, we didn't have the money. I did go to a dentist once and he removed the broken roots of my two front teeth.

I didn't sleep much at night but I still got up every morning to cook Jim's breakfast and make his lunch. One day Jim came home from work, took his sandwich out of his lunch box, and plopped it on the counter. "Are you stupid?" He asked. I didn't see anything wrong, it was just a sandwich. "Open it," he demanded. So, I opened it. Instead of putting a piece of lunch meat on the bread, I had put the paper picture of the meat that was on the top in the package. I laughed! I mean it was funny. Anyone could have made the same mistake when you are not wide awake. Not funny to Jim. He whacked me around to teach me to pay attention and after that, I was very careful to check for pictures.

Evelyn was my mother's friend who lived in the front house. She managed the property for the owner. On the first of the month, she came to collect the rent. Jim answered the door and invited her in. We were having dinner. She mentioned that the steak we were eating smelled really good. Jim cut off a piece of his steak and fed it to her off of his own fork. Honey could have dripped from his lips as he talked to her. After he paid the rent and she left he called her "a fat, nosey cow." I just could not understand his mood swings.

I took in a stray cat. I have always loved cats because they always brought me comfort. I loved it when they would lie in my lap and purr and I would stroke their silky fur. This cat wandered in one day and stayed. One day Jim became enraged with jealousy of the cat and drop kicked it out the door. He slapped me around for paying more attention to the cat than him and then begged me to forgive him. He said he didn't know what came over him; he just loved me so much. That was his pattern.

The cat was nearly dead so, I put it in a box and hid it in the garage. There wasn't anything I could do to help it but give it water and food. Cats are remarkable animals. It took a couple of weeks, but the cat lived and mended. Thereafter I tried to keep the cat outside when Jim was home.

Sometimes Jim raped me. At least today it would be considered rape. I had no choice other than to get beaten and it was not loving sex. It was only him taking what he wanted. Back then, men just about owned their wives. Men provided for the household and since he was the moneymaker, he was the king of the house. A woman would never think of complaining that her husband "raped" her. It was just not in the vocabulary. The police would have just laughed.

I think I became depressed and just numb. My twitching was bad and my OCD worse. I had no front teeth. I slept very little at night and was exhausted all day. I weighed about 95 pounds and my hands shook. I had to put up a front for other people. I was too embarrassed to admit I had made a mistake but, I was barely 17, where was I going? I'm sure there had to be some good times, but the bad just overshadows it.

How could I have married this man? What was wrong with me? Sometimes I would get a bit rebellious, but mostly I only wanted it to work. I blamed myself for making him mad and was always determined to be a better wife.

What I didn't understand at the time and what would take me many years to learn, is that I had no warning system to determine good and bad people. My father was a very mean and abusive man when he drank, but I knew that he loved me in some kind of twisted way. He had saved me from Fred and Mary Potter. He was so loving at times, like when he walked on his hands to give me money when I lost my Hoppy Taw. I just had nothing to tell me who was dangerous. There were never any red flags for me.

So why did I stay? To start with, I had no place to go. I was ashamed and embarrassed to let anyone know how bad it was. I hated my mother who had been married four times and I was determined not to be like her. Divorce was not an option.

Evelyn had a poodle dog that had babies and her dog "dried up." That means she had no milk. Five pups had to be fed by hand. I often went up to her house when Jim was at work and Evelyn asked me if I would help feed the pups. One of the pups was a runt. It was a tiny little thing. She thought it would probably die, but I was determined that it would not. I fed it every couple of hours in the daytime and as much as I could at night. I would wait till Jim went to sleep and sneak in and out of the house to feed the pups. The tiny runt lived and Evelyn gave it to me for helping her save the rest of the litter which she was able to sell for considerable money.

I begged Jim to let me have the pup. Eventually, he said yes. I named the puppy "Winki" because I was sure it had winked at me when I was feeding it. I trained it very well and it never barked. I kept it away from Jim as best I could and it seemed to work out. I had someone to who I could confide all my troubles to. Winki was a smart dog, it knew instinctively to stay away from Jim.

Sometime in about August of 1964, my dad came to visit me while Jim was at work. As it happened, I had a black eye. I told him I ran into a cabinet. My dad didn't buy that. He had been a wife-beater for years and was an expert on that kind of thing. I finally confessed to him what Jim did and everything that was going on.

I wouldn't leave with my dad as he wanted me to do. He was sober then, but I knew it wouldn't be long before he was drunk. My dad said if I wanted to leave, he would get me an attorney. I don't know why, but without thinking, I said yes.

A few days later my dad came to pick me up and take me to an attorney's office, Bolton, Groff & Dunne, in Los Angeles. Because my dad was an insurance adjuster, he knew a lot of attorneys. This one took my case for nothing. I talked with an attorney for quite some time and answered all his questions. They drew up papers and I signed them. Some of the papers were for a "Restraining Order." It took a few days, but it was granted. I was as nervous as a cat when I went home. I was sure Jim would know I had gone to an attorney and had filed for divorce. If he knew, he might kill me.

A process server came to the door one night and served the restraining order and divorce papers on Jim. He was shocked. I mean he was shocked speechless and just couldn't believe it. He started crying. I think he honestly couldn't understand why I would do such a thing.

When the shock wore off, he followed me around the house ranting at me. He was careful not to touch me, but he was bullying me as much as he could. We passed by a little room divider that had a miniature six-inch, oak, cheese cutting board hanging on it. I grabbed it down and hit him in the side of the head with it. "Now, you son of a bitch, go ahead and hit me because I have a restraining order and you will go to jail," I yelled at him. I should have known how dumb a move that was, but for some reason, I did not. His eyes got really big and for the first time, I saw fear in HIS eyes. He shook with rage. He could have killed me. Many women lose their lives every day to men like him. I was just one of the lucky ones.

As I said, I had no place to go and no money so I stayed in the house with him until our court date. I moved to sleeping on the couch. He kept trying to get me to go back to the bed, but I refused. One day he put flea powder all over the couch saying that it had fleas from the cat and dog. It didn't. It was only one of his tricks. I simply vacuumed it up and ignored him. My heart had hardened. All I could feel was pure hatred for him. Where before I had thought he was so handsome, I now just saw him as ugly.

I think my cat and dog picked up on the vibes as well, because they slept with me on the couch. Winki slept on my legs and the cat on my shoulders. If Jim came close the cat would hiss and the dog would growl. It was my alarm system that would wake me.

On December 17, 1964, I had my interlocutory Judgment. I was 17 years old. I was awarded $20.00 per week alimony for three months until March 21, 1965, when I would turn 18.

Jim moved out of the house and I moved in with Evelyn. I slept on her couch. I had no training and had only an 8th-grade education. My prospects were not good.

As luck would have it, the owner of the property, Lindsay, came a couple of days later to see that the house in the back was ready to rent. She offered me a job as a nanny to her granddaughter, Travis. She said her daughter worked and didn't have time to care for Travis so Lindsay was the one who cared for her. Lindsay and her husband owned an airport in Perris, California, and she had way too much to do to take care of Travis. She offered me $50.00 a month plus room and board. I of course took it.

Married to my first husband, Jim (JPO)
November 23, 1963 to October 15, 1965
Claudia age 16 - Jim age 25
(Jim was 9 years older than me)

Chapter 12
Perris, California

I moved to the Perris Valley Airport with Lindsay to care for her granddaughter, Travis, who I would share a room with. The food was great. I had a car anytime I needed one. I was really happy. Travis was a beautiful little girl about fifteen months old and I quickly fell in love with her. The house at the airport was a big stucco, ranch-style house. It was one of the nicest houses I had ever been in and Lindsay had a "color" TV.

The color TV had been invented in the 1950s but had not been affordable until the mid-1960s. Hers was the first I had ever seen. What a difference color was from black and white. Most of the shows were still filmed in black and white, but the nightly news was in color and I was fascinated. As more shows were filmed in color, more people would buy the color TV, but it was way into the 1970s before more color than black and white TVs were sold. You could watch black and white on a color TV, but you could not get color on a black and white model. Today, no one has a black and white TV but occasionally you will find an old black and white movie or cowboy show on TV.

TVs were large in size, because the big "picture tube" was over a foot deep, with the largest screen being only about twenty-five inches wide. TVs had "Vacuum Tubes" in them. If your TV went out, you had to find the "blown" tube and replace it. You had to take the tubes out of the back of the TV and go to your nearest drug store that had a "U-Test-M machine."

Color TVs brought a different kind of problem, in that sometimes the color would go all wonky and you would have to use a "degaussing" (demagnetizing) tool to get it right again.

Lindy gave me a credit card for gasoline and one for a department store. Credit cards were a new thing that had just come out in about 1962, but I had never seen one until then. Lindy letting me have her credit cards was a big thing. She would let me buy things for Travis and even tell me to get something for myself. The first time I used the credit card, my hands were shaking when I signed the paper. Today you simply stick your card into a "card reader", but back then, the clerk would lay your card on a small mechanical machine, then lay a sales slip, which had carbon copies inside it, on top and then slide a bar over it which would cause it to put an imprint of your card name and number on the sales slip. Until the advent of computers, everything was mechanical and done by hand.

In addition to everything provided to me, Lindsay paid me an additional $50.00 a month. Considering that $50.00 in 1964 equals $457 in 2022 money and that I had everything paid for, including rent, utilities, groceries, car, insurance, gasoline, and some clothing, this was a great job.

I had two days off a week in which I could take one of Lindsay's cars and go back to Hawthorne to visit my family and friends and go to my dentist, which was one of the first things I did. In arranging for my teeth to be fixed, I explained my circumstances to Dr. Bass and he agreed to work with me. I could pay as I could afford and he would do the work I needed. In those days, there were no “credit dentists,” so all my money went toward getting my teeth fixed.

The Airport was a whole new way of life for me. I was responsible for Travis from the time she got up to when she went to bed. I did everything for and with her. She and I played all day. Sometimes we drove into Riverside to go to stores to buy things that weren't available locally.

I liked to sing and used to sing Travis to sleep for her nap and at night. Lindsay said I had a beautiful voice. That gave me a bit of courage to sing more. Sometimes Travis fell asleep too soon, but I would just keep singing.

One day I heard a song on the radio and had to have the sheet music for it. It was a Petula Clark song called "Downtown." I decided to go into Riverside to the music store.

Lindsay and the airport had lots of cars, so there was always one available for me to use. That day there were no cars available except a "stick shift." I had been driving since I was about 14, but I did not know how to drive a stick shift. I told Lindsay and her husband about my plight while we were having lunch and her husband told me there was nothing to driving a stick shift. Easy for him to say!

He told me to take the car (actually a truck) and practice on the runway. Well, that was a bunch of fits and starts for a while. Boy, I killed that engine dozens of times before I got the hang of it. All the time, I had Travis standing behind my right shoulder. This may seem strange and dangerous, but that was what we did in those days.

Seat belts were not even in all new cars until 1964 and were not mandatory until way into the1980s. Any car made before 1964 did not have seatbelts unless you paid extra for them or unless you had them installed aftermarket. Before that, it was common to see kids standing in the front seat of the car. Scary!

At any rate, after I could go up and down the runway, shifting through all the gears, and not stalling out, I figured I was good to go.

Remember, I was seventeen years old.

Off to Riverside we went. On the flat roads I was fine, but the first hill I came to, I killed the engine and rolled back into the car behind me. There wasn't any damage to the car behind me because as soon as I saw I was rolling backward I panicked and slammed on the brakes throwing Travis forward into the dash. Travis was not hurt, but it scared her and she was crying. Fortunately, the man in the car behind me was nice and he could see I was terrified and was trying to console Travis. He told me to go on but be careful. What a scary experience that was. My heart was racing a mile a minute.

I turned around and went back to the airport. Eventually, I did learn to drive a stick shift, but I never drove one with Travis in the car. There was nothing I needed bad enough that I couldn't wait for an automatic shift car to be available.

Sometimes while Travis was down for a nap, I helped Lindsey in the little "Burger Trailer" at the airport. She sold burgers and fries to customers who had come for flying lessons or to take a ride in a "glider."

I enjoyed working at the airport for a couple of months, but then, shortly before I turned 18, Lindsay's husband caught me in the hall and tried to kiss me. I panicked and pushed him away. To me, he was an "old man."

I was too scared to tell Lindsay because I might lose my job, but he was afraid I was going to tell her and decided to strike first. That night he told Lindsay that I had hit Travis when she would not go to sleep, which was ridiculous because I loved Travis, and I loved to sing to get her to go to sleep. I told Lindsey what had really happened, but, it was his word against mine. Of course, she wouldn't want to believe that her husband was a cheater, but I have found that more men than one would believe are in fact cheaters. Lindsay had to let me go and I went back to Evelyn's house. I wonder if she ever found out the truth because I'm sure if he tried it with me, he did the same with others.

I had a hard time digesting that incident. What was it with men? Why would Lindsay's husband risk getting caught kissing a seventeen-year-old kid that had two missing front teeth?

Claudia age 17 with Travis
At Perris Valley Airport
With my new blond hair.

Chapter 13
The Dentist

As soon as I moved back to Inglewood, I went to the dentist. I gave him the last of the money that I had saved from working for Lindsay and the money Jim had given me for alimony. He had been taking out my top teeth as I paid for it and there were only four top front teeth left to take out and then he could fit me for a denture.

Since I had moved back to Hawthorne / Inglewood area I did not have a car. I had asked my mother, Peggy, to drive me to the dentist for the extractions and she had agreed. I was very excited to get my new teeth.

I showed up at the dentist and my mother asked how long it would be. Instead of waiting, she said she had some errands to run and would be back before I was done. So, she left.

Dr. Bass pulled the rest of the top teeth and was ready to put the plate in, but he needed to check the x-rays. He came back in and he almost had tears in his eyes when he said, "Honey, I'm so sorry, but you have two wisdom teeth that I forgot about. They have to come out."

Generally removing wisdom teeth would require an "Oral Surgeon," but that was not in my budget. He gave me Novocain and extracted the wisdom teeth. Novocain helped, but it didn't kill all the pain. The roots of the wisdom teeth had grown around the bone and had to be broken so they could be taken out in pieces. Trying to withstand the pain, every muscle in my body was tensed. I was a wreck, and exhausted by the time he got all the pieces out.

He put the plate in and told me not to remove it for a week because the gums would swell up and I wouldn't be able to put it back in until the swelling went down which might be several weeks.

So here I am, my face is swollen, it was kind of numb but I was still in pain. I went out to the waiting room and my mother had not come back. I sat down in a chair hoping she wouldn't be very long. I just wanted to get home and go to sleep. So, I sat....

After some time, the receptionist asked if she could call someone for me. I said I didn't have anyone but my mother that had a car. And I sat....

The office was about to close and she still had not come. I was naturally, in tears. Dr. Bass came out and asked if he could call a cab for me. I told him I didn't have any money because I had given him the last of what I had.

I think that if my mother had come in then, he would have ripped her a new one. I had been sitting for over two hours. He called a cab for me and gave me the money to pay for it.

Riding home in the cab I was just sad, sick, and lonely. Where was my mother? As it turned out, she had gone to a bar and was having so much fun, she had just forgotten about me!

Chapter 14
A New Life

I needed a job. Evelyn's daughter, Carol, worked for Eastman Kodak and thought I might get on there. I however was still 17. I went and applied and lied about my age. They required that you show them a birth certificate. I told them that I didn't have one, but I would send for one and bring it in as soon as I got it. They hired me on the condition of showing them the birth certificate when it came.

I worked in the "darkroom" for Kodak as a "film splicer." We would open the little cans of film, cut the end tab off the film, clamp the film down, and "heat seal" a splice to join them together, and then wind them onto a big 12" reel.

The cylinder-shaped can of film was about an inch across and one and a half inches long. To get the film out of the little sealed cans it came in, you had to use a "decapper" machine. You held the metal can to the machine, and it uncrimped the top of the can, then sucked the cap down a little round chute into the trash can below. It worked pretty good for most of the time, but sometimes it sucked the film out of the can and it all wound up in the trash can.

In those days, women were required to wear skirts and blouses or dresses. You were also required to wear nylons and high heel shoes .... Even if you worked in a "darkroom."

The darkroom was very hot being a tightly closed space with lots of heat seal machines. Many of the women took off their blouses while they worked. It was dark and unless someone was using a special "night vision" pair of glasses, you couldn't see anything. Even with the night vision, you couldn't see much because everything looked green. Nonetheless, every time someone lost a roll of film to the trash, you had to call out "cover your film," and everyone had to put a black casing over their spliced reel of film and then put their blouse back on so that the film could be located with a "green" flashlight. Even a flashlight could expose the film so there was always a chance that someone's pictures would be lost.

We wore "Nylon Hose" in those days. That is two separate stockings held up by a garter or garter belt. Pantyhose were a kind of new thing for regular ladies and weren't economically priced until into the 1970s. Before that, "pantyhose" were mostly used by film stars and such.

It didn't take me long to figure out that if I took off one of my nylons and rubber banned it to the trash chute, it would be very easy and safe to retrieve the film. That was what I used on my machine and soon everyone was doing it. I also put it into the suggestion box so that other branches of Kodak might adopt the idea.

There were several other machine modification ideas that I put in the suggestion box as well. For several years after that, I would, now and then, get a check in the mail for $50.00 or $100.00 for an idea that had been approved. Kodak was a very good and honest company to work for.

Carol and I got an apartment together. I finally turned eighteen, footloose and fancy-free.

For my birthday Carol and her boyfriend took me to an amusement park. I can't remember where it was because I only remember the disastrous ride we went on. It was the spinning teacups. I didn't want to go on the ride, but they coerced me into it. Being the obliging kind of person that I was, (never being able to say no) I got on the ride.

As soon as it started I knew it was a mistake. My stomach started going wonky. I tried to tell them that I was getting sick, but they just kept laughing. Pretty soon, I got really sick and started throwing up. So, the cups are spinning and I am throwing up and vomit is going everywhere!

Finally, the guy running the ride saw what was happening and stopped the ride. Vomit was everywhere and some of the people in other teacups had started to vomit as well. I was so weak and dizzy that Carol and her boyfriend had to almost carry me off. The ride had to be shut down for cleaning. What a lovely birthday that was.

I rode to work with Carol, but wanted my own car. I was able to buy a 1954 Ford Fairlane for $100.00. It needed a bit of work, but it was mine. That was a lot of money in 1965. ($900 in 2022 money) A new car in 1965 cost about $2,600 ($23,400 in 2022).

I only had the car for a few weeks when my dad came around and said he needed a car, so I gave him mine. I don't know why. I just felt sorry for him.

I made about $1.45 an hour plus what I made for "above standard" performance which was $0.10 to $0.25 an hour. That was about $62.00 to $70.00 a week before taxes. When you consider our rent was only about $90 per month ($810 in 2022 money) divided between the two of us, we were living on the high side of life. The apartment we rented even had a swimming pool. I had never had a swimming pool.

In 1965 Lyndon Johnson was President and Hubert Humphrey was Vice President. The population of the United States was around 200 million. Life expectancy was 70.2 years. Gasoline cost $0.31 per gallon, a dozen eggs was $0.53 and a gallon of milk was $0.95. "Remote controls" for TV had been invented, but would only work on new TVs.

I felt very lucky to have the job I had. Considering that I had only an eighth-grade education, I was very lucky indeed. Girls in my time weren't raised to get jobs, they were supposed to get married and have babies.

I still wanted a car, so I saved more money and bought a dark brown, 1949 Nash Ambassador Coupe. It was a stick shift and it looked like a big cockroach, but it was mine.

Driving to work could be a thrill in my Nash. To get to Hollywood where I worked, I drove up La Brea Ave. There is one place where there is a red light at the top of a hill. If I got caught at the red light, I better be the first or second car because any further back left me on a steep grade. My car did not have enough "pick-up" to make it up the hill from a stopped position so I would have to roll back down the long hill to get a running start.

One day, while I was going to work, the car's motor suddenly started running fast. I couldn't get it to go slow. It was like I had my foot on the gas full throttle even when I had the brake on. I made it a few more blocks to work. I forgot about it until it was time to go home. As soon as I started it, it revved up. I shut it off and opened the hood. One of the guys I worked with came up and asked if he could help. I was glad to have any help I could get.

I told him what it did and started it for him. I shut it back down and we looked under the hood. We finally found that I had broken the "accelerator spring." Not having an auto parts store handy, I saw that maybe I could put one of the big rubber bands that I used on the film reels. He thought it might work also. I went in and got one and we fitted it to it. It worked like a charm.

It was some weeks later that I lent my car to a friend that we called "Shaky Marlene." We called her that because her hands always shook, worse than mine. Doctors didn't seem to find anything wrong with her, but her hands just shook.

Marlene went to the store and when she got back she was shaking all over. "Oh, my God," she said. "Your car is possessed or something!" Her face was white. We could see that she was serious and quite traumatized. Still, we all looked at her like she was crazy. "No, Really, I'm not kidding. It would not stop! It just keeps going. When I got here, I had to shut it off to get it to stop." And then it dawned on me. "The rubber band broke!" I said. Now everyone was looking at me like I'm nuts. So, I explained it to them. I had forgotten all about it and had not replaced the accelerator spring. Marlene never asked to borrow my car again and everyone else was leery of it as well.

Those days were the most fun and carefree times of my life. I had a great job, money, a great place to live, a pretty smile, friends, and I ruled my own life.

After I turned 18, I still did not bring in my birth certificate to work because I was afraid I would get fired for lying in the first place. I lived under constant fear that they would call for that birth certificate any day.

Carol and I decided that I should become a blond. My hair was very dark brown so that was a huge job. Bleaching dark brown hair in those days required many processes and it burned your scalp. By the time we were finished, I was running around the block to cool my scalp, the bleach was so hot on my head. We did get it blond though. My head had scabs on it for a week.

Sometime later, we got the idea of making my hair orange to match a dress I had. There were no weird colored hair dyes in those days so we did it with food coloring. It turned out very pretty and of course, I got a lot of attention.

About this time, Carol introduced me to a guy she had dated in high school. His name was Mel (MJC) and he was only four years older than me. He was getting discharged from the Army and came over in his Army uniform. He was one of the fortunate soldiers who had been stationed in Germany rather than being sent to fight in Vietnam. He was very handsome. He and I hit it off right away.

One thing that had a huge influence on my meeting eligible men my age was the Vietnam war. By The mid-1960s, the number of troops in Vietnam had reached about 500,000. More than 58,000 men were killed and hundreds of thousands were wounded. Many more were injured that were not recognized by our government. They either had PTSD or had been sprayed with Agent Orange and, as my brother would be in later years, incapacitated as a result. More than 500,000 men became draft dodgers and moved to other countries like Canada. All in all, an entire generation of men was taken out of the marriage pool. Most of the men I dated were ten years older or ten years younger than me.

Mel was such a gentleman. He brought me flowers and cards and he was so attentive and polite. I of course was leery, It would take more than a bouquet of flowers to impress me.

When I had been working at the airport in Perris, I got a ticket, and they sent me a notice to appear in Hemet, California. Mel offered to take me.

We drove up together in Mel's car. At one point, he pulled off the road, got out of the car, and then got back in the car. He explained that he had to "pass gas" and didn't want to do it in front of me. I mean, how sweet can a guy be?

I and my orange hair showed up at court and certainly got a lot of attention. No one, and I mean no one, in those days had seen anyone with bright orange hair. Weird color hair dyes wouldn't come around until the 1980s.

The judge, after doing a "double-take," seemed to love the color and he let me off on the ticket. Although I was still a shy and introverted young woman, I loved the attention.

On the way home, Mel stopped at an overlook and we got out to enjoy the view. "Look at it, Mel," I said, "The whole world is ours for the taking!" And that is how I felt, on top of the world. The eternal optimist.

Mel and I continued to date, and of course, "we fell in love." I continued to work at Kodak and all was right with the world.

One day, I showed up to work with my hair "green." We had an employee meeting and my supervisor made a lot about my hair. They had never seen weird colored hair.

After the meeting, my boss came to me and asked if he could take some pictures of me and my lovely hair to see if "Quality Control" would pick it up thinking the color board was off. I said OK. Quality control did pick it up, and everyone was happy.

I met Mel's family and his mother and I became fast friends. His family never yelled and they were just a lovely family. You could tell his dad ruled the roost, but he seemed to be a good leader and he never drank alcohol. It would be a few years before I found out how wrong I was about the "good" family view.

In January of 1965, I started getting pains in my stomach when I rolled the spliced reels of film at work. The reel was on a spindle and I had to wind it with my right hand. When the reel got near full, I would get shooting pains.

Mel's mother, Connie, said I should go to the doctor. I did not have a doctor because I never went to a doctor. She told me she had a good one, Dr. Sloan, so I went with her recommendation.

He examined me and said that I had an abdominal hernia that would have to be repaired. He explained that he would cut me open and sew together the inside lining of my abdomen and then sew up the outside skin. He further explained that if I didn't have it done, my intestines might get strangled off and all kinds of bad things could happen. That was scary! I had seldom even been to a doctor and now this one wanted to cut me open.

Fortunately, I had medical insurance at work that would take care of most of the cost. So, we set the date of February 3rd to have it done.

Because Carol worked, she would not be able to take care of me after the surgery. Connie said I could stay at their house and someone would always be there for me.

I was very scared going into the hospital to have the surgery. One minute I'm looking up at nurses and doctors with covered faces and the next minute, I wake up in a bed with my stomach "on fire!" It just burned. I must have gone to sleep again because the next thing I remember was my sister and Mel at my bedside. Teri said, "Oh, God, look at her, she looks all gray and dead!"

Well, that scared me and I tried to move which made the pain worse. My take away from that is: if you go to someone's bedside in the hospital, don't say something like that, because they may be able to hear you and it will scare the hell out of the patient!

The next day, I saw my abdomen. There was an incision about four inches long and it was "stapled" shut. That spooked me. What if I moved when I was asleep and the staples came out?

Dr. Sloan came in to see me and assured me that that was the strongest part of my body. He also said that it wasn't only the hernia that was bothering me. He said that there is an "inside umbilical cord" that is supposed to dissolve after you are born, but mine did not. Instead, it had grown inward and had wrapped around my liver and bladder. He had to cut it off and get it out. He had also taken out my appendix. It seems like I was pretty lucky to have found it when we did.

They gave me pain meds and the pain got better. The second night, I had a reaction to the medicine. Every time I closed my eyes, I felt like I was falling. I would jump and grab the sides of the bed. That of course was painful. I called for the nurse who kind of poo-pooed it. I had a very tortured night. I called her several times through the night.

The next day, Dr. Sloan came in and I explained the symptoms to him. He asked me if I had taken anything other than what they had given me. I said, "No, of course not!" This conversation was beginning to irritate me.

That night, the same thing happened. I knew it was useless to tell the nurse, so I called her and asked for a pot of coffee. I stayed up reading all night.

The next day when Dr. Sloan came in, I told him what had happened. He again accused me of taking something. I was beside myself. Why wouldn't anyone listen to me? What was the nurse telling him?

Mel's mother came to see me and she questioned me also. She had been in that hospital several times and had never had a problem. Does that mean that I'm not having a problem?

That night, when I called the nurse because she had forgotten to bring my pain med, she said, "Doctor Sloan said not to give you any pain medicine, but then he relented," and she gave me the meds.

After the nurse left, the word "relented" kept ringing in my ears. The more I thought about it, the madder I got. I got out of bed and got my suitcase and threw it onto the bed. Yikes, I had forgotten the books I had packed. I never went anywhere without several books to read. Pain flared up in my abdomen and I guess I turned white and passed out. The girl next to me called for the nurse.

The next thing I know, Dr. Sloan was there and they were putting me back into the bed. I told them all what I thought about them and that I was leaving. Dr. Sloan said that if I stayed the night, he would release me in the morning. I agreed on the condition that they bring me a pot of coffee.

The girl who was in the bed next to mine came out of surgery and the next day, she started crying and I don't think she stopped. She had had a hysterectomy. I figured she was crying because she would no longer be able to have children. That was not the case. "Look at this," she said. "Just look at what that butcher did to me!"

I thought she must be exaggerating. She had a huge bandage on her stomach. She removed it to show me and it was gross! It looked like she had been ripped apart instead of cut. It wasn't just a straight line cut, it was crooked and went down and then to the side.

"I'll never be able to wear a bikini again," she said. I know that wasn't her main concern, it was just the only thing her traumatized brain could think of at the time. I couldn't see why any doctor would do that to a patient. It was a butchered job!

The whole experience of that hospital set my mind about trust and doctors. These men were not saviors. They were uncaring butchers as far as I was concerned. Lesson one: you have to thoroughly investigate a doctor before you let them cut on you.

I healed from the surgery and within a month was back to my old self. I had a pretty big scar above my belly button, but I was no longer in pain.

I did not go back to work at Eastman Kodak. My step-dad, Leroy, talked to me about watching Kim and Peppy. He was desperate because he didn't have anyone he could trust to watch them. I loved my job at Kodak, but I loved my siblings more and because of my upbringing, I understood his fear. So, I quit work and moved in with Leroy and the kids. I did however condition it on having nights to myself. I wasn't about to watch the kids so Leroy could go out and party at night.

One afternoon, Mel came to pick me up for a date and Leroy had not come home yet. Mel worked for his uncle in a construction company and he was tired, so he lay down on the couch and went to sleep. When Leroy got home, I needed to wake Mel up, so I put one of his "Camel" cigarettes in his mouth. That was what my sister did to me if she wanted to wake me. HE ATE THE CIGARETTE before I could light it and did not even wake up. After I got him awake and told him what had happened, he laughed and explained that he must have thought it was a fried potato. His mother put a fried potato in his mouth to wake him up.

Claudia age 18 when dating Mel 1965

Right: Mel 1965 age 22

Chapter 15

Second Marriage

Mel and I continued dating and then in January of 1966, I discovered I was pregnant. In those days, being pregnant before marriage was a huge shame. So, of course, we got married. It didn't bother us because "we were in love." Mel wanted children and his mom wanted grandchildren .... lots of grandchildren.

The apartment we moved into was one of Mel's uncle's apartments. His uncle, built apartment units in the Hawthorne to Redondo Beach area. They were mostly ten-unit buildings. After he built a unit, we would move into the manager's unit and rent out the other units. The rent was free for us in exchange for managing. He would sell the building and we would move on to the next. Of course, that meant that we were only in one place for a few months.

While Mel had been such an attentive gentleman when we dated, he changed rapidly after we got married. Though we had dated for over a year, I had not investigated how much Mel worked or how much money he made or anything. I was very naïve as to what that might mean.

Women were not trained to evaluate a man for his potential as a provider. It never occurred to me that when I chose a man, I was also choosing the future for my children and their welfare. Had I been able to see the future, I would have chosen very differently. Unfortunately, all young girls looked for at that time was "being in love." That's a stupid and costly mistake for yourself and your children. Once you have children with someone, you are stuck with them forever!

Mel, as it turned out, wasn't what you would call a great worker. He was supposed to go from project to project to see that the workers were getting it done and that there were no problems. If there was a problem, it was up to him to fix it. He was pretty much on his own.

Sometimes Mel didn't show up for work for several days. His uncle would call me and ask where he was and I would have to go and locate him. He was usually shooting pool and drinking beer at some bar.

Mel's work ethic got worse as the months went by. His uncle was getting very irritated and finally fired him. I was about seven months pregnant and he was out of a job. We would soon have to move out of our apartment because the building had been sold.

About this time, my obstetrician's office informed me that unless I had my bill paid by the time I delivered, I would not have a doctor. Not good and very scary for a nineteen-year-old young woman.

One of the apartments had become vacant and Mel was supposed to paint the interior and touch up some things on the outside of the building. The money would be enough to pay my doctor. Mel got lost in a pool game and failed to do the necessary painting, so I did it. I was not going to be without a doctor when I delivered. That was the beginning of what would become my painting career though I did not know it at the time.

I recall that when I was done painting the apartment, I was exhausted. I went upstairs to my apartment to lay down for a nap. When I went through my front room, on the way to my bedroom, I saw a piece of lint on the floor, under the bookcase. I went into my bedroom and lay down on the bed, but I could not get that piece of lint out of my mind. I could not sleep until I got up and picked up that piece of lint. I and my big belly had to get down on my hands and knees to get it. This was certainly a bit of insanity and I knew it, but OCD had me and there was nothing to do but go with it! When you cannot control much, you control what you can.

I paid my doctor with the money I got from the painting. Mel borrowed some money from his mother and we rented a little house in Inglewood.

When I started labor, Mel took me to the hospital, said he needed to go buy some cigarettes, and then disappeared. Labor was hard, very painful, and frightening. I didn't know what to expect.

There had been no training in school or anything about having a baby. Back then people didn't even talk about sex. If you didn't have a mother to teach you anything, you just did not know what to expect. I was so very naïve.

I was in labor for two full days. They wouldn't let me out of the bed and I thought my back would break. Crying most of the time, and screaming at others, I thought I was going to die. They said they couldn't give me anything for the pain because it would wear off before I delivered and they wouldn't be able to give me anything at that time. It takes about five minutes to "have a baby," but I had to lay for two days in excruciating pain. You cannot convince me that that makes sense.

I don't know if they understood how much pain I was in or if they just didn't care. I felt like I was being tortured to death.

At one point, my dad showed up. They wouldn't let anyone else in my room, but he got in? He had stolen a white coat from somewhere.

He came over to the bed and started to lift the sheet that covered me. "Let me see where it hurts," he slurred. He was drunk as a skunk. I started screaming and kicking him. The nurse came in but thought he was a doctor. By the time I got it through to her that he was my dad and not a doctor, I was exhausted and terrified. I could not believe it. How much more could happen to me? All I wanted was my husband, and he was nowhere to be found. Mel would say later that he just hated hospitals. "So do I, you moron!"

The doctor told me that I had a small birth canal and that was why it was taking so long. Today they would do a c-section. In those days, they let you lay in agony.

On September 28, 1966, my daughter, Tami Mel-lene was born. She weighed four pounds, fifteen ounces. She was beautiful and I fell in love. And yes, I did, somewhat, forget the pain I went through when I saw my child, (and the pain had stopped) but the trauma that surrounded it, I would never forget.

They tried to say that Tami was premature because of her small weight, but I knew when I became pregnant and she was not premature. When I brought Tami home from the hospital, she fit into a shoebox. She was tiny, delicate and beautiful.

Today, I know she was small because I smoked back then. Like I said, "everyone smoked back then." They even gave you an ashtray in your hospital room. It wasn't until the 1970s that smoking was forbidden in the rooms themselves, and into the 1990s that it was restricted to the outside of hospitals.

At any rate, I can remember feeding Tami with one hand and smoking with the other, a cloud of smoke encircling us both. I can't even imagine doing that today. Times change!

In those days, it was rare that women nursed their babies. At that time, it was thought that breastfeeding was only practiced by the uneducated and lower class. I tried anyway, but couldn't get her to "latch on," and no one was trying to encourage me or teach me how. She was too small to take the chance of her losing more weight and so she was put on formula. Manufactures thought they could do better than "Mother Nature," and hospitals probably got a kickback and free formula.

I seemed to have a lot of milk, and even though they gave me "dry-up" pills, I continued to produce milk for several months. When your breast gets too full, the milk leaks out, and if you don't have something to absorb the milk, it runs down your blouse and leaks all over. Breast pumps had been invented, but only hospitals had them, and they were big and expensive.

In those days, there was some kind of "disposable diapers," but they were nothing like what we have in 2022 and only the rich could afford them. It wouldn't be until the late 1970s that "disposables" caught on and prices came down a bit.

Most diapers were made of cloth and were either "flats" or "pre-folds." Flats were about 16" X 24" and had to be folded in half and then into a triangle and then was held by a "baby safety pin," which was only a big metal pin with a plastic head. Pre-folds were about 7" X 9" and were held by two safety pins, one on each side. We mostly used the pre-fold diapers because the flats were just too big for a five-pound baby.

Along with diapers, babies wore, "rubber Pants." They were a plastic or rubber panty that went over the diaper with elastic leg and waist to prevent "leaking" from diapers. They also kept all the heat, from the ammonia in urine, in the diaper, and against the baby's skin, causing "diaper rash." Some women used "Baby Powder" that helped absorb the wetness, but I used "corn starch" as recommended by my mother-in-law. It worked better and was a lot cheaper. In later years they would discover that the "asbestos" in baby powder can cause cancer so it was fortunate that we couldn't afford it.

Mel seemed to love his baby. He was very attentive to her but he would not change her diaper. He got a job and things were better. He still got lost in bars, but it was better. My optimistic self, thought, "having a baby might change him."

But, I remember one day, he dropped me off at the Laundromat to wash baby clothes. We did not have a washer and dryer, so several times a week I had to go to the Laundromat to wash baby clothes and diapers. I had Tami in a buggy. Mel went for "a pack of cigarettes." He of course did not come back. The clothes were done and I could only wait. My milk started coming in and I was leaking. I had no pads, so it ran down my blouse and dripped on the floor. I was so embarrassed. I put a diaper down my bra, but it was still a mess.

In those days, of course, we had no "cell phones." They wouldn't be available until the 1990s. (23 years away) The Laundromat did have a "payphone" on the wall. A payphone had slots at the top so you could deposit coins to make a call. I had no money left after I washed the clothes, so I had to borrow a dime from one of the people in the Laundromat to call Mel's mother. Fortunately, she was home and came and picked me up.

When Tami was a few months old, I saw a pair of baby shoes in the store and couldn't resist. It wasn't something she needed, I just wanted them. I bought them, and when we went to Mel's parent's house, I got scolded for wasting the money. His mom reminded me that Mel owed her money, and until that was paid, I had no right to waste money. I was so broken-hearted and sad. I looked at my precious baby and cried because I couldn't even buy her a little pair of shoes. At that moment, I just hated Mel!

Mel had made up with his uncle and by Thanksgiving, we had moved to one of his apartment buildings and were the permanent managers. My sister, Teri, and I decided we were going to make a real Thanksgiving dinner. Up to that point, we had always gone to a relative's house for holidays. We decided we wanted to have a Thanksgiving that was just for our family. I had Tami and Teri, married to Sam, had two little girls.

We were very excited. We were creating a perfect Thanksgiving. One like we never had at home. We bought all the groceries and Teri, Sam, and their kids came over to our apartment. We figured the "men" would watch football and we would cook and it would be like something out of a magazine.

The Turkey was cooking and we were almost finished with everything else when Mel and Sam decided to go get a six-pack of beer. They would be "right back" ....

"Right back," never came. We waited for hours. The Turkey was drying out and there we sat. We both just cried. It was such a letdown. We were broken-hearted. We eventually tried to eat but our beautiful Thanksgiving dinner tasted like dust in our mouths. Nothing tastes good with tears.

Other things were going on in our lives. My dad had gotten a "big rig," and was driving for "Mayflower Movers." This is a man who had had several "drunk driving" charges that I knew of and they gave him a license to drive a truck? I thought the world had gone stark raving mad.

It only took a few months for him to get drunk and turn the truck over on the highway. Luckily, he didn't kill anyone. He totaled his truck and took it out on Dodie, of course. Like it was her fault?

I learned to stay away from big trucks on the road as they can be very dangerous if a drunk is behind the wheel. You just never know what condition that driver is in.

Whenever I talked to Dodie on the phone she complained about dad. I felt sorry for her and begged her to leave him. I couldn't imagine why she wouldn't. I told her I would help her if she decided to leave and that it wasn't good for Nini, but she couldn't seem to do it. I think it might have had something to do with her religion. She always told me that people were supposed to suffer on this earth and "receive their reward in heaven." What kind of crap is that? What was the reward? A bale of hay you horse's ass!

Meanwhile, dad called me on the phone, also. He never made any sense, he just went on with crazy stuff. He didn't like Mel and often said he was going to shoot him in his knees. Knowing how crazy my dad was, I was afraid he would do it, and then I would be stuck supporting "a disabled Mel" for the rest of his life.

Mel was always quitting or getting fired from this or that job. Unemployment was not enough to live on. Most of the time he didn't qualify for benefits because he had quit his job. When Mel did work, I always put on my makeup and dressed Tami in a pretty dress and I would put her in her buggy and then go down to the end of the driveway to meet Mel when he came home. More often than not, he did not come home and I would go back home disappointed.

When Tami was less than a year old, I had had enough. We were about to be evicted from another apartment. I decided I would get a job which meant that I had to leave my baby with my mother-in-law while I worked. More than anything, I just wanted to stay home and raise my child, but I just had no choice.

I put in applications at several places and was offered jobs at three different places, so I took them all.

The first place was a donut shop. I worked that job on the weekends. I worked the "window" selling donuts. The minimum wage for women was about $1.40 per hour in 1967 in California. I was of course hired at minimum wage.

The first Saturday I worked, I had a customer who said I charged him too much for a dozen donuts. He said he bought donuts every week and it cost him $1.32 and I was charging him $1.42. A little flustered, I recalculated the donuts he had ordered. My price was correct. I told him I was sorry, but my price was accurate. I suggested that the person who had waited on him before might have made a mistake if he had made the same donut selections. He insisted I was wrong. I had a line of people waiting. Finally, I said, "OK, this is the price of these donuts this week, do you want them or not?" He started to walk away but then decided he wanted the donuts and paid for them.

I did not know that the owner was watching me, but he was. He came over to me and said I had done a good job and that that guy was always giving people a problem about the price. He said he liked the way I handled it and gave me a ten cent per hour raise on the spot. I was delighted.

It also taught me something that I never forgot. The customer is not always right. "Trust yourself" because people will cheat you if they can get away with it. That man had no consideration of whether I might get fired for that exchange. He did not consider or know how badly I needed that job. It was only a game to him, a sick, stupid game.

One job was as a part-time waitress, but that didn't last long because they wanted me to come in at all different times and that didn't make it with my other two jobs. I had nights open for that job and that was all. I had to quit that one after a couple of weeks.

The other job was with Hyack's Manufacturers. They made silk and burlap artificial flowers and arrangements.

When I went to apply, I asked Mel to apply with me. I figured he might make it to work a little better if I worked alongside him. We were both hired.

The first day we went to work, we got to the shop and Mel said he didn't have enough cigarettes and was going to go to the store down the street and would be right back……

Mel didn't come back. I was very embarrassed. I told the owner that he had car trouble and begged him to give Mel another chance. He agreed. The next day, the same thing! Mel dropped me off, went to park the car, and just left. He didn't get another chance with Hyack's, but I continued to work there.

Within a few months, I had worked myself up to being the "floor representative" at Flower Shows. I made my wage and a bit more depending on how many arrangements I sold. When there wasn't a flower show going on, I worked in the manufacturing warehouse making flowers or flower arrangements. They trained me in arranging flowers and it took very little time for me to become quite good.

Mel's mother picked me and Tami up in the morning and drove me to work and then took Tami to her house. Mel was supposed to pick me up from work but, more often than not, I had to walk home and hope that Mel would come home soon so we could go and get Tami from his mom's.

This was a tough time for me. When I was working all three jobs, I didn't have any time to even think. I got little sleep and Mel's mother kept Tami overnight many nights because I was too tired to take care of her and Mel was no help at all.

My mother-in-law, Connie, was not unhappy with this arrangement. She only had two boys and had always wanted a girl. Now she had one, but it was my little girl that she had.

My mother-in-law continued to give Mel money and there was no way that I could ever catch up. I was like a cat chasing its tail.

Eventually, the owner of Hyack's had to hire a supervisor to keep things running at the shop when we were away at flower shows. I thought they should have elevated one of the ladies that worked on the flower line, but in those days, a man was usually the foreman. Men thought that women were not capable of a job like that.

The man they hired was an insufferable, overbearing, bruit of a man who treated all the women with disrespect. He made sexual innuendoes toward the younger ones, berated the older ones, and was just a bully.

I was often at a show and was not aware of what was going on until one day that I didn't have a show and had to work the manufacturing floor. When I saw how things were, I complained to the owner. What I told him was completely disregarded.

About a week later, after having been the target of some of his abuse, I led a strike and everyone walked off the floor. Manufacturing came to a halt. The guy was eventually fired. Of course, I lost my job but I was not going to put up with abuse all day long. I needed that job, but I didn't need it that bad. Why were men such pigs and why did women have to put up with it?

Married second husband Mel (MJC) February 18, 1966
Claudia 19, Mel 22 Left to Right: Connie (Mel's mother)
Mel, Claudia, Dodie, my dad. (Mel about 3 years older than me)

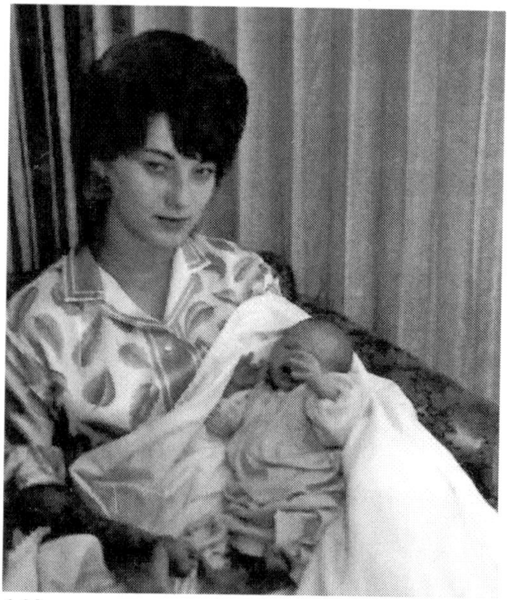

Birth of daughter
Tami Mel-lene
9-28-1966
She fit in a shoebox!

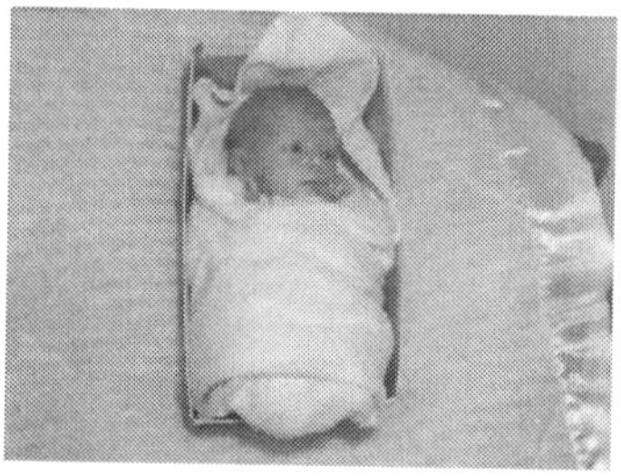

Chapter 16
Modeling and More

I read in the paper that a modeling agency was looking for new models. I decided to apply. I got an interview and went in. They were nice and the agency looked very professional. There was one girl in there getting an address for her modeling assignment.

They said I needed a "portfolio" and asked if I had any professional photographs. I said, “No." They said it wasn’t a problem; they would have the pictures done for me. It would only cost me $100. That doesn’t sound like much in 1967 money, but the equivalent in 2022 money would be $849. It was an enormous amount of money that I did not have.

Since leaving Hyack’s, I only had the donut shop job and while I was able to pick up some extra hours, it was not full-time.

Of course, I couldn’t ask Mel’s mother for the money. Instead, I asked my stepmother, Dodie for a loan. And she came through for me.

I went to the shoot and the pictures came out great. They had my makeup and hair done and I looked very professional. Now all I had to do was to get some jobs.

Nothing came. No phone calls, no jobs. I called the agency and just got a run-a-round. After a few months, it became apparent that I had been scammed. I was very upset and vowed they would not get away with it.

I decided to sue my agent for breach of contract, and I told the modeling agency what I was going to do. Now, you would think that if a client threatens to sue you, you would at least send them out on one shoot.

They did not.

It took a few more months to get the money to file but I managed. I had a court date set.

Their attorneys called me and wanted to meet. I told them I would see them in court.

Mel was not working and I was barely making the rent and groceries. The day we went to court, we barely had the money for gas; we did not have enough money to buy lunch. When we got to the courthouse, the agency's attorney asked for a meeting to see if we could come to an agreement. The court ordered an arbitration meeting.

So, we went into a little room and their attorney asked if I would accept a refund of $100. I declined the offer. Then the attorney put three pictures in front of me and asked me to pick out the picture of the man I had talked to. I have a great memory for faces, I'm not so good with names, but faces are my thing. Even though I had only seen him one time, it was no problem. Then he tried to say that I had not been promised a job. I got a little notebook out of my purse and read the date, time, and what exactly was said. That moved them. I would be a very convincing witness. Of course, I would, my dad had trained me in what was "best evidence," and my contemporaneous notes would carry a lot of weight with the court.

I don't remember exactly how much I sued for. It seems to me like it was $1000. I might have gotten it and I might not. I knew that if I went before the judge, he could order the return of my money, he could give me nothing or he could award "punitive damages."

The agency's attorney finally offered me $500 (about $4,250 in 2022 money). Considering I didn't have enough money for lunch, that was an enormous amount of money. I accepted it. They cut a check right there.

I paid Dodie back the money I owed her, and then I turned the case over to the police department's fraud team. They said they would investigate and keep an eye on the agency. Within two months, the agency went out of business.

This kind of scam still goes on today. Many young, hopeful women and men are taken in every day by crooks like this. I was twenty years old and naïve as hell. My advice to young women and men is: If an agency says they are interested in you but you need pictures, they will take them for free if it is legit. If they advise you to go to your own photographer and have some pictures taken, it may be OK. If they want money to take them for you ……. run to the exit.

One of my modeling pictures 1967

Claudia age 20

Tami came down with what I thought was "Scarlet Fever." At least, consulting my "Mother's Medical Book," she matched all the symptoms and pictures. Her hands and feet had not peeled, but that would happen in a few weeks. Mel's mother thought she had Measles. She was very concerned because Mel had not had measles and she was afraid that it was far more serious for an adult male, and might make him "sterile," if it was measles. The rash did not match any of the pictures, in the book, for measles. Remember, this was before the internet. So, I took Tami to the doctor to find out which it was. That was when I found out that doctors only "practice" medicine not much had been "perfected". They sometimes don't know or can't be sure. The doctor wasn't sure, but was leaning toward "Measles." There was no treatment or medicine for measles, but scarlet fever would require antibiotics. He prescribed the antibiotic because if it wasn't needed, it wouldn't hurt. In those days, they freely gave antibiotics because they had no idea, at that time, that they were creating, "superbugs," that would later plague our society.

A few days later, Mel came down with what did look like measles. His mother thought she had been vindicated, but a few weeks later, Tami's hands and feet pealed and Mel's never pealed. That was just bizarre. It appeared that Tami had scarlet fever, but Mel had measles!

That left a question in my mind of how that could happen. Mel obviously had not contracted measles from Tami, so how did he come down with it. Could the "mind" create measles from "belief?" This is a question that would stay on my mind for years and lead me to some of the greatest secrets in the universe and would quite possibly save my daughter, Tami's life later on.

Mel was more obsessed with sex than working and I was just too tired most of the time. I did not want a divorce, but I was getting to the breaking point. I figured I could make it by myself better than with Mel.

I struggled with this for some time. I didn't want to be like my mother, but I didn't think the arguing was good for Tami either. I remembered from my childhood how frightening that was, but I just couldn't get the fighting to stop. He wanted sex and I wanted him to work to support his family. I gave in, he did not.

Mel was never physically violent with me, but he was terribly abusive all the same. He called me bitch, slut, whore, and many other things and all in front of Tami. He couldn't fault me for my housekeeping, but he could compare my cooking to his mother's. I, of course, always fell short of her mark.

Then sometime in July or August of 1968, I discovered I was pregnant with our second child and I knew I was screwed. I thought I could support one baby, but how could I support two?

I hate to say it, but I was devastated. I did not want this baby. I only wanted out. I hoped I would miscarry. I hit my stomach to try to shake it loose. It was a dumb idea that fortunately didn't work.

Mel went to work at Bekins Moving and Storage as a mover and we rented the house behind Evelyn's that I had originally lived in with my first husband. It's a small world.

For some time, everything was going pretty good and I again became hopeful. I am the eternal optimist if nothing else!

My brother, Pat, graduated high school and joined the Army. He was sent to Vietnam and I was scared to death that something was going to happen to him.

Pat and I were very close. I wrote him faithfully every week. One time I wrote him a letter in code. When we were kids, we made up languages like "G" where you put a "G" after every syllable. We studied ciphers and codes and crazy things like that. It never occurred to me that I was writing a letter to a soldier in a war zone. The army did not appreciate my "code writing," and sent my letters back (decoded) with a stern warning not to do it again. I continued to write, but not in code.

I gave birth to my son, Andy Martin, on March 15, 1969. He weighed four pounds fifteen ounces just like Tami had. I don't even remember the labor or birth, I only remember that they gave me a "saddle block," which is the anesthesia that is put into the spine with a needle, and it numbs the lower part of your body, so you don‘t feel the pain of labor. Unfortunately, you have to lay flat for twenty-four hours after you give birth or you get a headache. I got a headache even though I laid flat for twenty-four hours. The thing I remember the most is my beautiful baby boy with a head full of dark hair.

They said he was premature, and this time they would not release him from the hospital until he weighed over five pounds. Tami had only been in the hospital a day and a half after being born. But Andy they kept over a week. I was sent home after two days.

It was really hard to leave my baby. I was only able to see him a couple of times a day. I did not breastfeed him even though the thinking was beginning to change on the issue.

In the hospital, they fed him formula so that he would get the "right" amount of nutrition. Most babies lose a little weight after they are born and he went down a few ounces. It took a full week before I could bring him home. I was twenty-two years old.

When I finally brought him home, the nurses were all disappointed. They loved to pick him up and comb his hair. Andy cried a lot and I just thought that I had a "colicky" baby. But the truth was, he just wanted to be held all the time which was pretty difficult with another child.

Tami did not appreciate her baby brother or his crying. "Get that baby out of my room," she screamed. Eventually, she came to love him, but it took a while.

That house had no washer and dryer. Instead, I washed the diapers in the bathtub on a "scrub board" and hung them outside on the clothesline to dry. It was a whole lot easier than packing up two kids and going to the Laundromat and it cost a lot less.

I was on edge because Mel had worked the longest he ever had at this job, but he was starting to go out more at night and was missing work some days. I was just waiting for the second shoe to drop.

My compulsive behavior kicked in. I started ironing everything in the house. It started out ironing the diapers, and remember, I had two kids in diapers. The diapers were stiff when I brought them in from the clothesline, so I started ironing them to make them soft. Then it was sheets and dishtowels. Yes, I was losing it. When there is little you can control, you control what you can.

Fabric softener was somewhat in use in the late 1960s but was not a commonly used product and was more of a luxury item. The dryer sheet wasn't invented until the late 1970s.

Within a few months, Mel lost (quit) his job and we moved in with his brother and sister-in-law. His brother had two kids and one on the way, but we moved into one of their three bedrooms.

Mel's parents had helped them buy the house and his parents had a small house on the back of the lot, so here we were just a bunch of peas in a pod.

In the 1960s it was recommended to get several shots for babies: Measles, Mumps, and Rubella in one shot (MMR) with a series of three. Diphtheria, Tetanus, and Pertussis in another (DPT) in a series of three. Polio was a separate one.

Tami had had her shots with no problem other than sometimes she cried when she got them. I never heard, in the news, of adverse effects from vaccines. There was no internet to consult. If you heard anything, it would have to be through the newspaper, TV or from a friend or family member. I was a naive twenty-two-year-old mother of two.

When Andy got one of his vaccines, it was a different story. A few hours after getting the shot, he started making a high-pitched wailing sound that was just piercing and eerie. You could tell he was in horrific pain. My heart shudders to think of how that sounded. I called the doctor, but was told it was a natural reaction and would get better. I held that poor baby for several days afterward.

I didn't connect it at the time, but at about six months old, he used to get on his hands and knees, in his crib, and rock, bumping his head against the end of the crib. He would scoot the crib clear across the floor. He never stopped doing that and still rocks in his sleep today, more than fifty years later. I know it was from that shot. The doctor told me it was just a coincidence.

There were, eventually, so many reports of vaccine injury to children that the "Childhood Vaccine Injury Act" was passed in 1986. If you can prove that your child is damaged by a vaccine, you get a certain amount of money. But it is a "no-fault" law as well, so the vaccine manufacturers are not held accountable for the problems and cannot be sued for damages. How many children were damaged and continue to be damaged today?

Vaccines may be needed, but there needs to be some way to identify those who might be damaged by them, like some kind of pre-test or DNA test or something. In those days, there were only about seven shots a child needed. Today, a child has about fifty-one doses of some foreign pathogen, put into their little bodies before they reach school age. It is very controversial as to whether this causes "autism" in children. I don't know the answer to that, but with the high rates of it showing up, I think we need people, not paid by the pharmaceutical companies, to investigate the matter more fully. As of 2022, one in about fifty-nine children will be diagnosed with autism. I am not against vaccines, I just think, perhaps, they have made into law, what should be an "informed parent's choice." I will now step down from my soapbox.

With two children it seemed impossible to leave Mel, and of course, I had that thing running in my head that I didn't want to be like my mother.

I enjoyed my kids and loved holidays. I always managed to make Christmas a special time. I saved my "Blue Chip" stamps and I would clean my neighbor's houses or babysit their kids for more stamps. No matter if Mel was working or not, my children never went without.

We moved to a "court" of houses. There were about eight houses that shared one driveway. I met the neighbors and it was a lot of fun there. The girl across from me, Karen, became my best friend. She had three kids and her husband worked at the post office.

On July 20, 1969, I sat with my two children and watched the televised event of Neil Armstrong walking on the moon. He was the first man to ever do that. It was amazing. I remember holding my breath.

Would a moon monster appear?

It seems commonplace now because everyone knows what the moon looks like up-close, thanks to “rovers” taking pictures of most of it. We know there are no moon men or monsters, but back then it was an event with an unknown outcome.

Before this event, people speculated on what was on the moon. Was it made of "green cheese?" Was there life there? When I was a kid, I spent many days and nights looking at the moon and wondering what was up there. It was a miraculous mystery. And now it was solved!

Mel worked sporadically. He often borrowed from his mom to make the rent which I refused to pay back. I had sat her down and had a talk with her and told her that if she gave him money, I would no longer be responsible for paying it back. I was done with that game and I would not feel guilty for buying something for my kids. The answer, I told her, was, "don’t lend him money!" If we need money, I will let you know.

My relationship with his mother was a "push me - pull me." I got along with her when Mel wasn’t involved. I loved her like the mother I never had. She taught me how to can fruit, how to make jelly, and how to cook. If only she would not lend her son money. She was the enabler in his undisciplined life.

Sometimes when Mel came up missing, she and I would get in the car and go look for him. I remember one time finding his car outside a bar. We got out of the car and went inside. I knew where Mel would be and headed for the pool table. Connie scampered along behind me. "Give me a quarter," I commanded her. Still shuffling behind me, she dug into her purse and forked over the quarter.

When we got to the pool table, Mel was spinning the cue ball on the table and saying, “Come on, there must be someone who wants to play." I walked up and flipped the quarter onto the table and said, "Here's a quarter if your kids and I have to pay for your time." With that, I turned and started walking out of the bar. Connie was still scampering behind me with big eyes. She had never been to a bar before in her life. It took a minute before it registered with Mel what had happened and then he ran after us.

One Saturday, Mel and Sam (Teri's husband) called us from the county jail. They had been pulled over for some reason and the police had found warrants for unpaid tickets on them both. They needed Teri and me to bring $35 ($270 in 2022 money) each and come to the Los Angeles County Jail and post their bail.

Well, that wasn't something we wanted to do, but they both had jobs and we were afraid they would lose their job if we didn't get them out. That was a lot of money back then and we didn't have money lying around waiting for something to spend it on. Fortunately, the ATM (automated teller machine) had recently been invented and you could get money out of them if you had money in the bank. We didn't have that much in the bank. We put in a phony deposit envelope saying there was a deposit in it and were able to draw some cash from that. We would have to deal with the consequences later.

So, we put all our kids in the car and drove to Los Angeles County jail. What an ordeal. That place was like a zoo with all kinds of derelict-looking people. We didn't feel safe and kept our kids as close to us as possible.

We got to the window to pay the fines and were told we didn't have enough money. The fines were now about $50 ($386 in 2022 money) for each of them because they had found more warrants. Neither one of us had that much money. The bank ATM trick would not work again. We had to drive from friend to friend and borrow whatever we could to get that much.

We were too afraid to spend any money on something to eat because we might not have enough money for the fines. We stopped home and made jelly sandwiches for us and the kids.

These were the very early days of computers. Police departments had some computers, but they weren't fast and if you were searching for warrants, it might take hours to get a response. That is why the warrants trickled in.

We finally got the money and went back to Los Angeles County Jail only to be told that the fines were now about $75 (over $579 in 2022 money).

So, we went back to Hawthorne / Inglewood area to try to find more money, crying all the time. We knew Mel and Sam were setting in a cell with food being delivered and not a care in the world. Why is it that women and children pay the price for what a man does? It's just not fair!

Of course, we were spending money on gas to go back and forth. The only place I had left to borrow was Mel's parents who thankfully gave me the money. They also took my two kids and Teri's as well so that we didn't have to keep driving them back and forth to the jail.

Eventually, we did post enough money to get them out of jail, but then we had to wait hours for them to be processed and released. They had been in Sam's car, which had been impounded, but that would have to wait until Sam could find more money. We were two pathetic little girls, twenty-six and twenty-four years old, being blown around by circumstances. This is not how I had envisioned my life. Feel sorry for myself? You bet I did!

My children were the most important thing in my life, and everything

I was, or did, revolved around them. Anything that took from my children was an enemy of mine. Their father was becoming my enemy.

There were, of course, some good times. We had parties and family get-togethers and holidays. Sometimes Mel was kind, caring, and attentive to his kids. But I never felt like we were a real priority. The bad seemed to wash out the good. I understood how Dodie felt. Boy, the crap women had to put up with!

Through the years, my dad continued to plague my life. He would call, drunk. If you hung up on him, he might show up at your door and that would be a big fight. So, you learned to just try to get him off the phone. Many nights I fell asleep with the phone next to my ear. All you had to do was to grunt now and then because you weren't going to get a word in edgewise anyway. He would eventually run out of BS and hang up on you.

In closing this chapter of my life, I want to note a few more things about this time in history. Though there is some controversy as to whom and how the microwave oven was invented, it was mostly only a theory or used for military technology for many years. The Microwave oven had been patented in 1947, the year I was born. It slowly advanced some, but was only used commercially and was prohibitively expensive for ordinary folks. By the mid-1960s you could buy a microwave oven but they cost about $500 (about $4,300 in 2022 money). Most people would not get one until the 1970s.

It was so much more difficult, before the microwave became affordable, for ordinary people. In order to reheat a cold cup of coffee, you had to get out a pan, put the coffee in it, heat it on the stove, and then wash the pan. Everything having to do with cooking, simply took a lot longer, and seldom did people, really, have a "hot" meal.

In those days, you saved for whatever you wanted, be it a couch, TV, or a bed. Mostly you bought for cash and what we bought was second-hand.

As far as "credit cards," there had been clothing store accounts, Diners Club and American Express cards, since the 1950s, but they were only for the very wealthy. Visa did not come out until about 1976 and MasterCard in 1979. Some people were able to get a loan through a company like, "Beneficial Finance," but that was a very risky and dangerous thing to do. If you missed your payments, they repossessed your furniture.

People just lived differently then. Young girls dreamed of the day they would be wealthy enough to buy a "brand new" refrigerator. Getting an iron or a set of cooking pans for Christmas was a "good" thing. That just shows you what the role of a woman was.

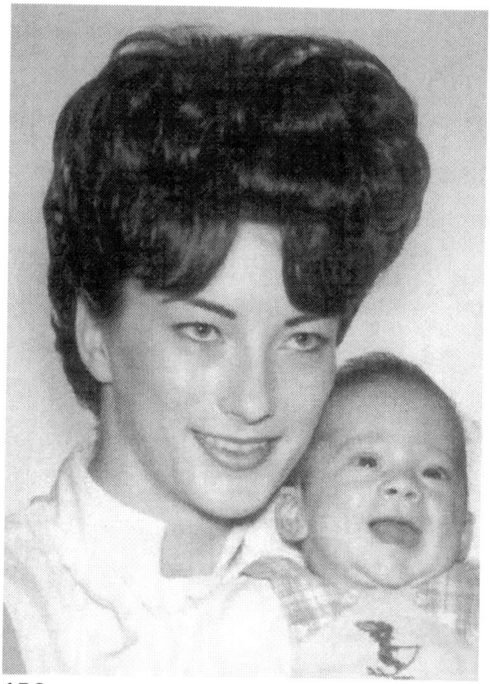

1969

Andy 1 month old

Claudia age 22

Chapter 17
Strange Stuff

I Thought my kids were OK, even though there was an awful lot of turmoil in our lives. I tried to give them everything I had never had. I kissed and cuddled them; I read to them and they had great holidays. I knew how to sew and made outfits that matched, including shirts for Mel. I spent as much time with them as I could. I had bought an old upright piano because I thought I could teach myself to play the piano. I used to play for the kids when they went to bed at night. It wasn't a song or anything, it was only some notes that I thought sounded pleasant and the kids loved it.

At some point, I was working and Mel was staying home with the kids. My brother, Kim, had come to stay with me for a few days. It was supposed to be a short time thing but turned into months. Then I came home from work and found him in bed with Mel. Now that was a total surprise. I threw Kim out!

Mel's excuse was that he was "only testing," to see if Kim was gay, as though that was a good reason. I didn't care if Kim was gay or not, he was in bed with my husband! How stupid do you think I am?

I can't begin to tell you how betrayed I felt. It would be one thing to cheat with a woman, but to cheat with my brother? Both of them were scum as far as I was concerned. Inside I felt abandoned all over again and just very sad. There was nothing to be done though. I was still a woman who had two children to raise, I still had only an eighth-grade education and it was still a man's world.

Mel's obsession with sex was getting a bit much. He brought home a "dildo" one day. In those days, there wasn't a "Sex Toy Shop" on every other corner, there was no internet and I had no idea what a dildo was. It wasn't shaped like a penis, it was only a plastic cylinder and it vibrated. I told him to get the thing out of my house. I was furious. Screaming mad: I knew what it means to scream at the top of your lungs. This lazy bastard did nothing but lie on his ass and think about sex. Not only did I not want to play his stupid games, but I also hated him for what he was doing to my children and our family.

Sister Teri was working at a place, called Dunn's Thermo Glass, as a secretary. She said they needed help and I might get a job. The owner, Mr. Schruben, had recently bought the company and had a huge order to fill, so he needed workers.

Dunn's made large "dual lite" thermo glass windows for skyscrapers that were about 80" X 100" inches. They also made veined, smoked mirrors that were about 60" X 100." I was hired as a "glass cleaner" in the mirror division.

To make the mirrors, pieces of clear glass were dipped in a huge vat made of wood and lined with plastic that was full of water and had the gold paint floating on the top. The "veinor" heated a mixture of "Ivory Snow" detergent and glycerin in a pan. In another pan, gold paint was mixed with a product called "Waterlox."

To do the veining, you sprinkled the detergent mixture on top of the water (because it floated), and then dipping a paint stir stick in the gold paint, you form a grid pattern on top of the water with the gold paint. Next, you swirled a thin stick through the grid of gold paint making a random vein pattern. Then two "handlers" dipped the clear glass directly onto the gold paint that floated on top of the water. Once you picked up the gold paint, you turned the glass over and set it on sawhorses to dry.

After the veining dried, I cleaned between the veining with a razor blade and then pumice. Then it went to the mirroring department. It is quite a process. I watched everything because I was fascinated with how it was done.

One of the things I learned very early on is that glass is dangerous, especially large pieces like we were working with. If you hear a "crack" sound, the glass was breaking and you should get away from it.

One day we had a new glass "handler" who wasn't quick enough. We heard the glass crack. Working together, the two handlers should have yelled "BREAK," and just dropped the glass while stepping back away from it. The new kid didn't respond correctly and when the other guy tried to drop the glass, the new guy tried to pull it to himself to keep it from falling. The glass went down his leg from the upper thigh to below his knee. It split his leg wide open.

Everyone was screaming and the kid was hopping on one leg with the blood running all over. My sister came out of the office to see what was going on. I grabbed a chair, motioned to Teri and she pushed him down into it. I put a tourniquet on his leg and Teri went to call an ambulance.

The young man wound up having two hundred and seventy-some stitches in his leg. I can assure you that I never forgot that lesson.

Mr. Schruben was a strange old man. He was a "mechanical engineer" of about 60 years old or so, who still remembered the "Roosevelt" years. He hated President Roosevelt so much because, during the depression, Roosevelt had sent army troops to their farm to kill all the chickens in an effort to keep prices up. He had such resentment that he refused to spend a dime with Roosevelt's image on it. He kept any dime he came across with Roosevelt's image in a special drawer in his desk. We thought he was a bit wacko, but he signed our paycheck.

Mr. Schruben was very wealthy and owned blocks of houses in the Hawthorne / Lawndale area. He had so many houses that he didn't even know who rented each house and would sometimes send me or Teri to collect rent only to find out that the original renter had vacated and a "squatter" had moved in. He might be an educated man, but he was not a very smart man. A smart man would have hired a property manager.

When I went to work at Dunn's, Mr. Schruben had recently bought the place. Part of the sale included a contract for these big, dual lite windows and hundreds of the veined mirrors. He was having a hard time filling the order for the contract.

It was obvious to me that the reason he was having a problem, with the mirrors, was that the guy that was doing the mirror veining was dragging his feet. Mr. Schruben had inherited the guy when he bought the place. The guy had a two-year contract for a set amount of money per month and his job was to do the veining. He took a lot of breaks and really worked much slower than need be.

Teri confided in me that Mr. Schruben was about to lose the contract and I told her what I had observed in the mirror department. Teri, in turn told Mr. Schruben and Mr. Schruben talked to the guy and threatened to fire him. The guy laughed and said Schruben couldn't fire him because he had a contract.

To make a long story short, Mr. Schruben did fire the guy and put me in charge of the mirror veining. We were churning out about twice what they had produced previously.

Then a few days later, the guy came back and walked into my area. I have to say, he was an imposing man of over six feet tall and all muscle.

When he saw how many lites of glass were drying, he got mad. He had figured I would not be able to handle it and Mr. Schruben would have to hire him back.

When he saw that wasn't going to happen, He picked me up by my shoulders and held me over the veining tank. I thought I was going to get a bath for sure. I looked him right in the eye and said, "Put me down and NOT in the water." He looked at me a moment then just put me back on the floor and walked out.

To finish this story out, we made the quota for the mirror contract only to find out that it was a phony contract. The plan, of the previous owner, with the help of the guy who did the veining, was that Mr. Schruben would not be able to fill the contract and it would be his fault that the contract was canceled. The previous owner would buy the place back at a lower price than he had sold it and he would find another sucker. Because I could make the contract date the whole thing unraveled. Mr. Schruben had paid big money for an ordinary glass shop that had no big contract. He still lost a lot of money, but he could have lost a whole lot more.

For all my diligence and for saving Mr. Schruben a ton of money, I was laid off due to "lack of work" and I moved on to another "minimum wage" job. The stupid man should have hired me to manage his properties, but like I said, "He was not a very smart man."

I got a job at "Frito Lay." The first job I was given was as a "pretzel sorter." I stood on a wooden box with a pole that had a hook on the end and I scooped up any of the "Knot" type pretzels that weren't shaped correctly.

After a couple of hours of doing this, I was getting pretty bored. I just couldn't see myself spending my life doing this day after day. I looked around at the women working there. Many were pretty old. It gave me chills to think of myself in twenty years. I wanted to cry.

Then some kind soul came by and whispered that no one had ever stood on that line for that long. Some women even passed out onto the line. She said that if it made me sick smelling the yeast and watching the conveyer of pretzels go by, they would put me on something else. All of a sudden, I felt …. Dizzy.

They moved me to the "Rod pretzel bagging" line. I had to scoop up a hand full of pretzel rods (about 8 inches long) and put them in a bag then weigh them and add or subtract rods to get the correct weight.

Today this is all done by machine, but back then it was hand packed by uneducated minimum wage workers (mostly women) who could never look forward to anything else. The poor stayed poor and the rich got richer. I always had too much fire in me to accept that, but for the time being, this is all I had and my kids depended on me. I worked every hour they would give me.

One day I came home from work and Mel was lying on the couch watching TV. Tami was sitting cross-legged about three feet away from the TV, like a zombie staring up at the it, and did not even notice when I came in. Andy was hanging over the side of his playpen, watching TV in a transfixed state also. I could smell Andy's dirty diaper from the door. I flew mad. I walked over to the TV, unplugged it, picked it up, went out the door, and smashed the TV in the driveway. I went back into the house. They hadn't moved and I can still see them all staring at me. "Now, let's see if we can do something different," I said. My patients had come to the end.

We had gotten a second car because I needed one to get to work and he needed one to get to … well, where ever it was that he went.

My car was a 1963 Buick Wildcat. It was red with a light tan vinyl top. It was only about nine years old. We had gotten it pretty cheap because the vinyl top was rotten and was falling apart. I looked under the vinyl and it looked like it was nice red paint on top of the car. I figured it would look a lot better if I simply took off the ripped-up and rotten vinyl top. I got it about halfway off when I discovered that it had been hiding big rust holes in the top of the car. There was nothing for it but to continue removing the vinyl.

We certainly couldn't afford to replace the vinyl top. At first, I left it with the rust holes in the top. Then one day it rained and I had to go out and put a moving pad on top of the car so it wouldn't leak inside. Now I knew I had to do something.

I came up with the "brilliant" idea of covering the top with "contact paper." So off I went to the store. I needed something that would go with the red. There wasn't much in my price range and then I found a perfect paper in the sales bin. It was pink with red velvet roses on it. Now I had a fancy car that Mel would not want to be seen in.

The "Fuller Brush" man used to come around occasionally and you could buy brushes, vanilla, and other items from him at the door.

One day, I was having an unusual and weird day. I was trying to go to the grocery store and when I started to put the kids in the car, it growled! Yup, you read it right. The car growled. I grabbed the kids and took them back into the house. I was shaking. I'm smart enough to know a car can't growl, but I certainly was not going to put my kids into a car that sounded like it did.

About this time, my Fuller Brush man came up. "Hi," he said, and then he saw I was in great distress. "Oh! What's going on?" he asked.

"My car is growling," I replied. Well, of course, he looked at me like

I was nuts. "Show me," he said. So, we walked out to the car. It WAS making a growling sound. He looked a little shaken now.

Then he kind of pulled it together. "Look," he said. "I know it sounds like a growl, but cars can't growl. Give me the key." I gladly handed over my keys!

He walked around the car and opened the driver's door. He got in and got out and put his ear to the side of the car, then went around to the back of the car. He opened the trunk. I was holding my breath. He moved the trunk padding and up in the corner by the gas tank hose he pulled out ….. That damn vibrator. Mel had hidden it in my car!

That definitely falls into the category of "Life's most embarrassing moments." I could feel my face turn bright red. I was beyond embarrassed.

"What is it?" I asked, as though I didn't know.

He played along and just put it in my trash can. I, of course, bought several things from him that day even though I could not afford them! Today, I would just laugh. But times have changed since the 1960s. That was who I was then.

I have always been a bit of an odd duck. I thought a bit different than most other people, it seemed. I was a mix of naivety and brilliance.

One time, I had a problem with sticker burrs in the front lawn. I tried to pull them out, but it was useless. If you got them out when they were green, it worked pretty well. But if they had dried out and dropped off the main plant, you just couldn't get all the burrs up. Whenever the kids were in the yard they wound up with their clothes full of these burrs. If they took a little blanket out into the yard it came back full of burrs. I would have to spend hours picking burrs off of clothes and blankets.

One day I was vacuuming the front room when Tami came in crying because she had gotten burrs on her. All of a sudden it occurred to me that I might be able to vacuum the burrs out of the yard with my "Kirby" vacuum. So, I took it out and vacuumed up the yard. And it worked wonderfully.

My neighbors came out while I was doing it and stood watching like I had lost my mind. However, after a few weeks when they saw that I no longer had the problem with the burrs, a couple of them came and ask to borrow my Kirby Vacuum. Eventually, we all eradicated the sticker burrs from our yards.

I played "Eek, Eek a Mouse" with the kids. They would chase me and I would run yelling, "eek, eek, a mouse," then I would jump into Andy's crib where they couldn't reach me. They just squealed with laughter.

Children's cribs were a lot different back then. There were no regulations in the 1960s and 70s for baby cribs. Regulations were not in effect, believe it or not, until 2011. Before that, the spaces between the slats were whatever the manufacturer designed. The bed Tami had was a hand-me-down, so we didn't have any choice and probably would not have even thought of checking the distance between slats if we did.

When Tami was less than a year old, her body slipped through the slats in her crib but her head did not. I heard her screaming and ran to check on her. She was dangling by her head with her neck pressed against the mattress. I almost panicked but realized that if I did, my child might die.

She was crying so hard that I could not stick her body back up through the bars and her head was too big to pass through the other way. I calmed her down as best I could, grabbed the pillows and bedspread from my bed, and folded it so she could stand on them. Then I ran like hell into the kitchen and got a case knife and ran back to the bedroom. I took the side off the bed and sat with her until she stopped crying, her chest got smaller and I was able to slip her body back through the slats. You have no idea how scary that is. I, of course, got rid of that crib.

I also became acutely aware that I was the only thing between my kids and danger. I became a mother hen after that, always suspicious as to what might be harmful that no one cared about or warned about.

Holidays were always my favorite time. I loved to make surprises for the kids. Sometimes, I would even make my own holiday celebrations that I called "Happy Happy Days." Kids often outgrow their clothes, so whenever I bought them new clothes or toys, I would wrap them up, make a cake and have a "Happy Happy Day" party. The kids loved it.

One Easter I had bought the kid's outfits to wear to Grandma Connie's house. I also got them a big blow-up rabbit and a bunch of other Easter stuff. I wanted to put everything in their basket, but it wouldn't fit. So, I bought a little plastic wading pool and made an Easter basket out of that. I put their new shoes and Easter outfits in it and all their Easter candy and toys. Then I tucked cellophane grass in between the items. I made the basket handle out of newspaper and wrapping paper then I made a big bow to put on it. It was beautiful and it was big!

I kept it in the garage until Easter morning. When the kids came out, there in the middle of the front room was the basket. They were so surprised and delighted. We put it on top of the car to take to Mel's parent's house to show them. The neighbors thought I was nuts!

My son loved to play in the mud, so later in the summer I took our little plastic wading pool and put mud in it so he could play. It solved the problem of the mess and I just hosed him off in the pool when he was done. One time I caught a frog and put it in with him. He was in heaven with his frog and his mud.

Tami was a quiet and shy little girl. Andy was a barnstormer, afraid of nothing. At Christmas when Tami was about five, I got her a bicycle. She could ride it up and down the court in safety and she loved it.

Then one day she came into the house crying. I asked her what was wrong and she said the little girl next door said she would knock her from her bike. The little girl next door was about the same age as Tami, but a lot bigger.

I told her to go out and get on her bike. I would be watching. As soon as Tami picked up her bike, the girl came out of her house and grabbed the handlebars. I went out and told her to let go of the bike. She would not. I couldn't hit the child, so I told Tami to hit her and make her let go of the bike.

Tami was too afraid to stand up for herself. I could see this as a problem that would permeate her life if it wasn't handled now.

I told Tami that if she didn't hit her and make her let go, I would spank Tami. Yes, I know that was brutal, but I didn't want my daughter to be bullied the way I had been and I didn't know any better.

Crying, Tami round housed her and hit her right in the face. The kid ran off crying much to Tami's surprise. Tami had no more problems with bullies.

The kid's mother came to my house and complained about Tami hitting her little girl. I explained what happened. She said she would whip the kid for being a bully.

Yes, things were different in those days. We were all just poor folks trying to make it as best we could. I didn't know if my decisions were right or wrong. I just did the best I could.

Left: Easter basket made from wading pool. 1972

Left: Andy and Tami sitting in wading pool basket.

Andy age 3
Tami age 5 1/2

Chapter 18

The End of Marriage Two

One night, Mel asked his mom if she would watch the kids so we could go out on a "date."

This was unusual. Mel seldom thought of me. He usually went out by himself, especially on a Saturday night. I was delighted and hopeful. Always the stupid optimist!

We went to a bar of course. I didn't drink much in those days, but I did occasionally have a few drinks.

Sitting at a table, Mel started asking me if I would be interested in "wife-swapping." I just looked at him. I couldn't believe what he was saying. I was the mother of his children. I was stunned. Inside me was a little girl who just felt betrayed.

I was not so naïve that I hadn't heard of it, but that was what weird people did. Not nice, regular people. In my opinion, it showed the state that our marriage was in that he would even think to ask such a thing. I was like a deer in the headlights.

Then my old childhood friend, Marty and her husband came in and sat down with us. I seldom saw Marty and never went drinking with her and had only met her husband once so this was very suspicious. I looked at Mel and asked, "So did you sell me to him or just give me to him?"

"Oh, come on, you know you want to," Mel replied.

Contrary to what he thought, I did not want to! I considered it wrong and filthy. Not only that, but you have to remember that birth control, other than unreliable "rubbers," was not on the market until 1982 and if you had sex with anyone, there was a good chance of getting pregnant. Let alone the “moral” issues, this was beyond my comprehension. My head was racing and my heart was pounding. I was angry, disappointed, betrayed, and heartbroken all at once. How could any man do this to the mother of his children?

I looked at Marty's husband and said, "Come on, let’s go!"

He got up and we left the bar. I got into his car. Mel and Marty came out and got into Mel’s car. They started following us. "Lose them," I commanded. The chase was on. We sped around the streets cutting into alleys and behind buildings and Mel stayed behind us.

Finally, I told Marty's husband to pull over. Mel came up to the window of the car. I rolled down the window and asked him why he was chasing us and he replied, "I want to watch!"

"In a pig’s ass," I responded.

By then, I was enraged. I smacked Mel in the face.

"Get the fuck out of my sight," I said through gritted teeth. Mel seemed shocked. He walked back to his car, got in, and drove away.

I started to get out of the car. I didn’t know how I would get home or if I would go home. I just knew I had no intention of having sex with Marty's husband. He grabbed my hand and contritely said, "I’m sorry, Mel made it seem like it was OK with you. I’ll take you home," he said. I got back in the car and he drove me home.

The next day, Mel’s mother brought the kids home. I was in a fog. I pretended as if nothing had happened. But I was stewing.

Later that day, my sister Teri, dropped off her three kids. She had a habit of doing that when she wanted some free time. She would drop them in the driveway and tell them to tell me she would be back in a bit. I knew the “bit" might be several days. Teri didn’t know what was going on in my life, but she didn’t come up because I might tell her, "no."

The kids were all playing and I was just stewing. My brain was scrambled. "How could he do that to me?" my mind kept saying. I don’t remember a lot after that. Just flashes.

I went to a neighbor’s house who had told me she had a gun. I asked her for it. I thought it was a handgun, but all she had was a shotgun. "How can I sneak up on him with that?" I screamed at her.

I went back to my house and the kids had all brought mud into the house and had, somehow, managed to get it on the ceiling. All I could see was mud. Mud everywhere. It was only a dirty world full of mud! I lost it.

I think one of Teri's kids must have called her, because Teri showed up and I was eventually taken to Hawthorne Community Hospital and admitted to the psychiatric ward. I was put on a suicide watch. I was labeled "depressive, homicidal, and suicidal."

I don’t remember a lot about the first few days. I was catatonic and they drugged me up to where I just stared at people. I could make no connection to anyone or anything. I remember watching people, thinking how funny they were going about their lives as though any of it mattered.

Little by little, I became more responsive. I got mad when they wouldn’t give me a razor to shave my legs. My psychiatrist thought that was progress because anger is a step up from depression.

My psychiatrist was weird. Whenever I had a session with him, he would tear off little pieces of paper and roll them into a ball. I told him he wanted to fuck his mother. It must have been true because it made him fidget more. Why were men the only psychiatrist to be found? I remember observing and thinking how strange it was. Where were the women?

I went to "occupational therapy." I was painting a "spring landscape."

Everyone thought it was quite good. The therapist was a nice man named "Lou," and I started talking to him and expressing some of my thoughts.

Then one day I went to therapy and he ignored me. It was blatant and obvious. His behavior had changed so radically and so quickly, that it just wasn't normal and it took me about two seconds to figure this was some psychiatric crap. I painted over my "spring" scene with snow, making it winter. Then I made a little card for it and named it, "In LOU of Spring." I left it on the easel and walked out. I was depressed, not stupid.

I did not do any more paintings and didn't talk to Lou anymore. Whatever game they were playing, I wasn't playing. The next project I did was sculpting with clay. Then one day I was mixing up my clay, and I was told to go stand in the corner. So, I went and stood in the corner. It was obvious to me that this rejection was supposed to make me angry but I wasn't angry. I knew what it was about so I just thought it was stupid.

For several days I stood in the corner. It didn't bother me because I didn't want to interact with anyone anyway.

Then one day, I got tired of it. My psychiatrist was visiting the OT that day. I walked up to him and dumped my mud and water batch right on his shoes.

"OK, I said. Now I'm mad!"

Well, now he was mad! You could see it in his face. He was furious. Isn't he supposed to be all in control? Sorry, but this was my thought process at the time.

I was sent to the "quiet room." So, I went in and they locked the door. The "quiet room" was a padded room with nothing but a bed bolted down to the floor.

I sat and stewed. I thought my psychiatrist was an idiot. I thought life was just stupid. I then started thinking of my mother and Mel and how stupid I was to stay in a marriage like this because I didn't want to be like my mother. On and on it went. I knew I would never get out of this psych ward unless I got mad. So, I tried to think about anything that would make me mad. I thought about my mother-in-law lending Mel money, my friend Marty being involved in this, Teri's kids getting mud on the ceiling, Mel, Mel, Mel!

Pretty soon I was mad and pounding the walls. I started thinking about my childhood and the Potters, Dad, Dodie, the Thanksgiving dinner, and on and on. It just all came up for me. I was not only mad, I was enraged. I pulled the bed out of the floor and threw it across the room.

An orderly came in the door and announced that my psychiatrist wanted to see me and he was supposed to escort me to him. For some reason, I decided I didn't want to see that idiot.

"I don't think you are big enough to make me," I said.

We had a bit of a tussle and he got my arm behind my back.

"Go ahead and break it you son of a bitch", I growled.

"I'm sorry," he replied, "I might have to."

He didn't break my arm and after I took a few breaths, I walked to my psychiatrist's office. As we sat talking, he busied himself rolling up little pieces of paper. "You have fantasies of fucking your mother," I told him and it sure got a reaction out of him.

"I'm going to release you," he said. "I can't help you any further."

"No, you can't," I spat. "But you need to get me someone else because if you release me, I'm going to kill myself"

He released me anyway. They gave me several bottles of tranquilizers and off I went.

I don't remember much after being released, I just remember sitting in a bar with my sister, Teri, and drinking. I took a hand full of pills every now and then. Then, I just remember the sound of my head hitting the concrete floor. It was like thumping a watermelon only I was inside the watermelon.

I "came-to" in the emergency room with my psychiatrist standing over me yelling, “You just did this to make me look bad!” Teri was telling them that I didn’t take any pills. It was all surreal. Why was she telling them that? Did she even know if I had or hadn’t taken any pills? Fortunately, they didn’t rely on her words.

They gave me a choice of syrup of ipecac or pumping my stomach. I drank the syrup and threw up the drugs. I told them I wanted to go back to the psych ward. I signed myself in and was readmitted. Now I had another question dancing through my mind. Did my sister want me to die?

I had a different psychiatrist. I didn’t make a lot of progress, but at least I was watched. My mind just wouldn’t think straight.

A few days later one of my neighbors came to visit and told me that Mel and some woman were moving everything out of my house. Now, that pissed me off. I decided that I was going to get out and put an end to that.

I went and talked to the head nurse. She informed me that I couldn’t leave. My psychiatrist was called. I informed them, that I had signed myself in and they could not keep me. I knew the law and as it turned out, I was right.

Today they could hold you, but at that time, they could not. They got my release papers and I left with my neighbor but by the time I got to my house, there was nothing left at my house but my car, my clothes, and a few personal items.

I had no place to go, so I went back to Evelyn's house. She said I could stay on her couch.

I found out that Mel had my kids at his brother's house. I called and told them I was coming over and I wanted my kids. Warning him was a stupid thing to do because, by the time I got there, they had moved them.

I went in anyway and tried to reason with Mel. He was not giving me the kids.

"Well, they certainly aren't staying with an asshole like you!" I said, as I walked to the phone and dialed the police. "I am making a citizen's arrest and request police officers to transport my prisoner!" I said, and I gave them the address.

Mel and his brother stood with their mouths hanging open. They couldn't believe that I could do this. Surely the police wouldn't arrest Mel.

It only took the police a few minutes to get there and they knocked on the door. Mel's brother went to open the door. I looked Mel straight in the eyes and then smacked myself across the face as hard as I could,.... then I blew him a kiss.

I had learned something from all those sleepless nights when my dad kept me up all night studying his law!

The police came in and I walked up to Mel and said, "Mel C, I place you under citizen's arrest for assault and battery." Then I turned to the police and asked them to transport my prisoner.

I explained to the police as briefly as possible that they were hiding my children and we got into a fight about it and Mel had hit me. I also explained many of his other attributes and pointed out that he probably had lots of warrants for tickets. They got the picture.

One of the cops was very quick on the uptake. He walked to Mel and asked him to put his hands behind his back.

"Wa wa wait," he and his brother both sputtered. "You can't do this!"

"Not only can we, but it is a felony under California Penal Code 142 if we don't transport you. And believe me, Mr. C, I will transport you. Now, do you want to give the lady her children?"

The policeman turned to me and asked if that was fair. Would I drop the charge if they gave me the children? I agreed if they had them there in fifteen minutes.

Of course, his mother came with my kids and I put them in the car and left. The police stayed until I got well away.

I went back to Evelyn's house. I was exhausted! We fed the kids and made beds for them on the floor, and I went to sleep on the couch.

About five o'clock in the morning there was a hellacious pounding on the front door. "Open the door, this is the FBI," someone yelled. Evelyn and her husband came to the door and opened it. The police rushed in with guns drawn.

My kids were scared to death and shaking. I was trying to calm them down. There were guns at every window and door around the house. The police quickly separated all of us. They asked my name and I told them who I was and they immediately put me in handcuffs. They took Evelyn and her husband into separate rooms to question them.

At first, I thought this had something to do with Mel. But then, they started asking me where I had been that day. Wow, how do you explain that one? "I was released from the Hawthorne Community Hospital at about two p.m.

“What were you in the hospital for?" they asked.

"Oh, shit, here goes… I was in the psychiatric ward for the last month!" Well, this is just a wonderful day!

After many questions and the assurance of Evelyn that I had been asleep on the couch since about nine p.m. they finally told us what it was about.

My dad was in the Sepulveda Veteran's Hospital for some reason that I cannot remember. My sister, Teri, had gotten drunk and decided that she would get his ass out of bed like he always got us out of bed.

Teri called Pacific Telephone Operator, Nicki Walter at 2:20 a.m. and said, "This is no joke. Sepulveda Veterans Hospital will be blown up at 4:14 this morning."

The operator was able to jamb open the circuit and telephone investigators traced the call to my sister's address, even though she had hung up.

Los Angeles police searched the hospital in Van Nuys and found nothing. The patients were not evacuated. My father later confirmed that he had slept through it all.

Deputies then went to Teri's house. Teri's husband, Sam, filled me in on some details later.

The police came to the door and asked for his wife. He said she wasn't home. The police went into the house and saw Teri passed out on the bed. The police asked who that was and Sam, knowing that Teri had warrants for traffic violations, said that was ….. You guessed it, ME. So now they have my name.

When they aroused Teri, Sam called her, Claudia. Seeing the police, she went along with it. They found her driver's license and thought she was Teri, but they weren't sure. Now they had to track me down.

They arrested her and booked her into the Lennox sheriff's station. Fortunately, the operator had recorded the conversation so they had a "voiceprint" of her. They needed to analyze both of our voices to determine which one of us made the threat.

I was shaking in my boots then because our voices are very alike.

They transported me to the station to "voiceprint" me. They assured me that, Teri was in a cell swearing that she was Claudia.

Fortunately, the voiceprint proved who was who and I was let go with the sympathy of the officers involved.

After everything behind the bomb threat was revealed to the FBI and the powers that be, Teri was eventually let go on a misdemeanor.

I felt betrayed by my sister, but I also knew that none of us kids were right in the head. She had been damaged by all we had gone through in childhood and as young women and she was drunk!

Bayan Held in Bomb Threat

A South Bay woman was arrested before dawn today after she reportedly made a bomb threat to Sepulveda Veterans Hospital in Van Nuys.

Booked at the Lennox sheriff's station on suspicion of making a false report of a bomb was Teresa Verda Stipsky, 27, of 3549 W. 147th St., Alondra Park area.

According to deputies, a woman called Pacific Telephone operator Nicki Walter, 22, at 2:20 a.m. today and said, "This is no joke. Sepulveda Veterans Hospital will be blown up at 4:14 this morning."

The operator was able to jam open the circuit, and telephone investigators traced the call to the suspect's home, deputies said, even though the caller had hung up.

Los Angeles police searched the large hospital in Van Nuys and found nothing. Patients were not evacuated.

Deputies then went to the suspect's home and arrested her at 4:15 a.m.

Newspaper article
My sister, Teri, made the bomb threat and blamed it on me.

Chapter 19
Getting Another Divorce

I was able to stay at Evelyn's house for a while, but I had no money and no job. I cleaned and did the cooking in exchange for room and board for me and my kids. We slept on the front room floor and got up very early so the front room was cleaned up when Evelyn and her husband got up.

I had no idea what I was going to do. The only thing I knew was that I needed custody of my kids and a divorce.

In those days, there were no "do it yourself" divorces. You had to be represented by an attorney because only an attorney could file the papers.

I got out the "phone book," which was a large book that contained everyone's number in your area. White pages were for residents and yellow pages were for commercial establishments. (remember, this was before the internet). I started at A. I called attorneys' offices and explained that I didn't have any money, but needed an attorney to file the paperwork for me. I would handle the court appearance. I finally got an appointment with an attorney and went to talk with him.

He was just starting out in business. He said he agreed to see me because he was curious to see what kind of person would take this on. He further said that he would take my case and he would make my husband pay for it.

I declined because I knew that even if the court awarded my attorney fees, Mel would never pay them, and, eventually, I would have to pay the bill myself and I didn't want that.

I would be willing to pay for the time it took for the attorney to file the papers, but that was it and that would have to be in payments.

I noticed that his office was very stark. He really was new. I told him I was an artist and offered that I could make him a painting for his office in return for him filing the papers. We struck a deal. I was 25 years old.

September 18, 1972, the paperwork was filed. I did a beautiful seascape for his office and he seemed quite pleased with it.

When I went to court for the hearing, Mel showed up with not one, but two attorneys. His mother had paid for them. She wanted my kids.

The judge inquired as to why I was representing myself "In Pro Per" (in the person of yourself). I explained. He asked me a few legal questions that I guess I answered OK. We proceeded.

The first thing I did was to apologize to the court in advance for anything I might do wrong and said it would only be through ignorance and not with intent.

I presented my case short and sweet. The judge asked why I was waving alimony and child support and I told him that Mel had barely worked in the seven years we were married and I had no hope that he would in the future. I didn't want the hassle.

Then Mel's attorneys started. The first thing they asked was if I had been in a hospital recently. Well, so there it is.

I knew they had to have the information on me and the only way to get through this was by telling the truth. So, I said, "Yes, I was in the Hawthorne Community Hospital Psychiatric ward for one month from, and I gave the dates. I was diagnosed as "depressive, homicidal and suicidal."

His attorneys were stunned. They had not expected that. They stopped and started whispering together. They had no questions to move forward because they had banked on me trying to hide it.

Mel's attorney tried to ask a question and just stammered. The judge interrupted and asked, " what is the purpose of this line of questioning?"

Mel's attorney replied, "We wish to demonstrate that Mrs. C is mentally and physically incapable of caring for her minor children."

The judge looked at me and winked. "Well," he said, "you aren't going to do it with her testimony!"

That was pretty much the end of the case. In the end, I was awarded custody of my children. I was further awarded all furniture and appliances, all household furnishings and my 1962 Buick Wildcat with red velvet rose contact paper on the top.

Mel was supposed to pay all community obligations and his attorney was ordered to file all paperwork necessary. Because he was "unemployed" he was ordered to pay $11 per child per week and spousal support was waved.

I felt very proud of myself. In some twisted way, I was thankful that my dad had made me study his law. Life takes some strange ass, unexpected turns.

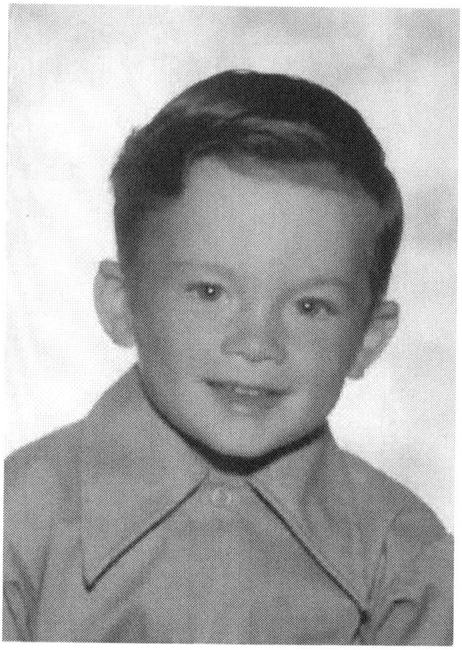

Pictures of the kids 1972
At the time of our divorce.

Tami age 6
Andy age 3 1/2

Chapter 20

Starting Over

I borrowed money from Evelyn and rented a house for $135 per month. I worked the money off cleaning her house, pulling weeds, and ironing at the minimum hourly wage of $1.65. It took a long time to pay it off, but I did.

I applied for welfare. I think I was awarded $225 per month but the amount Mel was "supposed" to pay in child support was deducted from that amount. That was about $88 per month. So, my grant, after deductions, was about $137 per month. That was exactly why I had tried to wave the child support.

Mel of course never paid his child support and, in those days, there was no one to try to collect it for you. After paying my rent, that left me with $2 per month for utilities, gas, and everything else.

Back then, if you worked, they deducted however much you made from your welfare grant. There was nothing to do but try to get a job and not report it.

I got a job as a seamstress for a company that made bicycle accessories. The pay was on "standards." The more I sewed, the more I made. The standards were set on how fast the owner of the company could sew but the minimum was "minimum wage."

When I was in my teens, my mother had a singer upholstery sewing machine. I had taken "Home Economics" in school. I learned to sew and I was good. At home, all I had to sew on was my mother's big upholstery machine. I could alter my gym shorts that had French seams and you couldn't tell they were altered. Our school dress code did not allow us to alter our gym outfits.

At any rate, on the second day of sewing, I hit his standards and passed them. I was making some good money.

On the third day, the owner called me into his office and told me that he was going to have to change my standards. I was making too much money. I was flabbergasted. I argued with him that the more money I made, the more he made. That was the whole point of the standards. He said I was making more money than him. It didn't make sense to me. He held fast. He was changing my standards to where I would be making minimum wage and I would be busting my ass. God, I needed that job!

I went back to my machine and started working, but my thoughts kept churning. Son of a bitch, this isn't fair. Tears came to my eyes and I couldn't see to sew. Finally, I got up, grabbed my purse, went to his office, and loudly, with his door open, told him to go fuck himself and I walked out.

Man, life just wasn't fair. Couldn't I ever get a break?

I went back to the "want ads" and found an ad for a cocktail waitress at a place called the "Lamplighter." So, I went to apply.

As it turned out, the two guys who owned the bar were from Gary, Indiana. Since I was born in Indiana, we hit it off. They were also Irish. I decided to confide in them what my situation was. I was on welfare, but it wasn't enough to pay my bills. Any money I made would be deducted from the amount I was awarded if I reported it. My ex was supposed to pay child support but did not. Could they pay me under the table?

They agreed. They would write me a check for a different name and I would sign it over and they would give me cash.

I was a good cocktail waitress. I never had any complaints. And with tips, I made decent money.

One night, Mel showed up. The only way he could have known I was working there was if he was following me. I had gotten off work and was sitting at the bar drinking a coke and waiting for my paycheck. Mel came over and sat down. He started talking very sweetly. I knew where this was going.

Since our divorce, Mel had never stopped trying to get me to go back with him. I was not having it. I didn't care how sweet he tried to be, I knew who he was. If he really wanted to do something, he could pay his damn child support!

When I explained that in no uncertain terms, he picked up my purse and headed to the door. I of course had to run after him. This became a big fracas. Big Mike came out of his office.

When I say "Big," I mean big. Mike was about six foot four and had to weigh 300 pounds and it wasn't fat. He reminds me very much of "The Beast" on the TV game show, "The Chase." He interceded and asked Mel to leave. Mel was all "yes sir" and crap like that and he left.

After I got my money, I went out to go home. My car wouldn't start. I opened the hood and the distributor cap was missing. Then Mel walked up. I went back inside and got Mike.

Mike and I went back to my car and he told Mel to put the distributor cap back. He said he didn't have it. Mike punched him and knocked him to the ground, and then he kicked him in the ass all the way to his car and made him get the distributor cap and then go back and put it on my car. Mike told him to leave and never come back.

About a week later, a big black woman came in and sat at one of the tables. This was unusual because it was rare that a black person came into the bar and a black woman, alone, in the middle of the afternoon just wasn't right, because in those days, a woman usually would not go into a bar unaccompanied.

I took her order and was going to the bar to fill it. "Oh, Claudia," she called as though she wanted to change her order or something.

I did not turn around. I sat my tray down, gave the bartender her order, and went into Mike's office. I told Mike I was pretty sure that there was a welfare investigator out there because she knew my first name without being told and I did not go by my first name in that bar. He went out and told the bartender to serve her drink to her. I went out the back door.

The bartender served her drink and she asked what happened to the waitress that had taken her order. He told her it was the end of my shift and I had left. Of course, I had to quit working there.

My next job was as a nursing assistant for a convalescent hospital. I really liked that job.

I tried to work nights, the 11 p.m. to 7 a.m. shift so that I could be with Andy in the daytime and Tami when she got home from school.

I also signed up for night school. I was determined to get my high school diploma. The school allowed students to do the class on their own time. I could put in as many or as few hours as I wanted.

My mother (of all people) was taking care of the kids and it was working for several months. I know it sounds a bit wacky, but she was older and never went out.

Then one night when I went to school, the teacher asked if he could talk to me in private. He said that someone had turned in a complaint that said he and I were in a relationship which was of course against school rules. He said, fortunately, that the school board had already investigated the complaint for months and had determined that it was not a valid complaint. The person who initiated the complaint was Mel.

I quit night school. I was so humiliated. My face must have been bright red and of course, I was enraged. How could he do this to me? All I wanted was to be left alone.

I always honored his visitation rights and even let him have the kids more often. I wanted the kids to have a relationship with him and their grandparents.

At work, I started dating a registered nurse. I'll call him Steve, though that is not his real name. He was a divorcee and was just a very nice man.

Eventually, Mel found out where I was working as a nurse assistant and turned me into welfare.

I was called in for an interview. The lady from welfare was very nice and she understood the trap I was in. In those days there was no way you could force a man to pay his support and there was no way you could wave the support through the courts. Women were, as usual, screwed! She quietly suggested that I not work under my name or my Social Security number.

I had to quit nursing, so I looked for another job as a cocktail waitress. That seemed to be the job that made the most money and I could work late so I could have my days with the kids for the most part.

Instead of using my name and Social Security, I made one up and went by the name of Lola. I of course had to cash my checks where I worked.

The bar I worked in was out of the city I lived in and I took elaborate precautions to be sure I wasn't being followed.

Steve and I broke up. He went back to his ex-wife because of his kids. I had no intention of doing that.

On Halloween, I dressed the kids up and took them Trick or Treating. They wanted to see their dad, so I decided I would let them spend some time with him and I drove to his mother's house.

We went to the door, and Mel's mother answered the door. I told her, that the kids wanted to see their dad.

I had been given a restraining order when I got the divorce and Mel was not allowed to have the kids if there was a person of the opposite sex present, between certain hours.

He had a girlfriend there that night. I told them I would make an exception for that night. The kids really wanted to see him. His mother told him, I was trying to set a trap for him.

"Look," I said, "how about her and I go to the local bar, and have a beer for an hour so he can visit his kids?"

They weren't having that either and she would not leave. So, I had to take my kids home with them broken-hearted and crying. I was so outrageously pissed. You can mess with me, but leave my kids alone.

I got a gallon of ice cream and took them to my sister's house. I asked my sister to watch them for a few hours. Then I went and waited at the bar that I knew Mel hung out at.

They came in about an hour later. As soon as she came in, I went up to her and told her there wasn't enough room in the bar for me and a slut like her. She was about a foot taller than me, but I did not care.

She swung on me and we started to fight. We were up against the bar and she grabbed me by the pubic hair. I was so mad, I didn't feel it. I put my shoulder under her and threw her over the bar. The fight was over. As I walked out past Mel, I said, "Go fetch your dumb ass girlfriend and don't ever do that to my kids again!" All 5 foot 2 inches of me felt like I was 6 foot tall.

The next day, it became obvious that I had paid a price for my actions as well, because I could not move my neck without being in horrible pain. It was almost like I couldn't move my eyes without having shooting pains up my neck. It took a couple of weeks to recoup, but it was worth it!

At some point, my dad came around sober. He was trying to get it together. I was so happy. He had been sober for about three months and looked better than I had ever seen him.

Mother had been taking care of my kids but was getting too sick to continue even though she was watching them mostly at night when they were asleep. I asked my dad if he would like to move in with me and take care of the kids. He was all for it. At least I knew that Mel would not be able to take the kids when I wasn't there because my dad wouldn't let him.

This worked great for about a month. Then one day I got a call at work from Mel ranting about my dad hitting him with a pool cue. He said my dad was drunk. I immediately left work and went home. My dad was not drinking and his side of the story was that Mel had tried to push his way in the house when dad happened to be trying to put a new tip on his pool cue. When Mel pushed into the house, dad had hit him in the head with the cue. I went back to work.

A couple of weeks later, Tami called me and said that grandpa was acting strange and she was scared. I went home to find him roaring drunk.

When I went into the house, my dad thought I was Teri for some reason. I told the kids to get into my bedroom and lock the door. Dad grabbed me by the hair and drug me across the room slapping me all the time. He kept saying that I shouldn't leave my kids alone. It was terrifying and confusing. I finally got away from him and ran to my bedroom. Tami opened the door and I went in and locked the door and pushed the dresser against it. Dad had ripped the wires to the phone out of the wall so I had to reconnect it before I could call for help. My hands were shaking so bad. I finally called the police and we hid in the closet until they got there. They arrested my dad and took him to jail. I went down the next day and filed charges against him for assault and battery.

I talked to the District Attorney to try to warn him about thinking that the case was a slam dunk, but he was not listening to what I had to say. I finally told him that my dad would outsmart him if he didn't listen to me. He was young and a bit arrogant and had no idea who he was up against.

When we showed up to court, I had a briefcase with me but the District Attorney only had a little folder. My father was representing himself, of course. The D.A. straightforwardly presented his case.

Next, my dad started and he testified that I was a "loose" daughter that ran out at night "partying and carousing." He paid the bills and watched my poor little neglected children.

The judge is not looking kindly at me. I opened my briefcase and started shoveling papers at the District Attorney. I had my work records, and letters of recommendation from people who knew me. I had rent receipts and bank records. I had my dad's records as well. I had everything to show he was a liar.

My dad was convicted for the first time in his life. As they led him away, he looked back, smiled and winked. He was proud of me. It was as though I had passed my bar exam.

Mother was too sick and or unwilling to take care of the kids, and Grandma Connie refused, so I had no choice but to hire a woman close to where we lived. She seemed very nice and I didn't have another choice. I had to switch to a day shift at the bar which didn't make as much money, but I could never find someone to watch them for the night shift. I would take the kids to the sitter in the morning and pick them up when I got off.

About two weeks into this, I noticed a mark on Andy's face. I asked him about it and he sheepishly said the woman had hit him. My heart dropped. I could envision all that I had gone through as a kid. That would not happen to my kids. I immediately fired her, no questions asked. My kids would not go back.

I called Mel and asked him if he or his mother would watch the kids. I explained that I had to work because he didn't pay support for them. I couldn't make it on $125 a month. I begged him to help. He finally said that they would take the kids, but it would be permanent. I would have to give him custody. I was so angry and told him to go piss up a rope.

I talked my friend Karen into taking them for a few nights and then my sister. I was too paranoid to leave them with someone I didn't know. I was missing some days of work when I didn't have anyone to watch them. Then I received an "10-day Notice to Pay Rent or Quit" because I couldn't pay my rent having lost so much time from work.

I was so tired, and I had just run out of options. I felt so beaten down, I couldn't take the chance on my kids being abused the way I was and I knew Grandma Connie would take good care of them. This was not an easy decision and it took several days to think it through. In the end, I decided that I would probably see them more if they lived with Connie and I could make enough money to support myself.

I let Mel and his mother have custody of the kids. I was supposed to sign a custody agreement when Mel's attorney had drawn up the papers.

I had not made it long on my own and felt totally defeated. The world was just set up that a woman could not make it without the help of a man, and at the same time men bitch because they have to pay child support!

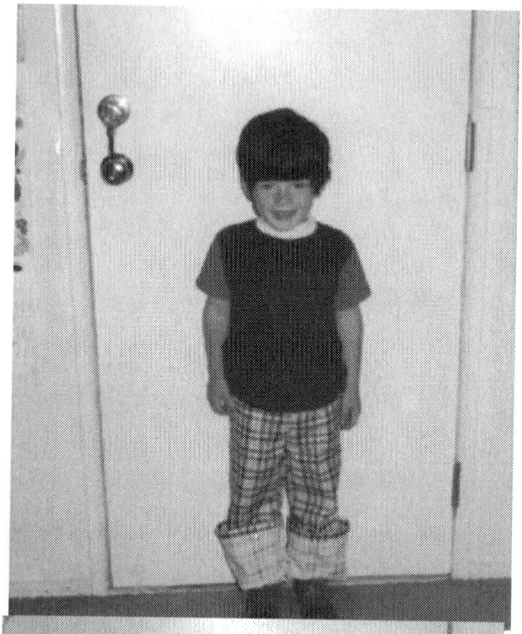

1973
Andy 4 years old

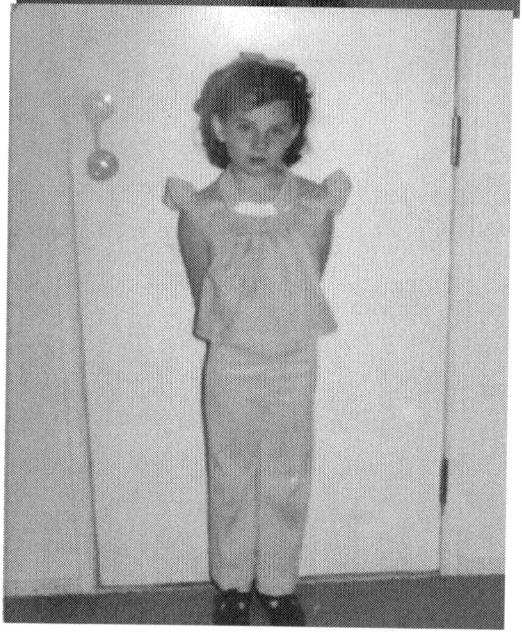

Tami 7 years old

Chapter 21
Husband Number Three

My mom said I could sleep on her couch and I was able to get my job back under my name and work nights where I could make better money.

In those days, women were not allowed to be bartenders. They could be cocktail waitresses, but they were not allowed behind the bar. Though the law was supposedly changed in 1971, there was litigation pending, and the day the law finally changed, I switched sides of the bar and became a bartender. Bartenders made a lot more money than waitresses. While men bartenders wore slacks, women wore “hot pants,” which are now called "booty shorts."

I, again, thought about going back to school so I would at least have a diploma. Somehow, I had it stuck in my mind that a High School diploma would make all the difference. That was only a fantasy. The truth was that women were discriminated against and no matter how you fought in those days, you just had all the odds against you.”

Without my kids, I started drinking. In some way, it was completing the cycle of becoming the one thing I didn’t want to be. Now, I had been divorced twice, didn’t have my kids and I drank.

I met bartender named Jack. He had two master's degrees, had worked as a defensive football coach for Cal State Long Beach, had been Governor Reagan’s campaign treasurer, and had dropped out of society to become a bartender because his rich father refused to give him the extra

$100,000 for his campaign as the President of the National JCs (Junior Chamber of Commerce). I just looked at him and thought he was a real pussy if that is all that happened in his life.

Jack and I dated and we took my kids places on weekends when I had visitation. The kids seemed to like him and after a while called him "Daddy Jack."

Then one night, Jack and I got drunk and decided to get married. I have no idea why we decided to get married. We picked up my brother and drove to Las Vegas. The bride wore white "hot pants."

As soon as we sobered up, we were baffled as to why we did it. I was too embarrassed to tell my brother that I didn't want to be married. The next day Jack and I got in an argument and I tore up the Marriage License. It was years before I knew the date of that marriage. I loved Jack in some way, but again, I still had the illusion that I didn't want to be like my mother who had been married four times!

I was drinking a lot. Let's face it, most of the time I was drinking. I couldn't stand to be without my kids and to kill that pain, I just drank.

At one point, I became so depressed, that I wanted to run my car into a telephone pole and have it done with. The bar was closed and I had to go home. As I started my car to go home, I spied a telephone pole and decided to end it all. I drove right at the pole, but at the last moment survival instinct took over and I swerved to miss the pole. I didn't see the guidewire a few feet away from the pole. I hit the wire and mashed in the front of my car. That pissed me off, so I threw the car in reverse and backed as fast as I could into the brick wall behind me.

I must have blacked out because all of a sudden there were cops all over. I got out of the car. The cop put me through a sobriety test and asked me to say my ABCs.

For most of my life, I have had insomnia. My mind just wanted to keep going over all the crap that had happened in my life. To get my mind to "shut up" at night, I would sing my little butterfly song, in my head, but pretty soon I could think and sing at the same time. Then I tried things that challenged my mind; I would say the ABCs backwards or do multiplication tables. A little weird, but it worked.

So, when the cop asked me to say my ABCs, I said them backwards. He looked at me a bit miffed.

"You're a real smart ass, aren't you?" It wasn't a question, it was a statement.

They were about to arrest me when I asked them to call the city manager; he would vouch for me. The city manager was one of the people Jack had introduced me to and we all often went bar hopping together. They called him, and he vouched for me and so the police drove me home.

The next day, my brother, Pat, and I went to get my car. The tire was impinged by the front quarter panel so we had to use a jack to straighten it out enough to drive. We finally got it going, but now it had one headlight aiming straight ahead and one aiming straight up, and a trunk that would not open. It was drivable, but it was a wreck. I didn't want the car anyway because it was about the last thing I had from the marriage to Mel.

I bought a 1964 Chevrolet Corvair from one of the customers in the bar. I paid all of $200 ($1357 in 2022 money) It was better than the 1962 Buick Wildcat that had the pink contact paper with red velvet roses on the top.

One of the waitresses at our bar had come from Texas. She had owned a beauty shop there. She was in the middle of a divorce from her husband in Texas. In those days, men in Texas had the upper hand. When they separated, he was awarded temporary custody of their two kids. He further got the beauty shop, house, cars, and everything else. She got nothing and it was taking all the money she could earn to pay her attorney. She moved to California to live with her sister while she waited for her court date.

After I bought the Corvair, I gave her my Buick Wild Cat with the contact paper roof, one headlight pointing up, and a trunk that wouldn't open. It was better than nothing and she was profusely thankful because she would no longer have to take the bus to work.

A couple of weeks later, she finally got her day in court. Oddly enough, her attorney proved that her husband had been cheating on her and everyone else. He was likely to be charged with embezzlement and was looking at jail time.

The judge gave her everything! Everything included his BMW car. He was awarded (drum roll please) her car. They exchanged keys in court. I would have loved to have seen the look on his face when he saw the car he had been awarded, with the lovely pink contact paper with red velvet roses on the roof, one headlight pointing up, and a trunk that wouldn't open. At least one woman got justice.

Jack and I decided to get an apartment together and eventually, we moved to Redondo Beach.

Sometimes, after I got off my shift, I would switch sides of the bar and get drunk. I was not a nice drunk. I had inherited my dad's attitude, not my mother's. I was a mean drunk. I often got eighty-sixed from my own bar (cut off from drinking).

I had several "biker" friends who often took me for a ride to "clear my head." One night getting off the bike I burned my left calf on the tailpipe. I wrapped it up, but it didn't seem to heal. One day my brother was in the bar and a nurse who knew me started talking to my brother. She told him that she suspected that the burn on my leg wasn't healing and she wanted to look at it. My brother talked me into letting her un-bandage my leg. It looked very bad. We decided to let my brother tend the bar while she took me to the hospital.

When I got to the hospital and they looked at my leg, they said I was lucky I had come in. I had gangrene in the burn and could lose my leg. They "scrubbed" the wound. It was very painful. They gave me a shot and a prescription and told me to see my regular doctor in a few days.

Of course, I never went back to the doctor but the leg did heal. Sometimes, someone is just watching over us.

I had a lot of fun at the bar because, when I wasn't drinking, I loved people and they loved me. Sometimes, I would send a customer to a neighboring bar and the bartender, there, would send a customer to me. Of course, the customer who we exchanged got a free drink out of it. I also had a trick to get people together so they would have a better time. I watched people come into the bar and noticed that the new person always sat as far away from anyone else as they could even though they all wanted to commune with other people. Most people just didn't know how. The first person who comes into a bar will take a seat at one end or the other of the bar. The next person will set at the opposite end. The next person will sit between the other two, and on and on, always sitting as far away from another person as possible. This is particularly true of men. What I would do, is when that second person came in, I would invite or cajole them into sitting at the end of the bar that the other person was sitting at and introduce them to each other, and then I would let them in on my observation. The next person would come in and, sure enough, they would head for the opposite end of the bar. Of course, we would laugh and then invite the new person to join us at the other end. By the time the bar was full everyone knew each other and everyone had a great time.

One night, about twenty-five of the teachers and their spouses, from a nearby high school came in all at once. One of them said they had been to their annual, end of the year teacher's party at the school, which turned out to be a dud, when one of them suggested they would have much more fun at the bar with Claudia. They all left and came to my bar. We had a great night and the bar made more money in one night than they usually did in three, and I made huge tips too!

The guy, who owned the cocktail lounge that I worked at, also owned a beer bar down the street. Sometimes, his beer "barmaid" would call in sick and he would have to work the bar himself. Then he asked me if I would help him out and do a double shift by working the beer bar after I finished my shift at the cocktail bar.

To accommodate him, I would work both shifts. The problem was, at the cocktail bar, I made $35 per shift plus tips and at the beer bar, he paid me minimum wage which was about $2.00 per hour or $16 for the shift. I'm doing him a favor and he treats me like that? I have to say, I resented it but felt I had to accommodate him.

I'm the kind of person who stews on things. You might not know what is going on with me. You might think you have pulled a fast one on me, but I am very aware. I was also very vengeful in some ways. I would smile at you while you are screwing me, but I'm going to get back at you eventually.

I started having a party when I worked at the beer bar. Many of my customers from the cocktail lounge would go with me to the beer bar and I would give away most of the beer. We rocked the music and danced and had a gay old time. I did not like drinking beer, so I took a bottle of scotch with me from the cocktail lounge and drank that. While I danced the customers would take turns tending the bar.

Sometimes, I got so drunk, that I forgot to set the alarm when I closed at 2 a.m. I can remember times my customers would clean up the bar and close for me. Sometimes they would all chip in and “donate” because there wasn’t anything in the till. They didn’t want me to get fired. Did I give a shit ….no!

Jack never tried to stop me from drinking. He understood. Sometimes he would try to distract me. Sometimes we would go out and I would shoot pool for money. He would make side bets and clean up. I was pretty good when I was drinking, but really bad when sober. I was known as "Little Irish" and my best competition was a woman named, "Santa Anna Rose." It was fun. But, of course, nothing filled the emptiness of not having my kids.

Then, one night, Jack and I got in a fight and I shot all the windows out of our apartment, with my gun. I don’t know why I did that. I think it was just because I didn’t care.

Jack hustled me out of the apartment before the police showed up. Later, in the middle of the night we went back and packed up everything into our two cars and moved to Phoenix, Arizona.

Third husband Jack (JPK)
He was a very good man, just not the right time. He later founded the Riverside Recovery Resources and devoted his life to helping others.

We married April 19, 1973
I was 26 and Jack was 37
(Jack was about 11 years older than me)

Chapter 22
Phoenix, Arizona

We drove all night and arrived in Phoenix, Arizona where I had lived as a teenager. We had very little money so we rented a cheap apartment and started looking for jobs.

Jack got a job at a "Jolly Roger's" restaurant as a bartender and I got a job as a cocktail waitress at a newly built “Roadhouse” restaurant and we settled into a routine. Working, drinking, working, drinking.

Jack and I got along pretty well most of the time, but when I drank, I was not a happy person. I was the type of person who didn‘t indulge in a lot of complaining. I held it all in and smiled in the face of adversity. I had learned early on not to show my true emotions. When you can’t face your true emotions, they get covered up with anger. I was, underneath, a very angry person. Still, Jack always reassured me that I wasn’t bad. That life had dealt me some bad hands.

At one point, I decided that I would do a painting to keep my mind off missing my kids and out of a bottle. I wanted to do an oil painting of Rodin’s statue, "The Kiss." I acquired all the things I needed and went to work. It was about three feet wide and five feet tall. I didn’t have money for all the colors of paint, so I decided to do it in a “sepia” technique which only required three colors; black, umber and white.

I worked on it for several weeks. It was about where I wanted it. I really liked it. It had a certain emotional feeling about it. Then I made the mistake of asking Jack what he thought. He was very impressed with my artistic abilities. He liked the painting very much but thought I needed to improve on one area of the painting. So, I went to work changing it to please him, but the more I worked the more unsatisfied I became.

Every night when I came home, I worked on the painting. Finally, I tried to put it back the way I had it to start with but just couldn't get it there. One night I came home drunk. I looked at the painting and was so disgusted with it. I grabbed a butcher knife and started slashing the painting. I just kept cutting it.

Somehow, I knew it wasn't the painting I was disgusted with, it was my life. I was trying to kill everyone and everything that had hurt me. Mostly, I was trying to kill myself.

Phoenix was not a good move for me. Jack and I started getting into arguments, mainly because I was miserable.

One night we went out drinking and got into an argument on the way home. Jack decided to get out of the car and walk home. Jack was a gentle creature who never raised a hand to me. Too bad he caught me at the wrong time in my life. It was quite a way for him to walk home. I started feeling sorry that I had started the argument and decided I would find him and talk him into letting me drive him home. It was about 2:30 a.m. I was driving down 7th street in Phoenix. Somehow, I thought it would be a good idea if I pulled my car onto the sidewalk so my headlights would spot him better. The next thing I heard was, "Lady in the Corvair, would you please pull your car OFF of the sidewalk?"

"Oh, Crap!"

I pulled the car into the street and parked it. The policeman came up and asked, what-the-hell I thought I was doing. I told him I was trying to find my husband. "It was a very wide sidewalk," I told him. "I couldn't see very well, so I drove up onto it. It seemed very reasonable at the time."

He asked me to get out of the car and put me up against his cruiser. He asked where I was going and I told him I was going to the "Canlin House Apartments" about a mile down on 7th street. He said there were no Canlin House Apartments on 7th. I argued that there was. Then I spotted his hat on the front seat. "I'll bet you your Smokey the Bear hat that there is," I said.

"Get in the car," he said and opened the back door. I figured I was going to jail.

He started driving. "So, show me where this Canlin House Apartments building is," he said. So, we went down the street and I showed him where it was. I really did know where I lived.

He stopped the car and shrugged his shoulders. "Well," he said, "I guess there is a Canlin House Apartment building on 7th, lucky you," he said. And he opened the cruiser door for me.

"I want you to go to your apartment, go to bed and sleep it off. Your husband can find his own way home and you can both walk to get your car in the morning."

"OK, but just remember, I own that Smokey the Bear hat," I said as I walked off.

I left my waitress job and got a job as a bartender in a cocktail bar on the outskirts of town. I was tired of being groped and having my ass patted. I wanted a bar between me and the men.

Arizona was an open carry state. That means you could strap on a gun and walk down the street. They could carry a gun into a bar, but they had to check their gun behind the bar while they drank. Then they would get drunk, get in an argument with someone and then ask for their guns back.

Good thing I had no fear of guns. The funny thing is; that no one ever got shot. I was very good at bringing some humor into the situation and they liked me.

I didn't work there long because it was just too far to drive for the extra money I was making as a bartender and it was cutting into my drinking time.

I got a job at a place called, "Terrie's English Pub." The lady who owned it was English. She cooked very tasty "Fish & Chips" with her own recipe for a beer batter. I did it all. I tended the bar, cooked, and served. I made good money and worked a lot of double shifts. I know this because I have a letter of recommendation that she gave me when she sold the place. I however barely remember working there.

I do remember when she sold the bar and the new owners took over. It was purchased by two Italian brothers. Because Terrie had worked the bar herself and I was the only other employee, they had no one to take her place when she left. At first, I worked any shifts that they couldn't cover until they found other people who could manage to do it all. Not everyone could handle bartending, cooking, serving, and cleanup.

When they finally hired someone who could handle it, I took a weekend off. The first weekend I had off in a couple of months. I remember switching sides of the bar. I had a drink in front of me and I was wearing a white dress that had red cherries on it.

The next thing I know, one of the brothers is screaming at me. Where had I been? Why hadn't I returned the keys? They had been calling me for two weeks! I looked down at my dress and it was just as clean as it had been. I thought they were pulling my leg, but they were not.

He said I had left and had forgotten to give them my set of keys to the bar. The owner had to call his brother who had to drive from the other side of town to bring his set of keys so they could close up.

I've been in a blackout drunk before, but not for two weeks. My dress was still crisp white. I was not dirty, nor had I anything wrong with me.

Jack confirmed that I had been missing for two weeks. He had not filed a missing person report on me because he thought I had left to go back to California. I just, to this day, cannot figure it out. I think I must have been abducted by aliens!

I didn't like the new owners of the bar, so I quit and went into a depressive funk. Jack bought me a quart of scotch every day and every day I drank it. The only time I was sober is the days when I talked to my kids on the phone.

I got pulled over on my way home, from a bar, one night. I ran a red light. There wasn't any traffic and my foot was just too slow on the brake. I stopped somewhere after the light. The lights of a police cruiser came on and I knew I was going to jail. I pulled over and stuck my hands out the window.

When the cop came up, I said, "You got me," put the cuffs on!"

"Oh, no, not you!" he said with disgust. It was my friendly cop with the "Smokey the Bear Hat."

I was only a few blocks from home. He told me to drive straight home. He would be right behind me and to not forget that he knew where I lived!

The thing about getting away with dangerous and illegal crap like that is: You never learn because there, seemingly, is no price to pay. You just slip through the cracks. I'm sure that cop thought he was doing me a favor, but was he?

I remember waking up one morning and every bottle was empty. My hands were shaking and I really needed something to drink. Finding nothing in our apartment, I went to a neighbor's apartment that I knew drank and partied all the time. I knocked on the door. Someone, in about as bad a condition as I was, opened the door. "Do you have anything to drink?" I asked. "We got nothing and I'm shaking like a dog shitting bones." He waved me in and we stepped over drunks lying all over the floor. The guy staggered to a table and picked up a warm beer. "This is about all I got," he said, and opening it, he handed it to me and opened one for himself. Nothing ever tasted so good!

I was getting sicker by the day. I was 5'2" and weighed about 85 pounds and looked like death warmed over. I was drinking at least a quart of scotch a day.

On Thanksgiving Day there was nothing in the house but popcorn and vodka. I went for the vodka. Pathetic!

In one of my more lucid moments, I finally told Jack I wanted to go back to California. I knew I wasn't going to make it much longer. So, we packed up and went back to California. Jack was such a good and decent man.

It had been a few months since I had seen my kids. I can't tell you how much I missed them and when I saw them I just clung to them. They had put on weight. That had been one of the things I was afraid of with Mel's mother. She fixed any problem with food; greasy food.

Jack and I moved in with my mother. I couldn't stop drinking. I was hooked. Then one day, I just couldn't get out of bed. I thought I was dying. I lay there wondering what happened to the sweet girl I used to be. I knew I could not go on. I had to stop drinking. I asked Jack to quit with me.

Jack always assured me that I was not an alcoholic, that I had had a lot of bad breaks in life. He said he didn't want to stop. I finally had to tell

Jack that I had to get away from him. I told him that if we didn't separate, I was going to die.

Reluctantly, Jack moved out and we ended our marriage. I had come to love Jack, and always will. He was there for me at a time when I needed him, but some people can love you to death and Jack was just not willing to quit drinking at that time.

A few weeks later, I found out I was pregnant. I cannot begin to tell you how hard of a time this was for me. I loved Jack and he loved me, but we both acknowledged that we weren't fit to have children. He had children that he didn't take care of and I couldn't take care of the kids I had. Was I going to be like my mother? It is funny that I could resent my mother so much when she was stuck in the same world I was. Everything is relative. Men owned the world and women were just allowed to be in it.

Jack and I agreed that we would get an abortion. He stayed with me until I had recovered. Then we started drinking again. My body would not make it much longer. I finally had to tell Jack again that we just had to separate.

After several days of drying out, I looked up the Hawthorne chapter of Alcoholics Anonymous and went to a meeting.

I had gone to AA some years before to try to get my dad into it. At that time, most of the people were old men and a few old women. The old men ruled the club. They laughed and told me they had spilled more than I ever drank. Well, now I was back and ready to fight for my seat. This was sometime in 1974.

Claudia age 27 , Tami 8 years, Andy 5 years
We don't look happy!

Chapter 23
Husband Number Four

One of the first people I met in AA was to become my next husband. Skip (AFW) was leading the meeting and greeted me when I walked in the door and hovered over me the rest of the evening.

I was still just a child looking for a parent I think. I just wanted to be loved. Any positive attention was love to me.

I didn't know anything about the program or getting sober and was willing to take direction from anyone.

Dating a newly sober alcoholic woman or man was what was called the "thirteenth step" in a twelve-step program. I'm thinking the guy is only being nice and trying to show me the ropes. Skip worked with me on "program," but his main focus, I now know, was getting me into his bed. Within a couple of months, we were "a couple." I was dry, but I certainly wasn't sober.

Skip worked as a Mortician at Utter McKinley Mortuary. He was a steady worker, sober and I quickly developed trust in him. He had custody of his two young boys and seemed like a caring father. Skip and his boys lived a "bachelor" life. They had little furniture. The house was pretty much a disaster and they ate mostly junk.

Skip and I had long talks about everything. My main goal was to get my kids back. He said he would do all he could to make that happen. Somehow, I thought I was supposed to be in that place at that time. I thought I would be a much better stepmother to these boys than Dodie had been to me and maybe I could get my kids back. I moved in with Skip when I was only a few months sober. Terrible mistake!

Skip and I were married on December 30, 1974. I had now caught up to my mother. She had been married four times.

I went to work making a decent home, for us, out of our little rental house. I had a front room set and some other furnishings that were in storage at Evelyn's house. I got that and transformed the house into a real nice home.

Skip bought a motorcycle and had a special seat, sissy bar and pegs put on it so we could go on long rides. One ride we took was From Hawthorne, California to Crater Lake, Oregon. Traveling up the coast, through the redwoods and San Francisco was a great ride. I felt like the wind was blowing the cobwebs out of my brain.

I got along with the boys pretty well, but the truth was they didn't want anyone telling them what to do. And it didn't seem like they wanted a clean home. They made it clear, that they weren't going to make concessions for my efforts. They did things like, one day I had just finished washing the kitchen floor on my hands and knees and one of the boys walked right on the wet floor to get some lemon aid out of the refrigerator. He poured some into a glass, spilling it on the counter and the clean floor, and walked away. I was a bit upset about it, but Skip brushed it off. They were just boys!

It wasn't long before the truth of this marriage was beginning to hit me when Skip told me that I had to go to work or I wouldn't get my kids. He wanted me to go to work in his mortuary.

Just the thought of going to work with dead people was traumatic to me. I still remembered my brother in his little casket. That trauma had never left me, but I dutifully did as I was told and went to work as a mortuary attendant.

In truth, I was hanging on by a ragged thread and didn‘t know it. Skip had changed after we were married and I had little hope of it working out. I just had no place to go and just couldn‘t think.

I was lucky enough to meet a woman named Paula. Paula was a hoot. She was innately funny and she was wise. Paula wasn’t highly educated, but she made the most of what she had. She had been sober for several years. After becoming sober she had gone to school to become a nursing assistant. When she wasn’t working at the hospital, she worked the "coffee bar" at the "Alano Club."

An "Alano Club" is a commercial building that has a room for AA meetings and usually a "Coffee Bar" where members can drink coffee, hang out and play cards.

Paula had three kids and an ex that didn’t pay support either. She was on welfare so most of the money she made was deducted from her grant, but she kept working anyway because it was the right thing to do. She at least got food stamps and medical for her kids. She was sober and taking care of her kids and that was good enough for her.

Paula and I became fast friends. In AA it is recommended that you get a sponsor who is someone with several years in the program, who maintains sobriety and is the same sex as you. Paula became my "real" sponsor. Up until that time, Skip had been my sponsor.

At work, Skip did, what I considered stupid and childish things like hiding behind a curtain and jumping out to scare me. Or send me into a room to tidy up for a "viewing" knowing that the corpse had one eye open and I would have to "super glue" the eye shut. God, I hated that.

My pride would not let me show how much this affected me. I did what I always did. I sucked it up and walked on. At some point, I talked it over with Paula. She told me I should quit, but hanging over my head were my kids.

I never saw a paycheck because Skip was the manager of the mortuary. He got my check, I had to sign it and he kept it all. The only thing I got out of it was a 15-year-old Cadillac and that was only because my Corvair had died and at times I had to drive myself to work.

Sometimes, I had to go to work earlier than Skip. To get into the mortuary in the morning, I had to go in through the "prep" room. If a "stiff" came in, during the night, that was where they put it. The light switch was across the room, so when I went in, I tried to run across the room before the door closed. More often than not, I was just feeling my way and running into bodies. That still gives me the willies. Walk on, walk on, I'm a happy merry butterfly....

I started losing it although I didn't know it. I remember one woman who was being viewed. Make-up artists and hairdressers came in and prepared the body. She wore glasses, so they put them on her with her eyes closed. For some reason, I thought she looked ridiculous and laughed when I saw her.

People from where she had worked came in to view the body and would stare at her. One woman said, "IT doesn't look like her."

I almost laughed. "What does IT look like?" I asked. Then I had to run out because I was about to laugh.

Another woman was out for viewing and one of her eyes popped open. I was not going to glue it shut. A woman came in to view her and I told her she wasn't there.

Another time we had a young man who had died from gunshot wounds. I was in the alcove, above the casket, turning on the music for the service when a woman came in wailing, "Oh, my boy. My poor Pinky boy, tell your mama what happened to you."

Everything in me wanted to quietly and in a spooky voice whisper, "I was shot by my drug dealer, ma!" Just the thought of doing that almost made me laugh. I ran out and down the stairs and out the front door before I just busted up laughing. I knew I was losing it, but I didn't know what to do.

The worst was the baby, of one of our neighbors, who had died. The baby was about the age my brother had been when he died. She was in a little casket. She looked so sweet, but I could not handle it. I just started crying when I saw her and had to leave the mortuary.

To further exacerbate things, Skip was becoming more controlling all the time. He didn't want me to spend so much time with Paula, my sister, my brother, my friends.

If an alcoholic hasn't learned ways of dealing with their trauma, they will revert to the only thing they know will kill the fear, pain, or guilt. Anesthetize with alcohol. So, with almost a year sober, I got drunk.

My humor had not improved with my year of sobriety. I was a raging drunk and I told Skip everything I thought of him, his job, and his kids. I told him I knew I was nothing more than a housekeeper, cook, bed partner, and a paycheck. Then I went into our bedroom, locked the door, and refused to come out.

After Skip could make no headway, he called Paula, who called several other people and they all arrived for an "intervention." The only problem was, I wasn't coming out for the party.

Skip told them that I had my gun in the bedroom. That kind of put a damper on anyone with ideas of picking the lock on the door. It was only a "privacy" lock that you use a little key that comes with all privacy locks in case some kid gets stuck in a bathroom. They were all afraid now.

After they all talked it over for an hour or so, Paula finally said, "screw it, I hope she doesn't hit anything vital if she does shoot me." And Paula picked the lock. I was lying on the bed passed out. I had never thought of the gun. I went home with Paula and spent a few days with her.

Eventually, I went back to Skip's house. Skip was all sugar, sweet, and program. Back came the kind man I had originally met. He was good at putting on that act. I didn't have anywhere else to go and I thought maybe it was just me, the trauma of my childhood and working in the mortuary. I thought maybe we could work things out.

I came across a book called "Applied Principles of Alcoholic Recovery" (APOR). I don't know where I had gotten it from. It was only a spiral-bound book by a man named (as I recall) Robert Rack. In essence, it said that you should write down "everything that ever hurt you."

The fourth step of AA is: "Make a searching and fearless moral inventory of yourself." I had done that, but that was about what I, the alcoholic, had done; my sins no one else's. I was still left with a bunch of resentment for what had been done "to" me.

This book seemed to address that. So, I did the exercise. The thing with it was to write your life story in the negative, then take it to someone you trusted and talk about each item and feel the emotion involved. You had to stay in the experience until it "cleared." When you could be in the memory but not feel the emotion, it was clear.

I was willing to give anything a try at this point. I wrote my life story in short sentences, just enough so I would know what I was talking about. Then I took it to Paula and explained what I wanted to do. This was not mainstream AA and she was a bit skeptical, but she went along anyway.

With each item, I would tell her what the incident was and her job was to keep me thinking about it. The mind wants to go away from anything unpleasant. It will fight you. I think the mind thinks that anything on the negative side is "death." It doesn't make any distinction between actual dying and something that is just very painful.

It took us hours. I'd cry and Paula cried with me. I would dwell on an item and sadness would come up. I wanted to squirm away from it, but I just stayed with it, and then all of a sudden, the emotion would just go away! It was miraculous. It was like viewing a movie. I might feel some sadness the way you feel empathy for an actor in a movie scene, but there wasn't that deep hurtful emotion.

By the time I was done, my brain was scrambled and I was exhausted. It was like all the connections in my brain had been unplugged. A thought would start and then just cut off. In a way, I was a mess, but I could see a lot clearer also.

I went home and went to bed and slept for two days. I told Skip to leave me alone, I was fine. He called Paula who told him to just let me sleep. When I did get up, I found a different world. My mind was clear. It was almost like I had never been awake. I had hope, real hope for the first time.

I made the mistake of sharing about the inventory I had done and how much it had helped me. People in the Alano Club and AA itself found out about my studying the APOR book and made a big deal of it. It wasn't what was taught by the "Big Book" and therefore the "Board of Directors" decided to "expel" me from the club and the meetings.

I got so mad; I almost tore the door off the club when I left. Oh, yes, I could still become enraged. It would take a couple of months before all this crap settled down and I was given back my club membership. This made me do a lot of thinking about AA. Were these people really "recovering" if they acted like that? And, really, "Did I want what they had?" as the big book asks. I would have to do some more thinking about that.

Shortly after this, Skip announced that he had been transferred by Utter McKinley to a job out of our area. We would be leaving within a few weeks. If nothing else had made up my mind, that was the straw that broke this camel's back. I was not going to leave my kids and move to another place, far from my friends and sponsor so he could control me.

I told him I wasn't going. We argued about it for a while, but nothing he could say would change my mind. I told him he could have my furniture because he needed it for the boys. He finally accepted that I was not going with him.

He packed up everything in a truck and I packed my clothes and a few other things in my 1960 Cadillac the night before they left. We slept in sleeping bags on the front room floor. The next morning, he got me up at the crack of dawn so he could take the sleeping bag I was sleeping in.

With all the grace I could muster, I got up and gave him the sleeping bag. He asked one more time if I would go with him, "After all," he said, "You don't really have anything or anywhere to go."

"You can throw me into the streets naked and I will prosper!" I said, and got into my car and drove off. OK, so I was a drama queen. I don't know where the quote came from, but I thought it was one of the Queens of England. For some reason, it just felt good saying it and at that moment I believed it.

I had my clothes, a 1960 Cadillac, sixty cents, and a warm Coke, but somehow, I knew I was OK.

Paula got so mad at Skip for leaving me without even enough money to buy food that she got mad at her boyfriend, Cliff. We were sitting in her kitchen drinking coffee and I had told her I had to borrow $20 from my brother for food. Paula was outraged. She got up and went to the phone, called her boyfriend, Cliff, and said something like, "You men are all alike. We're finished!" And then she hung up on him.

We both looked at each other. "Paula, what the hell did you just do?" I asked.

"I don't know," she said, "I'm just so mad at Skip, I got carried away."

In about fifteen minutes, Cliff road up on his motorcycle and threw it down in the front yard, and headed for the door. Paula looked like a deer in the headlights.

"What should I do?" she asked me.

"Just talk to him, Paula. Explain what happened."

When Cliff came in the door, Paula looked at him and said, "Did you come home to talk or to fight?"

That was my sponsor, Paula. Of course, they smoothed everything over, but it gave Cliff a good indication of what life with Paula could be like. As I said, she was a hoot!

Forth husband Skip (AFW)
Married December 30-1974 to November 1, 1975
Claudia age 27 - Skip age 37
(Skip was about 10 years older than me)

Chapter 24
Another New Beginning

I found a job at a place called "Computer Micrographics." They put documents on microfilm. I started as an "Intake Document Preparer." When documents came in they were usually in a big box. I took off any paper clips and took out the staples. The camera operators had to be able to pick up a document and shove it through the machine. It was also my job to see that the documents were all heading one way. Naturally, it was minimum wage.

It was better than some jobs I had had and of course, I was fast and accurate. Within a few weeks I was promoted to "Camera Operator." I did so well at that, I was elevated to "Density Inspector" and then to "Quality Control." By the time I had been there six months, I had reached the top of "my" possibilities. I was making a bit more than minimum wage, but it was a dead-end job.

Then the "Jet Propulsion Laboratory," in Pasadena, California bought the company. Most of the people who worked there would lose their jobs, but they wanted to keep a few. I was one of the ones they offered a job to.

It would require me to work in Pasadena which was over 40 miles away and which I thought was just too far. I didn't want to stray far from my AA and my kids. It would mean I was traveling an extra two hours a day just to go to work and back. I turned the job down.

I started painting apartments. At first, I was not that good or fast at it, but I got the job done. I worked out of my car and got enough work to eek by.

My brother-in-law, Sam, had gone to work for the motion picture industry. He was making over $7.00 an hour.

Since Sam was new in the union, he didn't work all the time. When he wasn't working on shows he contracted to paint the outside of houses, apartment buildings, or commercial buildings. Sometimes he asked me to work with him and he paid more money than I could make on my own.

Sam didn't always have the equipment we needed so we sometimes had to put a ladder on bricks or wood boxes to reach something. I remember once we were painting a building that was on a corner of a busy street and the building jutted out almost to the street. To reach some of it, we had to put the ladder on a box in the street. Sam put out some cones and then held the ladder while my scrawny ass climbed up the sixteen feet to paint the eave.

Then one week, we were supposed to paint a two-story apartment building and Sam got a call to the studios. I was left to scramble and find someone to help me paint the building. There wasn't anything to do, but get it done. And I did, but it made me think .... "Why can't I paint in the studios?"

Women were not allowed to join the "Set Painter's Local 729" union in those days.

The "Equal Rights Amendment," which would give women legal equality with men by an amendment to the constitution, had been introduced during every congressional session from 1923 to 1970, but it rarely made it to the vote. It finally passed the House of Representatives and the Senate in 1972 and went to the states for ratification. As the deadline for ratification got closer to the 1979 deadline only 30 of the 38 states required had ratified the amendment. Congress extended the deadline to 1982 but no additional states ratified it.

In the early 1970s, I walked many demonstration lines to get this bill passed. Men owned the world, but we were determined that we were as good as them.

There was a woman named Phillis Schlafly, who opposed the amendment and formed an organization called "STOP ERA" (Equal Rights Amendment). She did a lot of damage to the cause. This stupid woman traveled the country in protest of the amendment while she left her six children with others. In one speech she said that the Equal Rights Amendment would do away with much of the "SPECIAL" status granted to women, including the right to be "supported by her husband." For me, that was just "full-on ignorance" of the plight of many women She had to have been rich or paid a lot of money to turn against women the way she did. She became an attorney so there was money somewhere.

We were all poor women earning, mostly, minimum wages. Some had brutal husbands and some had no husband at all. I just wanted to find Phillis and slap the shit out of the stupid bitch!

At any rate, in about 1975 the IATSE Local 729 Motion Picture Set Painters opened up to women. And as soon as they did, I called. They took my information and said they would call me back.

Meanwhile, I went to work for a Chiropractor as a Chiropractor's Assistant. There was only the doctor and me, so I did everything but crack bones. I ran the office and did the insurance billing. I took the x-rays and marked them. I did the ultrasound. I tended to the patients except for the adjustments that the doctor did. I was good at what I did and really liked the job. Of course, it was still minimum wage.

The office had been very behind in insurance billing and I was able to get that in order very quickly. I was good at insurance because if I had a problem with an insurance claim, I called the insurance carrier and talked with someone (usually a woman) who could tell me exactly what I had to put down to get paid. The previous girl hadn't thought of that.

One time a man came in who said he had had a "spinal Fusion." That's where they fuse two or more vertebrae together so that they no longer flex. It was supposed to fix his back pain, but it did not.

We did "standing full spine x-rays." I was marking and measuring the x-rays when I noticed that he had no "fusion." I went back to the room where he lay and examined his back. There was a long scar on his spine. I asked him about the operation. He said he had to be in a cast for about six weeks afterward. It sounded legit, but still, there was nothing on the x-ray.

I went and told the doctor what I had found and asked him to look at the x-ray. I thought I might have missed something.

The doctor looked at the x-ray and told me I was right. He said the guy must have been in the "placebo" class. I did not understand this.

The doctor explained that just like drugs are tested, so are operations. This guy had been opened up and then just sewn back up. Then they put him in a cast for six weeks. This was all to see whether or not an operation worked or if the results were just a "placebo" effect. He said the guy had probably signed a consent form for it but didn't know what he was signing. How often do people read those consent forms they shove at you in the doctor's office or the hospital?

I was shocked that doctors would do such a thing and wanted to tell the guy. Doctor Don said I wasn't allowed to tell him because it might put us in the middle of a lawsuit and chiropractors were on a thin edge as it was. I didn't tell the guy, but I never forgot that either. I had learned in my studying law to always read before you sign, but this was a great example of why! I would certainly never trust a doctor again. I had just seen too much.

Another patient we had was a young girl of about sixteen. She could barely walk. She appeared to be "not right." She could barely talk and seemed brain-damaged in some way. Her mother did most of the talking.

The first thing we did in the chiropractic office was to get a list of all the medicines a patient was on. This girl had a list of at least twelve medicines. To make this short, this girl had gone to her doctor because she had pains when she had her period. They gave her medicine. She had a reaction to the medicine and they gave her another medicine. On and on it went until she was just nonfunctioning.

Dr. Don said he couldn't take the girl off medicines that he had not prescribed, but suggested that the mother call her doctor and find out what if any of the medicines were necessary to keep her alive and what she could be taken off of.

Slowly she was weaned off these medicines and she became a vibrant young girl with a bubbly personality and thankfully, no lasting effects.

I was waiting for that call from the Set Painters Union and still working at the chiropractor's office and did house painting on the side. After a couple of months, I called again. Same crap! After another few months, I figured I didn't have anything to lose and I started calling them every day and most days I called them twice. I am not one to be ignored.

I went to several of the major studios to apply for work in person. Most of them sent me to "Human Resources" and had me leave a resume. They would call me.

At one studio I got in to interview with the head of the paint department. I gave him my resume and told him of my experience in painting and my art background. He was very nice. Then he said he would give me a try. There was only one catch. I would be expected to go into the closet and give him a little "head" now and then! He had a sly, oily smile as he waited for my reply.

I sat very quietly for a moment, just smiling. My insides were boiling. I wanted to scratch his eyes out and feed them to him. Of course, I was afraid that any bridge I burned could be the end of any hopes of getting into the industry, at all. I had no idea how the industry worked.

My inner self, who is not 5'2" and 100 pounds, but is in fact 6'4" and weighs about 200 pounds, won out. I just looked him dead in the eyes and said, "Fuck you, you cock-sucking asshole. I will get into this industry and someday you will need a job, and I will be the boss, and trust me on this, I will remember you!" And with that, I got up and left holding my head high.

In June of 1976, I got a call from the union to go to work at Universal Studios, "Back Lot", nights. It was the worst job in the industry. I figured this was a ploy to get me to shut up and go away. They had no idea who they were dealing with.

The first night I went to work, the boss, Ed, took me to a high tower in the back lot. At the top was a tiny room. He gave me a spray gun full of "lacquer window tint" and showed me how to use the spray gun. I had only a cloth mask, no respirator or protective equipment. There was only one door for ventilation. I did the best I could, but the tint ran down the windows. There was so much spray in the room, that I could hardly see the windows and had a hard time breathing as well.

Ed and another guy that was with him sat down below watching, laughing, and drinking beer. I'm sure it was a hoot for them. When I was done, Ed said it wasn't good enough and gave me a gallon of lacquer thinner and told me to clean it off. No gloves, no nothing. I climbed back up and cleaned it off then started over. My lungs were burning and I was dizzy.

I had to spray those windows four or five times before I got it figured out, but figure it out I did. I think I was close to passing out, but, as my dad said, "I had moxie."

The guys were impressed that I just did the job and didn't complain. From then on, they treated me OK. I worked in the back lot for two weeks.

Ed was not usually the lead in the back lot but had been filling in for a guy named Bill, who was on vacation. When Bill came back from his vacation and took over from Ed, the first thing he did was to put me on lay off. He wasn't fond of women entering the industry.

I reported back to the "paint shop" and thankfully, they had a show that would eventually become, "Gray Lady Down." One of the sets was the inside of a small nuclear submarine. They needed "small" painters to fit in the sub. I was assigned to that set.

When I arrived at the set, I met two other women who had gotten into the union, Wanda and Jackie. The three of us worked on that set for several weeks. I was still on nights, but that was OK with me. We were the first three women in the union. I think I was the third. There were two other women who got into the "Sign Shop" portion of the industry, but at the time I got into the industry, the sign shop had not yet been admitted into our union.

I was "permit" status. To get "officially" into the union, I had to have thirty days as a permit. After thirty days, I would become a number three card, in another sixty days a number two card, and then in another ninety days, a number one card. At that point, I could become a "journeyman," but to do that, I had to have three journeymen sign that I had learned my trade to be accepted. Lastly, I had to pay the "Initiation fee."

I received my first paycheck on May 19, 1976. I had worked 24 straight time hours and 6.5 hours overtime. My gross amount was $268.31 ($1,337 in 2022 money) and after all the taxes they took out I had cleared $163.86. I had to look twice at that.

That was about 39% of my pay the government had taken! The Federal withholding alone was 23.5%! Something was wrong with this. I cleared only $5.37 per hour out of the $7.95 per hour I earned. It was still better than the minimum wage that I could make outside the union, but I wasn't happy.

It seemed to me that the game the government played was to just keep people poor. If you made more, they just took more. If you were on the minimum wage end, you had to scramble just to eat and pay rent. On the higher end, you could eat and pay rent, but you had to scramble to get up out of that poverty level. So how did rich people get rich?

I would ponder that question for some time, but the main thing was; I was making more money than I had ever thought I could with my education. I was making more money than anyone I knew. And you can be sure I worked every hour I could. Most days in the studios are 11.5 hours a day. Saturday or Sunday was double time. Any hours over eight on the weekend was "golden time" paid at 2 ½ times your hourly rate. That was almost $20 per hour ($100 an hour in 2022 money). Wow!

My brother, who was recently divorced, and I rented a house together. My brother had had some trouble with drinking since he came back from Vietnam. He was now in AA with me and it wasn't long before my sister, Teri, joined us in the program.

My sister, Teri, had been admitted to the same hospital I had been in. I went to the hospital and talked with a woman named Adel who was an AA member. I told her all about Teri and asked if she would stop by and give her a big book that I had brought. I knew if I tried to give it to her, she would throw it in my face. Adel agreed and as it turned out, Adel was a great teacher and sponsor. Teri took to Adel and the rest was history. All three of us kids were, miraculously, clean and sober.

Pretty much all I did was work, visit my kids, hang out at the AA club, and study.

In my reading, I came across a poem that I thought was so profound. It was written in 1895 by a man named, Sam Walter Foss. It spoke to me then and it still speaks to me today. It is called: "The Calf-Path." I put it below in honor of what I believe is a great writer and an awesome teacher.

The Calf-Path
By Sam Walter Foss

One day through the primeval wood
A calf walked home as good calves should;
But made a trail all bent askew,
A crooked trail as all calves do.
Since then three hundred years have fled,
And I infer the calf is dead.

But still he left behind his trail,
And thereby hangs my moral tale.
The trail was taken up next day,
By a lone dog that passed that way;
And then a wise bell-wether sheep
Pursued the trail o'er vale and steep,
And drew the flock behind him, too,
As good bell-wethers always do.
And from that day, o'er hill and glade.
Through those old woods a path was made.

And many men wound in and out,
And dodged, and turned, and bent about,
And uttered words of righteous wrath,
Because 'twas such a crooked path;
But still they followed—do not laugh—
The first migrations of that calf,
And through this winding wood-way stalked
Because he wobbled when he walked.

This forest path became a lane,
that bent and turned and turned again;
This crooked lane became a road,
Where many a poor horse with his load
Toiled on beneath the burning sun,
And traveled some three miles in one.
And thus a century and a half
They trod the footsteps of that calf.

The years passed on in swiftness fleet,
The road became a village street;
And this, before men were aware,
A city's crowded thoroughfare.
And soon the central street was this
Of a renowned metropolis;
And men two centuries and a half,
Trod in the footsteps of that calf.

Each day a hundred thousand rout
Followed the zigzag calf about
And o'er his crooked journey went
The traffic of a continent.
A Hundred thousand men were led,
By one calf near three centuries dead.

They followed still his crooked way,
And lost one hundred years a day;
For thus such reverence is lent,
To well established precedent.

A moral lesson this might teach
Were I ordained and called to preach;
For men are prone to go it blind
Along the calf-paths of the mind,
And work away from sun to sun,
To do what other men have done.
They follow in the beaten track,
And out and in, and forth and back,
And still their devious course pursue,
To keep the path that others do.

They keep the path a sacred groove,
Along which all their lives they move.
But how the wise old wood gods laugh,
Who saw the first primeval calf.
Ah, many things this tale might teach—
But I am not ordained to preach.

I was profoundly moved by this poem. What, I thought are the Calf-Paths of my life. What path was I wandering down because others, who had gone before me, had wandered down? What was the foundation for my life and beliefs?

I had decided to avoid men until I figured out what life was all about. It seemed to me that men and women just could not get along and I wanted to know why.

I remember some friends, Mel and I had, who seemed like they had the perfect marriage. He was a pipefitter, making good money and she was a stay-at-home mom. They had two kids, bought a house, had nice furniture, nice cars, and everything I ever dreamed of having. Then they up and got a divorce because she was "bored." I couldn't believe it.

I had never liked being single. I really wanted a life partner. I just didn't want to be "owned" by anyone or abused. It didn't make sense to me that I would go to work and have to turn my money over to a man and HE would decide what to do with it. Why did MEN rule the world?

One thing I knew was that there were some great flaws in my thinking. I knew I could not go on with the information I was working with. Insanity, I had read, was doing the same thing, in the same way, and expecting different results!

I had to do something drastic or I would keep getting the same results I had always gotten. I didn't think everything was my fault, but it was apparent that there had to be something I could NOT see. I had to accept that "I didn't know what I didn't know." I wanted to know what it was that I did not know.

I started reading books by all the great philosophers, psychologists, and psychiatrists throughout history. Adler, Freud, Jung, Heidegger, and many, many more. I studied every religion, cult, and philosophy.

I read the entire Bible because that is where so many of the beliefs seemed to come from. Eve originally sinned by leading Adam astray so they were forbidden the "Garden of Eden," and that is why men have lorded it over women ever since. Are you kidding me?

Mel's parents were "God-fearing Christians," and his dad often quoted something about how women should behave. The man is the head of the household and the woman is meant to "serve" him. He ordered Connie around like a slave. "Woman, get in that kitchen and make me some fried potatoes." And, she would scamper and do as she was ordered. If he had been joking, it would have been different, but he was dead serious. I do not doubt that Mel thought his wife would respond similarly, and I might have if he had been a good provider and protector.

When I read the book of Numbers, Chapter 5, lines 11 through 31, and I was outraged. You will have to look it up to see exactly what it says, but basically, it tells a man how to find out if his wife is cheating on him. There is no test to see if a man is cheating! People conveniently quote portions of the Bible, to fit whatever point they want to make, but they somehow never preach stuff like this. In essence, you go to the priest, take the dirt off of the tabernacle floor and put the dirt in a bowl of water. Then write the accusation of infidelity on paper, dipping the paper (poison ink?) in the bowl of water, and then making a woman drink it to see if she has cheated on her husband. If she has cheated, "her belly will swell and her thighs will rot off!"

I thought I needed to go back and ask, "why do people think what they think? Why is the Bible so weird and why do most people believe in it? This truly seemed to be a "Calves Path."

Skipping a lot of the in-between stuff that I had to study, here is what I came to believe.

Before the time of civilization, there was not much trouble about what belonged to whom. But then man began to settle into villages and he amassed an abundance of all the things necessary for survival. At first, certainly, a village of people with an abundance of food would stick out like a sore thumb. A man would certainly question why some had so much while others had little. And so, the divine blessings of the "gods" came into being.

The blood of man flows throughout the history of his gods. As man hoarded his food because it was survival, he explained it with his gods. At first, he may have used this only to frighten others away. But soon he very deeply believed in the power of his gods.

Earth became abundant with man, food, and gods. Soon man was being molded into his god's expectations and specifications. Soon, many were called but few were found worthy.

Men still sacked the cities to take the abundance of others, but he did it in the name of his god. His god was a jealous god. Man created horrible ways of dealing with those who believed in other gods. God spoke to them and told them how to deal with others. He demanded blood. When a city was taken, those who survived, no doubt, began to worship their captor's god. Those who did not were sacrificed to the honor of the victor's god.

Now gods empowered men to perform all kinds of miracles. Now we have magic, voodoo, witchcraft, priests, and prophets. Art became magic and magic became gods. God was power. Those who had power had to find a way to keep others believing in this exclusive power. If men found that the teachings of the gods were wrong, these chosen of the gods would lose their power. Soon men were forbidden to use their imagination. The keepers of the gods were the final authority. Blind faith in the gods became a dictate of the gods. Further questioning was forbidden and mere speculation could mean death.

Very early on, through the conquest of man, and the condensing of gods, there rose to the top only a few "religions." I think the main ones were Jewish, Catholic, Protestant, and Muslim. They all have vied to take over the others. One of the ways was to capture and then intimidate. The "Inquisition" was born.

For the most part, some of those in charge simply fined you for a heretical remark, but some went all the way to murder. You either believed their way or forfeited your life or liberty. A sample of this is found in the story of Galileo.

Galileo Galilei was an Italian born astronomer and physicist (1564 - 1642) who became a professor of mathematics in Padua, Italy.

In 1608 Galileo heard that a spyglass had been invented in Flanders by a man named Hans Lippershey of Holland. Being a man of science, he thought about the principles and shortly built an instrument with the magnification of three. Later he pushed the magnification up to eight or ten and this was, at the time, a high-powered telescope. Galileo began to look at the stars.

Now at this time, it was believed that the Earth was "stationary," and that it was the center of the universe. All other planets revolved around it. This was called the Ptolemaic System after the Greek astronomer Claudius Ptolemaeus of the second century B.C. The Ptolemaic System fit in nicely with religion because it affirmed that Earth was the center of the universe and was held in place by the power of God.

After Galileo had observed the heavens with his new telescope, he began to believe that this was incorrect. A Polish astronomer named Nicolaus Copernicus (1473 - 1543) had advanced a theory earlier whereby the Sun was the center of our universe and the Earth and other planets revolved around it. Further, the Earth was not stationary but spins on its north-south axis at a rate of one rotation per day. Based on Galileo's observations, he believed the Copernicus system to be right .... And he said so!

The religious leaders, did not allow men this type of speculation and they did not want anyone messing with their teachings of the powers of God. Man was not only told how he should BE, but how he should THINK. To think other than the way of the empowered religious leaders was the way of the heretic and it was the DUTY of these men to root out anyone who went against the word of God and destroy them. The universe was run by miracle, not by natural law. They reasoned that if the earth were spinning we would fly off. Galileo was "forbidden" to press this theory further.

But, Galileo did. He wrote a book called, "Dialogue of The Great World Systems." He was summoned before the inquisition in 1633. He was 70 years old at the time and he only had to be shown “the rack” to retract all he had written. Today we know he was correct in what he wrote, but the church did not agree.

Galileo was imprisoned in his own villa for the rest of his life, until he died in 1642. His book was on the "Index of Prohibited Books" for more than 200 years; long past the time that science had proven him right!

Galileo was luckier than many. Through the ages, many were tortured, mutilated, or burned alive for possessing knowledge other than that of the scriptures.

What resulted from the inquisitions was far more fateful than the loss of great minds and knowledge. The macabre brutalities of those times instilled fear in disbelief that rang in the hearts of mankind for more than 500 years.

The procedure of the inquisition was much the same as that used by the Nazis in Germany during the persecution of the Jews. Neighbor turned in neighbor, son turned in father, mother turned in daughter, etc. Woe be the un-liked man. The accusers for the most part remained anonymous and the accused was forced to testify against himself.

Most people, of course, learned to be very careful. It was perhaps safer to say nothing at all on the subject, and children would be fiercely disciplined in unquestioned belief lest what they say be construed as heresy of the parents.

In 1252 Pope Innocent IV officially sanctioned the use of torture to extract the TRUTH from suspects. The penalties for guilt ranged from mild penance to death. Public whippings and confiscation of property were common.

The last of the Inquisitions was in Spain as late as 1834. For more than 500 years man walked with the fear of God's ordained.

The teachings of those years linger today as a parent will fiercely attack a child for asking an improper question or voicing doubt. Though we live in an enlightened society, the shadows of the horror past and forgotten linger in the hearts of man passed on from one generation to another without question, without cause, and without doubt. What would man / woman think and believe if he was not constrained by the beliefs of the past?

So that was the answer I found. I was stunned. How do we know what is real? How can anyone's thoughts be their own? Do people ever stop to ask "why" they believe what they believe? How does one dump their thoughts and belief-systems, that don't seem to work, and adopt new ideas and beliefs? I knew that what I had wasn't working for me and I had to change MY thinking.

Claudia 1976
When I got into the studios
Claudia age 29

Chapter 25
My Search Continues

One of the first places to start was to not give people power over me. I had to make a stand for what I thought was right for me, and not shaped by someone else's concepts, judgments, and considerations. Well, at least, I now had a starting place. I felt impowered.

This was in the day before computers or Kindle E-readers. You had to go to a library and borrow books or go to a book store and buy a book. There were a few used book stores and those were my haunts.

I tried borrowing books from the library but found that if I wanted to go back and look something up in a book I would have to check it out repeatedly or spend hours in the library which I didn't have. And, if I owned the book, I could highlight or write in the margins. Buying books became my thing. I had stacks of books all over the house.

One of the things I learned early on is that most books have one central point that is very useful and then they fill the book with crap so it is sellable. How much would you pay for a 10-page book? I wanted that one nugget that the book was about. I wanted the meat and potatoes of the book, not all of the gobbledygook.

I enrolled in a course called, "Evelyn Woods Speed Reading." Wow, what a difference that made. And yes, you really can learn to read faster. The essence of that course was to quit saying the words in your head. That is what slows a reader down. When you come to a "stop sign" while driving, do you actually say the word "STOP" in your head or do you just understand the meaning? Anyway, after I quit saying words in my head, I was much faster at reading.

My brother, Pat, had PTSD from Vietnam. He had changed so much since he came back. When he was young he was energetic and vibrant. In Vietnam, he had been in an area that had been sprayed with "Agent Orange" which contained "Dioxin." When he came home, he had good times where he was a hard worker, and then he had deep depression states where he couldn't get out of bed. I knew my brother, he wasn't lazy! But it cost him his marriage which was why we got a place together.

One of Carl Jung's books talked about how some people didn't spend enough time "crawling" when they were babies and this had something to do with how they turned out. He described an exercise in his book, so my brother and I set up a maze of cardboard boxes in the front room and crawled through that maze for weeks. We figured we didn't know if it helped, but it couldn't hurt.

Another person I studied was Abraham Maslow. He believed that humans had a "Hierarchy of Needs" which consisted of physiological (air, food, water, shelter), Safety, love/belonging, esteem, self-actualization, and Self-transcendence.

In understanding this, I could see that my needs had never been met on the first level, let alone anything beyond that. I had been trying to get to "love/belonging" before I had secured shelter or safety. No wonder it didn't work. Anytime those first needs weren't being met, there was no way I could reach the stage of "love" for any length of time. I just kept getting pushed back to basic survival mode. I'd have to work on that.

I studied meditation. I would lie on the bed and try to feel like I was floating in water. That is what the book said to do. I would visualize it, but pretty soon a shark fin would come up. I guess I have a great imagination.

I would start squirming and it would break the "meditation" spell. I kept trying because the book, I had, told me that eventually I would be able to meditate. Not happening here!

Finally, one day I realized that I wasn't "actually" in a sea of water and I wondered what would happen if I just let the shark" get me." I said, "OK shark, come and get me!" As soon as I said that, the shark disappeared! It just disappeared!

In letting go, I found a big secret the universe had been hiding from me. And that secret is, "what you resist will persist." Would that work for other fears? Would that work for "guilt?" And so, I started working on anything I could think of. This was similar to the APOR book I had studied.

This was a lifelong study that never stopped. I think my brother and I made a lot of progress.

One of Pat's problems was that every time he went shopping, he would have to go to the bathroom and so he would often leave a store without purchasing anything. It was a frustration for him. We looked for: What might make this behavior "reasonable" to his unconscious mind?

At some point in our work, he remembered being afraid he was going to wet his pants. He had been beaten for it earlier. He still had that fear lurking in the back of his mind. He also, unconsciously, had fear of falling down the hole in the "outhouse." Which forms a "personal dichotomy."

So, what is a personal dichotomy?

It is not easy to get a person, who was born feeling good about themselves, to feel they are no good. It takes years of teaching. One of the ways that we teach people this is by setting up games where they have no choice but to be bad.

A child of four has been taught that he is really bad if he wets his pants. At the same time, raising children is a tiring task, and sometimes mommy needs a little nap. The child is taught that you don't wake mommy up when she is napping unless the house is on fire. The child is outside playing in the backyard. The door is locked so the child cannot get in and hurt himself. The child has to go to the bathroom. He comes to the screen door and he can see mommy napping on the couch. He has a problem. If he wakes her up, he is bad. If he wets his pants, he is bad. He loses no matter what he does.

Pat decided he wanted to challenge his beliefs. To start with, he had to do a meditation and go back to the outhouse. He had to let go in his "imagination" and fall down the hole. As soon as he let go, it cleared up. His mind finally realized that he was now an adult and had survived the outhouse. Now he had to face the "wetting" his pants.

We put a towel on a kitchen chair and he sat down fully clothed and "wet his pants." When it was done, he laughed and said it wasn't really a big deal, just kind of warm. That one process changed his whole world.

We started looking for ANYTHING that seemed "off" in our lives. Something that we were not allowed to do that seemed to not be a problem for others. Our "concepts, considerations and notions," form how we are "allowed" to act and interact in the world. When we caught something, we "processed" it.

One thing I discovered was I had a lot of problems around food. I had been told I wasn't deserving of food that someone else paid for. As a result, I never wanted to eat in front of people. It just made me uncomfortable. So, try to enjoy a dinner date, party or holiday with that crap running in your unconscious mind. We processed it and it seemed to be cleared.

About a week later, Pat and I and several friends went to a restaurant after an AA meeting. This was a usual thing for us to do. After we had sat down in the restaurant, and the waitress brought everyone's food, I noticed that Pat and I were the only ones who didn't order food. We sat with our little cup of coffee and watched as everyone enjoyed their meal.

I turned to my brother and said, "Pat, we are looking through the crack in the door!" I could see the light go on in his mind. "You're right. Let's process it."

I had a great job and lots of money. I could afford to order anything on the menu. I called the waitress over and told her that I wanted "everything" on the menu!

The waitress refused to order it for me, even after I pulled out my credit cards and the cash I had in my purse. She was willing to give me ten dishes. I think she thought we were crazy or drunk.

Pat and I were laughing. I tried to explain what I was talking about, but most everyone thought our "processing" was a bit strange. Well, it was, but it worked.

When the food was delivered, we invited everyone to dig in. Pat and I ate till we couldn't eat another mouthful.

Before that, I thought I had been at "choice" about what I ordered in a restaurant. Not even close! But now I was at choice. If I go out to dinner with someone, I usually ask what price range should I be looking at, realizing that it is about their financial situation, at the time, and has nothing to do with me personally, or my worth. If the other person is run by some programming in their head, it is not my problem. If they tell me to order what I want, I do! Pat and I would never look through the crack in the door again!

That is how life went for months. On weekends, if I wasn't working, I picked up my kids and we played. We went to amusement parks and movies and anything we wanted to do. My kids seemed OK.

I tried to share what I was finding out with my kids. I tried to teach them that we each need to decide what is right and make rules for ourselves. While they were young, I would have to guide them, but when you get older, you need to choose for yourself.

I remember one day Tami, Andy, and I were going somewhere and had stopped at a stop sign. A woman was walking across the street very slowly. "Get moving old woman," Andy yelled and then snickered. I was surprised to hear something like that come out of his mouth. I swear it sounded exactly like Mel's dad.

I pulled the car to the side and told the kids to get out. Then I walked them to the crossing where the old woman had been and told them we were going to walk across the street at the same speed she had walked when the next car stopped. A car stopped and we stepped into the street. I was holding each of their hands so they had to walk at my speed. We walked really slowly. The car driver revved its engine. Andy wanted to hurry up, but I kept him back.

I wanted Andy to know how hard it was for someone who couldn't move fast. It was a good learning experience and it taught him empathy. Today my son is a very sweet man who always considers what other people are going through.

At work, I was one of the "On-call, Stand-by Painters." In some major studios, some shows did not want to pay for a "full time" stand-by painter who could handle any problems that came up. Instead, they called the paint shop and they would contact one of the "on-call stand-by painters." This was of course before the day of the "cell phone." The boss would have to locate a qualified painter by calling to the stage; then someone would have to locate whoever they were calling. Then you had to go to the phone and then the boss would dispatch them to the problem stage. The nearest qualified painter might be clear across the lot and would have to walk to the location with a rolling toolbox. From the first call until the painter showed up on stage could be an hour. Not the fault of the painter, it was the fault of the system and the company who didn't want to pay for a full-time painter on set.

I got a call to go to the TV show, "The Six Million Dollar Man," clear across the studio lot. It took about 15 minutes to get there. They had called for a stand-by an hour ago. Walking in, the director was furious and blamed me for the delay. "Why the hell did it take you so long to get here?" That was the first thing he screamed at me. "I've got a hundred crew members, standing waiting for you. This is costing me $10,000 a minute."

I was embarrassed and totally pissed. It wasn't my fault, but he thought nothing of humiliating me in front of an entire shooting company. I don't think he would have done it if I had been a man.

I just smiled and held up my hand. "What is the problem that I'm needed for I asked?"

The set was a laboratory and some brilliant "art director" had designed an "electrical plug" right in the middle of the door. He wanted it removed because it's "stupid."

I looked at it and decided the fastest way to make it go away was to put masking tape over it and then paint it in with the door color. The only problem was that the walls and door were painted with gloss lacquer. Lacquer is very fast drying but is not easy to match even if you have the original color.

I went to find the original color in the "stand-by" paints behind the set. All the painter had left was a five-gallon bucket of the lacquer which weighed about 50 pounds. There were no small buckets to transfer a small amount into. I went to the "Craft Service" table, to see if they had a paper coffee cup. They only had "Styrofoam." Lacquer will eat through Styrofoam. I couldn't get it to the set fast enough to keep it from leaking onto the floor. That would ruin anything on which it might drip. And I still had this jerk yelling at me.

I went and put the tape on the outlet in the door. Ran to the craft table and grabbed a "stack" of the Styrofoam cups. I would have to put enough lacquer in the top cup so that I had some left when I reached the door. I put about a quarter cup of paint in the top cup and ran to the set. Quickly, I painted the tape and then ran off the set just as the lacquer was burning through the last cup. Mission accomplished!

I walked back to the stage I was originally assigned to and went back to work. About two hours later, I got another call to go back to "The Six Million Dollar Man." They had another problem. Hurray for me, another ass chewing!

When I arrived at the stage, the same director was again yelling that it had taken too long for me to get there, it was costing him….. Yada, yada, yada. Again, I held up my hand and asked what was wrong? He showed me the "breakaway" door they had now installed where the solid door had been. It also had an outlet in it. A breakaway door is made so the actor can bust it up easily. Breakaway items are usually made of "balsa wood."

I looked at the director and looked at the two doors. I walked to the original door and removed the piece of masking tape then I walked to the breakaway door and put the piece of masking tape on the electrical outlet. I looked back at the director and in my loudest voice said, "There, I just saved you a hundred thousand dollars." I waved my hand, pointing to all the people around the set and said, "This entire shooting company and no one could figure out how to move a piece of tape?" The people on the set, including Lee Majors, just laughed. The director had been shown to be a blowhard fool. I was not called back to that set, that day.

In July of that year, I went to a seminar called EST which stands for "Erhard Seminars Training" and also Latin for "it is"

It was a transformational seminar about "why life doesn't work for us." The seminar aims to "Transform one's ability to experience living so that the situations one had been trying to change or had been putting up with clear up just in the process of life itself."

The seminar is very Gestalt which is about the person of today, not a reflection of one's past. It is about "being here now." I had already studied much of this, but still, I found the seminar fascinating. Werner Erhard led the seminar; he was handsome and charismatic. I am certain every woman in the room fell in love with him. I know I did.

To get entry to the seminar, you had to pay your money, but you also had to sign an agreement as to what the rules were and attest that you would follow them. There were not a lot of rules as I remember. Show up on time, participate when asked to, and don't leave the room for any reason until you are instructed that you can.

That seems easy enough until about the third or fourth hour when you really need to pee. Boy, people's real character comes out when they need to pee and can't leave the room.

There were always several "assistants" at the door to stop anyone who wanted to leave. They would remind the person that they had made an "agreement" about leaving the room. They would do anything to get the person to go back to their seat. People would get angry or cry or cuss. They would explain how they were different. They had medical needs.

Nothing was an acceptable excuse. If you had a medical condition, you should have come with a note from your doctor or not signed the agreement. If you left the room, you could be ejected from the seminar without a refund. Worse yet, you could be confronted by Werner in front of everyone. There were hundreds of people at these seminars and many were challenged by Werner himself.

One assistant, who “ran a microphone” from person to person as the seminar progressed, peed her pants because she had also agreed not to leave the room. Werner made an example of her. "Look," he said, "this woman keeps her agreements! Unlike most of you, she doesn’t make excuses or whine, cry or try to explain, she simply keeps her agreements!"

Werner continued, "This is why your lives don‘t work. You don‘t live up to your agreements. You are always trying to change something or wheedle out of what you agreed to. You do this in your work, in your marriages, your relationships with others. Look, it doesn’t have to be an agreement you made with someone else. It can be an agreement you make with yourself. You choose YOUR rules of how you’re going to live your life. Do it consciously and stick to your agreement. That’s all, just show up in life AS your agreement." The woman stood before everyone and she received a standing ovation. We “got it.”

In the seminar, at one point, we split into small groups and discussed why we came to the seminar. What did we hope to get out of it? Then we took a "stand" and commit to something to start the ball rolling. My stand was that "men are safe, smart & fair and that I can tell on them." Further I committed to complete everything I had started writing, to write a book about my life, and to quit smoking. So, to Allen, Janice, Nica, Nicole and Jean, my commitments of 08-03-1986 are fulfilled. I am my agreements!

It is hard to describe everything that happened in the seminar and would certainly take too long to explain it here, but people were truly transformed. I am ever grateful that I could afford that experience.

At some point around this time, I decided that I needed to date men if I was going to be able to "process" the things that were going on in my relationships.

There was a man named Bob, who had asked me out a few times. It had started some months before when a friend of mine and I were cleaning people's houses for money. He was one of our clients. He was a member of the AA club as well. Though I no longer cleaned his apartment, I often saw him at meetings.

He again asked me out and I accepted. Bob was a school teacher. He was a Harvard graduate. Of course, I admired all that education.

Bob was, I thought, kind of serious. He had a dry sense of humor and I liked the way he laughed. The only thing "off" was that he was a bit slow on the uptake.

One time, Bob had wanted to throw a dinner party for some of the people at the club. He was going to cook "Chinese" food. We all showed up at about 6 PM and of course, asked if there was anything we could help with, but he said no, he had it under control. It would only be a bit before it was ready. Time dragged on. Paula was starving and at about 8:30 she asked, "Is this dinner going to happen tonight?" Everyone laughed. As it turned out, dinner did not appear until after 10 PM. On the way out, Paula whispered to me, "Good lord, remind me to eat before I come to his next dinner party!"

I had told Bob, right off, that I had two children and they were a big part of my life and more important than anything else. Bob loved kids. He really wanted kids of his own and was always willing to include my kids on our dates. We went to amusement parks like Universal Studios, to the beach, or to the movies.

One night, Bob said he wanted to take the kids and me to a "drive-in movie." There was a show playing called, "The Groove Tube," that he thought we would like.

I trusted that Bob would take us to something appropriate for my children, He was, after all, a school teacher, and I always thought that educated people were so much smarter than me.

The movie started and it was a collection of comedy skits making fun of movies and television. It was pretty funny, but I was becoming a bit uncomfortable as to the appropriateness of it for my kids who were, about seven and ten years old. Then a skit came up that made it quite clear that it was not.

I'm watching and all of a sudden, there is a "talking Penis" saying something about "venereal disease." It was a takeoff of the "talking tooth" in the "Ipana toothpaste" commercial. My kids both started giggling.

I turned to look at Bob. He was just staring at the screen. Then he got a questioning look on his face. (Slowly it dawns) In an incredulous tone of voice, he said, "Is that what I think it is?"

"Yes, Bob, it's a talking pecker!" I think maybe we should go. Poor Bob was just not that fast on the uptake.

Eventually, I could see that Bob wasn't the person for me. I knew I was a bit faster thinking and also knew I would eventually become impatient with him. It would simply never work.

Then my sister came to me and said she was interested in Bob. She accused me of "stealing him away from her." She had never dated him and certainly never told me she was interested in him. I didn't care because it was clear that he wasn't the person for me by that time. I was quite willing to step aside.

But, now, how would I tell him. I did not want to hurt his feelings; he was such a sweet person. I couldn't say, "My sister is interested in you more than I am." Cowardly, I just started being "unavailable." I wasn't really comfortable with that, and finally, I told him. "There is nothing wrong with you and nothing wrong with me, but something that doesn't fit with us." Eventually, Teri and Bob would get together.

Since I started working at the studios, I "chose" to pay "child support" to Mel's mom. I paid $100 per week (about $500 in 2022 money). I also paid for all of their medical, dental, clothes, school needs, and anything else that came up. I bought or gave Connie money for all their Christmas, Easter, Birthday, and any other holiday. At Thanksgiving, I bought Connie a big turkey. I felt I could little complain about men not paying support if I was unwilling to pay it myself. This was not mandated by a court, it was about my integrity. I decided what was fair and I lived up to my own expectations and self-agreements.

Mel still followed me, but he had nothing to hold over me. I wasn't on welfare, so he couldn't turn me in and control me or my money. He had no power. I just observed him as someone who never lived up to his agreements.

One night I saw his car behind me and I pulled over and flagged him down. I asked him why he was following me and he gave his usual speech about how much he loved me and missed me and all that crap. I was done with his following me.

"So, would having sex satisfy you?" I asked. He became like a kid, all giddy and smiling. I suggested we get a motel. You could just feel his excitement.

I drove to a little motel and he followed. I rented the room, of course, he had no money. He still didn‘t work and still lived off his parents! We went in and he started pawing at me. "Slow down," I said, "We got all night." He lay back on the bed playing with himself, smiling like he was a prize catch. I waited until he was busting with passion. Then I jumped up and looking down at him I said, "Do you really think I would ever have sex with you again you dumb bastard?" And I walked out the door leaving him with his dick in his hand and his eyes as big as saucers. He could not believe that he had been rejected. I laughed all the way to my car. I've become a more compassionate person since then, but at the time, that was who I was.

I think that was how my brain let go of the stupid childish dream of what a man was or should be. I no longer mourned the loss of a marriage that could never have worked out and I only had a small amount of resentment that I had ignorantly wasted seven years of my life trying to make it work.

I still didn't know what I needed to know about life, but I had a start. Life moves on if we want it to or not. I would have liked to stay in those days of enlightenment and euphoria, but as usual, something comes along to jog you back to reality.

In October of that year, I got a letter from my Aunt Dorothea in Arizona. It read:

Dear Claudia,

I have felt so terrible all this time because I did not know how to get in touch with you until Teri just happened to call mom the other day, to tell you about Doug's death. Please try to understand, the whole family agreed we could bear anything except having your dad here. Doug shot himself to death, after first killing Shirley (his wife). Their bodies were not discovered until the next day. The gunshot sounds were heard at 5:00 a.m. on Sunday morning. No one investigated. I think I was in shock for about three weeks, though it shouldn't have been such a complete surprise after all that had gone before.

I can't remember just when you left Phoenix, but I think I had told you some of his strange erratic behavior when you were here. But it seemed to culminate late in September of 1974 when he completely "flipped out" and ended up for a short time in the State Hospital. He was firing a gun out of the house they were living in because he was convinced that Kissinger was going to take him and torture him and that he was out there with his men ready to throw fire bombs into the house. When State released him it was to the care of a private psychiatrist that Doug had been seeing from time to time for years, but he didn't stay with him long, and always had fears that he had not completely recovered; was always uneasy about it.

Well, it's all over now and no one will ever know exactly what took place. There is a great deal of difficulty coming up in the future about the settlement of his estate, mainly life insurance and Shirley's father has hired his own lawyer and the law is on his side when a homicide has been committed. However, we want to protect our grandchildren living with Charlotte (Doug's ex-wife) and her husband in Las Vegas.

I have a new unlisted phone number and under no circumstance do I want your dad to have it, so I won't even tell you, then you won't have to lie. I knew you were the only one who cared, so I can only repeat that I am sorry to be so late telling you this sad news.

With Love, Dorothea

This had happened on May 17, 1976, and the latter was dated October

18, 1976. I was devastated.

I had seen Doug when I was in Arizona. He told me that he could never find a girl as "sweet" as me. As I sat looking at this letter, I wondered if things would have been different if we had been allowed to stay together. At this point, it didn't matter. Life had blown us in separate directions and the deed was done. Doug had an abusive father and had suffered much in life. I guess he just wasn't lucky enough to hit the guidewire.

I went outside and sat on the curb in the street. I looked around, taking in the sights, sounds, and smells of my little world. I looked at the dirt in the gutter and tire marks in the street. How real everything was in that moment of "now."

I sat in the realization of Doug's death. I experienced it in the "now," the way I had learned to do with all my crazy experiments. Not running from the pain, but experiencing it. It didn't take long and it cleared and the pain went away. I would miss Doug and could only view our time together as cherished moments. Not filled with negative emotion but with a love for what we shared.

I thought how lucky I was. I had two beautiful kids. I had a great job. I had survived through all the crap that the world had sent my way. And, I was still reasonably sane. How many times in my life could it have gone another way? I would not be put down or defeated! What doesn't kill us certainly makes us stronger.

Chapter 26

The Lessons I Learned

I had parted from Skip in November of 1975; I was 28 ½ years old. I would remain single for over three years. I didn't file for divorce until February of 1977 and it was final in August of that same year. It was a simple, straightforward divorce with nothing asked for, nothing given.

I was just trying to figure it all out. I dated, and believe it or not, I was proposed to again, but I turned him down. I knew he was fun, but he wasn't for me, I wasn't ready. Because I made enough money to take care of myself, my kids, my mother, and everything else that came along, I wasn't trapped like most women. I didn't need a man and I wanted to see what it was like to live without one. That was scary, but I wanted to be at "choice." You have to learn (experience) past your fear to get there.

The first year I was in the studio, I made over $11,000 (about $55,000 in 2022) and paid about 30% of that in various taxes. During tax season in 1977, I went to work, part-time with a well-known tax company to find out what it was all about. They trained me on how to do taxes. That is where I learned that the small guy could make his taxes go down by owning real estate. You might be able to make some money in other investments, but the rich people dodged taxes through "rental property."

Working at Universal, I met a few stars. I worked on "The Rockford Files" and met James Garner. He was a very nice man. He was also very tall at 6' 2", but he seemed much taller. He had very long legs and a small upper torso. His belt was almost up to my shoulders.

Also, while working at Universal I had the pleasure of working on the mini-series, "Captains and the Kings" where I met Henry Fonda. I was repairing some walls that the grips had taken out for camera angle when he walked up to me. Smiling, he said, "I used to do what you do."

"What's that?" I replied. I was a little taken back to have a big star talking to me and just didn't know what to say.

"I painted the sets. When I first started acting, we built the sets, painted the sets, dressed the sets, and then they let us act in the sets. I remember it well."

He was a very easy man to talk to. He was about 70 years old and quite tall. He was very grateful for his success, he was humble and just like an ordinary person. I don't know why that surprised me, but it did. He was the biggest star I had met and I was just overwhelmed that he would even talk to me.

He was only on the set for a couple of days because he played a very small part. He talked about how different things were from when he was young. I shared a bit about how difficult it was being a woman in the industry, but mostly he talked and I listened.

At some point, I asked him about his daughter, Jane. You could see his eyes cloud over a bit. It had only been a few years since Jane Fonda had gone to Vietnam and participated in a protest of the war. Most of the U.S. hated her for that participation. I had heard about it, but my life was so much about just surviving, that I didn't understand much of it. I was just grateful that I had my brother back safe and sound from the war.

I could see that Mr. Fonda was very saddened by her action, ashamed is more the word. "Some mistakes are bigger than others," he said. "But I think they are still just mistakes."

I let the subject drop. I didn't know enough about it to say anything anyway and did not want to stress him about it. When his part was finished he came by where I was working. "Well, I'm wrapped," he said. "I guess I might see you on another show at some point. So long Hollywood, keep your chin up," He said as he walked away.

I never worked on a show with him again but I worked with his daughter sometime later, on a couple of movies. One was "Coming Home," and the other was called "9 to 5."

I was fortunate enough to stay at Universal Studio until I got my "Journeyman" card. Then I went to work at "Fox Studio," and worked on many of Spelling-Goldberg productions including, San Pedro Bums, Family, The Love Boat, Starsky & Hutch and Fantasy Island.

I also worked on a movie called "High Anxiety" with Mel Brooks. I liked Movies better than TV shows because the work was much more professional. TV in those days was not the HD picture you get today, so you could get away with some pretty sloppy work. But movie productions, because they are on a much bigger screen, show every flaw in the job. I was a perfectionist so you can imagine my reaction when a boss told me "that's good enough," when the job was only half done, in my opinion.

When I switched from Universal to Fox Studio, I went on days. That meant that I had to be at work at 6 a.m. The hardest thing for me was to get up at 4:30 a.m. to get to work by 6. I just turned off the alarm clock and went back to sleep never remembering that I had done it. The first week I worked at Fox, I was late three days. I finally got three "Big Ben" wind-up alarm clocks and put them under my bed in cooking pans. To shut them off in the morning, I had to get the broom from the kitchen and push or pull the pan out from under the bed and then shut the alarms off. The clocks were set a few minutes apart. By the time I got them all out and off, I was awake.

The next thing was always deciding if I "felt" good enough to go to work. My mind really tried to trip me up with that. I finally decided that no matter how I felt, I HAD to go to work. Once there, if I was sick, I could go home, but I had to show up at work first. That solved that problem because I don't get sick and once I got there of course I wanted to earn that big money. I was finally able to transition to working in the daytime.

When I had first entered the industry, some men were very resentful. They made life hard for a woman. "Grips" would drop hammers from the overhead "grip beds" and it would land right beside me. At first, I tried not to look like a woman. I was rather flat-chested anyway, so I simply wore a couple of shirts and covered my hair with a hat. I wore no makeup and tried to blend in. I didn't fool many people because I was so petite, but at least I didn't draw as much attention as I could have.

In those days, when a woman walked onto a set, the first man to see her had to call out, "lady on the set." Then men would be required to put their shirts on and close their toolbox if they had a "girly pin-up" adorning the inside lid. This was very frustrating for me because I didn't want to be noticed and the men resented it greatly.

One day when I was on a set at Fox Studio, a wrench fell from the grip beds and nearly hit me. That morning, the head of construction for Fox had sent out a memo to all construction departments, stating that men should adhere to the studio rules as far as women were concerned even if those women were workers. Furthermore, it stated that the women were offended" by the nude pictures around their working environment. I was the only woman working in construction at Fox Studio, at the time. To the men, it meant, that I was the one who had complained, which was not true.

I don't know if whoever dropped the wrench intended to hit me or not, but by this time I had acquired my "Journeyman" card, I had the protection of the union, and was a bit more secure in my job, and that day I had had enough.

I walked to the center of the stage and yelled as loud as I could.

"OK, listen up. I'm not here to challenge men or to mess with your routine. I don't care if you have your shirts off or not. I don't care and have never been offended by whatever nudes you care to display; the truth is, I just don't see them because I am busy doing my work. That is someone else's bullshit, not mine. You can cuss all you want. I'm no fucking lady! If anyone gives you shit about it, send them to me. You can jack off in the middle of the stage for all I care, as long as you don't interfere with me or my work. I have two kids to support, by myself, and I need this job. Don't fuck with me and I won't fuck with you!"

While I was speaking, someone turned off a radio that I had been yelling over. You could have heard a pin drop on that stage. Then all of a sudden, a carpenter started clapping. And then another and another and then all the men on set were clapping. That was the last time anything fell from the grip beds. After that, I learned to cuss and cuss often. I wanted no mistake about who I was and what I was about.

The paint shop was set up so that when you rolled down the big garage-style door at night and locked it, the only way you could get out was through the men's toilet. I had to ask someone to go in and see if anyone was standing at the urinal before I could pass through. It was logical for a building that was all male, but it didn't work well for me.

That night I went home and bought some "Playgirl" magazines and cut out a picture of every dick I could find. I pinned them to the inside of my paint box and plastered them on the lockers in the paint shop. The person who had put out the memo, about the nudes, came down the stairs from the office above and stopped dead in his tracks as he saw the display I had put up.

"Very funny, Claudia. Very funny!"

"Well," I said, "if you really want to do something for me, put in an exit door in this paint shop so that I don't have to exit through the men's bathroom when I leave at night. But, don't put out stupid memos and attribute anything to me."

The door was never installed, but the men put their nudes back up, I took down my "dick pics" and everyone was happy.

I had discovered early on that unless I wanted to sand a lot of walls, I better specialize. In set painting, it is a lot easier and you earn more money if you know how to "marbleize, wood grain, and / or age."

I set out to learn all of those. I didn't like sanding! The trouble was, the men who knew how to do those things were very close with how and what they did. I finally approached one of the best wood grainers in the business, who liked to strut and brag about what he could do. I told him I would pay him a thousand dollars if he would teach me. I don't know if it was the offer of money or if it was just that no one had ever asked him to teach them, but he took the deal. He didn't give me the "right" formulas for the paint mixtures, but I figured out what he didn't want me to know. Being an artist already, I quickly became very good. That was the best $1000 I ever spent. I did the same for marbleizing and aging. I was as good as anyone in the business and better than most. And, I seldom sanded anything!

Brother, Pat, and I continued our studies of "Human Nature," and continued to "Process," what we found was not working for us in our lives. Pat had come back from Vietnam different than he had left. My brother was never lazy; he had always been very industrious. He had been sprayed with "Agent Orange" which was meant to defoliate the jungle of Vietnam, but it didn't differentiate between jungle and human. He would have bouts of deep depression and lethargy, and times when he just could not get out of bed. We tried processing it, but when it hit, we could find nothing that would move it. Some things are just physical.

Once you get that the mind and body are very connected, you can never look back. One of the things we got into was hypnosis. I had dabbled in it when I was a young kid and my dad made me stand with my arms out at my side. You would be amazed at what you can do with it. I remember one day Pat was putting a girlfriend under who had had an elbow problem. She was lying on the couch with her arm bent at the elbow. He was saying, "You are getting lighter and lighter." All was fine until I noticed her arm was getting "whiter and whiter." Pat had not noticed. I flagged him to notice the whiteness of the arm. He started saying, "your arm is getting darker and darker." What we discovered by that was that each person has their own interpretation of things. My question from then on was what were we interpreting differently than other people?

If you raised a child all its life calling a "bicycle" a "ball," that would be their set interpretation for the rest of their life unless someone interceded. That's fine for solid things, but what about abstract things in life like good, bad, love, etc. You will believe whatever your experience is. For me, "love" was my father who beat me, held guns on me, but also walked on his hands to give me money to replace a much-loved toy. This information would profoundly affect our lives because we now knew, at least in some part, where to look for what we didn't know that we didn't know.

Unfortunately, my brother was never able to resolve his "Agent Orange" problem. Nothing we could do would bring him out of it any faster than just going to bed. He might be incapacitated for days, weeks, or months. He would later be diagnosed with PTSD by the military and given a small disability pension, but they would not acknowledge it was from Agent Orange, but attributed it to all the trauma of his childhood.

When he was "on" he was very creative, industrious, and talented. But when this incapacitating depression and pain hit him, he was just useless.

Pat was further plagued with back problems. My dad had kicked all of us in the ass, literally, and as a result, we all have back problems that only got worse with time. When I worked at the chiropractic office, I ran some standing, full spine x-rays on Pat. His back was a mess. He had what we call a "military spine." Looking at his spine from the back it had the curve that you would normally see from the side and vice versa. I believe the condition is called "scoliosis." It was like his spine was rotated one quarter. At times his back and neck caused him excruciating pain.

Another contributing factor to Pat's condition could have been from when I was pregnant with Tami. At some point, I had gone to my dad's house. I must have been about eight months pregnant, I was big. Dad was drunk and started an argument with Dodie which I knew would escalate into violence, so I tried to divert his attention. He got mad at me. I was too stupid to shut my mouth and somehow hadn't taken into account that I was eight months pregnant. My dad came for me with every intention of beating me. I ran out the front door to try to get away from him, but because I was pregnant, I couldn't run that fast. My dad caught me in the front yard and started hitting me. Pat came flying out of nowhere yelling, "Leave my sister alone," as he flew at dad and attacked him. They rolled down the hill and over a four-foot wall and then on to the concrete walk below. That was pretty much the end of the fight. Dad was beaten pretty good and Pat was bloody and limping. My brother, my savior.

There were so many brutal times. Pat's condition, and ours as well, could have been caused by my dad kicking us, beating us or it could have been from not having proper nutrition for most of our life. We will never know.

Some things we could resolve for Pat and some things we could not. Because I have always known Pat's condition, I always tried to help him out when I could. If he needed money, I would help out. I took him on a trip to Hawaii with us and we had such fun together. In later years I would have liked to take him to Ireland, but his condition got so bad that he didn't think he could make it.

Pat's wives and children never understood any of this and of course, it is now part of their "back story." I'm sure they felt abandoned and neglected and that is probably true, but there are some extenuating circumstances and it wasn't because he didn't "love" them. That's one of those times we have to ask, "What were THEY taught love was?" Pat had three girls with three different wives. Pat loved all of his children even though he felt that, sometimes, they only looked for what he could do or give to them without trying to form a relationship. They had been taught to hate him. He probably didn't do well in showing his love, but he had had no model of a loving father or mother. I don't think Pat was ever kissed or cuddled as a child other than perhaps by Teri or me. Mother abandoned us when he was about three and a half years old. Who was ever there to show him how to love or be a loving father?

The same for Teri, she had back problems as well. And from being hit in the ears, she was nearly deaf. She yelled at her kids because she had no idea how loud she was. We didn't even find this out until she was over 50 years old. When she finally got hearing aids she said she was surprised the "newspaper" made noise. She had never heard it before. She was as broken as any of us.

We all have our "back story" and it is for each of us to find our own way to resolution. One thing I came to believe is that if we don't find a way to resolve that back story, it will "attract" more negative to our life until we resolve it and hold happy thoughts. Yes, that is what Tinkerbelle tried to teach us, and somehow that turned out to be profound advice.

Left: Brother Pat's Army picture. So young and innocent!

Chapter 27
Moving On

In May of 1977, I enrolled into Lumbleau Real Estate School. No computer classes in those days, you had to actually go to a physical building to get the schooling.

It is really hard to explain, or for people to imagine, how life was before "The Internet" and "Cell Phones." If you were going someplace that you had never been, you had to get a paper "map" and plot your way. Most people carried a "Thomas Guide" (book of area maps) in their car. If you needed to make a call, you had to find a "phone booth." Your car radio was the only way to get (unreliable) weather reports, no way of knowing where "McDonald's" was in a town you have never been in. No references as to whether a doctor is a quack or not or if a restaurant's food is good or bad. And, you seldom met someone who wasn't in your immediate surroundings. I think everyone should put down their cell phone and stay off the computer for a week to see what it is like. Somehow, we made it, but it would sure be hard to go back.

In December of 1977, I bought my first house. I found a house at 4056 W. 130th St in Hawthorne, California. I think I paid around $74,000 for it. Interest rates were 8.96% when I opened escrow, but the rate was going up. The loan company, I was going through, was dragging their feet in approving the loan. It went on for weeks. I finally called and asked them if they were dragging their feet until the rate went up or were they dragging their feet because I was a single woman? The loan was approved within days at the original rate.

The property was a two-bedroom one-bath with a one-bedroom one-bath rental in the rear. It had a huge backyard on which I thought I might build more units. The front house had a tiny kitchen, but I could see how I could make it functionally bigger.

I moved into the front house and rented the back house to a couple I knew from AA. I was on my way to riches.

In June 1978 I passed my real estate exam and I went to work as a real estate agent for Tarbell Realty in Redondo Beach, California. I was straight up with the broker and told him that I didn't have a lot of time to work in real estate. I told him that I wanted to learn about buying and selling for my own purposes, but I was sure I would make money for the office if he let me work with a woman that I knew who worked there. My friend, Rose, (who later became my brother's mother-in-law) had been an agent for some time and she was quite willing to run the paperwork for any listings or sales I might get. Rose could have all of my commission. He agreed and I worked there until the end of the year.

The reason that I did all of that, was because I was afraid when I bought that first house. I knew nothing about buying real estate and I was a woman alone. Working with fear and ignorance is the easiest way of making costly mistakes. I didn't trust myself and knowledge is power and of course, I always had this thing in the back of my head saying that I only had an eighth-grade education.

Working at Tarbell, I walked neighborhoods, talked to people, and got listings. I worked nights and weekends and any days I had off. I previewed houses and I showed houses. I began to understand real estate pricing. I sold some houses, and my partner, Rose, handled the rest of it. She went over all the paperwork with me so that I knew what each step was and how to work around problems.

Sometime in early 1978, Tami wanted to live with me. The kids were no longer with Grandma Connie because Mel had a girlfriend and wanted to live away from his mom. Tami didn't get along with his girlfriend and wanted to live with me. Mel, now having someone else to focus on, wasn't so interested in his kids. Tami was about eleven years old and very independent and, of course, she wouldn't get-on with someone replacing her mom or taking her dad away from her.

I was working on, "The Six Million Dollar Man", starring, Lee Majors. Lee is a very nice man and very down-to-earth.

At one point, we were doing sets for a back-room gambling casino and so we had all the tables and games. We all caught the gambling bug. At lunch and during slow times, we would usually get a poker game going and Lee would join in just like one of the crew. It just happened that we had some very pricy games going on and I was one of the winners and had been for a few weeks. It's not nice to quit when you have everyone's money, so anytime there was a game, someone would find me and asked if I wanted to join.

It also happened that I had a chance to bring Tami to the studio with me one day, and that was the day we had these poker games going on. Tami was about eleven years old. She came away thinking that that was what I did at work all day. She of course mentioned something to Grandma Connie and that gave them ammunition to goad me about what I "really" did for work. They had a hard time believing that I made the kind of money, that I made, by just painting.

One day, we were in the kitchen and Tami confided in me that her grandmother had told her several things about me, but she didn't know if were true or not. One thing was that I had beaten her with a hairbrush and locked her in a closet. I was floored by that statement. I asked Tami if she remembered it and she said, "No, but grandma said maybe I didn't remember it."

I was truly pissed at Connie for trying to turn my child against me. I asked Tami how Connie got this information? Well, that is an interesting question, isn't it? If Tami didn't remember it, she couldn't have told Connie. Is this something Connie witnessed? And, if so, why did she not stop me before I locked you in a closet? Fortunately, Tami was smart enough to figure it wasn't true. I could only assure her that I never had and would never "beat" either of my kids.

I asked her, "What else?"

"Grandma says, you are a queer, and wear men's underpants."

I was stunned. This is the crap they are telling my kids? I would never forgive them for that. In answer to that, I unzipped my slacks and dropped them so she could see that I wore little lace panties. "Do those look like men's underwear?" I asked.

After that, I kept asking my kids what had been said about me. I also had a talk with Mel's parents and told them that if they ever wanted to see their grandkids again, they better stop. I was no longer a frightened little girl with no money. I don't think they said anymore to my kids, but then I don't know all of my children's "back story" either. I know MY perception of their life; I don't know THEIR perception of their life.

That shows the mentality of people back then. If a woman works at anything other than a "woman's job." it must be because she was "queer!" Stupid, stupid people! If I were "gay," I would have been gay proudly. I simply wasn't, but at times, I have to say, I wished I was.

Tami moved in with me. She had her own room and I had a telephone put in for her. Knowing that kids like to talk on the phone, I thought it best for her to have her own phone, in her room. Phones were still hooked to the wall by a phone line, but now they had "push-button dialing" on a slimline, "princess" phone, in many colors.

That year, I also bought a brand-new car, a 1978 Chevrolet Monte Carlo. My first ever new car. I felt like I had arrived. I traded in my 1966 Oldsmobile Toronado that was on its last leg. I had bought the Toronado when my old Cadillac broke down. I had decided on the Toronado because when I was inspecting it at the car lot, it had a "paintbrush" in the trunk. I somehow saw that as a sign.

The Monte Carlo's design had one big flaw. The front bumper, which was made of rubber, just wouldn't stay on. I took it back to the dealer many times to have it fixed, but it just never worked. I was very disappointed. Then, I took it to the studios and had the special effects guys work on it. They used every glue they had, but nothing worked. Finally, they riveted it on, every six inches and that of course fixed it, but it didn't look the same.

The other thing about the car was, that I had gotten used to driving a "front-wheel drive" car, my Toronado. This new car was not front-wheel drive and it was "squirrelly." I had it for a couple of years and then sold it at a loss. I decided I would never buy another "new" car. I would let other people find the "bugs" in the design before I bought.

I went back to night school for a short time and took a class in "Beginning Spanish," because I needed five "elective" credits. Always working toward the goal of getting my high school diploma. I had a very busy life.

I had been pursued by a guy, Jim (JAA), from the club, off and on. He had been married, but they had called it quits he said. He was very handsome, but I wasn't sure he was done with his ex-wife, who was a member of the AA club we both belonged to.

He was very nice to me and brought me flowers and really tried to impress me. I have to say, I was flattered. But, a couple of times he went back with his ex. I don't know what that story was because most of the time she lived with her mother, sister, or somewhere else. I don't know that they ever lived together except for a very short time.

He worked as a "Scale Mechanic" for some company and talked about opening his own business. He seemed to be stable and responsible and he was several years sober in AA. Then, he bought a motorcycle. Little by little, he was winning me over.

I finally went and asked his ex-wife if they were in fact finished and she assured me that they were. I accepted what she said.

For a couple of years, Paula, Teri, Pat, and I had dragged my dad around to meetings, dances, and other AA functions. He was funny. He would start out sober, but by the end of the night, he was drunk. We would usually find that he had hidden a bottle, in the tank of the toilet in the men's room, wherever we were. I kind of thought he was a waste of time, but Paula thought otherwise and I just went along with her. As long as he wasn't violent, it was OK. Somewhere along the way, my dad got sober and it stuck.

I have to say, "hats off to Paula," who had the insight that none of the rest of us had. She is the one who got my dad sober. She had patience, faith, and love. She was a truly remarkable human being.

We all joined a square dance club and went each week to learn the moves. My dad was a good dancer and he became my partner. It was quite different with my dad sober. He was a lot of fun and was always volunteering to help with anything that anyone needed. He just became a very nice man and I was very proud of him.

I started remodeling my house. The kitchen was small and very narrow. I could see that if I used part of the big linen closet that was in the hall behind the kitchen, I could create an alcove for the refrigerator, and with it set back into the wall, the kitchen would be a lot larger, at least in appearance. The only problem was the "pocket door" that went from the kitchen to the hall. The door went into the wall between the refrigerator and the linen closet; that had to be removed.

I hired my dad for the job. I explained very carefully, what I wanted. I wanted the door "removed" and a solid door frame put in to replace the one with the slit that had been for the pocket door. I didn't think it was necessary to tell him my entire plan, and that was a mistake.

I came home from work and it looked to be all finished. He was so proud of the job he had done. So, I told him, "Now what I want to do is move the refrigerator into the dining area, and then cut a hole in the wall behind where the refrigerator is now to create an alcove for the refrigerator by using half of the linen closet in the hallway."

He looked a little upset. "What's wrong," I asked.

"You can't do that because the door is in the wall," he replied.

Grrrrrr. "Why didn't you take the door out as I asked?" I said.

"Because it seemed silly to take it out when I could just push it back into the wall and save you some money!"

I had to laugh. "OK, Dad, let's get something straight. From now on, if you are going to work for me, you have to do exactly as I ask, no figuring it out yourself. No saving me any money. Just as I ask, OK?" And sheepishly he agreed.

I was running my own shows by then and got a show called "Friends." Not the one that became popular from 1994 to 2004, This one was a comedy about three little boys from different backgrounds and they only shot five episodes before it went down.

I had an opportunity to get my dad into the business as a painter. Being sober, he needed to support himself. My dad was 59 years old and not in the best of condition. After all, he had been a "Skid Row" bum.

I talked to him before I hired him. He had to agree that no matter what went down on the set, he had to stay out of my business and I would call him Jim instead of dad. If I couldn't handle whatever went down, I shouldn't be there in the first place. He agreed and I brought him onto the show.

The "Construction Coordinator," who ran the carpenters, did not like the fact that I had been given the show. He had a son who was a painter and wanted him to get it, so it was a bit of a hostile situation.

Carpenters and painters were working on top of each other because of budget. One of the carpenters was a pretty nice guy. We had talked a few times and we had discovered that we were both from Indianapolis, Indiana. This guy was pretty easygoing and wore engineer bill coveralls. I put dad in the set with him because I thought he probably would not give him as hard of a time as some younger carpenters might. I went to deal with other things.

I checked back on my dad. When I went into the set, the carpenter said, "Hey, did you know this guy is from Indianapolis, Indiana also?"

"Yes, I did," I replied, "He's my dad!"

The carpenter turned white. He started apologizing to my dad, "I'm sorry, really, I'm sorry. I didn't mean anything by it," And on and on he went.

My dad started laughing. It was a rumble that started deep in his chest and built until it was just a huge belly laugh.

"No offense taken," my dad said. "We're cool."

I walked away but winked at my dad. My dad later explained what had happened. The guy had asked him, "So, how is it working for a cunt?" To which my dad had replied, "Oh she ain't so bad. She knows what she is doing."

I hired another woman for my crew. Her name was Terry Minch. She had come into the studios just after me and was a very hard worker and a very talented artist.

The coordinator put in a complaint to Mr. Spelling that his men couldn't work because they were "distracted by the women" on the set. That's the good old boys networking bullshit!

I knew he was only doing it because he wanted his son to take over the show. I was furious that I had been called to the office for such crap and told them what was behind it. They agreed and said that his son was not going to get the show, they and the "Art Director" were very happy with my work.

I went back to the stage and confronted the coordinator. In front of the carpenters, grips, and anyone else who happened to be there, I told him, he should take his little boys out and get them "laid," so they could come back and work like men! My dad got a good look at what I had to contend with. Fortunately, my dad lived up to our agreement of not interfering even though I know he had to grit his teeth at times to do it.

One day, I didn't have anything for my crew to do but I didn't want to lay my dad off because he needed to get the thirty days that it took to get into the union. I only had four painters, but they all volunteered to take off so I could keep my dad on. Now, I had to make him "look busy" so the coordinator couldn't complain. I had dad washing buckets and cleaning my equipment. When he finished all that, I told him we had to move the paint shop from the back of the stage to the front. When he was done with that, I told him I had changed my mind and had him move it back to where it was to start with!

At about this time my daughter, Tami, graduated from the 8th grade. I was so proud of her. She was 13 years old and just a wonderful girl. She looked all grown up in her gown. It really seemed that everything was going fine. I guess I didn't understand hormones, puberty, and the difficult road ahead.

My mother had had a stroke but was still drinking. She would often call me because she had fallen and hit her head or bruised some part of her body. She just couldn't quit drinking or moderate it. She would sit for hours trying to get her handwriting back with a "wine cooler" in front of her. By this time, her fourth husband had died of cirrhosis of the liver.

She was alone in a tiny little one-bedroom apartment, living on a tiny amount of Social Security. She was only 58 years old. I helped her as much as I could even though I had no real connection with her. I felt it was more of a "duty." While I did what I could for her, I had to live my life. One of the things that she had always talked about doing in her life was to go to Hawaii. I didn't tell her, but I had a trip planned to go myself.

A group of people from the Alano club were planning a trip to Hawaii. They asked me if I wanted to go along. Since I was single and thought I might never get another chance, I decided to go. My friend Jackie, who was gay, was one of the people and as it turned out everyone in the group was gay except me. I decided to go anyway. They called me the "token straight."

The men on the trip had a lot of fun when we would all go to a club together. I would find a guy that I thought was cute and one of our gay guys would ask them to dance.....and they would. I could not tell a straight from a gay which shows you how much I really saw other people.

On the airplane going to Hawaii, I found out that Jackie was terrified of flying. Her way of dealing with fear was to simply go to sleep …. And I mean sleep. One of the things the airline did was to have a game to guess the total miles we would fly to Hawaii. The winner would get "a bottle of Champagne." It was a great prize for AA members. Nonetheless, I played the game. Because I couldn't wake Jackie, I guessed for her as well. She won the bottle of Champagne!

Jackie and I got on fine. We shared a room, but that was all. She kept telling me she was interested in me, but I was not interested in her in that way. Jackie just saw women different than I did. I remember her staring at a painting of a young girl, in a gallery on Oahu. The girl had her hair over her bare breast standing in a field. I could see that Jackie thought it was a beautiful painting, but I just couldn't see it in the same way.

We had such fun in Hawaii. I made her climb Diamond Head, going up through someone's backyard. We were surprised to find a military installation inside the caldera.

We went to a place called "the toilet bowl," at Hanauma Bay, which is a tidal hole by the ocean where water comes up as the waves come in and then go out as the tide recedes. In order to get to it you had to cross a treacherous walk along a cliff. When we got there, a lot of people got in it and rode the tide. I was not a good swimmer and was afraid of water, but I told her to get in and she did. She had told me she was a very strong swimmer. When the tide came in and the hole was full she jumped in. Then the tide went out and people panicked. Jackie scrambled and finally was able to get out, but she was shaking. She said when the tide went out; it was, truly, like being sucked down a toilet. She had no control. She had grabbed onto the first thing she could, which happened to be some guy's swim trunks which, she said, probably saved her life, though she had almost pulled the trunks right off of him. We found out later that a good many people have died at Hanauma Bay.

I have no idea why Jackie agreed to it, but we went on an "Island Hopping" excursion in a small plane that held about twelve passengers. The passengers were allowed to take turns sitting in the copilot's seat. We went to all the islands. At one point it became Jackie's turn to be the copilot. She refused, but there were eleven passengers and the pilot in a 12-passenger plane. Everyone took their seat, so there was now nowhere else for her. As soon as we took off, she became drowsy. The pilot kept nudging her, but she was just comatose. It was fun for all of us, but not fun for her.

We went to the "Jim Neighbor's Show" and the "Don Ho" show. We also went to a luau and I fell in love with the "hula" dance. I even got up on the stage and tried it myself. I found it a lot harder than it looks.

That was a great time in my life. I felt like life was turning around for me. Here I was, a girl who had to beg for a pair of shoes as a child, and I had gone to Hawaii. I was my own master! This only goes to demonstrate how little it takes to impress a poor person. I really felt like I had arrived.

Me kissing Don Ho.
Hawaii July 1978

Claudia 31

Chapter 28
Marriage Number Five

The year 1979 was a disastrous year! It started out pretty good, but then the wheels fell off the bus, so to speak.

I had a girl come in and clean my house and I had bought a beautiful, brand new, upright Chickering Piano that I loved to play. I was running my own shows in the studios. That was the good things.

I was appointed to the "Rent Mediation Board of Hawthorne." I really enjoyed this position. It gave me a chance to see that the right thing was done at least in one area. I was a very fair mediator and it was an eye-opening experience.

At some point, Mel married a woman named Celeste. I don't know how long they were married, but it was long enough to cause a bit of havoc in my life. They and my son, Andy, had moved to Fernley, Nevada even though our custody agreement did not allow him to take the kids out of California without my permission, and he certainly did not have my permission.

My son, Andy, called me from a payphone in Fernley, crying because he was hungry and Celeste had hit him. My heart almost jumped out of my chest. I told Tami to bring me her phone. Thank the powers that be, that I had gotten her a twenty-five-foot cord for her phone.

While I kept Andy on the phone and got him calmed down, Tami called the operator and got the number for the Fernley Police Dept. She dialed the number and when the Desk Sergeant came on the line I explained that my son was in a phone booth somewhere in Fernley and he had been assaulted. I had Andy give me the phone number of the booth he was in and the name of the bar his father was in and the police were able to find the location.

The police found him and they got on the phone from his location. Andy pointed out the bar his father and Celeste were in. I told the policeman that I wanted my son to be put on a plane and sent to me and that our custody agreement forbade Mel from taking him out of the state of California. I would purchase the airplane ticket for him.

The police found Mel and told him they would arrest him for child neglect unless he would let them put Andy on a plane and send him to his mother. Mel acquiesced and Andy was sent to me.

Tami and I went to the airport to pick him up. A stewardess escorted him off the plane and checked my ID to be sure I was his mother. I could not believe how Andy looked. His clothes were filthy and he was filthy. I just cried for the poor little guy. He didn't seem to know how dirty and neglected he was, but I was reliving my childhood.

On the way home, I stopped and bought him new clothes. When we got home, he took a bath and put on clean, new clothes. It was a good day because I got my son, but a bad day because of the circumstances.

Unfortunately, I think this was only a game for Mel because a few months later, Mel came around and bought Andy a great big fire truck and talked him into wanting to live with him again. It also was partly because Mel found himself alone again.

When Mel came back from Nevada, he and Celeste had nowhere to go, so they made arrangements to stay with my ex-brother-in-law, Sam. In the middle of the night, Celeste switched beds and traded Mel for Sam. Celeste divorced Mel in August and Married Sam shortly thereafter.

Meanwhile, Jim, the guy I was dating, confided to me that he was going to lose his house because he was behind in his payments. He had bought a real, fixer-upper. He couldn't afford to fix it and he couldn't make the payments on it either. He wanted to sell it to me for what was owed plus some small amount of cash.

In those days, you could buy a house "subject to" the existing mortgage instead of getting a new one. Jim signed the deed to me and I brought the payments current.

I had decided to sell the house I had been living in so that I could buy a better rental property. I had found out that I could not legally build more units in the back of my house. Rose and I had partnered up and were buying several units and the money from my sale was my portion of the down payment. I had planned to remodel the house I had bought from Jim and then move into it.

In January of 1979, Jim wanted to get married. I ask him if he was crazy because I had been married and divorced four times. I would be his third or fourth wife. He assured me that he knew what he was doing. I was in love with him. I had known him for several years and he had been nothing but kind, so I said yes. I thought we would be a good match and I wanted a stable home for my kids.

Jim and I were married in Las Vegas on February 10, 1979. After we were married, I put him on my bank account and some of my credit cards. He still wanted to open his own business so he needed the credit. His story was that his credit was bad because of his ex-wife. I bought the story because I had had to pay a lot of Mel's bad credit to save my own. I also deeded half of the property I had purchased from him back to him.

Jim moved into my house and we started remodeling the house I had purchased from him which we now owned jointly. He was still working for the scale company but was in the process of getting his licenses and everything to open his own company.

I had sold my house and we were working as fast as we could to get our house ready. My escrow was to close in 45 days.

We had almost finished our joint-owned house when Jim all of a sudden changed. He was no longer the sweet man I had known for more than three years. All of a sudden, he was sulky, angry, and touchy.

One night he came home late. I was already in bed, it was about midnight. He sat down on the edge of the bed and I asked him where he was so late. He grabbed my wrist and said, "You know, I don't know what it is about you, but you really piss me off," and then he hit me. I was stunned. I had no idea of what had gone wrong. I think maybe I had too many irons in the fire to notice anything. We fought, but I was no match for him. I did get in some licks, but he just laughed and pushed me away.

Then he was nice and we made up. I was so busy with so many things and I just wanted the marriage to work. I asked him to go to counseling with me to see what had gone wrong. He wouldn't go.

One Sunday, my tenants in my rear house had their plumbing back up. I hated to call a plumber on a Sunday, so I decided I would look at it myself. Jim was lying on the couch watching TV. I told him I was going to the back house to look at the clogged plumbing. He flew mad. "You're just trying to make me look bad," he yelled. I was again stunned. Where had that come from? Look bad to whom?

I tried to explain to him that I didn't expect him to help me or anything. It was my house and my tenants and I needed to do something because I felt that they paid their rent faithfully and I was responsible to provide them with livable quarters. I of all people, being on the "Rent Mediation Board," knew the expectations of tenants and the responsibilities of landlords. And, that was, also, one of those "agreement" things that I lived by.

There was no explaining to him. He just got madder. He was working himself up and I was doing everything I could to deescalate the situation. "Please, let's go to counseling I cried, I love you and I don't want to argue."

He looked at me and said, "You want to know what the problem is? Your ugly, scrawny, sexless body turns me off!" Then he hit me and the fight was on.

Tami came in from her room and looked scared to death. She saw what was happening and I told her to run and lock herself in her bedroom. At this point, I had no idea what he might do to her. She ran and fortunately she crawled out her window and went to the back house to my tenants who in turn called the police.

I felt like I was in a fight for my life. He got me on the floor and had his legs wrapped around my waist. I heard my rib crack and a stabbing pain as he continued squeezing with his legs. He had his hands over my mouth and I was about to pass out. I reached back and tried to claw his eyes out. He finally had to release me. I pulled away and got up. I ran for the door just as the police came up. They arrested him on the spot.

They took him to jail. I was so shaken because I, for the life of me, could not figure out what had gone so wrong. I had not expected him to look at the plumbing. Was that what it was all about?

I knew I had a broken rib because I could not breathe deeply. I had broken ribs before thanks to my first husband and my dad. I needed to go to the doctor, but unfortunately, Jim had the keys to my car because he had used it to go to the store earlier. I had the keys to his truck, but that was owned by the company he worked for. I was afraid that if I took the truck he could have me arrested for auto theft. I was also afraid that if he bailed out of jail, he might come back and who knew what he might do. I decided not to go to the doctor but tough it out.

My tenants had taken Tami to their house to try to distract her. I got my gun and sat in the front room. I would have to wait and see. I had to think. I had to figure out what-the-hell had happened. I was just in disbelief. What had I missed? Why had he gone from Mr. Nice Guy to this raving maniac? What had I done to make him so crazy?

A few hours later, Jim pulled up in a taxi. He had bailed out of jail. I had set the deadbolts on the house and he couldn't get in. He came to the window and asked to switch keys and could he have his coat because it was cold outside?

Like a fool, I felt sorry for him. I told him, "Look, I have a broken rib and can't take the chance of fighting with you. You put my keys on the porch and then go out to the sidewalk. I will put your keys and coat on the porch chair. But, don't try anything because I have a gun,"

He agreed and I watched as he put my keys on the chair and then he went out to the street. I opened the door and grabbed my keys and threw down his coat and keys. I started back in the door when he came flying up the sidewalk and stuck his foot in the door. I held the door, but pulled my gun up under his chin and said, "Just blink mother fucker and I'll blow your fucking head off." I watched his face as the blood drained from it. Just like a thermometer going down. He turned white and slowly backed out of the door.

He left and that was the end of that marriage. That was March 24, 1979. We had been married for 43 days.

It wasn't long before I found out what it was all about. He tried suing me for alimony saying that I had talked him into opening a business and he couldn't support himself yet. What a load of bull. He also sued for the house I had bought from him, which I then put him back on the deed after we married. He said it was the other way around and that he had only put it in my name because we were getting married. What a lying crook! And, how stupid was I?

All this getting married, him getting mad, and everything else was about money. He saw a way that he could fix his credit, open a business and get his house caught up in payments and even remodeled. He married me for money! I felt so dumb! How had I not seen this? Were there signs that I should have picked-up-on?

I felt disgusted. I felt helpless and hopeless. Everything I thought I knew came into question. And, having no way of facing the truth, I got drunk. I went to our jointly owned house and put cement down the new sink. I tore the shit out of the house. I tore off all the wallpaper that I had just hung. I would be damned if he was going to enjoy all the work I had put into that house.

I only drank that one night. The next day, I was so sick. I just lay down on the couch, my head still spinning. My dad, of all people, came over to take care of me. I remember him bringing me a plate of eggs. "You need to eat," he said. I started laughing. "What a turnaround this is," I thought. I'm drunk and he's sober!

In all the turmoil, Tami wanted to go to Grandma Connie's and under the circumstances, I thought it best as well. I felt so bad that I had exposed her to the very thing that I hated about my childhood. Tami moved to Grandma's house. Now, Mel or rather Grandma Connie again had both kids.

My house was closing and Rose and I were supposed to close on the houses we were buying. I had to tell Rose that she would have to buy the houses by herself. I explained that if I completed the purchase, they might wind up being part of the divorce lawsuit. Jim could hold them up in court for years. She agreed.

One of the properties we were buying had a rear house that was a one-bedroom furnished house. I rented that from Rose and moved all my furniture into it as well. The house was packed to the ceiling with all my belongings. There was a small path to the bedroom and that was it. To get to the bathroom, you had to crawl over the bed to access it. LOVELY!

The alimony was the thing that got me. Other than my first husband that the court insisted I get alimony until I was eighteen, I had never asked for alimony. And now this man was trying to get it from me?

In the studios, I could take off whenever I wanted, or just not take a call for work. So, I did not work. He couldn't get any money if I didn't make any money and I had other things I needed to do. One thing was certain; I wasn't going to pay alimony!

I stayed in that little house for a couple of months. I hired a lawyer of course. The money I had made from the sale of my house would carry me through. The main thing I was stuck with, was, "Why do men beat the shit out of me?"

I decided that I needed help with that question, so I went to a psychologist. I did not like psychiatrists because of my previous experience, but maybe a psychologist would work.

I "interviewed" several psychologists before I found one that I liked and thought I could work with. Bob Halon was a charming man with a good sense of humor. I thought he might be just the ticket. I went to him weekly. My goal, when I started with him, was to answer the question, "Why do men beat the shit out of me?" Of course, we had to go over my childhood and all the crap of the past that I thought I had pretty well handled. He thought I had pretty well handled it also. I don’t know if he was helping me much, but I enjoyed having a safe place to talk about my "stuff."

Then one day my niece, "Sandie" who was about 15 years old, told me a joke. "Why does a doggy lick his pee-pee, Aunty?" she asked. "I don’t know, Sandie, why does a doggy lick his pee-pee? I replied. "BECAUSE HE CAN!" she yelled and giggled with all the charm of the teen she was. We laughed. But, something about that stuck with me.

I was sitting in the waiting room of Bob Halon’s office a few days later. I was reading a story in one of his magazines about an unruly little boy. The parents had taken him to a psychologist and he had observed the family unit as they waited in the waiting room. The mother would sit down and pick up a Good Housekeeping magazine and the father would pick up Sports Illustrated. The little boy would sit quietly for a few minutes and then he would get up and begin throwing magazines off the table onto the floor. This would go on for a bit and then escalate. The mother would finally whine "John, do something." At that point, the dad would get up and put the kid back in his chair and the whole thing would start over.

"Pay some attention to the kid," my head screamed. Give him something to play with. He is doing it because you don’t pay attention to him and so he can get away with it!” And a light went on in my head.

At that moment I was called in for my session with Bob. I was all excited. “I know the answer,” I said. "What answer?" he asked.

"The question I came in here with," I said. "Why do men beat the shit out of me? The answer is…..because they can!"

I told him about Sandie’s joke and the article I had read and how it all came together for me. I told him that I had been looking for some deep psychological answer to a question that had a much simpler answer.

"So, what are you going to do with that information?"

"I'm going to take the money I'm paying you and I'm going to take Karate lessons!"

Married fifth husband, Jim, (JAA) February 10, 1979
Divorced March 24, 1979 (married for 43 days)
Claudia age 31 - Jim age 33
(Jim was about 2 years older than me)

Chapter 29
I Want My Black Belt

The divorce dragged on. Every time we had a court date, his attorney would get a continuance. I was getting a bit antsy about the situation. I understood their game. Every time we were put off, I had to waste more money on my attorney, and eventually, I would be softened up and give in. It could be months or years. Meanwhile, he was living in my house and I wasn't working because I was not going to pay him alimony.

I was standing on a principle of righteous indignation. I thought it was outrageous for a man to try to take from a woman what she had earned. With the payments I had made up and the construction materials and labor that I had put into the house, I had about $75,000 equity in the place. But, eventually, I got tired of their game.

The last time I went to court they got another continuance, I blew it. My attorney was not going to object and I was supposed to just walk away.

"I object," I yelled at the judge. "Give him all of it. I just want my divorce, and leave me the hell alone. Give him the house, I'm done!"

"Now, Mrs. A, you'll get your day in court, just be patient," the judge said.

"No," I said, "I'm done, I want this finished today so I can get on with my life. I want it done NOW!"

The judge told my attorney to have a talk with me. We would recess for fifteen minutes. The men would handle the little woman!

Of course, my attorney wanted me to accept another postponement. I was his cash cow! I'm only an ignorant woman in a man's world, but I would not be put off.

I told him if he didn't go along with what I wanted, I would substitute myself "in pro per" and fire his ass. Eventually, he saw my point.

We reconvened and my attorney told the judge that he was sure I knew what I was doing. It was settled.

When I left the court, some guy ran after me and grabbed my hand. "I just have to tell you that I know you are going to be alright," he said. I was kind of taken back by it, but then I looked this man in the eyes and could see that he had no game, he really felt what he said. And at that moment, I knew he was right. I thanked him and calmly walked away.

Further down the corridor were my now ex and his attorney. They were laughing. They really thought they had won.

As I walked by, I said, "laugh you stupid bastards, but it won't last. I can make more money than you can steal and I will be on the way back up while you're on the way back down, because I know how to make money and you are just too ignorant to get it!"

I went back to work and moved out of my little one-bedroom prison. Back to the drawing board. Obviously, there were some things I still did not know that I did not know.

Interestingly, within a month I was made an offer I couldn't refuse.

One of the people I had gotten close to was a woman named Nova. She was kind of like a surrogate mother to me. Paula was my main sponsor, but Nova was like my conscience. She would sit beside me and say things like, you know, even when things aren't going your way, you still need to get up every morning and shower, put on your makeup and take care of yourself.

Nova had definite opinions about everything. She said I cussed too much. The length of Paula's skirt was too short. So and so wore too much make-up. But, beneath all of it, we all knew she cared.

I went into the club one day and she said she and her husband wanted to talk to me. I didn't know if it was an ass chewing or what.

I went over to a table and sat down with her and her husband, Les.

"You know," he started out, "Nova and I are going to retire and we're thinking of moving out of California, so we need to sell all our rental properties. We'd like to sell them to you."

"I'm sorry, Les," I said. But, I just gave my money away to Jim in our divorce and I haven't been working for months. I can't buy anything right now."

Les held up his hand. "We know all about that and we know it wasn't right what he did. That's why we are willing to sell our houses to you on assumed loans and second mortgages. You don't need any money and we know you are honest."

Wow, I was stunned. Of course, I agreed and bought three properties that had two houses on each lot. I was back on the top.

Unfortunately, Les and Nova moved away but we kept in contact. About six months after they had moved, Nova had a massive heart attack which left her disoriented. The only thing Les could think to do was to move her back to Hawthorne to people and places she knew. He asked if they could rent one of the houses that he had sold to me, and which they had lived in?

Unfortunately, the house in question, I had recently rented to a woman with a couple of kids. She hadn't been in the house for three weeks. I went to the woman and told her what was going on with Nova and I asked if she would be willing to vacate the house if I gave her back all her money and an extra month's rent and paid for her move. The woman was gracious enough to do it. She moved out and Les and Nova moved back in. I reversed our deal on the house so they again owned it.

About this time, Mel approached me about sharing a house. That way we could both share the kids. He had been working at construction for several months so I decided that I was willing as long as he understood that I was NOT available to him. He agreed.

I found a large four-bedroom house that was within our price range. I would pay two-thirds of the rent and Mel was to pay one-third in exchange for him watching the kids when I had to work. I also bought the groceries and paid the utilities. If it worked, it would be great.

One lesson I had taken from the marriage to Jim was, "If you aren't enjoying the ride, get off the bus." Since I had gotten into the Studios, I had done little else but work. Sometimes I had gone for months without a day off. My children, my Studio work, and real estate dictated my time. Everything I did was motivated by what I would have in the future. And now, it had all gone away in the blink of an eye. I made a decision that I would never do that again. No matter what happened, I always needed to take time to enjoy the journey. I would never be afraid of not having enough money and would never change my lifestyle.

Shortly after that, I decided to use some of the money I had left to get breast implants. I could still hear Jim saying "Your ugly, scrawny, sexless body turns me off." Talk about something that kills a sense of self-worth for a woman. I knew it was only because he had to justify getting away from me, so he could get the house and anything else he could, but it still hurt.

I had the operation done on May 4, 1979. After I had the implants, of course, Mel wanted to see the result. I told him he could go piss up a rope!

The hardest part of recovering, from the operation, was that I couldn't work and I couldn't drive for several weeks. Being the woman, I am, I bought a pair of roller skates and that was how I got to the AA club. Nothing keeps me down.

After I was healed from the operation, I made good on my promise to myself and found a karate school.

I joined the West Coast Shotokan Karate Association whose motto is "Respect, But Fear No Man." Well, that sounds like what I was looking for.

My sensei (teacher) was a retired police officer. I watched a session at his school. He had his five-year-old son in the class. I could see, right off, that that five-year-old could clean my clock and decided he was the teacher I wanted. I didn't know until months after I had joined that women were NOT allowed to achieve black belt status. It was still a man's world.

One day we had a visitor to our dojo (classroom). He was an old man of 80 years. No one figured he could teach us much. Boy, were we wrong. The sensei had a few of us go up against this old man one at a time and no one could get near him. The more we watched, the more amazed we became. He moved effortlessly. Then it was two of us against him and then three and eventually the whole class of about 15 members. It was incredible to see this man move and he was graceful as well. He didn't hurt any of us, but just gently put us on the mat.

That gave me great hope. Surely if this 80-year-old was able to defend himself, I could learn to defend myself. I poured myself into learning. I worked every spare hour I had to learn to defend myself.

I was a quick learner. When I was still a green belt, I entered into a

Karate competition. I came away with two trophies, one 3rd place for Kumite (sparring) and one 2nd place for Kata (form).

The competition was supposed to be a "NO contact" competition, but one school was out to draw blood and did not adhere to the rules. Even our little white belts were taking hits that should never have happened. The whole concept of no contact is to demonstrate your skill at delivering a blow where you wanted it. At any rate, it turned out not to be a no-contact event.

I was about 33 years old at the time and much older than most contestants who were 18 to about 25. I had several matches and won them and moved up in the ranks. The last match I had was for second or third place. The winner of this match would take on the highest rank competitor and they would be first and second. The girl I was matched with was about 18-year-old and in the very first round she hit me in the solar plexus. So much for "no contact."

When a contestant did not control their punch and hit someone, they had to turn around and kneel (in shame) until the other fighter was ready or the referee ended the match in which case it would be an invalid match.

I was humiliated but learned a big lesson. I should never consider that someone is NOT going to make contact. I had simply started with my guard down and had not defended fast enough. OK, game on.

I chose to continue even though it had knocked the breath out of me. The next round, I came out and hit her right in the throat. Oh, yea, I'll sit in shame while you recover.....bitch.

In order to win, you had to get two points on your opponent. There were no more mistakes of contact. We were both on guard. We just kept going. She got a point, I got a point, she got a point, I got a point. Contrary to what most people think or what appears in movies, real fighting is hard, exhausting work. After about 20 minutes, my lungs were burning. My muscles were tiring. I almost wanted to give her the point so I could quit, but I'm too stubborn for that. She finally, legitimately got the point and I wound up in third place. There had been about thirty competitors, so I didn't feel that bad. My kids were very impressed that mommy got two trophies.

I stayed in Karate for about two years. I kept trying to get them to let me test for black, but it just wasn't happening.

One of the young girls, of about fourteen years old, came to me and told me that one of the older men, a black belt, kept hitting on her. He wanted to date her! He was also touching her in places he shouldn't during practice and was laying it off to normal karate contact. He was about 25. She didn't know what to do and was thinking of quitting. Of course, I was very upset. I had a history from four years old with dirty old men.

I went to our sensei and told him what was going on, but he simply brushed it off. She must be mistaken. Then I went directly to the guy and talked to him. I advised him that she was underage and what he was doing was against the law. He just laughed and walked away.

Shortly afterward she quit our school. That really made me angry. It just wasn't right the way women were treated. It was a man's world and it sucked .... the shit young girls and women had to put up with!

A couple of weeks later, I was matched with him in sparring. My resentments followed me onto the mat. After a few rounds, I foot swept him, got him on the floor, and kneed him right in the groin. He rolled over in pain, crawling on the mat. I got up, bowed to him and my sensei, and said, "that was my black belt exam." Thank you and goodbye.

The interesting thing is that from the time I got into karate, I was never hit by a man again. I don't think it was because I knew karate, but because I did not telegraph fear. Another lesson of, "whatever we hold inside is what we attract." Fear attracts things that you should fear. I had always been in fear, even when I didn't show it or know it.

I was working on the TV show, "Starsky and Hutch" with Paul Michael Glaser and David Soul. Paul was into Karate and would practice in the parking lot behind the stages. I watched him when I could and refined some of my kata as a result.

Michael and David were a few years older than me, and I have to admit that I had a crush on David Soul. He was a sweetheart and a very good singer though most people did not even know he could sing.

We had a Christmas party on stage each year and the last year, I went home and dressed to the nines. When I walked onto the stage, no one on the show recognized me.....except David Soul. He hugged me and swung me around and yelled out, "Look everyone, it's our Claudia." I was so embarrassed but so thrilled at the same time.

Claudia with Karate trophies won in competition in 1980

Claudia age 33

Chapter 30
Europe and Weird Fun

At the end of 1979, I met a very nice guy by the name of John. Of course, he was in AA. The only place I could meet anyone was in AA or in the studios where I worked. I didn't date anyone from the studios because of possible complications. There was no internet or dating sites that I had access to like people have today.

At any rate, I had gone to an AA meeting in Culver City to hear different speakers. After the meeting, someone suggested a group of us go to a "Jazz club" to hear another AA member play. John and I had been eyeing each other. He was on the short side and I was probably the only girl that matched him. In the discussion, John asked me if I wanted to go to the jazz club. "Sure," I said. The truth was, I was not fond of most jazz music. It has too many "sharp" notes that hurt my ears. Some of the mellow stuff I can handle, but most of it ... no! I went along anyway.

Having arrived at the club, I ordered a soda and listened about as long as my ears could handle it. I was getting ready to go when John asked, "Would you like to get out of here?"

"Yes," I confessed. "I actually don't care for jazz, but only wanted to get to know you." He laughed and said, "that's funny because I hate jazz and just came to be with you!" That was the beginning of a relationship.

I had about had it with Mel not paying his share of the rent and we were beginning to fight. He was just never willing to give up on getting me back.

I told him I was moving out and taking my kids. He informed me that he had custody of the kids and he was taking them. He moved out and took the kids back to Grandma Connie's. I rented an apartment, but a few months later, I moved in with John.

John was an air traffic controller. I thought that was kind of scary because he had been a practicing alcoholic and an air traffic controller at the same time. I was certainly glad he was sober, but what about the rest of those controllers who handle all the airplanes in our skies?

John and I seemed to get on quite well. In August, we planned a trip to Europe. The countries we visited were; Ireland, England, Scotland, France, and Wales. I climbed the 287 steps up the Sir Walter Scott Monument and kissed the Blarney Stone. I went to the Tower of London, The Cathedral of Notre Dame, went to the top of the Eiffel Tower, and walked the Champs-Elysees.

Traveling to different countries is an eye-opening experience. I had no idea how other people in the world lived. I think it was in France that we were walking down some street and came across an open-air "meat market." It didn't even have a door that I could see; it was just like an alley with a roof. I was fascinated to see slabs of meat unwrapped, laying out for someone to purchase. We walked into the market and strolled down the row. It must have been about one hundred feet deep. It was stall after stall of chicken, lamb, pig, fish, beef and God only knows what else, and much of everything still had its head attached. As if in a trance, we kept walking. There were flies all over the place and especially on the meat. And then … the smell caught up with us. It was all I could do to run out before I threw up.

For someone used to U.S. meat that is sold in clear cellophane, in clean little cases in our supermarkets, this was a horrific experience.

It was a very interesting affair to get on the "Tube" in England. The cars did not stop long and when the doors closed, they closed. If your luggage was in and you weren't, say goodbye to your luggage. It became apparent that we had way overpacked for this vacation. I would get into the car and John would start shoveling suitcases to me. We had six altogether and two of them were huge. We were fortunate to get them all on.

I had acquired the habit of counting our cases where ever we went. One, two, three, four, five, six. Sometimes, I would have to ask John where a case was. I guess this got to him and he told me to "stop mothering him." I was a bit miffed as to why it bothered him, but finally made a deal with him. We separated the cases and he became responsible for half and I became responsible for half.

We went from England to France. This was before Eurostar was built which takes you under the ocean between the two countries. We went by hired car to the ferry, by ferry from Dover, England to Calais, France. From Calais port to Calais train station and then took the train into Paris. It was an exhausting journey.

We were sitting at a sidewalk café in Paris having just gotten off the train at Gare du Nord station. Getting off the train and getting a porter was a bit of a problem because neither John nor I spoke any French. Because of that, the cases he and I were responsible for, kind of got mixed up.

We were sitting, trying to catch our breath, and drinking a cup of coffee and I'm trying to, surreptitiously, count the suitcases. I could only see five. One was missing. I recounted ….five. I'm stretching my neck to see around John's feet.

"What's wrong with you?" he said. "What are you looking at?"

Well, John, I don't want to be "mothering" you, but I only see five suitcases and unless you are hiding the 'train case', we are missing one and it was one that you were responsible for."

Disconcerted, John looked around. Chagrined, he hung his head. "CRAP! So, what do we do now?" All our toiletries were in that case.

We went to the station and tried to fill out a lost suitcase report because the train had already left the station. Of course, all the forms were in French and we had not a clue what they said. In France, at that time, no one seemed to speak English. We were just lost.

I have great sympathy for people coming to America without being able to speak our language. You can't go far without needing language for some reason or another and without it you just have a great sense of helplessness.

"OK," John conceded, "I guess I needed a bit of mothering. I'm sorry,"

"Sorry is great, John, but we are still out of the things we need. We don't even have a toothbrush. I think that because you were the one who lost the case, it should be up to you to replace the items and the case." He agreed.

We went to our hotel and upon arriving in our room, we discovered there was no toilet, only a bidet. John called the front desk and when they couldn't understand what he was saying, John went out in the corridor and came back with a hotel employee. The guy was seemingly not understanding what John was talking about so John pats the guy on the butt and then makes like he is sitting on a toilet. I'm ready to bust a gut. Our journey to France was going to be a blast.

The light finally went on in the guy's eyes and he led John down the corridor to where a "shared" bathroom was.

Having gotten that out of the way, we ventured out to do some shopping. That was when we found out that we couldn't even identify a "drug store." It's called a "Pharmacie" in France, which is close enough that we should have figured it out, but we were looking for a "Drug Store". We walked around looking in windows, and, eventually, we found what looked like the right place.

The next thing is trying to identify the products we needed. Everything was in that train case. Toothbrushes, toothpaste, razors, shaving cream, soap, shampoo, Q-tips, tweezers .... Just think of all the toiletries one needs on a trip.

John went to the salesperson and in "English" tried to explain that we had lost a suitcase and needed to replace all the items. The guy just looked at John. John's solution for someone who didn't speak English was to ... "talk louder and slower." I've always marveled at people that think this will work.

John started playing "charades" with the guy. He starts talking very loudly, enunciating very distinctly, and was using exaggerated motions to demonstrate brushing his teeth. The clerk walks to a place and shows John what he is looking for. Whew! One item down. We got toothpaste from the same aisle. The same exaggerated motions, John is trying to get a razor, then shampoo. On and on it went. John was exhausted, but we had almost everything we needed.

"OK, John," I said smiling. "There is only one thing left to get."

"What's that?" John asked.

"Tampons," I replied, "and I can't wait to see how you ask for them!"

You could see John deflate. "You've got to be kidding," he said. He looked so helpless.

The clerk just stood silent. But, then I saw that the clerk couldn't hold it any longer. He busted up laughing. We had found, maybe, the only drug store clerk in Paris that spoke English!

When we got back to the hotel, we promptly brushed our teeth with something akin to "Brylcreem," which was a hair styling product for men. It came in a tube exactly like toothpaste!

I didn't care for France. The people were not friendly and I did not care for the food. The fact that we couldn't read a menu didn't help. After ordering some disastrous meals in some very fine restaurants, we gave up. It seemed to me that most of their meat was a bit "rancid." To cover that up, they applied ample quantities of cheese and sauce. We finally went to a grocery store and bought potato chips and grapes. At least we knew what we were eating. I think it was more a function of our unsophisticated palate than bad food.

When we were getting ready to leave France, a street vendor talked John into taking our picture with the streets of Paris in the background. We had already exchanged our remaining "Francs" for English pounds. The best the guy could do was to give us change in Irish money. So, he charged us in French Francs, we paid in English pounds and he gave us change in Irish Punts and Pence. While the guy is setting up the picture, I am trying to calculate to figure out what he charged us for two little Polaroid pictures. In the picture, it looks like I have a big smile on my face, but actually, I'm whispering to John, "He's screwing us John. I can't calculate it fast enough, but I know we're getting screwed," Later when we did calculate it, it turned out to be $25.00 US per each little Polaroid picture (about $97 in 2022 money). Yeah, we got screwed, but I figured that's just part of the fun of traveling.

We went back to England. We were next going to Ireland. This time, we repacked our suitcases and left most of our luggage with the "concierge" at the hotel at which we were staying. We also had him rent us a car and at his insistence, paid for the full coverage insurance.

John was pretty good at driving on "the wrong side of the road." Only the "roundabouts" were a bit of a problem and on a few of them, we had to go around and around before we could figure out how to get off, going the correct way.

I had given it a try but found that because I had been born left-handed but had to switch to the right, my brain had a harder time making the switch. At least that was what I figured.

Driving through the English countryside was amazing. We drove to a ferry line somewhere around Liverpool that went to Dublin, Ireland.

I wasn't fond of the English food, and the one thing I really missed was sugar. They only had "raw" sugar and it wasn't nearly as sweet as American "white" sugar. On the way, we stopped at a gas station and I went inside. They had candy for sale and one thing they had was five jelly candies in a pack that we called "Chuckles." They were; red, yellow, purple, orange, green and they were sprinkled with sugar. When I saw them, my mouth started watering.

I went back to the car with my prize. John and I tried one. After being a couple of weeks without our kind of sweet sugar, our taste buds had changed. Instead of being the sweet delight we were expecting, they were so sweet, they were sour! It was a very strange experience.

In Liverpool, John drove the car onto the ferry and the first place we went was to the dining area. We hadn't eaten since breakfast and we were hungry.

They had sit-down dining with table cloths and everything. They were serving corned beef and cabbage with potatoes. After eating the bland English food and the rancid French food, I thought I had died and gone to heaven. I didn't think it was because I'm Irish, but because it was just delicious food. I wanted to stay on that boat.

When we arrived in Ireland, it was in the middle of the night and there was a light misty rain. We drove the approximate 160 miles to Blarney Castle. Arriving as it opened, we felt very lucky that we were the first people to kiss the Blarney Stone that day, as it had been washed clean for us, by the rain. Soon the sun came out and we were able to thoroughly explore the castle and grounds.

Ireland is lovely. Like a big green patchwork quilt. The pastures have had all the stones removed and they form the perimeter walls of each field. We started driving and just kept being inspired by the next beautiful sight. There were houses with "thatched" roofs and quaint streets that were very narrow because they had once been only a calf's path.

Very soon, we came to a roadblock. There were guards ..... with guns! We had driven all the way to the border of Northern Ireland. This happened only a few days after Lord Mountbatten had been blown up by the Irish Republican Army. Because both John and I had Irish last names, they wanted to know why we were going to Northern Ireland. After someone explained what was going on, we decided that maybe it would be best to visit it another time. We turned around and went back to our bed and breakfast in Dublin.

Coming back from Ireland to England, we met a young man who was hitch-hiking. He was going to the USA to go to school in New York. It was very interesting talking to him, but I wasn't feeling comfortable with John turning his head, constantly, to look at the young man in the back seat. I finally had to say something and asked if it was OK if the guy got into the front seat so John didn't have to keep turning around.

I got into the back seat and tried to kind of barricade myself in, with luggage, in case we had an accident. It wasn't long before John rear-ended a car. I flew forward and hit my nose on the seat ahead of me, which really annoyed me. We pulled the car off the road, as you would in the USA, but a cop came up right away and yelled for us to get the car back on the road. In England, everyone has their own insurance, so there is no reason to stop, for small accidents. Kind of strange to us, but we just went on. When we got to the hotel, we took the keys to the concierge and said, "Broke, Broke, Fix, Fix!," thankful for that full coverage insurance he had talked us into.

Arriving home from Europe, we found our apartment had been broken into. The first indication was that there were "nude" pictures of me hanging all over the apartment. (Of course, I had some nude photos of myself; I was a young vibrant woman.) It scared me and gave me the chills at first. We thought some pervert had broken in. Checking out the apartment carefully we found, vinegar in the ice trays, labels torn off our can goods, and the bed had been short-sheeted. Obviously, we had been "Chivareed."

Recently, my brother remarried and my sponsor Paula had married her boyfriend, Cliff. A group of us from the AA club had gone to their houses and Chivareed each of them.

With Paula and Cliff, we had taken all the clothes in their closet and hung them all on about four hangers, buttoning each item up all the way as we went. Then we moved the mattress off their bed into the garage and put their dresser drawers where the mattress had been, making the bed up all nice and neat.

For Pat and Beth, we had stacked all their furniture up in their living room and put a bottle of “Nonalcoholic” Champagne on the very top of the stack. We also removed all labels off the cans and put vinegar in the ice trays.

Our apartment was only payback! I went to the phone to call my brother since I knew he was the only one who could pick the lock on our apartment. When I picked up the phone, it smelled horrendous. I could not for the life of me figure out what he had done to the phone. When he answered the phone, I said, very funny! Now, what-the-hell did you do to the phone?

"What?" he replied, "I can't hear you, there must be something wrong with your phone," and he hung up on me.

I finally figured out what was going on and unscrewed the "receiver cap" on the handset and found he had stuffed it full of "Limburger Cheese!" I knew that we would never get the pungent smell out of the telephone and we just threw it away.

Soon after that, John and I parted ways. It was over something quite trivial as I look back at it, but it was a red flag for me.

Some friends of John's invited us to go with them on a weekend getaway. I don't remember where we were going, but it was several hours away. They had decided that we would all go in their car. Because they did not smoke, there would be no smoking.

I objected to the plan. I smoked and I didn't like the setup and asked why we couldn't take one of our cars and let them go in theirs. We could simply meet at the destination.

It became an argument. The thing that was big for me is that he had NOT asked me if it was alright with me before agreeing to this plan and as he stated, "Having already committed to the plan, HE would be embarrassed to change the plan now."

So, what I'm getting from this is that John thought nothing about making a plan for ME without consulting ME and when it came down to it, HIS saving face was more important than ME. I chose to end the relationship before we got any further involved. He was truly surprised that I had chosen to go my way. I felt proud that at least I had seen a red flag before I wound up married to him. I'll admit it was a bit petty on my part, but I was just too gun shy at the time.

The next man I got involved with was Bruce. He worked at the studios. I finally decided that if I had a choice between a recovering alcoholic or someone I worked with, it would be smarter to choose someone I worked with. At least we both started on the same financial level.

Bruce was a very nice young man. He loved sailing and owned a 38-foot Morgan Sloop. We often took off on the weekend to sail to Catalina Island. This was a whole 'nother learning curve for me. I had never been on a sailboat before. About the only thing I knew was that I was still afraid of drowning.

There had been three incidences in my childhood where I felt like I was going to drown. The two I've already mentioned and one time at my grandmother's house in Phoenix, Arizona. We had all been in her pool and were just going in for lunch. I was about the last to go in when I felt someone push me into the pool. I had put my tennis shoes on because the deck was blistering hot. Somehow, the tennis shoes held me down at the bottom of the pool. I remember looking at the side of the pool but it was out of reach. Having no fat on me, I had no buoyancy. I thought I was going to die. At the last minute, my uncle grabbed my arm and pulled me out. Even with all of this in mind, I was going to go sailing! I never did find out who pushed me into the pool.

The first test of whether or not someone would be a good sailor is if they get seasick. I remember sitting at the table in rough weather stabbing my steak as I followed it across the table. Nope, no seasickness here.

I was a fast learner and, in a few months, I could pretty much sail it by myself. Handling the sheets (sails) was a bit tricky, but all in all, I had a good handle on it. Bruce was an excellent captain and an excellent teacher.

One Friday, we set out for Catalina and I was determined that I was going to sail the boat all the way without using any engine. That's pretty hard to do because there is one spot near the island where the wind just seems to die. Being a bit stubborn, I refused to give up and pretty much sat for about an hour before I conceded to the fact that nature overcame my determination. I used the engines to make it the rest of the way.

Another time we were on our way back from Catalina and another sailboat got in a race with us. I took the helm and Bruce took the sheets. I was so involved in winning, that I didn't notice that we were leaning way over to where I was standing in the side of the boat. Not a care in the world.

Another time we took off for Catalina after work. Bruce hadn't had much sleep for a couple of days and was just dog tired. He said he was going down to the V birth for a few minutes of shut-eye. He was down for several hours. I'm at the helm, singing and I just felt so free. After Bruce awoke, it dawned on me that I did not have on a harness and was not tethered to the boat. Anything could have happened. I could have been knocked overboard and Bruce would not even know it.

Bruce was a lot of fun for a while, but then something came up that told me he wasn't the one for me either. Moving on!

John and I and our $25 Polaroid picture in Paris, France 1979
Claudia age 32

Claudia sailing 38-foot Morgan Sloop1980

Claudia age 33

Chapter 31

Thirty-Four and Counting

Life always seemed to move fast for me. It seemed like I was always juggling children, several careers, education, and men.

My sister had married Bob and had had twins; a boy and a girl. Bob had always wanted kids and now he had them in spades. My sister had four children with Sam, the oldest of which was 16 and now Teri had twins as well. A repeat pattern emerged, her kids versus his. Teri and Bob decided to buy a donut shop that was located inside a supermarket. I think this further caused problems because Bob had a full-time job and with everything life involved, it just wasn't working very well. My sister came to me at times to help with kids. Six children are often overwhelming.

Meanwhile, my kids were changing rapidly. Half the time they were with me and other times with Grandma Connie. It was a continuation of the game, "pack and go, to and fro." My daughter wasn't making it to school and was running around with a boy who was older than her. I tried driving Tami to school, but she just went out the back door after I had left. When you are working about 11.5 hours a day plus driving two hours, there just are not enough hours in the day.

I worked as "standby" on the movie 9 to 5 with Dolly Pardon, Lily Tomlin, Jane Fonda, and Dabney Coleman. It was a great show to work on. Dabney Coleman, despite the characters he usually played, is the sweetest man.

Lily Tomlin is a great artist, often ad-libbing much of her part which made it a better film. It showed what an extraordinary talent she is.

Somehow this show became the "prankster show" and everyone was pulling pranks on someone. One day I made some "cat poo" out of plaster by pushing it through a hole in a Styrofoam cup, then painting it with brown hairspray. We put it in the middle of the set and then we called "craft service" to clean it up. The girl who came in must have had a weak stomach because she couldn't get close to what she thought was real cat poo without retching. She would turn her head away and try to sneak up on it with a huge wad of paper towels. I was watching from the side, holding my mouth to keep from laughing. When she finally got it we all busted up laughing.

The cat poo jokes continued; you never knew where I might put a bit. Sometimes I might put it on someone's desk or a side table. One day we were doing the scene where Mr. Hart (Dabney Coleman) gives Doralee (Dolly Parton) a box with a scarf in it. I don't remember whose idea it was, but I wound up making some "Cat Poo" and putting it in the box.

Dolly and Dabney were rehearsing the scene. The prop master switched the box with the scarf for the one with my cat poo. When Dolly opened the box, she started laughing and looked around and said, "Claudia, where are you?"

There was a grip on the show that played the guitar and Dolly invited him to play a song with her. He fell in love with her. One day she called him over and was blatantly flirting with him. He was just eating it up when Carl Dean (Dolly's real-life husband) came up behind him and tapping him on the shoulder and asked, "Are you flirting with my wife?" The poor guy almost fainted. Dolly was a real jokester too.

One day Dolly, her assistant, Judy Ogle, and I were standing outside a set while the grips and electricians were setting up a scene. We stood watching as guy after guy went in and out of the set. All of a sudden Dolly said, "Ninety miles of cock girls, and not an inch for any of us!" Judy and I laughed so hard, we could barely breathe. Dolly was always fun.

I brought my daughter, Tami, to work one day. I put a shirt on her that said, "I'm my mother's daughter." I was known for wearing T-shirts, with some slogan or another written on the front, so everyone knew right off whose kid she was. I introduced her to Dolly. Dolly was so kind to her and made her feel so special. Dolly did not have any children of her own, so I told her we would share. Tami had so much fun on the set that day and of course she fell in love, as we all did, with Dolly.

One night, all the ladies, who worked on the set, went to a studio and we recorded the background for the song, 9 to 5. We had wine and cheese and sang our little (off-key) hearts out. When Dolly sings she runs her fingernails on one hand over her fingernails of the other hand to keep beat. We all had a great time and it was such a treat that she gave us. I don't know if our version ever made it to the track, (I highly doubt it) but it was a great time anyway and just an example of what a great heart Dolly has.

At the wrap party, Jane Fonda made a toast to Dolly and said something like, "To Dolly, who walked onto the set and into our hearts and made better people out of us all." Jane Fonda could be such a generous person.

Also, in 1980 I had met a man at work named, "Tony" (ACT). Tony was about 10 years older than me and was on the short side, but he was very nice looking and had very nice manners. He asked me out, but I was pretty sure he was married from the conversations at work. I declined and told him I didn't date married men. He kept saying he and his wife were finished and he was going to leave but they were waiting until they could tell their children. I was not interested. Single men were bad enough, but married men were a whole different problem that I wasn't willing to take on.

I went on to another job and another studio and didn't see Tony again for a while.

Some months later, Tony called me and said he had left his wife, and he was calling because I had mentioned that I had some rental houses and he was wondering if I had a vacant one bedroom that he could rent.

I told him I didn't have a one-bedroom, but I had a very large bachelor for rent in Inglewood. It was a rear house that was furnished. We struck a deal and he moved into the bachelor house.

The tenant I had in the front house was a little strange. She always had all her windows open, even in the middle of winter. I didn't think a lot about it. I figured she was a hot-blooded person. I seldom went to her house because she never had problems and paid her rent like clockwork.

When she had rented the house, I had told her that her parking space was on the street in front of her house because the back house had the driveway for parking. That worked out fine at first, but then the back tenant had moved out and a single girl without a car had moved in for a few months. Because the driveway wasn't used, the front tenant took to parking in it.

Now that Tony had rented the back house and had a car, the front tenant was back to parking on the street, but she didn't like it. We had a discussion about it. I explained that the back house was so far back that it was a huge inconvenience for the back tenant to carry groceries or whatever, if they weren't allowed to use the drive way to park in front of their unit. She would have to stick with her original agreement and park on the street.

I started getting some calls from Tony about the front tenant. She was leaving things that blocked the driveway or yelled at him about different things. Truthfully, I had never had a problem with this tenant and I wasn't sure if Tony was trying to find reasons to talk to me or if he really had a problem.

Then one day, I got a call from a neighbor to the property that had my number in case of emergency. She said Tony was out in the yard, stark naked and yelling at my front tenant. I immediately jumped in my car a drove the short distance to the property.

Tony was indeed naked except for - Bubbles. Apparently, the front tenant had waited until Tony had gotten home from work and had gotten into the shower, and then she had turned the water off! Tony was so mad, but I just had to laugh. I suggested he go in and, at least, get a towel to cover himself. He was very embarrassed when he noticed he was, in fact, naked. He seemed to have a bad Italian temper.

I tried to talk to the front tenant, but there was no salving that savage beast either. For some reason, she thought it was OK to scream and cuss at me. I finally went to my car and found a scrap of paper and wrote out a thirty-day notice to vacate. She was on a month-to-month tenancy so it was legal. She had no option but to move.

I offered to take Tony out to dinner for his trouble and that was the start of our relationship. By now I had decided it was foolish not to date people I worked with because I was never on a show for very long and then moved on to a whole new group of people. And besides, other than the studios, the only place I went was AA and that meant I was going to date Alcoholics! What was I thinking?

After the front tenant moved I found out why she had her windows open all the time. She had about 5 cats and they urinated all over the house. I had to bleach and then shellac the entire house to get the smell out of it. Tony volunteered to help which made him a hero in my books.

Life went on. I went to work on E.T., The Extra-Terrestrial. It was a great show to work on. The construction painting was done by a man I had worked with quite a bit at Fox Studio. Jim was a big guy that was afraid of everything. I remember once we were working at an abandoned airport and he was afraid to go into a long dark building. I had to go in and be sure it was safe for him. At any rate, when the show started filming, I went on as the "standby" painter.

Steven Spielberg was the producer/director. This was pretty early in his career. He was very hands-on. In the scene where the corn stocks are rustling and Elliott throws the ball into the shed, it is Steven Spielberg and me lying behind the corn stocks, shaking them.

One of the main E.T. players was a dwarf named Pat Bilon. Pat and I discovered that we were about the same age, I was only a few months older. Pat was only 2 feet 10 inches tall, but he was a big man. He was an inspiration to watch because as he said, "I believe I can do just about anything .... but grow taller." He was also a very, very funny man, and while I, usually, had the title of "Jokester" on a set, on this show that title went to Pat.

One morning I was "on set" as grips and electricians were setting up. Pat walked up to me and hugged me around the legs. Because of my rather "short legs," Pat's face was right about at my "lady parts." He looked up and said, "Good morning Claudia, my, your hair smells good today!" And we all cracked up. "Ewe! Get away from my lady parts," I said and pushed him away. He had certainly set the tone for the day. I can't tell you how many grips and electricians mentioned how good my hair smelled that day.

Because of Pat's size, you almost forgot at times that he was a full-grown man. Sitting on set another day with some of the hair and makeup people, Pat crawled up on my lap. He had done that a few times, so I didn't think much of it. I was involved in a conversation with one of the grips and didn't pay much attention to Pat. He was just like any little child I might put up on my lap. Then all of a sudden, Pat starts "tweaking my breasts. I guess that with all the kids in our family, I was used to kids, touching parts that shouldn't be touched. I gently moved his hand away, but it went right back to what it had been doing. Then all of a sudden it dawned on me that this was not a kid!

"Well, you little shit," I said, picking him up and putting him on the ground. "Ladies," I said, "Watch this one; he's a randy little bastard!" Again, everyone cracked up.

Also, on that show was little Drew Barrymore. The first time I saw her was with her mother standing in a corner, talking. Her mother looked much like my mother; very small.

After Drew and her mother talked, Drew went right to Steven Spielberg and said something "apparently" clever for a seven-year-old because Spielberg laughed. And that was what I saw repeatedly. Her mother coached her in what to say and Drew dutifully carried it out. I felt sorry for Drew and felt she was being manipulated out of childhood. But who was I to talk; I wasn't doing so well with my own kids.

My daughter, Tami, was about fifteen and a hand full. She was failing all her school work and hanging out with the wrong people. And what was I going to do about it? I either worked to support my kids or I took care of them. Though I tried to do both, I just couldn't. Her father was drinking, doing drugs, and never had time to work. His mother and father were still providing for him.

I had a small apartment in the Hawthorne area, right across the street from my brother, Pat. My son, Andy, lived with me and Tami was still going from my house to Connie's house and back. Even as her mother, I didn't have much say because Mel still had custody, and she was old enough to choose.

Andy was not much of a problem when he lived with me. He liked to ride anything with wheels. If he wasn't in school, he was usually on his skateboard doing tricks in the driveway. He could spend hours doing the same trick over and over. He had my kind of determination to "get it right."

At work, I was working mostly as a "standby" on movies. The pay was great, but the hours were variable. The shooting company would start at 6 a.m. on Monday and shoot for however long it took to get the scenes. They had to give the crew an eight-hour turnaround, so each day the "Call" time got later and later to where by Friday we might be coming in a 6 p.m. My brother and his wife or my sister, Teri, who lived in the apartment below me, looked after Andy when I wasn't home. Andy was 13 and didn't need much supervision.

After Tony and I had dated for about a year, Tony and I were married on Christmas Eve 1981. He was 45 and I was 34 years old. I had been single for about three years and was ready to try marriage again.

Before we married, I sat Tony down and was very truthful with him. First of all, I couldn't believe any man would want to be husband number six! I told him that I was very fond of him and we got along great, I loved him, but I didn't think I was in love with him. He somehow thought that was OK. I told him further that we would only be together as long as we were happy together. He was OK with that also. We wrote up a "Pre-marital agreement," and the rest is history.

We had a small wedding with only family and a few of my AA

friends. Tony and I sent out a wedding announcement to the rest of our family and friends, in the form of a "Marriage --O -- Gram." It stated:

"Dateline: Hawthorne, California. December 24, 1981. STOP Good Morning Mr. & Mrs. America; Flash ------- It has been confirmed by reliable sources STOP Tony (Last Name) and Claudia Gilligan have just exchanged wedding vows. STOP Second for Tony, sixth for Claudia PLEASE STOP If you are thinking of sending a gift STOP Happy Holidays!!"

Tony seemed very refined. He always said "please and thank you." I had never been with a man that was so mannered. He spoke well and was fun to be with. He blended well with my family. His only drawback was his occasional temper, but it was not directed at me so I was OK with it.

I remember one time we were driving somewhere and a guy in another car was making eyes at me. I was driving. I think the guy thought Tony was my father. I thought Tony was going to crawl over me and out the window to get to the guy. When he got mad, he simply lost all awareness of where he was or what he was doing.

In 1982, I came across an IQ test and Tony and I decided to take it. His came out to be about 120, which is above average; the average being 100. Mine came out to be 151. I was a bit shocked but thought it probably wasn't an accurate test. I thought I was somewhat smart, but never thought I was that smart.

I decided to take the test for "Mensa," the high IQ society. To qualify, your IQ had to be in the top two percent of the population. Mensa set up a "proctor" test where someone from Mensa watches you take the test. I took two different tests with a proctor. When the results came back, I qualified above 99 percent of the population with a 149. I have to say, I had no idea. I had always thought I was smart enough, but I never thought

I was exceptional.

The thing that struck me was, "what a waste." No teacher ever thought I was smart. They were always too busy accusing me of cheating on tests, having someone else do my projects, or bothered about the fact that I didn't get along with others or I didn't "make friends easily." Today, they test kids for intelligence and put them in classes accordingly. My grandkids have qualified for "accelerated" learning.

This explained much about who I am and why I always wanted more knowledge. I've always felt like I was "Johnny Five" in the movie, "Short Circuit," just going through life saying "input, input!" I seemed, always, to need more information. It also explained why I would always be promoted in any job I took and within six months I would reach the highest level my "schooling" would allow.

I have to say, I felt cheated in life. If only I had had normal parents who supported me instead of being drunks!

High IQ and a couple of dollars might get you a cup of coffee, but that's about all the good it will do. I just wanted something more out of life.

February of 1983, I enrolled in West LA City College. I had been a sponsor to a woman, Claire, who was an English professor at the college. I had been talking to her about getting my high school diploma so I could take English in college because I wanted to be a writer. She suggested that I enroll in classes in City College for which I did not need a high school diploma. So, I enrolled in two classes of English.

I told Claire that I no longer cared if I got a diploma or even credit for the classes. I just wanted the information.

Claire was a delightful Irish lady and a very good teacher. We went to the school "Book Store" and she kept piling up the books. She said most students would only use one or two, but if I wanted to learn, I should read all those books. So, I did. I think the first time we went to that store it cost me about $300 (about $920 in 2022 money).

Claire was also the first teacher who figured out I was dyslectic. She returned a corrected paper on which she had circled all the "fo" and "ot." She explained that my mind sometimes doesn’t register the same as others. No wonder I had a hard time reading until I learned "Speed Reading." And it also explained why I always had a hard time writing school papers.

A large percentage of the population (about 75 to 80%) has some form of dyslexia and most will never know it. I was in good company because it was rumored that Leonardo De Vince was dyslexic also. I had learned that I could easily write in "mirror image" which was what Leonardo could do. I wasn’t ashamed of being dyslexic; I was annoyed by it.

Claire said, "Don’t worry about it. You can hire someone to type your work and they are used to people who can’t spell. Just keep writing."

I would struggle for a few more years until computers became mainstream and had great programs that could "spell check" anything I wrote.

At one point, I got a notice that I was "required" to take a class in "Beginning Psych" if I was to remain enrolled in my English classes. I took the letter to Claire and asked what that was about. She told me not to worry about it, she would fix it. She said that apparently, the class did not get enough students to keep the class open so they tried to badger new students into taking a class in which they had no interest.

A few days later, I received another letter telling me I was not required to take the "Psych" class. I went to Claire and thanked her for getting me out of the class. I told her that I didn't know how she did it, but I was very grateful because I barely had time for the two classes I was taking.

She said, "No problem, I went to the professor and told her that she didn't want you in her class because you would 'eat her alive'," and we both laughed.

I had met Claire in AA and, though sober for some time, she had a lot of phobias going on with her. She couldn't go to sleep at night unless there was a "potato" in the house. I don't know if being Irish had anything to do with that. She couldn't drive on a freeway because she was afraid a dog would run out and she would get in a wreck. I can't even imagine living in California and not being able to drive on a freeway.

At any rate, I spent a lot of time teaching her how to create "processes" to ameliorate these phobias. I drove with her on freeways telling her what to do if a dog ran out. "Just pretend that a dog is about to run out. Now, hold the wheel solidly, and "run over the dog," I said. She drove for many hours waiting for the dog and being prepared. In the experiencing of her fear, it soon went away. Of course, no dog ever came.

It is amazing how things get stuck in someone's mind. If you have a fear that other people don't seem to have, you might want to look at it as an "ingrained imaginary fear."

I was working with many alcoholics at the time and found I was explaining the same thing over and over. I decided to begin writing a book about the things I had learned. I originally called the book, "Imagination and Failure," because the imagination was where most of our failure originated. I later renamed the book: "Grandma's Human Repair Manual (How to Survive Your Parent's Mistakes)."

I eventually lost track of Claire after I had finished the English classes. Oddly enough, some years later, Claire and I became reacquainted and she told me that one day a dog did, in fact, run out in front of her. She said in a split second, she heard my voice say, “hold the wheel solidly, and run over the dog,” which is what she did, except for the fact that the dog dodged out of the way. She laughed." All the time I was afraid of running over a dog and the truth was I couldn’t if I tried." Claire continued to enjoy driving on the freeways.

My daughter had been dating a boy named Clay. He was five years older than Tami. When I first became aware of it, I threatened to have him arrested for contributing to a minor or whatever else I could get him on. Her father seemed to think it was just fine that they were dating. I’m reliving my childhood.

I still had hopes for my son. He was still such a sweet boy who liked to skateboard.

For Christmas 1982, I bought my son the new "Commodore 64" computer. It was the newest thing and it was the first home computer. The 64 was for the 64 K of Ram, which is laughable in light of today’s computers but was a big deal then. You could run an entire business on about 15K of memory. I knew next to nothing about computers; only what I had read in science magazines. But if it was something that would give my son an advantage in life, I was all for it.

The trouble with it was, it was very hard for a 13-year-old kid who had never heard of a computer to figure it out and I didn’t have enough time to figure it out for him. He had no friends who were into learning this new technology. You could play a few games on it, but they were not what he was interested in. With the accessories I had bought with the computer, I had spent over $800. (About $2,300 in 2022 money).

Eventually, I would be the one who loved computers. They were magical as far as I was concerned and little by little, I figured them out.

Christmas of 1982 was a bit much for Tony living in the area we were in. I had lived all my life in the Hawthorne, Inglewood area. It was a rather ruff area, but when you grow up in it, you don't notice. But, Tony had lived in the San Fernando Valley which was a whole level above Hawthorne.

Christmas day, we watched from our apartment windows as the police carted out a dead person from the apartment across the street and two doors down from my brother. It had been a gang killing. To visit my brother across the street, I took my 38-special with me in my pocket. Tony was aghast.

I decided it was time to get my son out of this area and into a place where he didn't have to contend with the violence of the times. Tony and I decided to buy a house and started looking around.

I tried everything I could think of to keep Tami in school. I bribed her. I didn't have TIME to give to my kids and the only thing I could do with problems was throw money at them. I just wanted her to get her damn high school diploma. That was my dream, not hers.

The more I pushed with Tami, the worse the situation became. She finally said that she and Clay wanted to get married. Tami was only 16 and Clay was 22. Looking at her, I could not believe how young she looked and I flashed on how young I had been when I got married at that age. It wasn't that I didn't like Clay. He seemed like a nice enough guy. I just didn't approve of my 16-year-old getting married. Her father approved and there wasn't much to do, but consent. Tami and Clay were married on May 14, 1983.

They had a lovely church wedding and my daughter looked very beautiful. I was proud that I could pay for her wedding and of course, her father contributed nothing but did, surprisingly show up sober.

In July, I went to visit my mother in the convalescent home where I had placed her. She had been in there for several years since she couldn't take care of herself. I visited whenever my lifestyle allowed and saw to it that her bills were paid and she had the clothing she needed. I no longer thought about it as a chore, I simply didn't think about it. I just did what was needed.

At one point, my brother, Kim, had taken her out of the home and moved her in with him. By the time I was notified, they were gone and I had no idea where she was. Nova and I did some snooping around and finally located him through the Social Security Department. That was, of course, why Kim had taken her. He wanted her Social Security check. When Nova and I went to his house, he was not at home and Mother was in a dirty bed, she was cyanotic and had lost weight. I called an ambulance and sent her to the hospital. That had been some months back, but I still kept a close watch on her.

Anyway, the day I went to visit, my mother was in kind of a panicked state. She was afraid of dying. She wanted me to take her home with me. That didn't seem like an option, I had to work and there was no one to take care of her. but eventually, I felt sorry for her, I told her she could come and stay with me for the weekend. I packed up what she needed, put her in my car, and took her home with me.

I called Teri and asked her to come over and visit with Mother if she wanted. She said she would the next day. Mother ate little and only sat and watched TV. We didn't have much interaction, but then we never did.

Sometime in the middle of the night Mother got sick and she couldn't breathe. I couldn't handle her, so I called an ambulance. I called Teri to meet me at the hospital. I didn't call Pat because he didn't know his mother at all. Since she had come back into our life, Pat had always lived with dad and although he had visited with her for a few hours here and there, he did not know her.

When we got to the hospital, Mother was on a gurney in the hallway. I tried to get a doctor to talk to me, but they were just too busy. They directed us to a waiting room where we could stay until the doctor had time to see us. We had to sit and wait for hours.

Eventually, the doctor came in and told us, "Your mother has a broken 'schnozz'."

"What are you talking about?" I asked. "She was brought in because she couldn't breathe?"

He flipped some pages on his clipboard and asked, "Is your mother Pearl Helen Webster?"

"Yes," I affirmed.

"Then she has a broken nose! They are putting her in a room and keeping her overnight for observation. You can come back tomorrow and pick her up." And with that, he turned and left.

I thought "What a rude and arrogant asshole!" There wasn't anything to do but come back the next day. I was just too young and dumb to question further. Teri and I went home.

In the middle of the night, I got a call from the hospital informing me that my mother had died. I would need to make arrangements for a funeral home to come and get her. I was speechless. It was like I was in an altered universe where weird things were happening and no one cared. The only thing that can explain it is that somehow the universe was acting in the same manner as Mother had lived; "Indifference to others feelings." It was just bizarre.

I had no idea what Mother wanted to be done with her after she had passed. It was never a topic of conversation that I could recall. I called "The Neptune Society," and had her cremated and her ashes spread at sea. I let the rest of the kids know and asked if any of them wanted to have any kind of service for her, but they had no interest.

In the blink of an eye, the mother I barely knew and never understood was gone and it left no deficit in my life.

Between Mother dying, Tami getting married, looking for a house, and work, I was run pretty ragged.

I was working as the lead painter on a movie called "Smorgasbord" with Jerry Lewis. It was a tough show because many days we were constructing on the same stage they were filming on and could only make noise between shots or when they were on break. It was tedious and very stressful. I was a bit run down from the fast-paced life I seemed to live, and everything I was juggling. I didn't have an option of leaving work because I was the lead on the show. I just had to tough it out. Since I was on call for both construction and production, I had a two-way radio and I talked them into giving me a second radio for my second in command.

Most all the people that were on the show, I had worked with on other shows and we all got on well. Terry Bousman was the Art Director.

Terry noticed I was looking a bit ill and said I should go home and get better. I had never ducked out on a show and bull headedly was reluctant to give up the baton. A few days later I had been reduced to laying on a couch in a mobile dressing room and was running the show by radio. My second was covering for me on the set. Terry knew where I was and we did our consulting in the dressing room if he needed to show me anything.

Later in the day, the door of the dressing room opened, and in came Terry Bousman with Jerry Lewis. I struggled to get up off the couch. I was running a fever and was weak as a kitten.

Jerry took one look at me and said, "I'm going to call for my car and you are going to go home. Someone else can take over for a few days. You need to take care of yourself."

I just didn't have enough strength to argue. One driver drove me home and another drove my car home. I took about three days off and was as good as new.

When I went back to the studio, I went and thanked Jerry for intervening and for his kindness in lending me his car and driver. We had an interesting talk. He said that years before when he thought he was a "hot star," he had not been kind to people, but life had taught him some hard lessons. He knew the value of all the people it took to make him a success. He was a very humble and sincere man. He was also a remarkable man in that he memorized the name of everyone that he worked with and never forgot anyone. I had heard those rumors but wasn't sure I believed it because we work with hundreds of people on every show. But, I ran into him a few years later and he actually remembered my name.

One of the coordinators, Mort, which I had worked with, lived in a place called Simi Valley. It was about 45 miles from Hawthorne on the other side of the San Fernando Valley. It was a fairly new suburb. I had gone to his house to paint something for him and his wife and was very impressed with the area. The 118 freeway was brand new and I was about the only car on it.

Mort's wife, Arlene, was a school teacher and told me how great the schools were. I was sold and started looking for a suitable house.

On July 29, we closed on a nice three-bedroom, two-and-a-half-bath home on Rosita Drive. It had a huge backyard with a swimming pool which thrilled Andy. And so, we moved to Simi Valley, California.

I had great plans for the Rosita house. I could see room for improvement that I could make to it. I loved designing and redesigning houses. I had and still have a good eye for it.

Married my sixth husband, Tony (ACT) December 24, 1981
Claudia age 34 - Tony age 46
(Tony was about 12 years older than me)

Claudia Gilligan

american
mensa
limited

a not for profit corporation of new york state / 1701 west 3 st., brooklyn ny 11223 – (212) 376-1925 – cables: usmensa

1/4/82

C. Gilligan

Dear Prospective Candidate:

We are pleased to advise you that your score on the supervised test indicates an I.Q. of 134 on the [illegible] scale; which is higher than 99 % of the population in general would achieve on this test.

We are happy to tell you that this is above the minimum level MENSA requires for its panel, and that we can now offer you membership in the Society.

We offer you congratulations on your success. As soon as we receive your membership dues, we shall add your name to the mailing list for publications and surveys, and you will then be welcome to join any of the Society's activities.

Sincerely yours,

AMERICAN MENSA LTD.

STP/81

(P.S. Although our admission standards were satisfied by the test scores indicated above, we thought you might like to learn the results of the second supervised test that you took. Your score there indicates an I.Q. of 149 on the Cattell scale, and this places you in the 99 % of the general population.)

I am a life member of American Mensa (98th percentile IQ), Intertel (99th percentile IQ), and also of the International Society for Philosophical Enquiry, (ISPE) The Thousand® (at or above 99.9% IQ Organization). The highest I have tested on an IQ exam is 151.

Chapter 32
Simi Valley and Treasure

I was very hopeful about moving to Simi Valley and making a new start for us all. Andy was in a good school and all was well with the world.

The month after we moved into Rosita, my niece, Merrie, came to me in tears because she was unmarried and pregnant and had no place to go and no money. Her mom couldn't help her and I was the only one she could turn to. And so, she moved in with me until the baby was born.

Merrie had an extraordinary sense of humor. She was just innately funny and was a delight to be around for that reason, but Merrie was also …. Loud. She had been raised by my sister who always screamed because, as we found out later, she was almost deaf. Because of my sister screaming, her first four kids have very loud voices. With my sensitive hearing, it hurts my ears when people talk loudly. Merrie tried her best to remember to hold her voice down and I tried to be understanding, but it was difficult for us both.

On December 20, 1983 Merrie gave birth to a son who she named, Todd. In the hospital Merrie and I joked about how "fat" little Todd was and Merrie, jokingly said, "We'll put the little shit on a diet when we get him home," and we both laughed.

The day after Merrie and Todd came home from the hospital, a "welfare worker" showed up at my door demanding to inspect my house because she had a report of child abuse. I was floored! What-he-hell was she talking about? Was this another trick of Andy's dad, Mel?

I told her I wasn't going to let her in and she could go back and tell Mel to kiss my ass. She showed me her credentials and said that if I didn't let her in, she would come back with a court order and the police. I asked who had made the complaint. She said she couldn't disclose who it was. I told her I would let her in if after she inspected, she disclosed who made the complaint. She agreed and I let her in to inspect my house.

I gave her a tour of the entire house. I explained that my niece lived with us and we toured their room as well as Andy's room and the rest of the house. I'm proud to say, my house has always been immaculate. My brother used to say that if there weren't enough dishes for everyone he would just use the toilet seat because he was sure it was clean enough to eat off of.

The welfare worker opened every cabinet in the house. I was beginning to wonder what, exactly, had been said about me and my house.

After the inspection, she sat and asked us questions about everything and anything you can imagine. Merrie was feeding Todd at the table and after several questions, Merrie "loudly" came to my defense and told the woman that she was being duped by Mel, and that her Aunt Claudia was never neglectful and always provided for everyone.

The woman finally said that she was satisfied that the complaint was erroneous. Then she said she didn't know who this "Mel" was, but he was not the one who filed the complaint. It had been a NURSE at the hospital where Merrie gave birth to Todd. Apparently, the nurse had "overheard" Merrie say we would put Todd on a diet when we got him home and she had filed the complaint.

How times had changed since I was a kid. With all the abuse and starvation, we children had endured with no one investigating and now they crawl up your ass for something said as a joke! Grrrrrr

We enjoyed watching Todd grow as a baby. He was so adorable. Merrie stayed with us a few more months and then moved on.

I was hired as the lead on a new show, "Oh, God! You Devil." Mort. was the construction coordinator and Peter Wooley was the Production Designer. I had worked with both of them several times before.

The first week of the show, I got a call from a friend in the Hawthorne area saying that Clay and Tami were living in a motel on Century Boulevard and that Clay and Tami's father, Mel, had her "working the streets." I had no idea if it was true or not, but could think of nothing else.

This was, again, before the advent of the cell phone. I had to try to make phone calls from a "stage phone," which wasn't easy to use, wasn't private, and was interfering with getting the show organized. I finally went to Mort's office to talk with him. I told him what I had heard. I told him I didn't know if it was true or not, but that I had to leave the show to figure it out. Mort confided knew what it was like to raise a daughter. He said he would replace me right away but if I got it figured out and wanted to come back, give him a call. So, I left the show.

I went home to Rosita and made phone calls from there. I didn't know Tami's exact address and that was the first thing I had to find out. My friend Paula was one of the people who gave me information and I trusted what she said. I finally got the address of the motel in which she was living.

I got in my car and drove to Hawthorne. I took my gun, a 38-special with me. The one thing I knew about Clay was that he was a level three Black Belt in Karate and I had tested him a few times to see how fast he was. I thought in a match, he would easily take me and I wasn't taking any chances.

When I got to the motel, I knocked on the door and announced who it was. It took a few minutes before Tami opened the door. I looked around for Clay. She told me he had "locked himself in the bathroom." Did, I need to know anymore?"

I told Tami to get her things together, she was coming home with me until her husband could provide a proper home for her. She didn't question anything but just started packing. We loaded her things into my car and left.

I took Tami home to Rosita and got her settled in. Of course, she denied the rumors but said she was done with Clay anyway. She said he "didn't treat her right." I left it at that.

When Tony came home from his job, I explained what had happened. So far, people just kept moving in with us and we were supporting them.

Tami said she wanted to go to "Beauty School" and become a manicurist. For her to get into a school for that, she needed a High School diploma. A GED would be acceptable so Tami and I enrolled in the Simi Valley Adult School for a preparatory class for the GED. I was going to stick to Tami like glue to be sure she stayed on the straight and narrow.

On November 16, 1984, she and I both took the test. We waited afterward while the tests were graded. Then the teacher came and told me to go to the office. I was sweating it. I thought for sure that I had flunked the test and they were being kind enough to tell me in private.

When I got to the office, the entire staff was there. As I went in, the rest of the class came in from the back. Then the principal announced that I had gotten one of the highest scores, ever, in the state of California. I was amazed. But that simply shows how skewed my thinking was about myself. I thought I had failed when I had excelled. I guess, I had been called stupid, by my dad and ex-husbands, so long, that I had started to believe it. My daughter was so proud of her mom.

Tami had passed all but one portion of the test and was allowed to retake that portion and passed the second time. We both received our GED. We were both so proud of each other.

I enrolled Tami in the Beauty School and bought her a little car to go back and forth to school. Things seemed to settle in, but that only lasted a short time, and then I started having problems with Andy.

I opened a phone bill one day and it was for over $500.00 (about $1,445 in 2022 money). There was a string of charges for 900 prefix phone numbers that were most of the bill. I investigated and found out that 900 numbers were for phone sex. I thought it might be something Tony had done, but when confronted, he denied it.

Later when Andy came in, I asked him if he knew what the calls were. He immediately started apologizing and said when he did it, he didn't know it would cost that much. He and a friend had recorded the calls and then put them on his school principal's answering machine .... As a joke! He further said he was going to sell his bike to repay me for the calls. His bike was very expensive and he loved it, but I let him sell it because I wanted him to take responsibility for his actions.

Andy was not doing well in school. They sent home a notice that unless he completed his homework assignments, he would be failing. I called him up on it. "You are 15 years old Andy. I was on my own by your age. What are you going to do with your life?" He would just shrug his shoulders.

It wasn't like I had a lot of time to deal with this kind of thing. I was working on a TV show named, "Streetcar Named Desire," which, as always, was 11 ½ hours a day plus driving two hours. It was also a show that had an asshole grip that seemed to hate women working in "a man's job." Tony and I had painted the sets and now, I was working as the stand-by painter and this jerk took every opportunity to screw up a set and then loudly complain about how long it took me to fix it while the entire shooting company watched. The entire set was plastered, so if they ripped a big chunk out of it while "wilding" (removing) a wall, I had to repair it when they put it back. If grips were careful and cut the corners, I could simply run a piece of painted tape down it and be done in minutes. But if they busted it apart, it was a lot more work.

One day they had busted the hell out of the set and when they put it back together, there were huge areas where the plaster had fallen off. I would have to mix plaster and put it on, let it dry and then paint and age it. There was no excuse for it. I'm fast, but plaster drying isn't. I mixed the plaster very tight so it would dry fast and was putting it on when the lead grip started to heckle me. "How long can it take to fix one damn seam?" he chided me.

I think most people knew it was bullshit, but it was nerve-racking to me. I wanted to stomp a mudhole in his ass. About the time I was ready to unload on this guy, Ann Margaret climbed up the opposite side of my ladder and said to the jackass "Now you just shush, quality takes time." Then she turned to me and said, "You take your time sugar and don't let him get under your skin. They can't film anything while I'm on this ladder!" and she winked at me. That certainly made my day. Ann Margaret is, truly, a class act.

Ann Margaret knew about women being pushed around and she would have none of it. If something wasn't right on the set or they didn't give her enough time in makeup, she just walked off and her husband, Roger Smith, would step in and nothing moved until he was satisfied that she was taken care of.

Meanwhile, at home, I made a deal with Andy that I would help him complete his homework and get him caught up if he would promise to take it from there. He agreed.

In dealing with his homework, there was one assignment that required you to; "Read an article in TIME magazine and write an “opinion” on the article." My opinion was that the articles were too damn short. I went and bought a Time magazine and read the entire thing. Nearly every article was but a paragraph or two. There certainly wasn’t enough information in ANY article on which I would want my son to form an opinion. I, personally, had some strong feelings about this assignment. I’ve seen too many people that have formed an opinion without having any real “facts.” That was not who I wanted my son to be.

I called the school and talked to the teacher who stood behind her assignment saying that "Children of Andy’s age need to start to form opinions on things and need to take an interest in what goes on in the world!" She was obviously an idiot! I informed her that Andy would NOT be turning in that assignment and if she failed him because of it, she would hear from me further. He did not fail the class.

The rest of the homework, we did together. I did most of it because I didn’t have the time or strength to sit for hours with him. I probably did him a disservice by doing so much of it myself, but I just wanted it done so I could go to bed.

The other problem with Andy was that all of a sudden, he was not clean. I had to tell him to shower. His room was a mess with dirty clothes all over the floor. It smelled like a locker room. When I said something about it, he would get mad and scream, "I LIKE DIRT!" So, now I have to deal with testosterone!

Andy knew how to use the washing machine since he was about ten years old. There was no excuse for dirty clothes. I told him that obviously, he had too many clothes and that unless he started washing his clothes every few days, I was going to take away all his clothes except for two outfits; One to wear and one in the wash. If that didn't work, he would only have one set. Andy had never been like this before and I was beside myself with how to deal with him.

Andy's bedroom had been decorated in what I thought he would like. Unfortunately, in my mind, he was still a little boy. Tony and I decided that maybe if we decorated his room the way he wanted it, he might take better care of it.

We asked him how he would like his room done. He said, "I want it to look like a dungeon!"

Well, that wasn't what I was expecting. I thought maybe some bicycle theme or something along the sports line. But, dungeon it was.

Being scenic artists, it didn't take long to complete the room. We lined the walls and made them look like blocks suitable for a dungeon with moss and lime in between. The corners of the room had what looked like big wooden beams. The ceiling was black and I found a chandelier that had little flickering candlelight bulbs and painted it black. I painted plastic chains black and then like they were rusted. We hung the chains from the wall on one end and they tucked under his mattress to look like a fold-down cot. The inside of his door looked like an old timber door. It turned out to be a great room.

That solved the problem with his room and wonder of wonder, he kept it clean. He was very proud of it and liked to bring his friends in to see it.

Tony and I remodeled the Rosita house quite a bit. Tony and my brother, Pat, remodeled the front of the house changing it from an ordinary stucco to a "Tudor" style with decorative half-timbering. The wood was dark brown and the stucco was white. It was beautiful.

There was a good size space behind the pool and Tony built a white Gazebo. Most of our "spare" time went into one project or another.

We had a couple of parties each year. July 4th was my dad's birthday so we always made a combined holiday out of it with a pool party. The other party was Christmas. I always tried to get all our family together least we all become estranged. Our parties were always a load of fun and I put in a lot of work to ensure it. I did all the cooking and decorating. Christmas was my favorite time of year. From the time I was on my own, I had always seen to it that we had a great Christmas. There would never be a repeat of my childhood.

One year my stepmother, Dodie, remarked to me, "Oh Claudia, look at all the money you're wasting on this party!" I looked around at all the family laughing and having fun and said, "It's not wasted mom, look at all the happy faces." I felt sorry for Dodie. Even though she had inherited plenty of money from the man she had married after she divorced my dad, she couldn't spend a penny of it to make even herself and her daughter, Nini, happy. I had always thought her miserly ways had something to do with me, but, in reality, it was just about her. I later found out that my sister, Nini, was as unhappy in her childhood as I had been and for the same reasons.

It seemed like no matter what I did; Andy wasn't making it at school. Now he was getting in a different kind of trouble. One day I was at work and got a call, from the Simi Police Department, that Andy had been arrested for having a knife at school and threatening a teacher. Wow, that was way far out of anything I thought possible with my son.

In talking to the policeman, I explained that I was the lead painter on the show I worked on and I could not just leave a crew and come get my son. The officer had a hard time understanding what I was saying. He asked what he was supposed to do with Andy? "Well," I said, "keep him. If he did what you said he did, I guess he needs to learn a lesson, or take him back where you got him from." And with that, I hung up.

The cop went and told Andy what had happened and Andy said, "See, I told you she wouldn't get me out!"

Within a short time, they took him back to the school and released him.

When I got the time, I used the stage phone to call the school and talk to the principal who gave me a long, convoluted story of what happened. This started when the teacher called the principal and said, "Andy had threatened to cut her with a knife." I could hardly believe that Andy, out of the blue, would threaten a teacher. I asked the circumstances. It seems like he didn't "personally" threaten the teacher. I'm standing in the middle of a stage trying to keep people working and talking on the phone at the same time. This question and answer crap went on for about 15 minutes. When the whole story came out, it went something like this. Andy had a fishing knife in his backpack, some kid saw it and asked Andy if he was going to stab someone. The kid then went to the teacher and told her that Andy was going to cut her and so the teacher called the principal.

What a bunch of crap! Why couldn't the teacher and principal have figured out that it was a lie? For me, the bottom line was; if I were a man, no one would expect me to drop everything and come and get my "little boy."

I put Andy on restriction for a week because he should have removed the knife before he went to school. Of course, I had no way of enforcing the restriction because I didn't get home until seven or eight at night. I didn't have a babysitter for Andy because he was sixteen years old. Hell, I was married at that age!

Another day, I came home from work early and found that Andy and his friends had erected a bike ramp against the block wall in the backyard. At the point that I saw it, the block wall was leaning and dangerously close to toppling over. We had to have the wall repaired and reinforced. I hired my neighbor to check on Andy when I wasn't there. He was to check in with her regularly.

Late in 1984 a book came out called, "Treasure." It was a game with a prize of a golden horse worth $500,000. I was so intrigued by it.

In the front of the book it states:

Somewhere in the earth is buried a horse of gold. Buried in the story are the clues that will lead you to that secret place. Find, link, and then follow the clues that lay hidden in this tale and you will come to understand the map… For it shows you exactly where to dig. But do not dig too deep. Break no law. Take no risk. It is in a safe place. And when you find it, look into the heart of the golden horse, for there hides the key to a great fortune … Waiting for you.

I hoped to get Andy interested in doing it with me. I worked on deciphering the clues every chance I got. It was a great escape for me and I couldn't think about problems when I was working on the puzzle.

Although I had bought a new IBM Pc Jr. in 1984, it wasn't much help because you had to write a program for everything and that took time. As far as the "Treasure Hunt" was concerned, it wasn't very much help. There was NO internet in those days, so most everything you did was by hand and with local, library help. I was still very engrossed in it.

The other thing that I was using the computer for was to write my book, "Imagination and Failure," (Grandma's Human Handbook). When I wasn't working, dealing with kids, or remodeling the house, I was working on one of these two projects.

One day Tony came into the den where I was working on something. He stood before my desk and announced, "Are you ever going to get off that? You're not entertaining me!" It wasn't what he said, but it was the angry way he said it. As, though I was, truly, shirking my duties.

"Did I hear that right?" I took a moment because I was truly baffled. My brain was spinning. Finally, I looked at Tony and said, "Tony, I wasn't put on this earth to 'entertain' you. Can you not find something to entertain yourself?" Between kids, work, cooking, keeping up with the house, and "entertaining Tony," where was the time for what I wanted or needed? He certainly wasn't making any attempt to "entertain" me.

He thought about that a minute and then turned and walked out of the room. That may well have been the turning point in the relationship but I just did not know it at the time.

It seems like all relationships start with such promise. Everyone puts their best foot forward. After the wedding, and the "new" begins to wears off, people start to relax and become who they really are. That is when as they say, "The honeymoon is over." I've thought a lot about that and have come up with what I believe happens.

The job of the mind is to keep us safe. The job of the hormone system is to keep us together so we can procreate. Both of these instincts are required for the survival of the species. Unfortunately, "the urge to merge" continues long after people have any desire or ability to have children. Heaven knows that if men didn't fuck, there'd be a bounty on them (just kidding). And as far as a man is concerned, if he wasn't so sexually-driven, a woman simply would not be seen by him. Like most things in a man's life, she just wouldn't be seen … like the bottle of olive oil right in front of him, on the shelf that he looks right at and swears he can't find it.

Because of this ancient setup, we are forced to gravitate toward each other for mating purposes. When we first meet, we don't know anything about each other. The mind abhors a vacuum. How does the mind know we will survive? To the extent that information is absent, our minds will simply, "fill in the blanks." Our "imagination" will create the other person to be nearly everything we want them to be. That's only a trick of the mind to get us to mate. Sometimes, the person turns out to be exactly what we wanted. But, more often than not, it just tricks us.

When man walked away from our ape ancestors, he developed, at some point, "language" and with that, he "invented" all kinds of things that truly don't exist without agreement.

Marriage is a construct of man. It only lives in his words. It lives only through our description of what it (marriage) is. That description has changed throughout history and certainly varies from person to person. As far as I can tell, the only reason for marriage is to "share resources" of some kind. ("Sex" is a resource.) Were it not for the need to "share resources" I think people would just be together when they choose to and would just walk away when they wanted something different. Of course, that would require both partners to be self-sufficient.

Certainly, at that point in my life, I had learned to "entertain" myself and really didn't "need" anyone in my life, I just "preferred" someone in my life. But, that someone had to be as independent at I was. Tony was welcome to join in with whatever I was doing, and I welcomed the opportunity to join in something he was doing. Unfortunately, he didn't seem to have any interest aside from me. For me to have to stop what I was doing to "entertain" him? Probably not going to happen!

The "Treasure" hunt became a great passion of mine and at one point, I decided I needed more information about a place near, "Wildhorse, Idaho." I could have done more research and not gone to Wildhorse, but where's the fun in that and, I needed to "entertain" Tony.

I told Tony about it and we decided to take my son and go on an adventure in Tony's classic, red, 1960 Ford Thunderbird. So, in March of 1984, we took off. We took turns driving.

While it was seasonably warm weather in Southern California, a freak storm had hit Idaho. We came to a road that was blocked off, but looking down the road, it looked like the road was clear and that they just hadn't taken down the roadblocks yet. I was driving. What we didn't know is that they put the roadblocks up way before the snow. I went around the roadblock. About 10 miles down the road, we started seeing snowdrifts in the middle of the road. Not a problem, I just drove through them. Then finally I hit one that threw snow up onto the windshield and froze the wipers. The car drifted a bit to the left and I could get no traction to right it. It came to rest on the opposite side of the road with the back end sticking out into the oncoming lane.

Luckily, within a few minutes, a little tiny car came from the direction we were headed. They stopped to help and confirmed that the road only got worse. They, fortunately, had a tow chain and were able to get us out and we got turned around. We pulled to the side of the road and within a few minutes, a Greyhound bus came barreling by from the direction we had been trying to go. If the little car had not towed us out of the drift, that Greyhound would have annihilated us. So much for our adventure.

We turned around and headed back down the mountain.

Unfortunately, coming down I lost the breaks on the T-Bird. Not even the emergency brake would stop it. I had to stop it by running the T-Bird into the side of the mountain to finally bring it to a stop. My son thoroughly enjoyed the trip and thought it was quite "wicked." Back to the drawing board and wait for some warmer weather.

When Andy turned 16, I got him a car for his birthday. It was a classic 1975 "Mustang Ghia." I was hoping to give him some incentive to do well in school and make something of himself. I think it only took a few weeks before he crashed it. And the incentive plan didn't work. Andy became more distant and belligerent. I guess that is the age that the testosterone kicks in. He started yelling at me when I asked him to do something. Tony tried to help by telling him to not talk to his mother that way, but it did no good.

One day Andy stormed out of the house and stopped at his car long enough to yell, "You've never done anything for me. My grandma paid for me when I was growing up, not you!"

Wow. Where did that come from? Was that another one of Mel's parents lying to my kids? I have to say, my feelings were hurt. No one will ever know how hard it was, at times, to give money to Mel's mother when I knew it only enabled her to give him more money. I did it because it was the right thing to do, not because I liked it, and now this kid is yelling at me for not supporting him?

Fortunately, I am a saver. I have saved every receipt and canceled check since I started on my own. I got out all the receipts and canceled checks for all the money I had given Connie; All the support, the clothes, the schooling, everything. When Andy came home, I quietly told him I wanted him to look at something. I showed him the receipts.

He was truly surprised. I told him to look at them good because I wouldn't show them to him twice. I wanted him to be truly satisfied that I had always paid for his upkeep and it wasn't because there was a court order.

"Your father on the other hand," I said, "has never contributed a dime to you."

My father was now 65 years old and he retired from the motion picture industry. I felt proud that I had gotten him into the industry in time for him to earn enough retirement and Social Security to live a comfortable life. He had been sober for quite a few years and had found a very sweet Mormon woman to share his life with.

Unfortunately, Tony and I did not last. Between kid problems, work, and everything else, we just drifted to indifference. I finally had a talk with him and we decided (maybe me more than him) to go our separate ways. It was a very amicable separation. Tony wanted to keep the house and I would take cash to equal the equity, but also stipulated that if he ever wanted to sell the house, I would have the first option to buy it. Most of the furniture he kept and again, I took the monetary equivalent. I signed a Quit Claim deed over to him. I had my wedding rings made into a "friendship" ring for him engraved with, "For the Good Times."

As I have continued to study human nature, I have, come to the conclusion that a good relationship could only be formed when two people are independent and secure in themselves.

I have come to pretty well understand myself. I like to learn and I like to travel, I like to cook and I like a clean house. Family and friends have always been important to me, so I like parties and get togethers. At the same time, I like my alone time. I don't need someone around, "All the time," and I don't need someone to entertain me. As far as the love languages, I think I'm "Words of Affirmation." Nothing else seems to fit.

Physical touch: That seems like it requires, too much holding on. I feel stifled. I'm not the clingy type. I like sex, occasionally, but let's face it, I'm not a teenager. I like nice long hugs except when I'm busy, which is often because I am the creative type and time flies when you are absorbed in something you love to do.

Receiving gifts: I get more out of giving than receiving. I delight in someone's else's happiness. A small, well thought out gift for my birthday or odd holiday is appreciated. I don't like to be forgotten altogether. A card or phone call is sufficient.

Quality time: I like some of that. Uninterrupted and focused conversation. A nice dinner out. I just don't need it very often.

Acts of Service: I don't like help unless I ask for it. Don't take a box out of my hands because you think it's too heavy for me. I'll ask if I need help.

Claudia with the book from "Treasure" 1983 -1988.

Me in front of the helicopter I rented

My piolet who thought maybe he should just shoot the crazy lady. It was only a pellet gun, so we just decided to shoot the giant grasshoppers instead. Claudia age 36.

Chapter 33
Moving Right Along

Of course, I met another man right away.... Ron (RDK). We worked on a show together. Tony, I, and Ron worked on the same show. Tony and I were still friends and saw no reason not to work together. Tony introduced me to Ron and we hit it off.

Part of our show was done on location in Flagstaff and Phoenix, Arizona, and Ron and I went to do the location work. We formed a relationship and the rest is history. Well, almost!

After the show was finished, we went to Cado Lake, Texas for some R&R. We did a lot of fishing and had a great time. Ron seemed to be the perfect man. I've never laughed so hard or enjoyed myself so much in my life. We seemed to be natural together.

Andy was living back with Grandma Connie, while I was on location, but she wasn't able to keep him interested in school any more than I was.

Ron was a widower. His wife had died as the result of falling off a horse. He had been single for many years.

Ron lived on several acres of property that a developer wanted. They had made an offer to him for the property. He was going to accept the offer. From my estimation, they were lowballing him. I thought he could get much more.

Ron knew my background in real estate and investing. He asked if I would handle it for him. I explained that I no longer had my license with a broker and couldn't represent him officially, but I could investigate and tell him what he should counter offer. He told me that if I could get anything over the $500,000 that they had offered, he would give me half of the amount over. Well, that was a deal I couldn't pass up.

It took several weeks, but I thought I pretty well understood the market in his area and I estimated that he should ask for $700,000. I made out a proposal that they could choose their deal. One was for them to pay $600,000 and give Ron two finished houses after the build. There were several scenarios like that to choose from.

We sat on the steps of his house while he talked to the developer. I wrote out exactly what he should say. No more, no less. He wasn't good at dealing, but I kept coaching him how he should respond. Finally, they said they would consider all options and get back to him.

In a few days, they called back and offered him $650,000. That was $150,000 more than he was originally going to accept and $75,000 extra for each of us. He was delighted and so was I.

A few weeks after that, Ron presented me with an engagement ring and asked me to marry him. I was a bit floored because we had only been going together for five or six months. I told him I would have to think about it. He responded that I had married six other men, what was wrong with him?

A week later I accepted his proposal with the same stipulations as I did with Tony; only as long as we were happy and we would maintain a separation of property. He agreed and we were married in Las Vegas, Nevada on January 31, 1986. He was my seventh husband.

Ron was very interested in my "Treasure" hunt and wanted to go along as I explored Idaho. When we got back from Las Vegas, Ron bought a small travel trailer and a jeep. We would be exploring in style.

This same week, one of Ron's family members came to me and told me that they thought Ron had a hand in his previous wife dying. They shared that Ron and his wife had been going through a divorce when she died. Oh, this is just what I wanted to hear.

Andy, Ron, and I went on a trip to Idaho to the area where I thought the "Treasure" was buried. Ron was starting to act a little distant from me. I thought maybe it was because Andy was with us. Except for Tony, men in the past had not taken to my kids. It's kind of like with animals; the new male wants to get rid of the pups of the previous male. I would just have to watch and see. Unfortunately for whatever man I was with, my kids came first.

This was not the fun adventure I thought it would be. There was snow on the ground, but Ron insisted we keep going. We packed into an area I had been interested in, but could not find the geological survey markers I needed to triangulate the position. Ron just started digging holes everywhere.

Our car got stuck in a mud hole with no brush or anything around with which to dig it out. We thought maybe if we waited overnight the ground would freeze and we could then get traction to get out. We bundled up as best we could and waited. I couldn't sleep. It was just too cold and I hate the cold! The only food we had was a thermos of chicken noodle soup. It was cold and not appealing but I can remember thinking, "I wonder how long it will take before this soup seems like a feast?"

Ron would occasionally start the engine to heat the car a bit, but it was still freezing. He never tried to cuddle me or keep me warm, he was distant and it almost seemed like he was mad at me. He was just cold and sullen.

The next morning, we tried to get the Jeep to pull itself out but to no avail. Ron sent Andy over a hill with a pair of pliers to where he thought there was an old corral so he could steal a piece of wood to put under the tire. I started to feel very sick and just sat in the car. I was getting weaker by the minute and had no idea what was wrong. Andy could take care of himself, but I wasn't sure about me.

My mind started racing with the information that Ron's relative had told me and I think I started to panic.

Andy came back with a two-by-four and we got the car out of the mud. We went back to the trailer and I just fell asleep. The next day we headed back home but something had shifted with Ron and me. He was not the same man I had married.

Andy went back down to Connie's house and school and Ron and I went to his house. It was still a week or more before the developer would close the deal with Ron.

On my birthday, March 21, Ron announced that he wanted a divorce. We had been married for 49 days. I just could not believe it. I asked him what the problem was, but he was only vague with his answers saying things like, "he just didn't think it would work." I asked if he would go to marriage counseling with me. He refused. Hummmm sounds familiar.

At some point, it dawned on me what this was about. I asked him if he was going to give me the $75,000 that we had agreed on from the sale of his property and he said, "Hell no, and no one is going to believe you if you say anything because you have been married SEVEN times." Well, there it was. The whole marriage thing was a setup so he wouldn't have to pay the money he had promised me. He could have reneged on the bargain without putting me through all this crap. It was his idea to split the money in the first place. I would have been quite willing to renegotiate or just help him out for free as I had done with many people. I was furious. I was madder at ME than him because I had been duped … again!

I moved out and filed for divorce.

Sometime later, I talked with Tony about what happened and he said he had overheard part of the conversations about the property when we were all working together. He had heard me advise Ron he could do better. Tony thought I should sue Ron for fraud. I told him that I knew from studying law with my dad that "Fraud" was one of the hardest things to prove. But in the end, I decided to go for it anyway. I wasn't interested in the money, but at least I would expose Ron for the fraud he was.

It took a couple of years to get to court. Ron came to court looking like an old decrepit man, with his hair grown out gray and just bent over like a cripple. This was of course just a ploy to make it look like a younger woman was trying to take advantage of an old man. After we presented the evidence, the judge said, "I don't know, do you think there is such a thing as "accidental fraud?"

The judge ordered us to try to get together and try to come to an agreement. The lawyers went into a room and when mine came out, he said they offered me $5,000. I really did not care about the money at that point. It was fraud as far as I was concerned and I wanted him nailed. I turned down the offer.

When we went back into the court, the judge ruled in his favor. Like I said, I realized that fraud was the hardest thing to prove. I just thought it was more of the "good old boys" network. I left the court feeling OK. I had stood up for myself and that was the most important thing. Ron knows what he did and he can take that to the grave.

Married seventh husband Ron (RDK)
January 31, 1986 Separated March 21, 1986 (married 49 days!)

Notice that he has dark brown hair when we got married!
Claudia 38 Ron 51
(Ron was About 13 years older than me)

Chapter 34
Next!

I have to laugh at women who can't find a man. Shit, they fall out of the sky as far as I'm concerned. It wasn't long after I moved to Torrance that I met another man named, "Bill." He was from AA and was a lineman for the telephone company. He laughed all the time and I needed to laugh.

We met at a meeting of "Hands Across America." Hands Across America was a public fundraising event to raise money for the hungry and homeless. It was staged to take place on May 25, 1986. Millions of people were to hold hands clear across the United States for fifteen minutes. To secure your place in line you paid $10.00. ($25.00 in 2022 money) I bought lots of places in line so my family and friends could join in.

It was a fabulous day and when we finally joined hands for the fifteen minutes, it was like electricity was flowing through the chain. You could physically feel the love that flowed from hand to hand. Magical!

I dated Bill for several months, but I wasn't into getting into anything permanent. I was done with that! (I think I've said that before).

My sister and Bob had divorced sometime back. She had at first fought to keep the twins, but I talked with her. At the time, she was still trying to raise a couple of those first four she had with Sam. I just didn't see her continuing to struggle. Sure, Bob would pay support, but that didn't solve the problems of sibling resentment. I couldn't see this turning out well and I had begged Teri to let Bob have the twins. Trust me, I told her, you will see them just as much or more than if you are working and trying to do everything yourself and these are Bob's only children and he will be devoted to them. I know she loved them and it was a difficult choice, but she finally agreed.

She had moved on and married a guy named Roy. It didn't last long, so now she was single again as well. She now dated a guy from AA, Jerry, and they seemed perfect together. Jerry was a sign-writer and Teri decided to become a sign-writer as well, so she enrolled in school. I thought maybe she could go to work with me in the studios.

My brother, Pat, had started dating a new girl. We were all in new relationships. All three of us seemed to be happy at the same time and my Dad was sober. I was just waiting for the second shoe to drop.

Bill and I dated for about six months and then split up for some reason, I can't remember what it was. It must not have been important.

I started dating a guy from Jamaica named, "Patrick." He was very intelligent and I enjoyed that he was so quick on the uptake. He loved to dance and so did I. He had a beautiful Jamaican accent.

I was still working eleven and a half hours a day in the studios. Andy was living with me and he decided to quit school. He wasn't attending regularly anyway, so I told him that if he quit school, he would have to hold down a full-time job. He didn't have to pay rent or anything; he needed to save his money until he could move out on his own when he turned eighteen. I tried to explain how difficult it was to make it in life without a high school diploma, but he wasn't listening. Andy got a job as a painter for a construction company and all seemed well.

I was in between movies and wasn't working. I had gone shopping and when I came home, Andy was sitting on the couch watching TV. When I walked in, for a flash, I thought it was Mel, Andy's father, sitting on my couch. It wasn't, it was Andy.

"What are you doing home from work so early?" I asked.

"Well, I was caulking stuff and my fingers got sore, and I thought, I hate this....so I quit!"

Oh, God, that was something I had heard from his dad many a time. I was raising another Mel!

"So, let me get this straight. It's good enough for your mother to work at jobs like that to support you, but you are too good to do it?"

After thinking about it for a few days, I talked to my boyfriend, Patrick, who had asked me to move in with him. I had turned the offer down, but after the incident with Andy, I changed my mind and I decided I would. I told Andy that I was moving on the first of the month and he was NOT moving with me.

Andy recalls that he came home one day and there was a new set of luggage sitting there. He asked if we were moving and I said, "No, we aren't, but you are!" Same thing!

Within two months of moving in with Patrick, that relationship fell apart. Patrick had gone to the doctor because he wasn't feeling right. The doctor had run tests and he was diagnosed with "AIDS." Wow, that was a shock. AIDS was a disease that only "gay" people were supposed to get and Patrick was not gay to my knowledge.

Because AIDS was very new and little understood, researchers came out of the woodwork to ask Patrick questions. They asked him if he had participated in sexual activities that I had never even heard of. For Patrick, it was embarrassing and humiliating.

As best we could figure out, Patrick had gone to the hospital to visit his mother who had been sick. He found her room in a mess and went about cleaning it up. There was a bunch of paper and cotton on a tray table and he had just swept it into a trash can. In doing so, he had been stuck with a hypodermic needle that was in the mess. He had reported it to the nurse and they had him do tests, but nothing ever came of it. That had been months ago. I have a lot of questions about where AIDS "really" came from. There is something a bit "hinky" about all of it.

Because of AIDS, our relationship changed. He did not want to have sex and I couldn't blame him. Sex wasn't everything and I thought there was a lot more to the relationship than that.

But then, Patrick got a little weird. He came to me and accused me of hiding my toothbrush in the shower because, as he said, I was afraid of getting AIDS. True, I had a toothbrush in the shower, but it was for scrubbing the paint out from under my fingernails. I showed him that my toothbrush, for my teeth, was in the medicine cabinet. He was becoming very paranoid and that is what eventually broke up our relationship.

I moved into a small apartment. I made sure it was too small for any kids to move in with me. Those birds had to stand on their own. I had not done a good job of raising them, but I had done the best I could. I felt guilty for all that I wasn't able to do for them, but I couldn't make it up to them by crippling them like Mel's mother had done with him. I just had to release them to the care of the universe and believe in their safety.

About this time, Paula and Cliff had split. She had moved to Bullhead City to live with her mother after she had run them into debt with her gambling. I felt bad for Paula. She was sober, but she had switched addictions. I saw this with many AA members who started eating or dieting, or going to meetings incessantly or doing any number of things. If I had to identify with an addiction, I'd say mine was men. Unfortunately, my Paula had fallen into gambling.

It started innocently when a bunch of us from the AA club had gone to Las Vegas. Paula had played the slot machines and had won. I think winning is about the worst thing that can happen to a new gambler. It seems easy to win and they will chase that first win forever.

When I went to Las Vegas, I usually went shopping for diamonds at the pawn shops while everyone else went to the casinos. I tried to get Paula interested, but even diamonds wouldn't divert her.

You could see Paula change the minute we would get to Vegas or even talk about going. I mean, I watched her and saw her face change. She became obsessed with the slots. What no one knew was that Paula was gambling when she was home. She was buying "lottery" scratch-off cards.

Paula was able to get credit cards because of Cliff's income and she ran the cards up to the max. When it finally came out how addicted she was, she had run up about a hundred thousand dollars in debt and they were going to lose their house. Paula moved in with her mother in a trailer in Bullhead City, Arizona.

Cliff remained in the Lawndale, California area and he started calling me wanting to talk. I couldn't believe it. What was he up to? Was he hitting on me? I talked to Paula by phone and told her what I thought was going on and what he was up to. She said they were finished and that if I was interested to go for it. I assured her that I had no interest in Cliff.

The truth be told, I never liked Cliff. He was gruff and insulting to most people. I thought he loved Paula in some way, but it didn't seem like a passionate love. It seemed to me that he put her down to make himself look better. Reminds me of that diving pool when I was a kid.

Paula could tell a story about something, quite ordinary, that happened, but make it hilarious. Cliff often interrupted her to correct the record when she was telling one of her funny stories. I think he was jealous of the attention she received. No one really cared if the story was accurate or not, we just loved to listen to her way of telling it. One time, when he interrupted her, Paula took off her shoe and threw it right at his head. Wham! It whizzed right by his ear and hit the wall.

At any rate, I confronted him and told him that I knew he wasn't just coming around for the conversation and asked him what the deal was? He confessed that he was in love with me. He said he had always been in love with me. While I didn't like him much, I knew Paula really loved him. I didn't care what she said, I knew she wanted him back.

I didn't run Cliff off completely but decided to talk to him. I wanted to understand exactly who he was. Why was Paula so in love with him? I gave him a copy of my book, "Imagination and Failure." I thought it might help him find some insight as to why he was so mean-sounding all the time. Eventually, in talking with him, I finally got his background story. I could so identify with Cliff. It nearly broke my heart to hear about his childhood.

Cliff had been abandoned by his parents. He lived with his grandparents. He had been clubfooted and that made him different from other kids and he had suffered from bullying. When he was bad, as a child, his grandmother locked him in a closet. When I heard the story, my heart went out to him. I understood why he appeared to be such a gruff person. I had become mean and uncaring at one point in my life, but I had grown from that and moved on. Cliff had gotten stuck being the "bully." That was his defense mechanism. The real Cliff was lost in the cover. I guess Paula, with all her instinct, knew that somewhere inside that gruff exterior was just another little boy that hurt. But what could I do to help him?

I came up with an idea. I bought a small leather trunk and I took it to a florist. I ordered one hundred red roses and had them make a huge arrangement in the trunk. I wrote a poem for Cliff which was attached to the arrangement and I had it sent to his work. It looked magnificent. He was the head of a large department for a chemical company and I knew everyone in his office would see it when it was delivered. Here is the poem:

The Old Trunk

He was a poor little fellow,
Carrot topped, freckled and wee,
And his feet turned in at an angle,
Not like regular feet should be.

He sat on a trunk in the closet,
He was a lonely little guy,
Punished for childish mischief,
A tear slid down from his eye.

Why was he there in the closet,
Frightened, alone and sad?
Did Grandma and Grandpa not love him?
And where were his mom and dad?

Life is unkind to some children,
They have too much trouble to bear.
To their gentle hearts, it is painful,
When they think there's no one to care.

Alone was the boy in the closet.

On the trunk he sat and cried,
Till his gentle spirit was broken,
And there it withered and died.

His sobs were stifled by anger,
His tears were all wiped away,
And in that old trunk he put childhood.
And he left it there that day.

The boy went on to manhood,
The battered old trunk left behind,
But it seemed he was always searching,
For something he could not find.

Years are but fleeting moments,
And a half of a century passed,
Before the man would notice,
The dark shadow that he cast.

One day while searching around,
To see what he could find.
He stumbled across that old trunk,
In the closet of his mind.

It seemed somehow so familiar,
So he lifted up its old lid.
And there he found all the treasures,
With childhood he had hid.

Love, understanding, compassion.
In the trunk he had hidden his heart.
And there were all his old dreams,
In fullness, not fragment or part.

He searched the musty old corners,
And tucked way down and behind,
He found a small gentle soul,
In that trunk had been confined.

He took out all of those treasures,
And a tear slid down from his eye,
His heart was filled up with love,
And a dream was born from a sigh.

The trunk was now dark and empty,
But he couldn't just throw it away.
So he decided to fill it with memories,
That he came across day by day.

He put in a memory of Grandpa,
His Grandma and Mom and Dad,
And all of the others he loved,
Fond memories, not the sad.

It was still a chest of treasure,
But now of a different kind.

Filled with memories for keeping,
In the closet of his mind.

No longer a sad little fellow,
Carrot topped, freckled and wee,
But a man with the heart of a child,
And a gentle soul set free.

Cliff later told me the story of what happened when the arrangement was delivered. It took two delivery people to carry the arrangement. Walking in with the trunk full of 100 red roses, no one could imagine who they were for. All eyes were on that arrangement as they walked the length of the entire front office, all the way to the back where Cliff had his office. He stood at the door looking displeased at the interruption to his day. But, then the flowers were delivered to him. He was embarrassed and didn't know what to do. So, he had the arrangement put on his desk. Then he found the poem and read it. He said he sat and cried for half an hour. Eventually, he took handfuls of the roses and gave them to his workers, and thanked them for working for him. He gave them to the men as well as the women. As he gave out the roses, he just felt lighter and lighter. He said something changed in him that could never change back.

Paula moved back to our area and she and Cliff rented a house. They stayed together until they died many years later. He didn't interrupt Paula when she told a funny story and I never saw him bully anyone again. He was still somewhat gruff, but he was gruff with a smile and a twinkle in his eye. I like to think that I had something to do with that twinkle.

Above: Claudia with the "Chest of 100 Roses" for Cliff. Poem "The Old Trunk" is attached. March 1987. Claudia 39

Left: Cliff and BFF Paula happily back together again.

Chapter 35
A Rusty Motorcycle

Having survived the marriage and divorce from Ron and numerous other fiascos of 1986, I had a shirt made that said "Phuck 1986." Just my little protest. I was 39 years old and had no hope of ever having a successful relationship.

In the early part of 1987, I went to "Appraisal School." It was another learning thing I thought might be helpful for me in my real estate adventures.

Then, of course, I started dating someone else. His name was "Rusty" (RJC). Rusty rode a motorcycle and one day he was at the Alano club and I was in a bad mood and he said, "Hop on. I'll take you for a ride. It will help clear whatever is bothering you." That was the beginning. Why is it (nearly) always a guy with a motorcycle?

Rusty was about five years younger than me. Paula said I was a cougar! Whatever, at least he was probably safe. I knew he hadn't been dating much or at least no one from the club. He had been married and divorced, but I think he preferred to be married.

The AIDS epidemic was becoming headline news and it wasn't only in the gay community. There had been a few arrests of men, who had AIDS, who were purposely infecting women. It was a scary time and certainly a turn-off to think that you might have sex with someone today and be dead in two months. Rusty was a sweet young man and at least he was probably safe.

Then I found out that Rusty was behind on the payments for the house that he had inherited when his parents died. I'm a sucker for a sad story. I wound up loaning him some money to catch up on the payments. I also advised him to sell the house because it was too big for him and he wasn't able to pay for the mortgage, taxes, insurance, and upkeep. His house was not in good shape and I told him the more it fell apart, the less equity he would have. He was not the kind of guy that could do construction or repairs. Rusty was a printer by trade. With the equity he had at that time, I told him, he could put a large down payment on something he could afford and take the stress off himself.

I was between shows and told him, I would help him by painting and doing some remodeling to bring the value up. He could pay me back for the actual expenses when he sold the house. He didn't need to pay for my labor, I would donate it. He had no doors on his kitchen cabinets so I had my brother, Pat, who worked construction, pitch in and make him some cabinet doors. Pat made the doors out of cheap plywood which I wood "grained" to look like Oak. I wood-grained all the woodwork in the house to look like Oak also. I painted the walls and put in new wall-to-wall carpeting.

We had been dating about six months when Rusty decided we should get married. When he first said it, I almost laughed, but after thinking about it, I thought, "Why not?" Rusty was not a violent person, so I was safe there. I also thought he was so different than the "Man's Man" type that I usually went for that maybe it could work.

We were married on June 12, 1987. I moved in with Rusty and continued to remodel his house.

Sometime in about October, my niece, Merrie, asked to borrow my car. I don't remember why she needed it, but I said OK. I had a 1976

Cadillac Deville. I loved that car. It was BIG. At any rate, I loaned her the car and she blew the engine in it. I needed a new engine.

Rusty said he had a friend down the street that worked on cars and he could get me a deal. So, I agreed. We towed the car to the guy and I rented a car to get to work. I was working standby on a show called, "Prince of Darkness."

As it turned out, Rusty's "mechanic" friend was not very fast at fixing the car. Rusty was not the kind of man to go "lean" on the guy, about what the holdup was, so it was left for me to deal with. I had paid him upfront for a new engine, so I was in too much to get out.

About the third week, I asked Rusty if I could use his car, instead of putting out all the money that I was, for a rental car every week. He rode his bike to work so his car wasn't used. He looked at me like I had told him I killed his dog.

"Well, no." he said, "I've never loaned my car anyone!"

I was dumbfounded. I said, "Rusty, I'm not just anyone, I'm your wife!"

He looked blank.

"Rusty, I'm also the one who has lent you thousands of dollars to catch up payments on your mortgage and the same person who is fixing your house so you can sell it and be OK. And you can't lend me your car until mine is fixed?"

At some point, later, he decided I could use his car, but I have to say, my feelings were so hurt that the marriage had no chance of surviving. Rusty didn't live in a "you AND me" world, but rather in a "you OR me world." I was not the young, patient person I once was. He was just too thoughtless for me and the worst part was that he was too naïve to even understand what he had done.

I guess I have my fairytale ideas of what a marriage is supposed to be. I had never had a model of a successful marriage because my parents fought constantly, cheated on each other, and showed no stability. My idea of marriage was from TV shows like, "Dennis the Menace" where no matter what, the husband and wife were there for each other. They worked together for the common good. They certainly never said, "No, you can't use my car because I don't lend it to anyone."

It took months more before I got my car back, but the marriage was over. As soon as I could get his house sold and find him a viable place to buy, I would be gone. I had told him the marriage was over and not recoverable so we were only looking at places that he could handle by himself. I only asked that when he sold his house, that he give me back $5,000 of the nearly $10,000 I had put into his house. He agreed and I saw him through his sale and move.

I walked away feeling OK with it. I had helped him and not harmed him, which is more than I could say about how some of my ex-husbands had treated me. The fact that we are still friends today at least says something about it. Rusty, not long after our divorce, married a very nice woman and they remain married today.

Eighth husband Rusty (RJC)
May 12, 1987 to November 1, 1987

Claudia age 40, Rusty age 34
(I am 6 years older)

A Rusty Motorcycle

I had gone to work at Lorimar Studio. I was between movies so I was working out of the paint shop where ever they needed me. I was mostly running the "Spray Booth" where we painted anything that needed spray painting but also needed an enclosed shop; like cars, trucks, airplanes, etc.

The day, I met Tom. I had been working on a “Max Headroom” set. I was doing some marbleizing and Tom rode up on his bicycle. He introduced himself and said that he was the lead painter on a show called, “Matlock.” He said he needed someone who could do marbleizing and a guy on his crew had told him he should check me out because I was about the best in the industry. He sat and watched me for a bit and then asked, “Are you available to work this weekend?” I said, he would have to ask the boss in the paint shop if they had anything for me for the weekend and if not, I would be available.

The Lorimar boss said I was free, so I worked the weekend doing the marble. Then Tom wanted me to continue, during the week, doing more marble and some wood-graining. I told Tom that I didn’t want to burn a bridge by quitting Lorimar so he would have to see if they would loan me to his show. I was looking for Lorimar to give me my own show.

Tom went and talked to the Lorimar Studio paint boss and he had told Tom that they had planned offer me a full-time job running the "spray booth."

I was used to running my own shows and had no intention of taking that job. It didn’t pay as much as I was used to making and I wouldn’t be my own boss. I went and talked to the paint boss and explained that I wouldn’t be interested in the job and asked that they lay me off, so I could take the job Tom was offering. The boss agreed and I left Lorimar with goodwill.

I have to mention that Lorimar paint shop, at that time, was not generally popular with the few women who were in the industry. It was definitely a man's world and they had little respect for most women. One day one of the under-bosses stuck his head out of the paint shop door and yelled, "Hey cunt, get in here." Fortunately for him, he wasn't talking to me or I would have ripped off his head and stuck it up his ass. The poor girl he was yelling at came scurrying. She was an "apprentice" painter. I later tried to talk to her about letting anyone talk to her like that, but she was too meek and mild to stand up for herself.

Tom was a sober member of AA. As it happened, so were several members of the crew, so I felt right at home. During breaks and lunch, the topic usually turned to the AA program.

When I met Tom, he was about thirty pounds overweight, had long hair and a big, bushy mustache. He was over six feet tall. He wasn't what I considered attractive. I could tell that Tom was very smart and at some point, I asked him to take an IQ test. He eventually qualified for Mensa with a 141 which was in the 99th percentile. His IQ was only eight points below mine.

There is much more to the beginning of Tom and me, but that is best left for his autobiography. Suffice it to say that Tom and I married on August 18, 1988. I was his third wife, and he was my ninth husband!

Tom and I when we first met.
October 1987

Married ninth husband Tom (TRI)
Me and Tom's wedding picture 8-18-1988
Claudia 41 - Tom 36 (I am five years older than Tom)

Chapter 36
A High IQ Man

Being married to Tom was different than any marriage that I had been in before because of his high IQ. I had no idea what a difference it could make. I never had to back up and explain anything to him. He got it! Too bad we didn't get together many years ago, but then I guess we wouldn't have been the people we were when we did meet.

Tom was a "take charge" kind of guy. The first thing he took charge of was my alarm clock. I like to be responsible for myself. You can't get mad at someone else for letting you down if you don't allow them to be responsible for something that is important to you. Getting to work on time was important to me.

One day WE had overslept and so WE were in a hurry. We didn't have time to make coffee at home, so Tom said he would stop at a donut shop and get coffee on the way. I was used to having my coffee when I woke up. We stopped at a donut shop and Tom went in for the coffee. He brought the coffee and handed me a cup. The cup was "boiling" hot. I tried to open it just as he was taking off. His truck was a stick shift. The truck lurched, and the coffee scalded my hand, at which time I tried to throw the cup out the passenger window, but since the window was up, the coffee went all over me which only pissed me off further. Tom started yelling at me and I started to kick the windshield out of his truck. Lesson #1 Tom: "get your own alarm clock and don't mess with my coffee time in the morning."

There were a few things that had to be ironed out in the beginning. He was, definitely, a strong personality and had always been the smartest in a relationship. He had ruled the roost and did not seem to have much respect for women. He was used to telling women what to do and they, for the most part, just did it. That wasn't going to work with me, those days were long over.

When Tom had asked me to marry him, I had laughed and asked him if he was nuts. I related to him all my faults; at least the ones I was aware of like intractable stubbornness, independence, and the ability to explain, quite clearly, what I did not like. He was already acquainted with my temper. I told him I was a high-dollar lady and wasn't about to change. I told him, I would take him apart mentally and put him back together if I found any weird problems with his thinking. That was simply who I was, but I guess he thought I was kidding.

I found a mobile home in Dominguez Hills that was a "rent with an option" to buy. I thought that it would do for a start. It was about 26 miles from the Lorimar Studio where we were working. It took about 35 minutes to get to work but much longer coming home.

I talked to Tom about investing in real estate. Not wanting to would have been a deal-breaker to me. He had bought a house before but, really knew nothing about investing in real estate and, he had bought in what I thought was the wrong area. I could see he was, as most people are, very afraid of making a mistake. I suggested that he study real estate and he agreed and enrolled into Lumbleau Real Estate School.

It wasn't long before we decided that Dominguez Hills was too far from the studios and not the right area for us. About this time, Tony let me know he wanted to sell Rosita, so we made a deal with him and closed on December 29, 1988. We moved to Simi Valley.

Tom and I had a lot of fun together. In January of 1989, we entered a "Millionaire Cash Quiz," which was a game with Winston Cigarette Company. We both smoked Winston. You received an entry ticket in each pack of cigarettes and had to answer trivia questions to return the entry. We bought cases of cigarettes and won $1,000. It probably worked out that we got our cigarettes for free, but it was fun to have someone to play with.

I know it seems like a trivial thing, but I was so delighted to be married to a smart man. I never knew it would make such a difference in a relationship.

I had met Tom's parents and I thought his mom was a sweetheart. You would have thought she would be a bit leery of someone who had been married eight times before marrying her son. I'm sure she probably was, but she never showed it to me. She was just so accepting and non-judgmental. I tried to call her occasionally, to check in with her and update her as to what we were doing since her son seldom thought to do it.

I was on the phone with his Mom, "Faye," one day and we had talked for probably twenty minutes when Tom came in and informed me that I had been on the phone long enough and that I needed to hang up.

I asked his mom to hold on for a moment and told Tom, "I make the same money as you, Tom. I pay the bills the same as you. Don't ever tell me to get off the phone again. I will be on here as long as I want. You are not my daddy. Now shut up and go away!" His mom cheered.

He bristled a bit, but he went away. We talked about it in more detail later, and came to an "understanding." I had certainly changed from the person I had started out being.

Another incident happened in our swimming pool. Tom came up to me very fast and went to grab me. I was taken by surprise and hit him in the solar plexus. He was shocked, but I explained my background and that I reacted automatically. He was trying to be cute and loving, but my unconscious mind did not know that and didn't have time to analyze further. I had done that lesson and never assumed that someone was not going to make contact.

Tom had a bit of a temper also and while he was never violent, he sounded violent. He also had a habit of putting his finger in my face when he was trying to get his way.

One day we had a disagreement and Tom puffed up his chest and got within a few inches of me, poking his finger in my face trying to intimidate me. I told him to step back and get his finger out of my face. He continued his intimidation. I foot swept him and knocked him to the floor. On the floor, his six-foot-one height makes no difference. I scratched the hell out of his face. He did his best to just get away from me. The fight didn't last long.

Tom came out of it saying that I "didn't fight fair." I had to laugh. "Who the fuck makes the rules?" I asked. Then I informed him that if he ever got in my face like that again, I would do the same thing or worse because "I make my own rules!" I also told him that I knew he was bigger than me and could probably whip my ass just on size alone, but he should remember that while "you might get dinner, I'll be getting a sandwich!"

He had to go to work and explain how he got all those scratches on his face. We have never had any more problems like that and when we argue, he makes sure he is a safe distance away from me.

It didn't take Tom long to drop that extra weight he had been carrying, cut his hair and shave off the mustache. The reaction of his brothers and sisters was to speculate if he was doing drugs or if he had AIDS. So much for family support.

One of the things that I loved to do was fish and Tom loved it also. I took him to my favorite fishing holes in the Eastern Sierra's by Independence, California. It was a place I took my son to have some quality time and it was just a favorite spot. Whenever we were off work for a few days, you could usually find us there.

Other things we enjoyed were traveling and exploring. Of course, there was also the "Treasure Hunt," and Tom joined right in with that.

Tom had passed his real estate exam in October of 1989 and we decided he should go to work at a real estate office, so he joined the Coldwell Banker Real Estate office in Simi Valley. That's when Tom's jealousy started to show. He did not want me to go to work in the studios without him. He wanted me to stay home. He was afraid someone would steal me away from him. You have to be kidding me!

I had always wanted to stay home and take care of my kids, but my kids were grown, but I thought it might be fun, so I said OK.

I was off work for over a year and what I found out was that my identity was very wrapped up in my being a worker. I became depressed. I had to work on separating myself from my job. "I am not what I do to earn money." I was also not willing to give over my life to Tom because he was now supporting me. I no longer had "my own money" and he started to dictate what we spent money on. That wasn't going to work. "Again, no, you don't get to be my daddy!"

I did do several projects while I was off. One thing I did was crochet an afghan for each of my sisters, my brother, and my dad.

I also earned an award from the "National League of American Pen Women" for a short story I wrote called, "The Fish Pond."

Tom and I joined a "Square Dance" club that was lots of fun and that is where I met the woman who would become another "best friend" for many years. Marlene and her husband Gary were angels (helpers) in the square dance club and we quickly became friends. Looking back, I was really busy but it didn't seem like I was doing enough.

Our Rosita house was the center of family and at least twice a year we gave big parties and everyone came. No one was a stranger. Anyone who had company show up at the last minute were told to bring them along, no questions asked. We always had way too much food just to be sure any surprise guests were covered.

My kids were out on their own by now. Tami was about 24 and Andy was about 21. Unfortunately, they both were into drugs. The parent who had to work to support them had little influence on them while the father who didn't work, sponged off his parents, and did drugs had too much influence. Though I never counted on it, the kids sometimes showed up to our parties. Sometimes sober, but sometimes it was obvious to me that they were high. They also had a bit of "attitude". There was not a lot I could do about it. I had struggled with this for some time when I reaffirmed my conclusion that my children were NOT one of the things that I had control over. Instead of resisting, I needed to release them with love to the universe and just believe that they were safe. That is the hardest thing in the world to do, but it was the only chance there was for any of us to be happy.

My friend, Marlene, was opening a "square dance" apparel store and needed a sign for the front of the building. The store was named "Denim and Lace." I made a big sign with the background looking like (faux finish) denim fabric and edged in painted lace. Marlene loved it and I was happy that I could do something for her.

April 8, 1989, my sister married her fourth husband, Jerry. Sometimes we would go camping or fishing with them. Teri didn't like fishing, but she was willing to do it just so we had time together. Brother, Pat, was on his third or fourth marriage as well. And here I was on my ninth and I'm sure there was much speculation on how long it would last.

May 26, 1989, my Treasure Hunt ended with no one finding the horse. The money would be given to charity. I was saddened, not because of the money, but because of the wonderful adventures I had gone on. My area of interest had always been the Wildhorse area of Idaho. I had made many trips there with many different people.

One time I went there with a guy I was dating and there was a snow storm so I couldn't drive through. I called to hire a helicopter. I told the pilot I wanted to get up to the Wildhorse area and asked him if he could fly there. He said, "You do realize there is a blizzard up there, don't you?"

"Yes," I replied, "Can you fly in it?"

"Yes, unless we get into a whiteout!"

"What is a whiteout?" I asked.

"That's where it is white up, white down, white in, white out and you don't know where the hell you are."

"What do you do in that case?"

"You try to set down and hope it's on the ground!"

"OK, I'm game!"

I also told the pilot that I was carrying a fire arm. He said he didn't care as long as it wasn't to shoot the pilot. He was as much of an adventurer as I was.

So, we took off in the helicopter and were lucky enough that the blizzard cleared. We got to the area I wanted to investigate, but everything was covered with snow so he couldn't set down because you couldn't tell what was under the snow. "Can you hover?" I asked, "So I can jump out."

I'm sure the guy thought I was nuts, but he obliged me anyway. We found a spot that looked promising and I got out on the skid and jumped. I landed in a couple of feet of snow. It was not possible to find the markers I was looking for, so I crawled back onto the skid and my boyfriend gave me a hand to get back into the helicopter. It was a great experience.

I would be back and I hired that same helicopter many times.

One of the most fun trips was with my son Andy and my brother Pat, and his dog, a Doberman Pincer, and the guy I was dating. I rented two Dodge Ram vehicles and we packed in. We were miles from anything. Andy was about 16 years old and he was just at that age where "Treasure Hunting" is really fun and exciting.

We found one of the geological survey markers that I needed so we set up camp. We had packed enough food, but we would need water which we would get from a small pond a mile away. It was a great adventure.

Another time, I went again with my boyfriend and I hired the helicopter and a surveyor. The helicopter would fly the surveyor to a couple of different mountains so he could triangulate the exact coordinates that I had come up with. By now, the pilot and I were friends. We both carried weapons, but his was a little pellet gun. He gave my boyfriend his gun and said, "Here, just shoot the crazy bitch." We all laughed and then staged some pictures for good effect. There were a lot of grasshoppers at that time of year and he gave me his gun and said I had the sole right to shoot grasshoppers in the area. While we waited for the surveyor to do his thing, I went grasshopper hunting.

After I met Tom, he and I made several trips to the area. We dug many holes and came up with nothing. In some of the holes we dug, I left a time capsule. It had my business card and a bit about what we were doing. Someday, someone will dig up one of those time capsules and wonder at the crazy lady who was on a Treasure Hunt in the middle of nowhere. The treasure hunt was an awesome adventure and I have so many memories that I will forever "treasure."

After about a year of being off, I was antsy to get back to work. I recognized my depression and knew I had to go back to work to fix it. Tom was confident in real estate, had won many awards, but we decided it was time for him to go back to the studios as well. While the real estate business was fun for him and he certainly looked very handsome in his suits, we were not making enough money for our lifestyle without me working and he had learned what he needed to be an investor. Besides that, when I decided to go back to work, he was afraid someone would steal me away from him. Oh yeah, someone is out there just looking for someone who had been married nine times! I had to laugh.

My ex-husband, Tony, had gotten a show called, "Three Men and A Little Lady," and he wanted me to come in as his second. He said he would hire Tom as a painter on the crew, so we went to work on the show.

Whenever I hired workers on a show, I always requested that the union ask the painter if they had any problem taking orders from a woman. If they did, I didn't want to deal with them. Come with your big boy pants and we'll get along just fine. I usually didn't have many problems. I worked right alongside the men and never asked them to do anything that I wouldn't do myself. I could carry two five-gallon buckets of paint that weighed about fifty-five pounds each (110 pounds) and I only weighed 105 pounds. I was a skilled artist and it usually wasn't long before I earned the men's respect.

We needed workers on "Three Men and a Little Lady," and most people worth anything were already working. We had to put in a "cattle call" for any painter on the books. We had hired about eight painters for the day.

When I came on the stage, there was a group of new men. I went to the shop to get a cup of coffee. It was about fifteen minutes before we were to start work. Tony, Tom and I were sitting looking over the workers when I thought I recognized one of them as being RM (initials), the guy who I had originally interviewed with that wanted me to give him "head in the closet." I told Tom and Tony who I thought the man was. I kept staring at him. Was it him or wasn't it him? Finally, I got up and walked up to him to get a better look. It had been about fifteen years since I had seen him, but it was definitely him. I asked him, "Did the union tell you who you would be working for?"

He looked like a deer in the headlights. "Only that it would be a woman running the crew, he responded.

"You don't recognize me, do you?" I asked. It's been about fifteen years. As I was speaking, I was re-living that day fifteen years ago when I had been desperate for a job and this man was in between me and getting that job. I was no longer that desperate little girl.

I explained to him exactly who I was. "Now, pick up your toolbox and get the fuck off of my stage." I backed him right out the stage door.

When the door closed behind him I turned and saw that every man on that stage, about 70 of them, carpenters, grips, electricians, painters, and laborers were standing watching. "Isn't it about time you men were working?" I yelled. Everyone scrambled to get out of my way. That was the best crew I ever had. There were no questions asked, they simply did as told. They were all afraid of me and I knew it. Let them all be afraid of the crazy lady. The best part was that I had gotten my pound of flesh for the indignities he had put upon me so many years before.

July 4th, 1990, we gave a big party for my dad who was celebrating his 70th birthday. It was a fabulous party. My dad had been sober for quite a few years and his brothers and sisters had come from Arizona to celebrate with him. At some point, I looked around and thought about all the miracles that had taken place to get us all to this place in time. I was very proud of my dad. While he had never been a good father, he had, at least, always been present in my life and now he was a beloved member of our family.

For my dad's birthday (July 4) and for Teri's (August 13) birthday, we sent them on a trip to Ireland. I had been there in 1979, but they had never had the opportunity. I figured they would take care of each other. That's not exactly the way it went. We had rented them a car and made arrangements for them to stay at Bed & Breakfast places. The day after they got to Dublin, I got a call first from Teri yelling at me because dad was being an asshole and, she didn't like the way he was driving. She had gotten out of the car and he had driven off. I could only try to calm her down and find a way for her to get to the bed and breakfast place. He had the itinerary and would show up eventually. Teri was able to get to the B&B and found a lovely lady who owned the place that made Teri a cup of tea and was able to talk her down from the cliff.

Next, I got a call from Dad saying that Teri had gone ballistic and had gotten out of the car. He didn't know what to do. I told him to go on to the B&B. Eventually they got back together and worked it out, but it was tough being in the USA trying to arbitrate a fight going on in Ireland. Just goes to show you that, "no good deed goes un-punished."

I figured it was more Teri than Dad, because I had worked with him under a lot of pressure and he never lost his cool. Dad, just wasn't the type to lose it under pressure. Teri on the other hand had a history of "blowing up" when you least expected it.

At about this same time, Teri, had gotten me into doing some crafts and she wanted to go to the Simi Valley Craft Fair to sell our wares. I had agreed to do it, but when it came time for the fair in August, I was sick as a dog with bronchitis. Marlene had volunteered to help me by loading all the boxes, driving me there, and helping me set up.

When we got there, Teri seemed distant. She wasn't talking to me. I didn't know what was wrong. At one point after we had set up, Marlene went to look around the fair. Teri took this opportunity to confront me with, "This day was supposed to be a day for you and me, not you me and your friend Marlene. You need to tell her to leave!"

I was shocked. I told Teri that Marlene was not staying and had only come to help because I was so sick. That did not appease her. When Marlene returned, Teri walked right up to her and said, "This day is supposed to be for me and my sister, I think you should leave!"

I was so embarrassed, but Marlene calmly said, "It's no problem, Teri, I didn't intend on staying." Then she told me she would be back at 4:00 p.m. when the fair was over to pack me up and take me home. With that, she left.

Teri continued to stew. I had done some unforgivable thing and she was not letting it go. It wasn't long before she started cussing me out and was tearing down her tent that was holding our display. Everyone around us was watching and I wanted to hide under one of the tables. I tried to talk to her, but it just got worse. Finally, I was left with all my decorated baskets and crap thrown on the ground and she was gone.

This was before the day of the cell phone and I had to walk the length of a football field to get to a payphone to call Marlene. By the time she got there, I was sweating and running a fever. I could barely move.

Marlene assured me it would be ok and had me sit while she packed everything up and carted it all to her car. Marlene had a calming way about her and I thought she was amazing. Teri didn't speak to me for months.

BFF Marlene and I in 2005. She was the greatest friend.

Claudia's 4 1/2-pound rainbow trout caught at Diaz Lake
Claudia age 40

Chapter 37
A Moment in Time

Lots of fishing, lots of parties, and lots of work was the theme for the next several years.

My favorite "Coordinator," Mort, asked us to do a show called, "Doc Hollywood. We built a hospital set on stage in Hollywood.

At some point, our regular "standby painter" had to take some time off from the show, so Mort asked if I could step in to do the job. Mort said I needed to go and talk to the UPM (unit production manager) to make my deal for the money. His name was Robert Cohen. I went in to talk to him and he flipped through some book that supposedly had the pay schedule for each job on a show. Finally, he said, OK so we will pay you the "production painter" rate.

Let me explain what that is. That is the rate you would pay someone who was painting an office. It is sand, brush, and roll only. They are not allowed to do anything that a "decorator" or "sign-writer" does.

When he told me that they would pay me the lowest rate in the book, I just looked at him. "Well, get another fucking painter," I said and got up to leave. I acted angry, which I wasn't. I had just learned to do that as a way to back people off. Underneath it I was watching to see what reaction I would get. I always had to take a hard stand about what they paid me because if I didn't, I would never be respected.

He started spitting and sputtering. "Wa wa wait," he said. "What do you mean?"

"I mean, I'm not going to take that kind of cut in pay to do you a favor. My rate to do your sets is "Sign-writer supervisor. Pay that or get someone else!"

He decided he could pay what I asked. The deal was done. By the time I got back to the stage, Robert Cohen had called Mort on the phone and said, "Man, why didn't you warn me about that woman!" Mort laughed his ass off.

A few months after the show wrapped, Mort called to ask if we would like to go on "location," to Micanopy, Florida where they would be doing "reshoots," for the hospital exterior. We would both work on the sets and then when they started shooting, I would do the "standby." We would be lodged in Gainesville, Florida. Mort made it clear that he was taking us as a reward for all our hard work and because the painters who had originally done the Florida sets had gotten drunk and pissed the town off. He knew we would be able to get along with the town and maybe smooth things over a bit. He said to bring our fishing kit because we would have time for lots of fishing.

At the last minute, Mort had some family problems and couldn't go, so he got another coordinator to go in his stead.

A man named, Bobby, was Mort's substitute coordinator and he had different ideas. When we got to Florida, he expected us to "hang around" the paint shop even when we didn't have anything to do. We told him that Mort had told us different and if he wanted us, the Driver Captain knew where we were and they could send a truck for us at any time. Bobby wasn't happy, but we were.

The place where we fished was where a pond went under the highway and had a small pond on each side of the road. We were new to Florida and all the birds and bugs were something to behold. Tom had great fun throwing a "Rattlin-Rapala fishing lure at an alligator. He just kept tossing it right before the gator's nose. Then all of a sudden, the gator snapped his head and bit the bate. I laughed so hard watching Tom and the gator.

"What should I do?" He asked. I suggested cutting the line. Just then the gator spit out the lure. The hard-plastic lure had a hole clean through it. Tom has a great souvenir from our trip to Florida.

One day, the shoot was called off because of rain. We were doing outside shots and they couldn't shoot in the rain. It was only sprinkling, so we packed up and went to the fishing hole.

At the bridge where we fished was a little spit of land below and a gator was sitting there. We were watching him and he was watching us. All of a sudden lightning hit close by. Tom tried to grab me and throw me over the bridge. Since I learned Karate, that wasn't an easy task and fortunately, he quit before one of us got hurt.

"What the hell are you doing?" I yelled at him.

"I was trying to save you from the lightning. They say to get as low to the ground as possible."

"So, you thought I would be safer with the alligator?" I quipped. NOTE TO SELF: This man is an idiot, I don't care what his IQ is!

About 15 minutes later "Ball Lightning" hit on the telephone wire across the street. It was about three feet in diameter and rolled down the line and when it got to the pole, it exploded. I had never seen ball lightning before. It was amazing.

Another weekend, we hired a fishing guide named Buck Bray. He seemed to be the best in Florida and we really wanted to catch some bass while we were there. We chartered him for the day which usually ended about 3:00 p.m. but after he saw how we fished, he said he would stay out as long as we wanted. I guess that day was just not a good day for fishing because we never got a nibble and we used everything we had and everything Buck had. It just wasn't happening.

At some point, we pulled into a fish camp to get a soda and some snacks. In the "livewell" there was a huge bass. It looked to be over ten pounds. Buck said, "Claudia, just reach in there and pull that bass up where we can see it." So, I did. It wasn't that easy to catch even in the live well but eventually, I pulled it out and we took a picture of it.

"Now," he said, "You can legitimately say you caught a huge bass." Buck was a lot of fun.

On the way back to the hotel, we stopped at a "One-Hour Photo" developing store and got prints made. The next day at the shooting company, we showed everyone the picture of the fish I caught!

Claudia with big fish!

Buck Bray was a load of fun!

We explored the town of Micanopy and had lots of fun meeting the locals. The producers remarked that it seemed that everyone in Micanopy knew us and we had done a lot of goodwill for the shooting company. They even gave us special credits on the movie ahead of everyone but producers, directors, Production Designer, and Art Director. Usually, we come after everyone on the show if we got credit at all. We thanked our production designer, Larry Miller because we thought he had done it, but he said it was the producers who had done it because they were so grateful for us interacting with the town and setting things right.

We took a trip to "Cedar Key," with Bobby and had a great time until the weather, within about ten minutes, went from sunshine and a calm sea to a black sky and rolling whitecaps.

Onset, I got a picture of Michael J. Fox taking a picture of me taking a picture of Michael J. Fox. He was a lot of fun and I was saddened to later hear of his diagnosis of Parkinson's disease. I sincerely hope that "Stem Cell Therapy" will be in time to help him.

Florida was great fishing, but Tom and I decided we would never want to live there because it was muggy, buggy and we weren't that fond of the gators.

We got back to California in time to have a big "Baby Shower" for my sister, Nini, and a 50th wedding anniversary party for Tom's mom and dad.

I had planted a vegetable garden in the back corner of our yard and got a radish the size of a grapefruit out of it. I guess I have a green thumb. The truth was that we were going from one show to the next so fast that I didn't have time to mess with the garden so it just kept growing.

1992 brought us to do the movie, "Buffy the Vampire Slayer." Tom, and I traded off, on who would get the top credits for the show, but we still did the same jobs no matter who was on top. Tom's job was to get me: Men, material, and information. My job was to run the crew and do the art. On this show, it was my turn for top billing, so I was the "Lead Paint Foreman and Head Scenic Artist."

We had been trying to get my kids, my sister Teri and her husband, Jerry, my brother-in-law, and a few other people into the industry for some time. The trouble was that all the available painters in the local had to be working before you could bring in a permit. On this show, it just happened that the industry was, finally, down to permits. I talked to my Designer and told him what I wanted to do. He said as long as I got the work done, he was fine with whatever I did. We brought in five inexperienced painters, and, I got the "Carpenter Foreman" to hire my brother, Pat, as a carpenter. Now, I needed for them to get thirty days so that they could get into the union. Fortunately, times had changed since I had gotten into the union. Instead of working months to get each card level and then having to have three Journeymen sign for you, now all you had to do was get thirty days and you were in. I had three journeyman painters, five permits, and Tom and me. I had Paula's son, John, as one of the permits. It was like herding cats!

Somehow, I got the sets done, although I had to do a lot more work than I usually would, to make up for my permits. The three journeyman painters were there because they were longtime friends and they said if it came to a layoff, they would quit so that I could keep my permits. It worked great.

The only fly in the ointment was my kids, Tami and Andy. They weren't real keen on working "every day." We tried to explain how every day counted, but they just didn't understand. We were just babying them to get their thirty days. I told them that once they got their days in, they could take off for six months as far as I was concerned, but they had to work every day possible until they got the thirty days. The last week just met with resistance and some days, they were pretty useless.

We had the kids staying at our house because we didn't trust them to get to work unless they were with us. They had a real hard time waking up at 4:30 a.m. and it sometimes took a fight. They said they couldn't make it another day and we insisted that they could. One morning Andy got up late. He was in the kitchen and was going to make some eggs for his breakfast. "You don't have time for that," I said. "If you want breakfast, get up when your alarm goes off." Turning half asleep with the eggs in his hand, the eggs rolled off his hand and landed on the floor. Without missing a beat, Andy said, "I guess I'll just lay them there!" This shows what a great sense of humor he has, which is why, I guess, I never just wrung his neck.

We babied the hell out of the kids and they did all get their union cards. I was so relieved because I knew that each one of them had the ability to support them self in a high-paying job. I felt that I had gotten my job done at last. I had made an ignorant mistake in choosing who their father was, but at least I had given them the tools to overcome that mistake.

It was not only my kids that I had been worried about, but Teri and Jerry as well. Jerry was a brilliant sign-writer, but he had worked in his parent's sign shop and had never saved for retirement. All he would have is a small amount of Social Security when he and Teri retired; the same for my sister. I dreaded what might happen to them if they did not have a pension other than Social Security. In recent years they had lived in Bullhead City and were barely scraping by. Now, I no longer had to worry that my sister would have to do without.

My brother did not get his thirty days in as a carpenter. Where I had backed myself up by hiring people that were willing to quit, so that I could keep family, there was no such luck with the carpenters.

So far, I had gotten my dad into the union as well as my kids, my sister and her husband, my friend's son, my neighbor's son and at one point I had even given Mel a chance to get into the union. A chance which he blew because he was too lazy to show up and though he was a talented and intelligent man, he would just never amount to anything.

My dad had worked in the motion picture and TV industry until he retired at age 65 in 1985. He had eventually moved to Big Bear Lake with my brother, Pat, and his wife. He had enjoyed a good sober life, but in April of 1992, he came down with what they thought was bronchitis. He went to the hospital and my brother called me and Teri.

Tom drove me to the hospital in Riverside. By that time, they had found that he had lung cancer. He was now on a ventilator. This was a horribly confusing time. Teri, Pat, and I were faced with the dilemma of unplugging him or not. They were pushing us to make a quick decision and if not, they were going to ship him off to some other place.

Tom stepped in and called his brother who is an attorney. His brother, Larry, thankfully wrote a letter to the hospital that changed their mind on shipping him off. I will be ever grateful for Larry's intervening on our behalf. It gave us breathing room to think.

At one point the doctors told us that dad not only had "oat cell" (small cell) lung cancer in the Trachea where it splits off to each bronchial tube to the lung, and was inoperable, but it had metastasized to his brain and he had a tumor at the anterior of the brain. Teri, Pat, and I looked at each other and burst out laughing and said, "No, that's just his computer chip!"

Let me explain.

Throughout most of our childhood, when drunk, my dad would tell us stories of how he wasn't who we thought he was. He was not Jim Gilligan, but "Captain Cormorant," an alien, from a planet called, "Quintomosa," who took over my father's body by implanting a "chip" in the base of my father's brain. This was before the advent of the computer, and we had no idea of what this "chip" was, but that was how he had taken over my father's body. He said someday, when my father's body died, he would go back to his home planet. He was just here to do research.

This wasn't a one-time story that he told. It was such a part of him that for his birthday, one year, I bought him his own star named "Quintomosa." Of course, we laughed when the doctor told us he had a tumor at the base of his brain!

After a little research, we asked to talk to the oncologist in charge of his case. They had wanted to do chemotherapy. I asked the man point-blank, "If this was your parent, would you put him through this?" The doctor stared at us a minute and then said that he would love to do the chemo because it would be an "interesting" case, but truthfully, no he wouldn't want it done to his father because there was almost no chance of survival, and it would be brutal on him to do it.

The doctors said they could give dad some medicine that would wake him from his coma and we could let him make the decision. I thought that was a terrible idea, if he was in fact as hopeless as they said he was, it would only serve to terrorize him and I was pretty sure that he wouldn't want it done to him anyway.

Teri, Pat, and I had a private meeting. The one thing we knew dad would say was, "Do something, even if it's wrong!"

We decided to take him off the ventilator and let nature do what it would. Either he would survive or he wouldn't.

When it came time to take him off, my brother Pat chose to stay with him because dad had always told him that if you were going to do something, be a man and observe the consequences of your actions. I thought that was rich from a man who had brutalized us most of our lives, and I would have rather spared Pat that experience, but he insisted.

Teri and I went out of the room while the ventilator was removed. In a few minutes, we were admitted back in. Dad took one small breath and was gone. I held his hand for a moment. His hands were big and the knuckles were swollen with arthritis. This is the hand that had thrown the dictionary at me. Who backhanded me when I wasn't smart enough to suit him or at age eleven couldn't, quite understand the legal concept he was trying to explain. This is the hand that had held a gun to my head. The hand that had handed me naked pictures of himself. This is the hand that had done so many wrong things. And yet, it was the hand of the man who had walked on his hands so I could get money for a new "Hoppy Taw." It was the hand of the man who had cooked eggs for me when I was hungover. It was the hand of the man who I had partnered with for square dancing. But, most of all it was just the hand of my father. A man like many men in this world who got lost, for whatever reason, in the hell his own mind had created. A man who was as much a victim of his time on this earth as I was. He was a man who truly loved me and in that moment I knew it, and I forgave him for all his shortcomings. I kissed him on the forehead and walked away. "Goodbye Daddy."

I don't think I mourned him much because my relationship with him was complete. He hadn't been the best father, but I had been a good daughter. I had no regrets.

I thought how strange it is that I had such intimate knowledge of this man and yet, in some ways, I did not know him at all and in a few years, my children would barely remember him and my grandchildren would never know of him. For them, he would only be a name. Most of the information about him will die when those who knew him die as well. One life passes and the next one is born like ships passing in the night.

Dad and I on his 70th birthday 1990

My dad, James Emmett (Jim) Gilligan
He became known as the beloved grandpa to many grandchildren.

Dad on his 70 birthday 1990

Dad and his siblings after many years of estrangement, thanks to Paula, he was able to recover his relationship with them and become an important part of the family. Billy, Dorothea, Dad, Jack.

Dad's70th Birthday Party 1990
Back: Nini 36, Pat 41, Teri 45, Claudia 43
Cousin Mary Bishop is in bottom left corner
and Dad is in the center.

Chapter 38
Another Generation

Tom and I got a movie called "The Firm," through Paramount Studios. We had been recommended by a set decorator named, Casey, who we had done some pick-up shots with, for "Swing Kids." Apparently, we had impressed Casey enough that he put in a good word for us.

Tom went to make our deal with the "Vice President in Charge of Motion Pictures for Paramount Studios." The guy had a problem with Tom and me having the same last name. He didn't think it looked right. What a bunch of crap. If it was two brothers, they would have no problem. It was just a man's thing as far as I'm concerned.

I remember one time, years ago, when I was running a show on the Fox Studio lot. I don't remember the name of it, but I had set it up for a woman to do the "stand-by" on the show. The woman's name was Terry Minch. She was a ballsy lady and could do anything. She owned horses and could toss a bale of hay over a fence like it was balsa wood. She was an all-around good painter and I was confident that she could handle anything the stand-by might throw at her.

I got a call from the producer of the show who wanted to know if I thought this woman was qualified to do the stand-by job?

"Well," I responded, "She's the second-best stand-by painter I know."

There was a pregnant pause and then he asked, "Who's the first?"

"I am," I replied, "And I am running your sets! Any more questions?"

The next week, the same man called and apologized. He said he couldn't believe the job she did under very difficult circumstances, and thanked me for putting her in the position.

Unfortunately, about a year later, Terry was diagnosed with breast cancer. She was so depressed and shared with me that her boyfriend had told her that "if she had her tit cut off, he would break up with her." Terry, tired of the bullshit in the industry, and the abuse she put up with in her relationship as well, put a gun to her head and blew her brains out. What a fucked-up world is that?

Anyway, back to the story. Tom suggested that I could go by my maiden name, which I had gone by for years in the industry. Tom would be listed by his name and I would be listed as Claudia Gilligan.

We did the show on location in Memphis, Tennessee. Usually, on location, the studio will give each worker a hotel room. Because Tom and I were "together," they, at first, tried to give us one hotel room to share. Tom told them we would probably kill each other and talked them into getting us a two-bedroom apartment overlooking the Mississippi River, which included a full kitchen and maid service. This is what Tom excels at: negotiations and numbers. I would kind of "intimidate" my way through to get what I wanted, but Tom had more finesse.

When a show is just getting started, the painters usually lag behind the carpenters. They have to build something before we can paint it. Because of this, when we first got to Memphis, we had quite a bit of free time. We took the opportunity to see some sights. We went to Graceland, visited Beale Street, and anything that sounded interesting.

We had, some years back, invested in a piece of property on the "Little Red River," in Arkansas. We had bought it sight unseen when our good friends and neighbors bought the piece next to ours. Since it was only a short drive from Memphis, we took a trip, to our property, to check it out. It was a good investment.

When we had first taken the job, we were told that there would be a lot of "marbleizing," on the show, but not to worry, there were lots of "faux finish artists," in the Memphis area. That turned out to be erroneous!

When we went to hire people for the marble, we found that they were all "artists." I set up two-foot by two-foot pieces of Masonite that had been laid in with the background color. I demonstrated what I wanted and set them to work. It took most of them over thirty minutes to do one piece. I had 10,000 pieces of Verde Indio Green marble to do. I tried to get them to go faster, but they just couldn't. I was the only faux artist we could afford. Where they took 30 minutes for one board, I took less than 30 seconds. Yes, I'm that good.

The Production Designer was Richard Macdonald. He was a famous designer and a talented artist as well. Richard loved my work. When he saw the marble I did, he asked if I could do a "little" faux granite. I gave him a sample. The granite he wanted was an "Alaska Red Granite," and I remember him saying he wanted it dark with "pools of black." So, I gave him a sample. What started out to be a "little" bit of granite became a mile of granite.

At one point, he came and asked if I could do a 14 X 20 foot wall of granite? I flippantly said, "Sure, just have the carpenters lay it down." Before I knew it, the carpenters were tearing apart the set to lay down a large wall! The more I did, the more he wanted. I did so much granite on that show that my shoes looked like the granite. At the end of the show, I mounted my shoes on a one-foot square of the green marble and presented them to the Art Director. Unfortunately, Richard became very ill while working on "The Firm," and had to leave the show. The next year he would pass at the age of seventy-three. It was a privilege and a pleasure to have worked for him. Our Art Director, John Willett took over the show.

When we worked in Hollywood I always had my "second." That was a person who worked right alongside me when I had to do the painting myself. His job was to fetch whatever I needed. He didn't ask questions or suggest anything, he just did what I asked. Sometimes, I would get mad and throw my tools. That might happen when a pressure pot wasn't cleaned properly or a spray gun didn't work right. His job is to pick them up, see that they were fixed, and put them away. It takes a pretty special man to do that.

Since we weren't allowed to bring any journeymen painters from Hollywood, we would be working with, mostly, "house painters." I didn't have much hope of finding a good second in Memphis, but I did. The man's name was Victor and he was perfect. I could not have completed, all that we had to do, if it wasn't for him.

In contrast to Victor, there was one guy Tom hired because he was supposed to know how to run an "airless" paint sprayer. We had a load of doors to do and I wanted to spray them out with an airless. So, this big burly guy shows up and I start to show him what I wanted to be done. He put out his arm and pushed me aside saying, "here little lady, let me show YOU how it's done. Of course, I was burning.

The first door he sprayed was a running mess. Before he could screw up another door I grabbed the gun and backed him off. "If you want this job," I said, "You're going to have to start with the assumption that I might know a little more than you which is why I am the boss. I adjusted the gun and sprayed a door without a run. He was suitably impressed. I later told Tom to get rid of him. I didn't need or have time to deal with his, southern, male ego.

It was nice and warm in Memphis when we first got there, but a few weeks later it got downright cold. I remember I walked outside our apartment one morning and had to look down to see if I had forgotten to put on my jeans. My ass was freezing! Do I need to say, "I hate the cold?" Looking across the street, there were beads of ice draping the trees and telephone wires, like a string of fine diamonds shining in the sun. There had been an ice storm overnight. It was absolutely beautiful, but damn, it was cold!"

At one point we had trouble with the finish on the marble pieces. We were using lacquer to seal them, but there were fogged stripes on some of the boards. That was Tom's bailiwick. He called the paint company we were using and they replaced all the clear lacquer we were using. Still the same results. They sent new lacquer thinner. Nothing seemed to work.

Then one night, I woke out of a sound sleep and said, "It's the rebar, the rebar in the floor!" The next day proved I was right. There was a metered line on the boards that fogged. Because it had turned cold, the rebar, being metal, stayed cold longer than the concrete. That is just how my mind worked. Go to bed with a problem and wake up with an answer. By changing how we dried the boards the problem was solved.

We went home on hiatus for Christmas in time for the birth of Andy's first daughter and our first granddaughter, Shailyn, on December 30, 1992. She had a head full of dark brown hair just like Andy had when he was born.

Shailyn's mother, Cathy, had never been Andy's girlfriend. She was one of the kids that hung together and she had been in love with Andy since their teenage years. At some point when Josett, Andy's girlfriend for a couple of years, and Andy had been broken up for a night, Andy took the opportunity to sleep with Shailyn's mother only to go back with Josett the next day, if I remember right. One night was enough for Cathy to become pregnant.

Josett had a little boy from a previous relationship and her son, David, became our first grandchild. He was a sweet little boy and we were glad to have him in our family. At any rate, Andy had told Josett that he didn't want any kids when they first got together, but then when Shailyn was born, Josett said screw that and got pregnant with our next granddaughter, Chantel, who was born November 6, 1993. That made three for Andy.

We returned to the frozen south and worked a few more months in Memphis and then we went to Grand Cayman Island in the Caribbean. The difference in the temperatures was astounding. When we went to the airport it was in the 30s in Memphis. When we arrived at the airport, we took off our Down winter coats and asked our driver if he would see that they got into our luggage that would be sent home. When we arrived on Cayman Island, it was in the high 80s and I, almost, kissed the ground I was so delighted to be warm again.

Of course, the first thing we did was to get a sunburn. I found a t-shirt that went down to my ankles and wore that for a few days because I couldn't stand anything else on my tender skin.

On one of our days off the shooting company was shooting a scene where Tom Cruise is riding in a Limo with Gene Hackman, by the ocean. My Tom and I had been in town on that day and asked if we could be in the scene, so they told us to go stand by the sea wall on the other side of the street. If you look fast enough you can identify us because I am wearing that long t-shirt.

On Grand Cayman, we were given a two-bedroom condominium on

the beach that was beautiful. We were there for one month. Towards the end of the show, we had about a week that we wouldn't have anything to do. Tom went and talked to the producer and asked if it was alright that we take the week off and have our kids come to visit. Tom told him they didn't need to pay us. The producer was fine with our request. We could keep the condo, rental car, and our per diem. So, Tom made arrangements for Tami and Andy to come to Grand Cayman.

While the kids were there, we explored every inch of the island. Tami had burnt her arm and leg when a candle had caught fire in her bedroom before she came to the island, so she was hampered in some of the things she could do, but it was all fun.

One of the things we did was to "swim with the stingrays." It was funny to see that Andy was very hesitant to get off the boat to "play" with them. Our guide kept saying, "They are just like puppies!" We had so much fun and I was so happy I could share this with my kids.

We left Grand Cayman in time to celebrate Tom's 41st birthday at home in our Rosita house.

About this time, we had a problem with a "cat burglar." It really was a cat that kept sneaking into the house, through the "cat door" that we put in for our cats. He was coming in to eat our cat's food. We couldn't catch the cat, because he always raced out the cat door when we came in. This became a game for Tom. He wanted to catch that cat so bad.

One day we came home from work and there that cat was. Tom ran to the cat door and put the lock on it so the cat couldn't get out. Now, Tom had him trapped in the house. The cat was a huge, black, feral cat. It was all muscle and had to weigh nearly twenty pounds. The cat ran into my office bathroom which was very tiny. It had only a sink and toilet, and barely enough room in which to turn around. It was so small that instead of putting a big door on it, we put two, small, louvered closet doors that opened out.

Tom chased the cat into the tiny bathroom and then slammed the louvered doors shut. Next, Tom got a big bath towel.

"Come here Claudia," he said. "I'm going to go into the bathroom and wrap this towel around the cat. I need you to hold the doors shut while I get the cat. Don't open the doors for anything!"

"Uh, I'm not sure I like this idea," I said.

"Trust me," Tom said. So, like the dumb ass I am, I consented to do as asked.

Tom opened the door, switched on the light and I closed the doors and leaned against them. It was all silent for a moment and then there was a big yowl and the doors exploded and out came two hundred pounds of Tom, and a pissed-off cat. Tom was screaming, the cat was yowling and my skinny ass was thrown about fifteen feet across the room, clear to the doorway. I landed on my shoulder, breaking my clavicle! The cat ran over my back as he raced out of my office into another room.

Tom ran to me and started to help me up, but I was in so much pain, that I couldn't move until I could catch my breath. As he bent down to grab hold of me, I growled, "If you so much as touch me, I'm going to kill you!"

Tom, backed off and it took me a couple of minutes to get up. The cat had run down our hall into our big bathroom. Tom had changed his mind about trying to get the cat himself and decided to call the "Humane Society" for help. Unfortunately, this was on a Saturday evening and there was no answer at the Humane Society. Next, he called the police. The dispatcher, who took the call, told him they could do nothing and he would have to wait until Monday to call the Humane Society.

"I can't wait until Monday," Tom snarled, "The cat is in my main bathroom." Then he spat, "Never mind, I'll just shoot the cat." The dispatcher warned him that he couldn't do that, it was against the law. Tom hung up the phone.

Just as we were speculating what we could do, an animal handler came to the door with a snare pole. Apparently, the police did have someone they could call.

The guy came in and Tom showed him where the bathroom was. The guy went in and "shut the door." Deja vu, I thought. I can't see this ending well. I stood way back, in the kitchen for obvious reasons.

There was a yowl, a yell and then the door opened. The guy had the cat in the noose, but he didn't have control of him. The cat was too big and too strong. The cat ran up the wall, across the ceiling and back down the other wall. All the way down the hall, the guy fought the cat. Tom opened the front door and the man finally got the cat outside. It took a bit to get him into a cage on his truck, but eventually, off he went with the cat and we never saw either of them again.

After everything quieted down, I looked at Tom and said, "Don't ever say 'TRUST ME' again!"

In June of 1993, Tom and I decided to make the "grass island," that we called Gilligan's Island, in our back yard into a huge fish pond. It was about half the size of our swimming pool and certainly different than most people had ever seen. I always think big. I made a big rock waterfall out of AB foam to cover the filter system. The whole thing came out beautifully and became the showpiece of the yard with huge Koi fish and water lilies. We had our annual 4th of July party for dad, even though he had passed. Most of Tom's family and mine came to see our new feature.

The next few years flew by. Work, parties, and fishing were about what we did. It was a good life at last.

Les and Nova had always been a part of my life. They were like parents to me. A few days after Christmas, 1994, Les died of a heart attack. A neighbor, who helped him care for Nova, found him in his chair with a notice that his "Options" had gone down and there was a "call" on them. That just means that he was buying stock on "margin" (with borrowed money) and he didn't have enough money in to cover his stock purchases. At any rate, the neighbor called me.

Tom and I jumped in the car and drove to Lawndale. On the way, I used my new Motorola "cell phone" to call the police and coroner from the car. We arrived just after the authorities did. That was a heart-breaking scene. Nova was laying on the couch asleep and didn't know he had died. They had been married for forty-three years and were, truly, lovers. Les had cared for her since she had had the heart attack. Now it would be for Tom and me to care for her.

After they had taken Les' body out, I woke Nova and tried, as gently as I could, to explain that Les was gone. She was of course devastated. "What am I going to do?" She asked.

"You're going to come and live with me, of course," I said and hugged her.

We packed up Nova's things and moved her in with us at Rosita. We turned the den into her room. She seemed content to watch her TV and visit with me. I hired Tami to come in when we wanted to go somewhere. Nova and Tami got on just great. Nova had always thought of my kids as her grandkids. Nova had never had any children of her own. Les had a couple of daughters that didn't really like Nova. One of them was in prison for murdering her boyfriend.

I made arrangements for Les' body to be sent back to West Frankfort, Illinois. He had bought a plot for him and Nova some time ago and had directions for all the arrangements. I wasn't able to go with him because I needed to stay with Nova who was not strong enough to make the trip.

Tom put in grab bars in the shower for Nova while she and I sat at my dining room table and went through her photo albums. She would tell me the names of her family and point out old boyfriends she had before she met Les. "When I met Les, it was all over with," she said. "I knew I would spend the rest of my life with him," she reminisced.

Sadly, in February of 1995, just 45 days after Les passed, Nova also died from lung cancer that she had had for years. This time, I went with her to Illinois. Before they interred her with her beloved husband, I tucked a little baby blanket over her so she wouldn't be cold. Nova hated the cold as much as I did.

In 1995 we did the sets for a "Disney" attraction called, "Ellen's Energy Crisis." It stared Ellen DeGeneres, Alex Trebek, Jamie Lee Curtis and Bill Nye, the Science Guy. John DeCuir jr. was the Production Designer, who we had worked with before and I just always loved his creative talents. Among others, we built a very space aged, science lab set, and duplicated the set from "Jeopardy." Bill Nye was a bundle of energy and we all had to have our picture taken with him. In talking with Alex Trebek, he noticed the Mensa metal I wear, and we talked about Mensa people on Jeopardy. He said they didn't do very well and he didn't understand why, so I explained it to him. I said, "just because your mind works fast, it doesn't mean you know anything. Mensa doesn't give you the ability to pull answers from the ethers. If you haven't studied something, how could you ever know it?" The light went on for Alex. Tom and I had a good laugh.

In Florida, we went on the ride many times and never tired of it. It was a ride through Dinosaur land with very lifelike dinosaurs. It has since been replaced with something else, but at least, for a while we enjoyed it.

Claudia, age 48, with Bill Nye the Science Guy
On set of Ellen's Energy Crisis - a Disney Adventure for Epcot Park.

Chapter 39
Your Alligator Mouth

In 1996 my daughter Tami had her first baby. She had been trying to get pregnant for a long time so this was a very happy time. On St. Patrick's Day, March 17, 1996, my third granddaughter was born. Tami named her after me. Now we had Li'l Claudia and Big Claudia. I was still 5'2" and 105 pounds, but I was BIG Claudia now.

In June Tami, Andy, Teri, and Jerry went back to work with us on the movie, "The Beautician and the Beast." That was a very fun show with lots of interesting sets. In one set that was supposed to be an underground dungeon, we had four twelve-foot pillars. When the show was over, I asked the construction coordinator what they were going to do with the pillars. He said they were going to trash them, so I asked if I could have them. He said, "no problem," and we acquired about $10,000 worth of huge pillars. Tom thought I was nuts but I had a plan.

We remodeled the fishpond, putting in a bigger filter, a concrete waterfall, and a pergola style cover, over the filter, held up by my four 12-foot pillars. Right up front was a replica of Michelangelo's statue of David. It was authentic which meant it was nude so all the grandkids got to snicker at that. It came out beautiful and now it was truly a showpiece.

Tom and I had made it eight years which was longer than any other husband I had had. All was good most of the time, but some things started to get annoying. It's really hard to pinpoint when the problem started, but it seemed that Tom became almost resentful of my talents and started to kind of sabotage me at work. I don't know why and could only put it off to "Mans Ego."

He became a bit pushy about who was the "lead" on the credits. I was usually aced out. It wasn't too big a deal, but I knew that if he and I were ever to split up I needed to maintain my credentials as a lead painter. Otherwise, I would wind up working for someone else. A position I did not want to put myself in and a position I did not deserve. I had won my place as a lead scenic on shows and I was just not willing to give it up without a fight. The other part of that problem is that I finally had a good relationship. It comes down to choices, doesn't it?

Other than who was supposed to be lead painter, Tom would talk to the coordinator and tell him a set would be done at such and such time without consulting me, and then when it couldn't be done at that time, Tom would start getting antsy and try to run the crew, moving my men where I didn't want them. When you work with a crew of people, you learn what they are good at and what they are not good at.

Trying to get Tom out of my business without embarrassing him was very tricky and not always possible. People started calling us "the Bickersons." More and more I had to "stifle" my frustrations. I was under more and more stress and it just wasn't necessary.

1997 witnessed a ground-breaking event as Madeleine Albright became the first woman to hold the office of "Secretary of State for the United States of America." She was such a strong woman and really showed the world that women could hold their own right along-side men. I may not have agreed with all her politics, but I have to admire her stamina. Bill Clinton was president and was having an affair with "Monica Lewinski". He was also selling overnight stays in the "Lincoln

Bedroom" at the White House. He apparently made over five million dollars for the democratic party. Honest Abe might have frowned on that. It didn't seem to matter which party got into office, the American people got screwed somehow!

Meanwhile at home, it was more parties, fishing, holidays, and travel. Shailyn's mother, Cathy had finally found a guy and they had a baby boy named, Jaron. It would be hard to heap presents on Shailyn and leave the little boy out. I could imagine how it would make him feel because he would not understand that he wasn't our grandchild. I was afraid it would be damaging to him, so I decided that to keep her new baby from feeling left out, we would just kind of adopt him as our own. At least until he was old enough to understand. So, he became our fifth grandchild.

For my 50th birthday in 1997, we made it a double celebration because Li'l Claudia was turning one year old. It was a huge party for about 100 people. We had a band in the gazebo, A clown on the patio to do face painting and entertain the kids, a portrait artist to do comedy sketches of the adults and it was all catered.

The kids all went together and got me a family portrait with all the kids, grandkids, Tom, and me. It was just a great time to be me.

That year we were doing an outside job for Veronica Hamel. Among many other parts, she played the part of "Lily Munster," in the TV movie, "Here Come the Munsters."

Veronica hired us to paint the interior of her house in an "Italian style" with bright orange and yellows with cracks running down the walls. It was just a huge canvas to me. Veronica and I got along very well. She said she wanted to keep me which was very flattering. We had told her we had a trip to Italy planned for the next month and she gave me a book of all the costumes that the Italians wore during "Carnival." Veronica was a beautiful and delightful woman.

Tom and I took our trip to Italy. It was a most amazing adventure and I got to see Michelangelo's "original" Statue of David. We went to Vatican City, Sorrento, Florence, Naples, the Isle of Capri, and many other places. We went to the Coliseum, The Leaning Tower of Pisa, The Pitti Palace, and Boboli Gardens. And, of course, we went to The Trevy Fountain and threw our pennies in so that we would someday return. We walked in the footsteps of so many famous people in the world that I had read about in my "Stoddard's Lectures" when I was a child. When we went to the Vatican, I was amazed at the opulence. I was also a bit disgusted. I thought of all the starving people who gave their money for this "show of power." I had to let that thought go, and enjoy what I could.

The Vatican is so big, that you have to follow a line on the floor to get to what you want to see. My destination was the "Sistine Chapel" painted by several important artists, but the most famous was Michelangelo. We followed the yellow line through gallery after gallery of art. At first, we were stopping to truly admire the works of all the famous artists down through history, but at some point, you just hit sensory overload and we were running through galleries saying, "Oh, yeah, another famous painting, move on!"

When we finally got to the chapel, I was surprised at how small it was. I don't know why my mind thought it would be huge, but it was not. I was filming the ceiling when a guard came up and put his hand over the lens of my camera. “Arresto, arresto,” he yelled. Then he pointed to a sign that said "recording was not allowed." He motioned for us to follow him. Walking behind him, Tom reached over and took the camera. When we got to where the guard wanted us to stop, he took the camera and tried to find the footage, but could not. Tom had rewound the film to way before we came into the chapel. The guard shoved the camera back at me in disgust and signaled for us to leave. Thanks to Tom's fast thinking, I have great footage of the Sistine Chapel.

The other places I wanted to see were "Pompeii" and "The Blue Grotto" on the isle of Capri. We didn't get to see Pompeii because the ticket takers were on strike. We were advised to go and see Herculaneum instead. We did go there and it was great, but I wanted to see Pompeii!

We didn't get to see The Blue Grotto, either, because the sea was too high. In high seas or rough weather, you cannot get into the Blue Grotto because to get into it you have to lie back in a rowboat to go through the opening. In high or rough seas, the boat could be smashed against the rocks.

In Venice, we went to Piazza San Marco (St. Mark's Square) where for a few lira you can buy a bag of birdfeed and be attacked by a thousand pigeons, and as a thank you they will poop all over you. Fun!

Of course, we took a gondola ride through the canals of Venice where our "gondolier" sang to us as we cruised the antique alleys of the town. From a set painter's view, the aging of the buildings was remarkable and something to remember.

The days we were in Venice were "Carnival" days. People started coming in from all over Italy for the celebration. There was a long parade through the town of people gaily dressed in the ancient robes and the famous masks of Venetians of long ago. We had our faces painted to join in the fun. Thousands of people filled St. Mark's Square to watch a piñata travel down a wire from the topmost part of the clock tower.

One day, Tom went for a "walkabout" by himself. He likes to do that whenever we go someplace new. He would just walkabout to see what he could find that might interest me. This time he came back with some pears which he set out on the window sill to keep cool. The next morning, we ate those pears and they were the best pears I had ever tasted. The juice just ran out of them and they were soooo tender and sweet! We decided to go get some more.

Tom led us down some streets and when he got to where he thought he had bought the pears, the store was not there. In the streets of Venice, the buildings have small stores cut into the side of buildings with garage doors that lift when they are open and leave no trace when they are closed. There is no signage of what store is there; there is only a closed door. We never did find the store again but will always remember those delicious pears.

Sadly, we left Italy. There was so much we had seen, but so much more I wanted to see. Travel is such a treasured gift.

Fortunately, we were able to go back the next year and I finally got to see Pompeii and The Blue Grotto.

Pompeii is a small town with the surrounding walls measuring about two miles. However, if you are walking up and down every street. It then seems to be a very large town. The houses were amazing with tile floors and mural painted walls. It was easy to envision being in that town when it was vibrant and alive.

Going to the Blue Grotto we first took a large boat, then when we got close to the grotto, we climbed down a ladder and got into small rowboats. From there we were rowed to the cavern entrance where we had to lay back a bit so the boat would clear the entrance. Fortunately, the day we went, the sea was very calm and smooth. I was so excited as we approached the entrance. I had waited forty years to see this.

As we entered, the water became azure blue with diamond-like sparkles of silver, but once we got inside it was just a small cave with blue reflections. It wasn't that spectacular. The man who rowed our boat knew it wasn't much and tried to make the most of our experience. He rowed around the eighty by two-hundred-foot cave singing "Oh Solo Mio," with his rich tenor voice. I leaned into Tom and said, "Years of dreams and thousands of dollars and it looks like our swimming pool at night." It was just too funny. We both started laughing. I think it was more because we had worked in the motion picture industry for too many years. We had made much better sets than this one. It took a lot to impress us. Ah, Hollywood!

On January 5, 1998, Paula lost Cliff. He died of some strange infection that they couldn't cure. I had traveled to Bullhead City to be with her. There wasn't anything I could do but be there for her.

On March 14, 1998, my daughter gave birth to her second daughter, Brandi Mel-lene. Again, one life is passing and a new life is beginning.

In August Tami married the father of Brandi. I wasn't sure about the match but hoped for the best. Tami looked beautiful and so happy. I knew the dreams she had and could only hope that her dreams would come true.

We had the wedding in the back yard of our house. My children's father, Mel, had to be invited. He looked old and spent.

October of 1998, we took Tom's mom to Hawaii. She was in a wheelchair, but we made it to all the things that she wanted to see. She had a special picture taken with Don Ho. We went to a Luau and I got up on stage to do the hula. I loved hula.

We were hired for the TV remake of the movie "Psycho." That was a grueling show for me. Often, Tom's alligator mouth overloaded my bluebird ass.

We had about twenty-five painters including Tami and Andy and some days we had to add depending on the amount of work that had to get done. I remember one guy we hired had never worked in the studio before. I took him out in front of the motel set and set him up with an airless sprayer.

"What I want you to do," I said, "Is to paint the dirt as far as the eye can see. He thought I was kidding, but that's Hollywood.

As big as the show was, we were under a constant crunch for time. They were just asking impossible things of us. Of course, the push comes to me and where I needed Tom to step up and take the heat off of me, he just added to it.

Tom had a habit of coming in and "helping" on a set by painting out big runs of walls without them being fully prepped properly, leaving the rest for me. Which meant that I had to go back and "sweeten" the finish and do all the labor-intensive work. It made him look like Mr. Speedo and left me to look like the laggard. Tom only wanted it to look like we were getting things done. I tried to explain that when you just run big walls it makes it look like we are nearly done and then the coordinator and art directors decide they can heap a bunch more work on me. The art department starts making changes and adding detail. At the same time, the coordinator is up our ass to get out of the set. For me, it was a no-win.

I was proficient at computers at this point. At times, I had gone home at night and Photoshopped changes they wanted to do to the outside of the Psycho house or inside some set, so they could see the finished product without me spending innumerable man-hours painting the outside of a huge building or redoing a set. That alone saved them days and yet, they just added somewhere else. And Tom kept coming to me and yelling about we needed to speed up. What he should have been doing is to corral that art department so the pressure wasn't on me. I was never a slacker on the job and always turned out the work as fast as possible. Unfortunately, he was too afraid to confront them, but had no problem coming at me. I was just in a no-win situation. Boy, how Tom had changed.

Sometimes, when you have so many men working, several will finish a task at the same time. I will sometimes tell a painter to sit or stand "over there" until I can get to them for reassignment. It would only be a few minutes to assign someone else and then I would get back to the other painter. If Tom came into the set and found someone standing, he would put them to doing something that wasn't what I wanted them to do. Then when I went to find that painter, I would have to go hunt them down. I would accuse them of not doing what I had asked and they would become defensive because "they couldn't take orders from two people at once." This undermined me as the crew leader and again, it just looked bad. If I said anything to Tom, he would argue with me and that was even worse.

One day our art director, Carlos, came onto a set on which I was working. I was helping with some wallpapering because it was a hand-painted wallpaper ($125 per roll) and I could not afford to have anyone screw it up. I had a pair of scissors in my hand when he came in with his clipboard. I had just about had it with Tom pushing for us to be out of a set that still had a mammoth amount of detail work to be done and the art department asking for more. I looked at Carlos and knew he was bringing more changes. I clicked the scissors a couple of times and said, "One more change and I'm going to cut your dick off!"

Poor Carlos stopped for a moment, turn around, and left the set. He at least understood. Later, Carlos told me how much he admired me.

At one point, I went to the paint shop to try to talk to Tom in private about the problem. I explained that it was his job to advise these art directors when they were going over budget and get me some breathing room. He just didn't get it and tried to defend himself. I was done and when I went out I threw the lock on the hasp and locked Tom in the paint shop. "If you can't do your job," I said, "At least, stay out of my way!" I got on my "two-way radio," and told the crew that if anyone let him out, I would fire them. No one on that crew would dare let him out except my daughter, Tami, who "felt sorry for dad," and unlocked the door. Grrrrrrr she knew I wouldn't fire her.

June of 1999 found us in Hawaii again. We took a great vacation on the island of Maui with Tom's sister and her husband. Tom and I started speculating about retiring to Hawaii. We both loved the weather and everything else about it. We just weren't sure which island we would choose.

Coming back from Hawaii, we found a good little investment house on Brandon Avenue in Simi Valley. It was a small four-bedroom two-bath home. We rented it to Andy and his family for a very reasonable rent and they lived in it for quite a few years.

In January of 2000, my stepmother, Dodie died. I don't know if there was a service for her, I only know that I didn't go to one. I loved Dodie, but I did not agree with her philosophy of life, that we were supposed to suffer here on earth to "earn" our reward in heaven. Nonetheless, she was a good woman who did the best she could with the crap she was taught. I felt bad for my sister, Nini, because Dodie was about the only person she had. To my knowledge, Nini had never reestablished a relationship with our father even after he got sober and had been sober for many years.

My nose had been broken since my first marriage. I had a deviated septum and often had sinus infections because of it. In 2000 I decided to have my nose corrected. I had no intention of having anything else done to my nose until my sister, Teri, said I should have the end of my nose changed. It was a bit bulbous! I had never thought anything of the shape of my nose until she said something, but after looking at it, I decided to have that done while I was having the deviated septum and the break fixed.

The year 2000 was the year when all the computers were supposed to go down because the onboard clocks could not go beyond 1999. There were all kinds of speculation as to what would happen at that stroke of midnight. There were many medical machines that had computer chips in them. Because of this, I scheduled the operation for after January first.

The operation was successful and I could breathe out of both sides of my nose for the first time since I was 16 years old. I had no idea the difference it would make or I would have had it done a lot sooner.

Because of the operation, I decided it would be a good time to stop smoking. My brain had been constantly reminding me that I had lost my dad to lung cancer. Most other aspects of my life were what I considered healthy so there were just no more excuses. I was fortunate in that by the time I got the bandages off my nose, the urge to smoke had gone away and has never returned. My only regret is that I smoked for all those years and so, of course, both of my kids smoked. I cringe thinking about those two little kids being in confined spaces filled with smoke as they grew up. Of course, that was how I was raised as well. Fortunately, none of our grandkids smoke, but I've spent a good amount of time talking about the evils of smoking.

Tom and I landed a show called, "Manchester Prep," which came out as "Cruel Intentions 2." It was another tough show. At one point we had a huge "Interior of the School" set that our Production Designer, Cameron Birnie, wanted to be all wood grain. We also had a coordinator that played games with the money, taking money off one set to put on another. He was, I think, trying to cover the number of carpenters he had and did not care about the paint department. It had nothing to do with the amount of work on a set.

He came to Tom and told him we had to be out of the set by the end of the day because there was no more money left for the set. This set was a huge staircase and hall with a dado. We had just painted the "lay-in" color for the wood graining. The coordinator said that was good enough. It would not be good enough for the Production Designer!

As it happened, the Production Designer was someone we had worked for several times before and we didn't want to disappoint him. It might mean the difference in rather he hired us again. I think the coordinator knew that the onus would fall on Tom and me rather than him. I was determined that we would get that set grained by the end of the day.

The problem with wood-graining a set is that you have to match people's abilities. Some people were good at graining and some aren't. Wood graining is not just a skill; it is an art. It takes years to learn to do it properly and some people will never be able to learn it. When I teach graining to other people I tell them not to let their brains tell them what to do. Just let it come naturally. I try to get them to whistle so that they can't think. Many painters wood graining looks cartoonish and fake. I certainly didn't have time to go back in and redo someone's crap, so I decided that most of the "wood growth" graining, I would have to do myself. No brag, I was just the best and the fastest.

I pulled painters from other sets and divided them into teams. One team would apply the graining material; it was just a thin glaze that was transparent. The next team would "flog" the glaze. To do that you use a brush that has bristles about six inches long and you hit the glaze removing most of it and just leaving the small grain marks in the wood. It doesn't take an artistic eye, it just takes muscle. Those brushes get loaded with paint and need to be cleaned and dried frequently so another team would clean and dry the brushes. My job was last and was to put in the growth. That is the bigger swirl marks in the grain. The job of my second was to keep the teams moving. The timing was everything.

I was fortunate to have a great team of painters who were willing to move at that pace. Many painters in our union would have walked out and refused to do it. We made it a game and called it "ants on a donut." We laughed and yelled at each other to keep moving. A set like this would usually take about three - eleven and a half hour days to grain with an eight-man crew. We did it in six hours with a crew of nine. About halfway through people from around the stage and offices were gathering to watch. No one had ever seen anything like it. When we finished, we were all exhausted, but exhilarated. We dried it with fans and put a finish seal coat on it.

That would be about the last show that Tom and I did together. I had just had enough. I wanted to strike out on my own. In recent years, he had edged me out as the lead on shows and was throwing me under the bus to make himself feel important or because he was just afraid. The reason didn't matter to me. It was making both of us look bad. I finally told him, I wasn't working with him anymore.

While Nova was still with us, we got a call to do a show named, "The Truth About Cats and Dogs." The Production Designer preferred women painters and I had worked with the Art Director before. They wanted me as the lead painter. Because of Nova, I could not do the show and Tom wound up doing it. I got some satisfaction from the fact that the first show Tom did by himself, he got fired.

In May of 2000, our swimming pool was getting to look a bit shabby.

Teri, Jerry, and I had painted dolphins in the bottom of it several years back, but time was fading them. The pool needed painting. I decided that it should look like the bottom of the ocean. Then I started adding. I wound up making a complete underwater world out of the entire pool. I painted a cave entrance where dolphins emerged. A mermaid sat on a rock reading "Moby Dick" to baby whales, sharks, sea lions, and others while their mothers stood guard over them. The pool light was transformed into the light of a diver who was seen in silhouette. The whole pool was filled with stingrays, conch, turtles, and every fish imaginable. Then, I got the idea to make "dive cards" for the grandkids so I painted in "Cartoon and Pokemon characters: Tweety, Roadrunner, Sylvester the Cat, Bugs Bunny, Garfield. They were all there. There were about forty cartoon characters in all and then there were cards for all kinds of fish.

Tom called our local newspaper and invited them to come and take a look at the mural I was painting. They put it on the front page of The Simi Valley edition of The Daily News complete with pictures, and on the third page of the LA Daily News covering a circulation of about two million readers.

Our neighbors, family, and friends were amazed and asked if taking on a project of that size scared me. I never thought about it. I've never thought about "if" I could do something, I just start and go until I'm finished. I may fail several times, but that is just part of the "doing it" process. It never occurs to me that something was difficult or couldn't be done. I think that if I stopped to think about some of the things I have done in my life, I might be terrified and paralyzed. Perhaps that is what keeps some people from doing amazing things; they just think themselves out of it.

Claudia and Tom at the Trevy Fountain in Rome, Italy 1998
Back in the day, before furs went out of fashion.
Claudia age 51

Tom and I with brother, Pat, in Hawaii 2001
Tom, Claudia, Pat and Hawaiian Girl
Claudia 53

Ventura County Star

HOME & LIVING

SUNDAY, MARCH 10, 2002

UNER THE SEA: The custom-painted pool offers hours of visual and physical enjoyment. A variety of sea creatures, both mythical and real, can be found beneath the sparkling water.

Destination: the back yard

Simi Valley home offers a little flavor of the Caribbean and Europe just outside the door.

By Amy Stroba,
Special Sections writer

"When you're an artist you have to create," says Claudia Gilligan-Ivanjack, a Simi Valley resident and artists.

One of her many canvases, so to speak, is the back yard of the three-bedroom home she shares with her husband Tom Ivanjack in Simi Valley.

It features a custom-painted pool complete with sea creatures and hidden cartoon characters, two gazebos and fountains with cascading waterfalls.

The Ivanjacks have lived in the home since 1983, creating a backyard destination that is a little bit Caribbean and a little bit Europe.

A few years ago while swimming with the stingrays in the Cayman Islands, she was

Please see **BACK YARD** *on* **H22**

Claudia Ivanjack, who works as a movie set painter, puts the finishing touches on the mural in her swimming pool.

At left is Claudia Gilligan-Ivanjack's version of one of her favorite spots in Rome — the Trevi Fountain.

Newspaper article of the mural I did in our pool
Also has a picture of our fishpond with pillars from the movie "Beautician and the Beast."

SUNKEN TREASURE

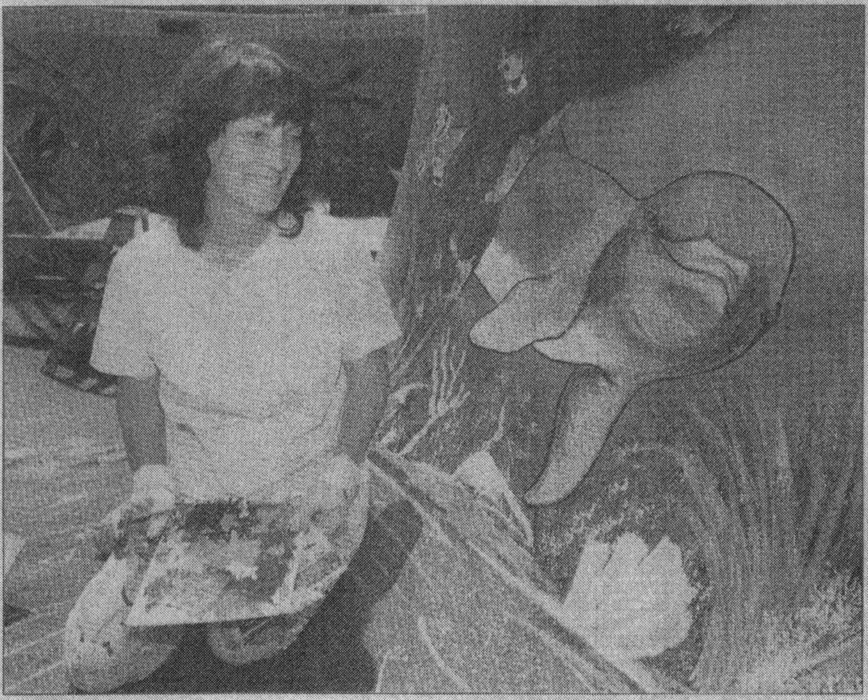

Tina Burch/Staff Photographer

Claudia Ivanjack, who works as a movie set painter, puts the finishing touches on the mural in her swimming pool.

Simi couple creates underwater mural

By Joseph Giordono
Staff Writer

SIMI VALLEY

If you know any of Tom and Claudia Ivanjack's six grandchildren, do not show them this article until this weekend. You wouldn't want to ruin the surprise.

Combining their love for the ocean and their talents as movie set painters, the Simi Valley couple is repainting the bottom of their swimming pool with a sprawling underwater mural — complete with a reef, whales, innumerable fish, sunken treasure and, of course, a mermaid.

And they are looking forward to the reactions of their grandkids when the painting is complete and the surprise is revealed.

"The pool is so big that it has been quite a challenge, but I cannot wait to see

See POOL / Page 4

Claudia age 52

Chapter 40
911 Attack and More

Having parted from Tom, as far as work went, I had landed a TV show called, "That's Life" (2000-2002), with Heather Dubrow, Ellen Burstyn, and Paul Sorvino. We were on our second year. I had my son working with me and life was good again. At home, of course, Tom and I were getting along much better because I didn't have to come home emotionally exhausted and pissed at him every night. My show was doing well and I was content.

In June of 2001, Tom and I took my brother, Pat, to Hawaii with us. It was kind of a birthday / Christmas / I must have missed something gift. On the island of Oahu, we went to all the usual tourist sites and we all had great fun.

September 11, 2001, I was sitting in my paint shop for "That's Life," catching up on some of my set accounting. I had a small TV on my desk and had it tuned to the news. At about nine o'clock, just as Andy walked into the shop, I saw what looked like a little airplane hit a building. "Look at this Andy, a plane flew right through a building," I said,

Andy took a look as it was replayed. "That's no little plane mom," Andy said. "That's a jumbo jet and we're under attack!" He was right!

We kept watching. Pretty soon I looked around and most of the workers and actors on the show were standing in my shop watching the TV. I must have had about the only TV in the area. I can tell you that not that much work got done that day. Everyone was watching the TV.

Shooting continued, but between shots, people came back to my shop to see what was happening. There had never been this kind of attack on the United States and we were all truly in shock.

I, like many artists, just had to do something. I did a large painting of New York with the smoke billowing past the Statue of Liberty. It also featured a large bald eagle flying across it. Coming from the eagle's eye is a tear with the reflection of the twin towers in it. The eagle holds a ribbon with the date on one end and, "We Will Never Forget," on the other. The painting was placed in one of the New York City Fire Departments that lost a lot of men in the horrendous event.

The beginning of 2002 was very sad for me. My friend of 28 years, Paula, died. I was able to spend a short time with her before she passed. She sat and read her Bible. It seemed to bring her comfort and she seemed to be just waiting. I think she was tired of life without Cliff.

I remember once when she came to visit me at the Rosita house. Several times I sent Tom to the store for one thing or another. About the fourth time I sent him, Paula scolded me. "You shouldn't do that, Claudia, men don't like to run to the store all the time."

I laughed. "Well, this one does," I replied. I told her to just watch. I stopped asking him to go to the store and yet, now and then, Tom would say he was going to the store for something and asked if I needed anything. I mean he would go four or five times a day. Paula finally got it. The next thing I knew she was sending him to the store for her. "Get me some oranges, Tom," she would say. I laughed and gave her a look. "Don't look at me like that," she said, "You know he loves it!"

When Paula and I had met, she said that she thought God had sent me to her as a comfort because she had recently lost her beloved brother. Paula was as much a sister as I could ever have. I cherish the time we spent together and will always hold her close to my heart. I know that if there are angles, Paula is one and she is watching out for me.

I had always wished my sister, Teri, and I were as close as Paula and I or Marlene and I were, but for some reason it seemed that Teri always got mad at me for some reason and I was always walking on egg shells. As soon as I forgot to be wary of her, she would explode about something that just took me by surprise. There was something about her explosions that I could just never understand. A small thing was so big to her and there was no appeasing her once the deed was done. It would usually take months before she would speak to me again. I, of course, always forgave her because I knew she was as damaged as I had been.

In the middle of 2003, we decided we needed to look for more investment property. I called our real estate agent and asked him to find listings and we would go view a few houses. We both found what we thought was a good investment, so we bought them both.

The one Tom found was on El Lado Drive with two houses on a lot that was being foreclosed on. It was kind of a run-down place, but he quickly cleaned it up and put on a new roof. We rented it to Tami and her family.

The house I found was a 3700 square foot, two-story house right out of the 1960s, but had been added onto in the 1980s. Tom scoffed at me when I said I wanted to buy it, but he went along anyway. I planned to completely remodel the house and that was what I did. I hired some of my carpenters from the studios and we treated it like a set, tearing it apart and building it new. When finished it was modern and beautiful. It had faux marble pillars and fireplace, and I did a trompe l'oeil on the ceiling with beams and sky. It was so beautiful that we decided to move into it. So, we put our beloved Rosita house up for sale and moved to Hewitt Place. The

Rosita house had so many great memories and it was sad to see it go, but life moves on.

Claudia, "Alias" Designer, Scott Chambliss and Tom at the Emmy Awards 2003. Claudia age 55

Chapter 41
All New Things

I took a course in Wilton Cake Decorating and also became a "Certified Law of Attraction Practitioner". I always had to be studying something.

I had read books such as Robert Collier's "The Secret of the Ages," dealing with the law of attraction. Which basically states that; Whatever you hold in your mind, be it belief or fear, you will attract like matter into your life.

I first came across this in books written by Robert Collier (1885 - 1950) back in the 1980s. I had tried to apply his principles. It seemed like life got in the way but I've never stopped studying the philosophy.

When we moved into the Hewitt house I pared my library down by getting rid of about two thousand books. I still had at least that many that I just couldn't part with. My books had always been a joke to my family. In my younger years, my brother, Pat, would groan every time he helped me move. "Anything but these damn books," he would say. The first time Tom and I went to a bookstore I came out with about $200 worth of books. He looked at me a bit funny, but I had warned him. Tom likes to read as much as I do. But he prefers to find his at garage sales at a much better price.

In 2003 at the age of 56, I decided to get an eyelid lift and have my face lasered. The troubles of the years were beginning to take a toll on me. When you work in Hollywood, you don't want to look "expired." The young people get the jobs whether it is for construction or acting.

That year we were invited to the Emmys. The show on which we were working, "Alias," was up for nomination for set design and we were all hopeful that it would win an award. I had worked a bit on the show, but not as Tom's second. I would only work, occasionally, on a crew; you can go yell at someone else. Scott Chambliss was the Production Designer and he invited us to the gala event. Since Tom and I each received an invitation, my son, Andy and his wife went along with us as our "plus ones." It was great fun walking the "red carpet." Tom and Andy looked so handsome in their tuxedos. Unfortunately, we didn't win that year, but we have great memories.

One of the sets on Alias required a 10 by 75-foot wall to be solid wood grained. That is not an easy trick and I think only a master grainer could do it and have it look good. I was the one to do the graining. I had one person put the glaze on, another flog it for the small grain, one to clean brushes as they got full and I ran up and down a ladder to put in the growth, before it all dried out. This time they sent in a cameraman to film the action. I could do things that very few in the industry could do and I could do it faster. Not brag, just fact. They said that the clip of my work would be on one of the season's disks, but I never looked to see if it made it.

Cell phones were becoming mainstream and we had traded in our old walkie-talkies for the latest model.

We had our annual Christmas party and had about 100 people in the Hewitt house. I just love big parties.

Occasionally I would be commissioned to do a painting for people in and around the studios. I don't know how they heard about me, but they did. Usually, I charge between $2000 and $4000 for a large painting. Tom thinks I charge outrageously, but that isn't a function of my worth, it is about his frugality.

I had a bit of time and a big empty spot on my front room wall so I decided to do a painting for myself for a change. I painted a 5' x 6' tiger that looked like stained glass. It came out to be a piece that everyone wanted. Everyone was amazed that its eyes followed you wherever you viewed the painting from. It of course became the conversation piece for the Hewitt house.

In October Tom's mother passed away. Of all my mothers-in-law, Faye was my favorite. We visited often by phone or in-person and I just always enjoyed her "realness." She just called them as she saw them. At one point she told Tom that if he and I were to divorce, she would keep me and let him go. Faye died at age 84. She is certainly worth mentioning in my story because she was always so loving toward me.

My daughter, Tami, became pregnant with her third child. She had divorced her second husband because he was heavy into drugs. Tami had been prescribed drugs because of a back problem and had become addicted. Because of the pregnancy, she had given up all drugs.

Tami had a new boyfriend named, David, and they were very excited to have a new baby. Following in her mother's footsteps, her ex-husband would not go away. Where ever she moved, he was close by.

May 1, 2004, we took my sister, Teri, and her husband Jerry to Hawaii for two weeks as a birthday present. We had finally decided that we wanted to retire to the island of Oahu. We had six weeks to scour the island and determine which area we wanted to live in.

We had a blast showing Teri and Jerry all the great places Hawaii had to offer. We saw and did everything you could do on the island in two weeks. Then Teri and Jerry went home and our hunt began.

We finally found a house in a place called Ko Olina Resort along the Waianae Mountains. It had miles of white sand beaches and four beautiful alcoves for swimming. We found a beautiful three-bedroom place with a room over the garage which would be my art studio. It was perfect, but when we went to sign the papers, they would not sell on the contingency of selling our properties in California. We had to choose one that was the same style house but did not have the art studio. That was disappointing, but at least we would have our foot in the door. We could look for better later.

We decided to fly out early so we could go to Florida to visit Tom's brother, Dennis, and his wife, Marsha, in a retirement community called, "The Villages." Dennis had been on us to come and see his place for some time. June 21st, we landed in Florida.

Even though we had said we would never live in Florida, we were very impressed with The Villages. It seemed to have everything. We decided to investigate buying a house there. It would be a rental house until we retired between five to eight years away. In selling a property in California without paying high capital gains taxes, we would have to find a like piece of property, so, we were looking for a house of about four hundred fifty thousand dollars. At that time, most of the houses were priced at about two hundred fifty thousand. We tried to get The Villages to sell us two houses, but they would not do it. They reasoned that if they sold houses to investors, they would buy up blocks of houses isolating the few residents that lived there. The alternative to the smaller houses was to buy something in the million-dollar range. We just wanted the happy medium but it didn't look like there were any.

Then, Marsha's son went on the internet and located a house in our price range. It was the original home of the creator of The Villages. We went to look at it and we fell in love. The property was on a 1.07-acre lot and the house was four bedrooms, 2.5 baths, and was about 3433 sq. foot on one level. It had twelve huge oak trees. It also had a huge, screen-caged pool and a pool house for parties and entertaining. It was our dream house.

For some reason, the stars aligned and we knew we were supposed to buy that piece of property. If we had gotten the original property I wanted in Hawaii I doubt that we would have changed our mind. But change our minds we did. We called Hawaii and closed that escrow and bought the house in The Villages. We would rent it out until we could move there.

Having our offer for the Hickory Head Hammock house (HHH) accepted, we jumped on a plane and headed home to California to see our new grandson, Wyatt Connor. We had been in Hawaii when Wyatt was born and he was about one month old by the time we returned.

He was adorable. Holding that precious baby, I could only think, "Oh sweet baby, what will your story be?" A new life holds so much promise. Three weeks and three days later Wyatt died of SIDS (sudden infant death). SIDS is where there is nothing wrong with a baby, they just don't survive.

Tami's husband had just gone back to work, as a machinist, after being off on "Paternity Leave." Tami had put the baby down for a nap and laid down herself. A short time later she woke and found the baby dead. She grabbed the baby and ran out into the hall of the apartment complex she lived in. Screaming and crying the person who took the baby from her was her ex-husband. Paramedics were called, but he was just gone. I can't even imagine the devastation she experienced. I could only hold her and cry with her. There is so little comfort to offer in such a situation.

In July we had a memorial service in a park and we let blue balloons go, and float up to heaven in some kind of symbolic gesture that was supposed to make us feel better. It was really only something to do when nothing could be done. A kind of goodbye that you never had time to say.

My children's father, Mel, came to the memorial. He looked very bad. He had Lou Gehrig's disease and he passed away in February of 2005. What a wasted life of a talented man.

In October of 2004, I went to Florida to furnish our new house so we could put it up for rent. I had a hard time finding the curtains that would fit all the windows. I was talking to my friend, Marlene, on the phone complaining about it. There weren't many stores in the area and I didn't know what I was going to do. Marlene said, "I'll be there in four days!" She was in Texas with her motor home visiting her sister. She would drive on to Florida and we would figure the curtains out.

Marlene, being a seamstress always carried a sewing machine with her and we got to work remaking the curtains that I had found, to fit my windows. Not everyone has a friend that will drive clear across the country to help you out. Marlene was one of a kind.

I had a lot of yard work to do and couldn't find anyone to do it. I had hired a couple of people, but they only made it a day or two and then didn't show up the next day. It seemed like Florida didn't have very diligent workers.

I had a guy in California named, Tim, that worked for me at times as a general laborer and or gardener for our properties. I put in a call to him and asked if he could come out for a few weeks. He was good to go and I bought him an airplane ticket.

Between the three of us, the house was coming together. On Halloween, our neighbors had a costume party and we were invited. I bought a t-shirt and on it, I drew a box and put some dots in it. That was

Tim's costume. Marlene and I put on cat whiskers. I didn't tell them what we were until we got to the party. We were two old pussies and Tim was our "litter box." Everyone had a laugh.

We returned home to California in Marlene's motor home in time for Thanksgiving.

My sister, Teri, and I had been talking about her trying to get Social Security Disability because she had several conditions including, Emphysema and Fibromyalgia. She really had Emphysema and had a hard time breathing and she was in pain somewhere in her body most of the time. I felt sorry for her but, at the same time, I remember when she told me that she thought she might get Permanent Social Security Disability, my brain said, "Oh, I'm so envious of you. I wish I could retire." I remember the "feeling" that I had. It was a deep yearning to just be free from the work and worry and problems.

Emmy Awards 2004 Claudia age 57

Left: Claudia & Tom at Emmy Awards 2004 Claudia age 57

Below: Me and one of my paintings. 2004 Claudia age 56

Chapter 42

You Get a Stent and You Get a Stent

In March of 2005 my ex-husband Jack would pass away. He went to the hospital for a routine stent placement as prophylactic against having a heart attack. He died getting the stent. Jack was such a good man and in the later years of his life, he founded the Riverside Recovery Resources, a drug and alcohol non-profit organization. Jack had ceased drinking in 1988 shortly after Tom and I had married. He had used the rest of his life well, by trying to help others in need.

I finished-up on "Torque," the show I was working on and the last show I would do. In June of 2005, I had a heart attack and they placed a stent in my heart. Fortunately, I survived.

We had flown nonstop to Florida to check on our property there. The next morning, we played "Pickle Ball," which is like playing ping pong, on a tennis court, with a "Wiffle Ball". Never suspecting I had a problem, and not drinking enough water, I had played hard for hours.

When we were finished with Pickle Ball, we went back to the house and I fixed breakfast. We had an appointment with a realtor to look at possible income property, so I went to shower. All of a sudden, I felt tired. When I say tired, I mean tired. My arms felt like lead. I told Tom I had just hit the wall and wanted to lie down for a few minutes before I got ready. A few minutes later I started getting nauseous. I went into the bathroom and put a cold washcloth on my neck and just sat on the floor by the toilet. Then all of a sudden it passed. I mean the tiredness and nausea cleared and I felt great. So, I got up and we met with the realtor.

The house we were interested in was close by. We went into the house and all of a sudden, I had a sharp pain across my lower jaw. I knew immediately what that meant. I sat down on a chair and told Tom he needed to get me to the hospital because I was having a heart attack.

The hospital was only a couple of blocks away so we drove to the emergency room. They quickly verified that it was a heart attack and gave me four aspirin. The next bit is a little fuzzy. I remember being in a room and a doctor explaining that he had to put a stent in my right coronary artery. It wasn't a choice. That's what they had to do. I was overwhelmed because I couldn't even understand that at 58 years old, I had a heart attack. I just said, "OK," and went with it. I remember before they put me under that I said, "I am a survivor."

When I woke up, there was a bit of pain in my legs but nothing I couldn't handle. I was hooked up to a morphine pump, which I told them to take out. The nurse who was caring for me had just come back to work after having four stints placed in each of her legs. Stints, stints, stints, everyone gets a stint!

They had me up and walking within hours. I was on four different medications. Aspirin, Plavix, Zocor, and Protonix. I was released from the hospital a few days later. I could go back to California where I should follow up with a cardiologist and gastroenterologist. At the time of the incident, my total cholesterol was 152. Fortunately, there was no damage to my heart.

I had been studying health and medicine most of my life ever since Mel came down with Measles when Tami had Scarlet Fever. That was too bizarre and I wanted answers. I subscribed to several magazines on health. I had read many books on different conditions. I had cured arthritis in my hands by stopping dairy products. I had worked in Chiropractics and had been a nursing assistant. I had seen miracles happen. I had taken courses in diet and stress management. I was not a novice to health and yet, here I was with a stint in my heart and on four medications.

In talking to Tom, I found out that I didn't HAVE to have the stint. It was recommended that I have it placed. Tom had approved it.

I have gone over my medical reports and this is what I found. In the ER at the hospital where I was evaluated, there were several erroneous things on the report, such as: "The patient had some chest discomfort. The pressure type of pain in the chest continued. Since the patient continued to have these symptoms, she came to the emergency room."

None of those statements are true unless Tom told that to them, in which case he was not telling the truth. I suspect that he may have told them that I had chest pain to get them to pay more attention to me. I have heard people say that if you want attention "quickly" in the hospital, tell them that you have chest pain. What people don't realize is that the doctors may use that information in diagnosing you and you may wind up having a procedure that you don't need. I also suspect that the earlier nausea and tiredness may have been a blood clot passing.

The report continues, the patient was evaluated: "The patient was found to have very minor ST-elevation in II, III, aVF with normal cardiac enzymes. With the diagnosis of POSSIBLE acute myocardial infarction, acute coronary syndrome, unstable angina (I had no angina) inferior leads inferior part of the heart, immediately transferred to the hospital and underwent emergency heart catheterization which was found to have a 90% blockage in the RCA and 30%-40% in LAD. The patient received proximal stent in RCA. The ejection fraction at that time was 60%."

So much of this report is wrong or at least, not reported by me that I question the entire procedure. I know that in recent years, there has been a lot of investigation into the unnecessary placing of stints. It is a lucrative business. This procedure cost almost $100,000. I also have to warn people that if you have great insurance, you are more apt to NEED this type of procedure. I have two insurance policies. I am DOUBLE covered, so I am 100% covered. Most patients will go along with whatever a doctor says, if it cost them nothing.... Nothing that is, except their health, but they don't know that.

I went back to California, but could not return to work. I felt tired and out of breath. That had only come on since the stint placement and had never happened before. I used to wear a pedometer at work and averaged walking about 15 miles a day. Now, I could barely walk across the room. I could not walk up the stairs to my bedroom; I had to crawl up the stairs. I was in shock for about the first six weeks.

During this time, I went to the cardiologist I had been assigned to by my insurance. I told him that I had extreme muscle weakness in both my arms and legs. He referred me to a Pulmonologist (lung specialist), who in turn diagnosed me with Emphysema and put me on another four medications including an inhaled steroid. Then, I was sent to a GP for my back pain and was given another two drugs. He first prescribed Oxycotin which I declined. That was the drug that got Tami addicted. I had taken Vicodin before and agreed on that plus a muscle relaxant. Shit, am I falling apart?

I had watched my mother die while taking about twelve different medications. I had watched Nova die who was on about the same amount. There is no way they can tell the interactions that can happen with that many drugs.

I was not feeling any better and I finally got a clear thought. "Claudia, you know this is bullshit. Wake up and do something about it before they kill you!"

I hit the books and the internet. I was looking for supplements to replace the drugs I was on. It was a bit scary because my husband and my sister were afraid I was going to do something drastic and would die. That's the support system, I didn't need.

I found that red yeast rice could be used instead of Zocor: a cholesterol-lowering drug. I was also on Protonix: for "Acute gastro ulcer with hemorrhaging." Had they prescribed it to me because they had me on Heparin in the hospital and it started bleeding in my stomach? Plavix: (High priced aspirin) prevent blood clots. Aspirin: More blood thinner. Vitamin E is a natural blood thinner.

To start with, my cholesterol was only 152 which is high for me because I usually don't eat meat. I had had eggs and bacon that morning which might be why it was so high. In my research, I had found that the Zocor could CAUSE pain in muscles. When I had told my cardiologist about the muscle pain he said none of the drugs I was on could cause it. As I said, Vitamin E and garlic are natural blood thinners. I would substitute Red Yeast Rice, Vitamin E and garlic for most of the heart medications. I would eliminate the Protonix because without taking all the blood thinners, I shouldn't worry about ulcers or stomach bleeding.

I made up a little booklet that showed natural supplements that could be used instead of the drugs. It included studies and medical analysis.

When I went in to talk to the doctor, He thumbed through the booklet but didn't, really, read it. He didn't have to because he knew that it was true.

"I don't understand," he said. "Why do you want to spend your hard-earned money on all these supplements when you have good insurance that will pay for your medications?" Well, there is it, isn't it? He was well aware of what insurance coverage I had. That was why he always wanted to run some very expensive test on me. I'm just a cash cow!

"Because," I replied, I intend to cure my problems, not mask them and cause more."

I took myself off of all medication, ignoring all the dire warnings from my doctor, my sister, and my husband. "Screw it," I said. "If I die, I die!"

Within about two weeks I started feeling like my old self. My brain began to clear and I started to remember what had happened that morning.

When we were playing Pickle Ball my legs started hurting. Being stubborn as I am, I just ignored them. At the last, just before we quit, my calves were in tremendous pain, and pretty soon I couldn't bend my knees. I was walking like I had pipes on my legs. By the time I stopped, my legs were extremely painful. When we went back home, I sat down for a few minutes and it seemed to pass. Everything else ensued within a half-hour of the leg pains. You just can't tell me that there is no correlation.

I don't trust most doctors. I have been misdiagnosed too many times. Just recently I had an incident that will show you what I mean.

I was in my backyard when I was stung on the hand by a wasp. My hand swelled up pretty quickly and my heart raced. I took my blood pressure and it was 180/100. I called the paramedics because I did not have an EpiPen and was concerned that I might be having a very allergic reaction. The paramedics took me to the hospital where I sat for several hours. I couldn't get any answers. They were probably huddled trying to figure out what expensive test they could run on me besides the blood test they had already run.

I finally had enough and told them I was leaving. They said that I couldn't because my blood pressure was so high. "Then give me something for it!" I said. "You have about five minutes to figure it out because I'm leaving." They gave me a shot of who the hell knows what, and discharged me.

When I got home, I called my cardiologist who prescribed a "blood pressure-lowering drug."

"How long will I need to be on this?" I asked.

"Oh, you'll need to take it the rest of your life!" WTF

I looked the drug up and found it to be a "Calcium Channel Blocker" that could decrease the pumping strength of the heart and relax the blood vessels. The drug also increases the risk of dying from heart disease. I declined his medicine.

I looked up, on the internet, what some of the Top and well-known "alternative" doctors would recommend on a "temporary" basis, for high blood pressure. Chlorthalidone is the name of the drug I came up with. It was pretty strong and so I would only take ½ the lowest dose.

I called my cardiologist back and ask him to prescribe Chlorthalidone. "You can't take that, it's too strong," he said.

"Yes, I know," I replied. "I'll have to cut the pill down. I'm only going to take it for a few days at the most." We had a bit of a "discussion" about what I would and would not take. I finally told him, "Look, either prescribe what I want or don't. I can go to someone else." Reluctantly, he gave me three pills. I might add that these pills cost about sixteen cents each whereas the calcium channel blockers can cost $20 a pill. Of course, insurance would be paying for them so who cares, right?

I just have to mention here that all people should object to unnecessary medical procedures or overpriced drugs. I don't care if you think your insurance is paying for it, it isn't! In the long run, we are all paying for it. We are paying for it through our taxes every time they jack up what we pay for Medicare. Employers pay for our insurance instead of putting money in our pockets.

When I got the pills home, I cut one down to about 1/3. I took it. A short time later, my blood pressure went down to about 90/60 which is Low Blood pressure. I didn't take any more pills. Within a day, my blood pressure returned to normal 120/70 and that was the end of it. It was just the wasp sting and yet no one was willing to listen to me.

Another incident I had recently is a further demonstration of why I don't trust doctors. I had had some sinus drainage for a few weeks and I was taking, over the counter, Zyrtec for several days. Zyrtec can affect your liver, kidneys, and heart and I just don't like taking any medicine for longer than for a few days. Since I had had a bit of a problem off and on for months, I decided to go to an allergy specialist, to get tested, to find out what I might be allergic to.

When I went in for the appointment, before I went in to see the doctor, they had me do a breathing test. Apparently, EVERYONE must do a breathing test before they see the doctor! The test showed that I had reduced O2 (Oxygen). So, the nurse said I needed to do a breathing treatment and then retest. WTF? I have to add that I have a "Pulse Oximeter" at home and my O2 is usually at about 98%!

So, I do the treatment and then retest which shows that my breathing is better. Now, I'm finally admitted in to see the doctor. The doctor promptly announces that I have "Asthma." Not allergic asthma, but just asthma. Again, WTF?

"Look," I said, "I just want to get some tests to see what I might be allergic to." At which time I am informed that I will have to wait for a couple of weeks because of something in the breathing treatment. Meanwhile, he prescribed THREE medications, including an inhaled steroid, for my "Asthma."

I left and had the prescriptions filled. I had them filled because, I believe, the drug stores report who gets their meds and who doesn't. If you don't get them filled, you will be listed as a "Non-Compliant patient," and that will be on your medical record forever. I don't give a shit because I'm sure I'm already labeled, but still, I play the game. I could be wrong, but I don't think so.

Of course, I did not take any of the meds. They were put in a big box I have that contains ALL the crap the doctors prescribe for me. The only meds I take, that is not over the counter, is an antibiotic, if absolutely necessary, or a half of one of my Vicodin for recurring back pain and then only if it might affect my blood pressure which pain can do.

The only reason I am willing to take Vicodin is that it was synthesized in Germany in 1920 (when my father was born) and approved for use in the united states in 1943 (before I was born). It is older than my Dad and has been used in the United States since before I was born. It works and it also costs pennies for a prescription while the "NEW replacement drug, extended-release Vicodin" cost about $300 for a 30-day prescription. Of course, they are saying that it is "safer" and will keep people from getting "addicted!" WKOBSIT? (What kind of bull shit is that?). As soon as this "Opioid Epidemic" stuff came out, I told my husband that the drug companies finally figured out that they could make more money by getting rid of these old drugs, that cost nothing, then tweak them a tiny bit and bring, basically, the same drug out as a new and improved drug for big profits. Now people with chronic pain have to jump through hoop s to get relief and are considered drug-addicted. Many of them aren't drug-addicted; they are just addicted to being out of pain. My brother was one of those people. He had to drive miles every month to go to the VA hospital to get his pain meds. If he was late or missed his appointment, for any reason, the doctor would "punish him" by not refilling his pain meds. Thank You for your service!

End of my tirade and back to my story. I left the allergy specialist and went home for a few weeks and then returned for my re-check. The first thing they did was another breathing test. I pass with flying colors so I am now admitted to the doctor's "throne room." He looks at my test results and is all smiles. "Well, I see your breathing has much improved, the medicine is working."

What a smug asshole! I hadn't planned to tell him that I didn't take ANY of his medicine, but I just couldn't resist.

"I didn't take the medicine," I said. Now his manner changed. Mr. Nice guy is gone.

"What do you mean you didn't take your medicine?" he growled.

"Just that," I replied. "You said I couldn't do the allergy test because of the breathing treatment so I thought I shouldn't take the meds either until after we did the allergy tests." I won't belabor the point. After much conversation he finally instructed me to "take my meds." He left the room and sent the nurse in for the allergy screening.

They stuck my back with about 64 different possible allergens. I had NO reaction to any of them. I had told the nurse that I thought I reacted to feathers so she used a hypodermic needle to inject me under the skin on my arm for feathers and about ten other items that are often the culprit. Nothing! Just nothing! I think we could have drilled down further, testing for food allergens, but I was satisfied that what I had was not an allergy to the most common items. I left the office never to return.

Chapter 43
Retirement at Last

I had been on temporary disability since having the heart attack in June of 2005. My doctor said he didn't think I should return to work because of the "fumes" and chemicals I was inhaling. He put in for my Permanent Disability Retirement.

I hadn't seen my daughter in a while, since Wyatt had died. She called occasionally, but with having a heart attack and everything, I was not aware of what was going on with her.

The first part of November 2005, I got a call from the police department, that my daughter, Tami, and her husband had been arrested, and I needed to take temporary custody of her two girls or they would be placed in the foster care system. You can imagine what kind of horrible images came up for me. Would the drama never stop?

Of course, we took my granddaughters. Having recently had the heart attack, I didn't feel I was in good shape to take them, but there is no way they were going to go to foster care. So, my sweet little granddaughters, Claudia and Brandi, moved in with us. When they delivered them to us, they looked so frightened and lost. L'il Claudia was nine and Brandy was seven years old.

The girls came to live with us and now I had to figure out what was going on. To top it off, Tami was pregnant, but because of the trauma of her baby, Wyatt, dying, her brain just denied it. It would take months and thousands of dollars to get the kids back with their mother and everything straightened out.

The big problem was Tami's ex-husband, who kept following her, and who still did drugs. I needed to get Tami out of California. Fortunately, the children's welfare worker, who was assigned to the case, agreed. None of them would have a chance unless we could get them away from Tami's ex-husband.

In the last part of December 2005, Tami gave birth to twins! She had another girl and a boy; Angela and Little David.

Where my sister continued to fight for Social Security, my disability was granted very quickly and in January of 2006 I retired from the Motion Picture and Television Industry.

Because the girls had been removed from Tami's custody, they investigated for months. The court was having a hard time separating Tami's ex-husband, Dennis' actions from Tami's because of the proximity of where they lived. It was past February 2006 before the girls were given back to Tami and, it took months after that before we got to court and the court finally gave Tami full custody of the girls, and made an allowance for her to get the kids out of the state.

As soon as I had that paper in hand, I took the girls and flew to Florida with them. Tami would follow in one week and her husband would follow in another month. So, off to Florida we went.

Tom and I found a three-bedroom mobile home for sale and made a quick deal for it. Tami and her family would temporarily live in it until they got established and then we would use it for a rental. We bought Tami and Dave cars because the one they had in California wouldn't make it to Florida. Dave and Tami were settling in. I could only pray that they would stay clean and sober.

The stress of the past year had taken a toll on me and my back and hip problems were getting worse. I figured it was more from stress than from a physical condition, but who knew.

Since my retirement and Tami necessitating our move, it took a minute to figure out what Tom and I were doing. While I was retired, Tom wasn't and he was only 54 years old. We had sold all our properties in California and our house was paid for so we weren't in bad shape if Tom didn't work, but he still needed to contribute to his Social Security.

Tom is the kind of person who can't sit still. Tom started a painting business in Florida and that would do for a bit.

I had been studying a lot of different "Energy" medicine because of my back problem. No doctor seemed to be able to help me. I had already had surgery and would not do that again. Chiropractics only brought temporary relief and I didn't want to stay on pain meds until my liver gave out. Often it felt like I was being stabbed in the middle of my low back with an ice pick.

I heard about a movie named, "The Secret", produced by Rhonda Byrne. It was about the "Law of Attraction." Watching the trailer to it, I was amazed that so many of the people I had followed for years were in it; Bob Proctor, Jack Canfield, Bob Doyle, and Mike Dooley to name a few. This movie spoke to my soul. All the reading and researching I had done and here it was in a very easy-to-understand movie. Of course, I bought dozens of copies and gave them to every family member and friend I had. I had been preaching this stuff for years and people just couldn't understand what I was talking about. This movie was a great explanation. Of course, people look at my life and wonder why it has always been so screwed up if I understood this stuff. I wondered the same thing myself, but I just kept studying, processing and singing. "I'm a happy, merry butterfly…"

I became a Reiki Master. I completed Advanced training in EFT (Emotional Freedom Technique - Tapping) and in December of 2006, Tom and I also completed our training in B.E.S.T. (Bio Energetic Synchronization Technique) with Dr. M.T, Morter and became "Master Practitioners." It cost us over $25,000 to learn this technique, but I felt it was worth it.

Tom and I also completed some courses with Sue Morter who I found to be the most loving person I have ever met. There was something that happened, that everyone was up in arms about. Everyone was voicing an opinion on how bad the person was; the hatred was thick. I can't remember what it was, but I do remember Sue's response. She told us that now, more than any other time in life, we needed to hold love in our hearts. We could contribute love to the universe or we could contribute negative energy which could only create more negative. She was powerful and I learned a lot about "The law of attraction" in that one incident. What an incredible woman.

Claudia and Tom with Sue Morter 2006
Claudia age 59

I knew how all this stuff worked and I could see it work for others, but I couldn't make it work for me. While Tom was a master practitioner also, he couldn't help but change the method that was taught. In doing that, he was just no help to me.

One thing I noticed was that whenever a B.E.S.T. doctor worked on me, I could get out of pain for a day, but then when I went to sleep, it reset and I would be in pain again. Dr. M.T. Morter thought it might be a repressed memory or emotion from something that happened while I was asleep. There had been plenty of trauma while I was asleep, like when my dad used to pick up my bed and dump me on the floor so I could get up and study law with him, but we couldn't get it to clear.

In 2006, we also remodeled our HHH house. We put in a new kitchen and made one room into an office.

David, our oldest grandchild graduated from high school. I was so happy. Maybe this generation of kids will get to graduate. We flew to Missouri to attend the ceremony.

About this time, I found a very fun computer game for my Play Station 2 called "Jak & Daxter; The Precursor Legacy." I have always loved this kind of game which is a "figure out the puzzle" type of game. The first computer game I ever got was back in 1972 called "Pong." It was only a ball being hit back and forth across my TV screen. Not a lot of skill to that, so, it wasn't very stimulating even though it was a very new concept. I think I and my son wasted about 12 hours straight racking up the points and then I asked, "So what do we have here? The answer was, several thousand points." I was already bored. I unplugged it and took it back for a refund. In 1994 I came across a really fun game called, "Mist." I spent weeks figuring that one out but I loved it because it makes the mind set up and take notice. I love things that take figuring out. Now, a game like that makes you feel like you have accomplished something. We never played a bunch of board games when I was a child because you never knew when a drunk might come in and upset everything. We preferred to stay outside as long as possible.

Our friends Marlene and Gary sold their house in California and moved to Florida. I was bowled over, but so happy. It had been so sad to leave my best friend behind. They wound up buying a property in the same complex as we had bought the rental house that Tami was in.

The Villages were a lot of fun. There are always parades, festivals, and activities. I enjoyed taking the girls to all the events and Tom and I took them to all the Florida attractions. Life was good for a very short time.

On April 21, 2007, I got a call from Dave that Tami had really bad back and neck pains and he needed to take her to the hospital, and asked if I could come over and take care of the kids. I jumped in the car and when I got there, Tami was already in their car waiting. She wouldn't even let me evaluate her because she was in so much pain. That is something a mother just never wants to see.

A couple of hours later Dave called and said that they had diagnosed her as having a gall bladder attack and they were keeping her until the morning when a specialist would come in to see her. I didn't buy it. I have seen people with gall bladder attacks and the pain can refer to the back, but not like she had.

I remember a time when my kids were very young and my neighbor's son fell on his bike and was taken to the hospital. Karen called me from the hospital in a panic. She couldn't get hold of her husband and they were saying that they wanted her to sign a form so they could remove her son's spleen. She didn't know what to do. I asked if he was in any immediate danger of dying if they waited until I got there? She said, "no." I advised her not to sign until I got to the hospital and could talk to the doctor. When I got to the hospital we went to talk to the doctor to get more information. The doctor staff had "changed shifts" and another doctor had taken over. When we asked the newly assigned doctor why her son needed his spleen removed, the doctor consulted his chart and said he didn't know what we were talking about. Her son had bruised the area of the spleen, but certainly did not need it removed. Just makes you think, doesn't it? I don't trust a diagnosis and would always want a second opinion for anything important. Back to my story.

I asked Dave to come home and take care of the kids so I could go to the hospital.

When I got to the hospital, Tami was in a room but was in excruciating pain. I mean, I could not touch the pillow her head was on without her crying out. This was not gall bladder. I suspected meningitis.

I went and talked to the head nurse but was told that the doctors had diagnosed her and that if I wanted a second opinion, I would have to bring in my own doctor. I went back to Tami's room to call, but didn't know who I would call. When I got to her room, she said. "Mom, my legs feel funny, like when your leg goes to sleep and is just waking up. It feels like little pins and needles. Now I'm about to panic.

I went back to the nurse but was again told there was nothing they would do. We would have to wait until the morning which was at that time only a few hours away. I kept Dave updated, that is all I could do. No doctor would come out.

The next morning, fortunately, a woman doctor came in to see Tami. Before she could touch Tami, I stopped her and told her what was happening with her legs and that she couldn't touch Tami's neck without her screaming. I said I thought she might have meningitis.

The woman listened and said, before she did anything else she was going to run some blood tests. The blood tests came back and Tami had a massive MRSA (Methicillin-resistant staphylococcus aureus) infection.

The doctor immediately called another woman doctor who was an infectious disease specialist. By this time Tami was paralyzed from just under the breast down. They transferred her to another hospital and ran tests for a couple of days trying to find the infection. The doctor finally told me that it was in her spine and her chance of survival was very slim. By this time, Tami was in a coma from all the drugs they had given her for pain.

I asked if they could open the spine and clean out the infection. They contacted a neurosurgeon who after reviewing the case declined to do the surgery. Then the infectious disease specialist took me aside and explained what was happening. Tami and Dave had no medical insurance. Their health insurance, that Dave had with his job, had expired. Without insurance, no doctor would touch her. Tami would probably die.

I was shocked beyond belief. Doctors would just watch a mother of four die because there wasn't enough money in it for them? DMF (I won't translate that, but it starts with dirty)!

I told the doctor that my daughter had four little children that needed her and asked the doctor what I could do. She said my best bet would be to get her on state insurance and get her into Shands Hospital in Gainesville, Florida.

I had no idea how to go about it. Dave was busy taking care of four kids and I was too afraid to leave Tami. Tom was working on a show in North Carolina. I called him and told him what was going on and told him to come home. He said he would be there by nightfall.

It took Tom a couple of days to get the insurance and to secure her a spot in Shands. They kept her on antibiotics constantly.

I stayed with Tami all the time. At one point they even took the visitor's chair out of the ICU room trying to get me to leave, but I refused. I sat or lay on the floor. Tom had gotten me a hotel room close by and I would go over to it and take a shower and change clothes while Tom stayed with Tami. I wasn't taking a chance with my baby. I monitored everything they did and questioned every med. They called me "Mama Bear." At night, when no medical personnel were looking, I would use all the methods of energy medicine, that I knew, on her. No one had much hope of her making it. The infection was just so massive.

At one point, while Tom stayed with Tami, I went home and printed out a bunch of signs that said, "TAMI HEALS QUICKLY AND COMPLETELY." I went back to the hospital and plastered them all over her room, the window and the door. No one could walk by or enter her room without reading that sign. That was about the "Law of Attraction."

On May 23rd an orthopedic surgeon cut Tami open and cleaned out the infection. There was about an eight-inch incision at the base of her neck down and one in the mid-back about a foot long. Within two days, Tami was alert and talking. Unfortunately, her legs were still paralyzed, but at least she would live.

Life can turn on a dime and we never really get how vulnerable we are. Tami was 41 years old with four kids and paralyzed. The doctor couldn't even tell why she was paralyzed because there was no infection in the part of the spine where the paralyzes started. He speculated that she might have had a stroke in the spine. He also told me that the infection couldn't get in the spine unless it was put there. They sometimes see it in people that have pain management things put into their back. The only time she had anything in her back was the spinal when she had the twins by Caesarian section. That would mean that it had been in her spine for over a year. It seems oxymoronic to say “lucky” and “paralysis” in the same sentence, but Tami was truly lucky that she was only paralyzed. I thank Shands Hospital from the bottom of my heart for giving me back my baby.

Tami was transferred to a rehab center where she would have to learn to care for herself. Meanwhile, there was much we had to do at Tami’s house. One of my HHH neighbors called her church and they came out to Tami's house and built a wheelchair ramp for her.

Dave couldn’t work and take care of Tami and the kids so we had to step in and support them. It wasn’t what we had planned for retirement, but we were just grateful to have the money to do it. Tom never balked or complained. It was only what we had to do.

We settled down somewhat into a routine. Dave took care of the babies and I took care of the two older girls. I wanted their life to be as normal as possible. Heaven knows they had been through hell.

I took them places and did craft projects with them. Every Christmas, we did a special craft project and made something for everyone. We always had a lot of fun.

Christmas of 2007, I sent my sister, Peppy, a ticket to fly out from Virginia for the holidays. I also had my son, Andy fly out from California. My sister, Teri, and her husband, also flew in from California at their own expense. Tami's medical problems reminded me just how fast life can change and I needed to connect with family that was away from me. I thought it would be a great Christmas.

We wanted to take Andy and Peppy to some of the sights in Florida that Teri and Jerry had already seen and Teri informed me that she had no interest to see again. That was when I first got a hint that Teri was not happy. I was thinking she was just having an off day.

We had decided to go to Homosassa Springs to see the manatees. Teri said, her and Jerry would go over to the "Town Square" and spend the day. They wanted to take our golf cart. Not a problem, because it was right across the street from where we lived. We cautioned her that our golf cart was battery driven and we didn't know how far it would go so she shouldn't go any further than the Town Square.

Homosassa was about an hour and ten-minute drive. Just as we were pulling into the parking lot, Teri called me on my cell phone and she was pissed. She started out by saying, "Why do you have such a piece of shit golf cart?" I couldn't even imagine answering that question, so I asked, "What is the problem?"

She yelled, "We don't know where we are and we called the police but they didn't know where we are, and this piece of shit cart has run out of battery. "

WTF am I supposed to do if she didn't know where they were, and I'm over an hour away? I told her to describe where she was, and asked if there was a guard shack anywhere around her or a house where she could inquire? I was, eventually, able to figure out, approximately, where they were. I called, Tami's husband, Dave, and asked him to get our utility trailer and go and get them and the cart, which he did. We continued on with the manatees and had a great day.

When we got home later, we called Teri on the phone and found that they were at a restaurant in the Town Square. We said that we would be there in a few minutes. She said, "We've already eaten!"

I suggested that they could have a cup of coffee while we ate and we could all be together.

When we got to the restaurant she went off on me. Yelling about my "piece of shit" golf cart. I tried to calm her down and I tried to tell her that there was nothing wrong with the cart, and that she had taken it clear across town about eleven miles from our house and we had told her not to go anywhere but the town square. We, finally, all had to leave because she just didn't care that she was disturbing everyone else in the restaurant. When we got home, it continued. Eventually, it came out that Teri didn't like the guest room because it didn't have cable TV, only local channels and a VCR. She was also mad because I had flown Peppy out for the holiday. Once Teri gets mad, there is no appeasing her. We didn't speak the rest of the night. She stayed in the guest room with the door closed.

In the middle of the night, I went to go to the kitchen and almost fell over Jerry, who was sleeping on the floor in the hallway. He said he had a bad back and couldn't sleep in the bed.

The next morning was more of the same. This was turning into a disaster. Later in the afternoon, her and Jerry packed up and left to go back to California. It was months before we spoke again. The rest of us had a great Christmas.

In May of 2008, I became a Minister in the Universal Life Church. The school was bugging us about the girls getting a bunch of vaccinations and we needed a minister to sign the papers. If I had to form a church, they would not be putting a bunch of poisons in my grandkids. I was pretty sure Wyatt was given a Hepatitis B vaccine when he was born. They never mentioned it in his autopsy, but it was standard practice in California at the time. I just have a lot of issues with the 50 something vaccine poisons that they want to jab into our kids. Sorry, everyone is entitled to their opinion.

In May our grandson, David decided to go into the Army. I tried to talk him out of it. I knew what they had done to my brother and then just dumped him when he was sick, but David said, “I know grandma, but I need the discipline!” It is so hard to be supportive when your kids or grandkids want to do something that frightens you. Keeping in mind the "Law of Attraction," I could only keep good thoughts for him.

August 18, 2008 was our 20th wedding anniversary and Tom planned a great trip to Cancun Mexico. We had such a great time. We went to the Mayan ruins of Chichen Itza (we call it, “Chicken Eats You)" and explored every inch of it. On the way to the ruins, we stopped at Cenote (say-no-tay), a water filled limestone sinkhole for a swim. Well, Tom swam, I watched.

Tom had, in recent years put on quite a bit of weight. I had been on him about it, but he didn’t realize how much it was affecting him until he went to pull himself out of the water with a rope ladder. He almost didn’t make it.

We also went to a Mexican amusement park called "Xcaret." It has a “gentle” river that advertising says, "Let the gentle current float you along in one of our underground rivers." It was great fun. It offers far too much to list here.

At night they have a big show called, "Xcaret Mexico Espectacular." It is advertised as, “Encounter of Two Worlds.” Our ancestors invite you to revive the Pre-Hispanic Ball Game and follow little "Lol-beh" as she travels through Mexican history. It really was a spectacular performance and a memory of a lifetime.

One thing that I definitely took away from Mexico was a great sense of gratitude for all that I have been blessed with. When you see people, who live in houses that have only a dirt floor and a hammock for a bed, you just have to be grateful. When you think life treats you bad, just visit some other, poorer, countries. We are so fortunate.

Tom & Claudia on our 20th Anniversary 2008
We took a trip to Cancun, Mexico
Claudia age 61

Chapter 44
No More Cheese!

In February of 2006, my sweet Tom was diagnosed with colon cancer. This was such a shock to us. You never think it can happen to you. And again, life turns on a dime.

He went to Shands Hospital in Gainesville, Florida and had a "resection" performed. That is where they cut out the cancerous portion. The doctor explained to Tom the possible things that could happen as a result of the operation. He could be on a colostomy bag for the rest of his life, he could lose sexual function, he could die on the table or any number of terrible things. He felt he had no choice. I thought there were other options and told him about all the alternatives, but I think he was too frightened to try anything else. I think he was afraid that if they didn't get rid of it fast they would want to give him chemotherapy. There were consequences from the operation, but nothing we couldn't live with and like he said, at least he is alive.

During his recovery, his incision split open. That was pretty ghastly. It had to remain open and several times a day I would clean it out, pack it with gauze and bandage it up. It made the recovery much longer, but eventually he did recover.

I have tried to talk to him about the cheese in his diet. Cheese is binding which greatly slows the transit time of food and elimination. Much research has come from T. Colin Campbell who is an American biochemist who specializes in the effect of nutrition on long term health.

He is the Jacob Gould Schuman Professor Emeritus of Nutritional Biochemistry at Cornell University. He had done experiments on the amount of "casein" in dairy that a person consumes. He found in experiments that cancer cells could be turned on and off by the amount of casein in the diet of mice. Twenty percent turned cancer cells on and five percent turned them off.

At the time of Tom's cancer diagnosis, his diet was atrocious and he ate an unbelievable amount of cheese, as many people do. Not to be too personal, but he suffered from constipation most of his life. Why do I put this in this book? Any way I can get this information to people is good enough for me. I think people might be able to eat a little cheese now and then, if you have no contra indication, but not the amount that people eat today. If you had one little bit of cheese, once a month, it might be OK. Cheese is on everything including salad! OK, off the soap box!

Tom went back to work and life went on. He was now mostly residing in California. We decided he could make more money there than on the east coast. We still had an extra family of six to support. Tom maintained a bachelor apartment in California and frequently flew home to be with family. It was a very difficult thing for him to do, but he did it for more than ten years.

We tried our best to maintain a normal life for the grandkids and whenever papa was home we took them to do all the fun things Florida had to offer.

In early August my oldest granddaughter, Shailyn, drove all the way from Missouri to visit grandma. I was not comfortable with that. It was such a long way for a 17-year-old to travel by herself. I called her mother and offered to fly Shailyn out instead, but they were fine with her driving. I did not sleep much until she arrived. Was I the only one that knew what could happen to young girls?

It was great to visit with Shailyn and we went to some of the fun amusement parks. I remember at one point, when she was holding her phone over water to take a picture and I had cautioned her not to drop it, she turned and told me, “Grandma, I’m almost eighteen. Don’t you think it’s time I decide for myself? At that moment I realized that my grandchildren were indeed growing up. They had a right to do things on their own, as they decided. We can only raise them so far and hopefully they have learned to take care of themselves. The rest of the visit went fine, but I noticed how much I wanted to “guide her” and I just had to learn to keep my mouth shut.

After Shailyn left, I got a call from Marlene. She had been having problems with her stomach lately and I couldn't seem to fix it with energy medicine. Marlene disliked doctors as much as I did, but I finally convinced her to just get it checked out.

Since they had Kaiser Insurance, they had to travel to California to see a doctor. At Kaiser, they had diagnosed her with cancer of the "Omentum" (area in front of the stomach and lower abdomen). They removed a liter of fluid from the area. She was having a hard time keeping food down. Marlene wanted to go home to Florida and didn’t want them to do anything. She was very opposed to having Chemotherapy. She had seen someone die from it. They had driven their motorhome to California and Gary would have to drive it back, but it would be too long and hard of a trip for Marlene. I flew to California to bring her back to Florida.

I was shocked to see how frail she had become in just a few weeks. We flew back and I put her in my guest room. Our plan was for me to get her well enough to go to the Gerson Clinic in Mexico. We both had studied and believed in the Gerson treatment and that was what she wanted. I had called the clinic and had made arrangements for her to have a bed once we got her there. The problem was, we couldn't get her well enough to make the flight. At that point, she couldn't even keep water down. She threw up anything she ate. I would hear her in the middle of the night and go in to her. There she was, trying to take a bucket of vomit to the bathroom. I took the bucket from her. She kept saying how grateful she was. It just broke my heart. I hugged her. She was my precious friend.

Marlene had had a horrendous childhood and had suffered much abuse by men in her life. When she found Gary, she felt like she had finally hit the jackpot. She said we were both so lucky to have the men we had. She loved Tom.

Gary made it back to Florida, but Marlene wasn't getting any better. We decided she would have to go to Shands hospital. The same hospital that had saved Tami. At the hospital they said she had gall stones which might be causing the nausea. She consented to having her gall bladder removed, but when she woke up, she had a chemo port in her chest. I could see the terror in her eyes. I demanded that they take the port out. "Can't you see how terrorized she feels?" I asked.

Removing the gall bladder did help with the nausea, but thinking back, I think Marlene just decided she was done with it all. I was supposed to be flying back to California for Tom's brother's birthday party. I was going to cancel it, but Marlene insisted that I go. "I'll be here when you get back," she said. Before I left, I hugged her so hard and told her what a special friend she was. Marlene died the next day on August 27, 2009. I think she knew she was dying and didn't want me there to witness it.

Marlene's passing was a great loss to me. She had been such a good friend for over twenty years and would be missed for a long time. Marlene was the third cherished friend that I had lost. Most people will be lucky to have one good friend in life and I had lost three. I guess, if you live long enough, you will lose a good many loved ones.

Our neighbors, Lorraine and Maurice, gave a luau and had a hula troupe come and perform. It was magical for me. I loved the hula. I talked to the leader of the group and signed up for lessons. She was not Hawaiian, but I was able to learn some basics.

Then I switched to another group that performed in The Villages and stayed with that group for several years doing many, many performances and many parades. Our group was often in the newspaper and I was often featured in one of the largest pictures because they seemed to like my smile. Some performers have a hard time smiling but dancing brings me such joy that I can't help it. When I teach, I always say that "a smile IS a hula move."

I also joined a modern kind of dance group called "The Shaka Crew." I have always loved dance. It has always allowed me to escape a world that I didn't like or trust. We performed in many of the businesses around town doing dances like St. Patty dances, 60s sox hop dances and on Halloween we performed, "Thriller." It was a lot of fun and with all the dancing, taking kids to and from school, and everything else I was doing, life was very full. I had no time to think of anything but what I was doing at the moment.

Next, I switched to a true Hawaiian instructor, Kewehi Punahele and his wife, Kamai. I joined their "Kaleo'okaiwa" dance troupe. What a great bunch of people they are.

I have performed in many "Hoike" (to show or display) competitions and our "halau" (school, academy or group) has won many of them. Before "Covid-19" hit, our group performed at Disney's Polynesian Resort on a regular basis.

My Kumu (teacher) gave me the Hawaiian name of Kamalamalama which means light of knowledge or child of light.

I eventually got my granddaughters into hula. That just made it perfect. We did some of our pae'aina together (public performance to show your level of dancing). Our group has four levels and I have completed all of mine. I also got my young grandson into hula, but it wasn't his thing. I had to laugh at the look he gave me the first time I took him.

My oldest grandson got married on August 14, 2010. Tom and I flew to Missouri for the ceremony. It was interesting to see my son, Andy, all grown up and responsible for a grown family. He was the proud father of the Groom.

My neighbor, Lorraine, became my close friend and her and I have traveled quite a bit to see different things in Florida. We went to St. Augustine, The Florida Aquarium and the Salvador Dali Museum. Places that our husbands probably wouldn't be as interested in. Her and her husband, Maurice, kind of took me under wing and included me in many of their outings while Tom was working in Hollywood. Lorraine and Maurice travel extensively to many of the places that Tom and I had hoped to go to before life stepped in and changed our plans. They always bring me back some little something that tells me they are thinking of me. Someday we might still get to some of those places, but for now I live vicariously through them. They are now my "Stoddard's Lectures."

The Villages Newspaper did an article of my work through the years in Hollywood. It was a lot of fun and I felt very flattered that they would think me worthy of a large article.

In 2010, I studied with the author, David Wolfe (expert on Raw Nutrition). I was lucky enough to be invited to a small meeting of people at a private home. I found David to be authentic, energetic and very knowledgeable about health, healing, and food. In 2011, I completed his course in "Ultimate Raw Nutrition," and became a "Certified Raw Nutritionist." Of course, I have read all of his books. I just always need more "Input." While I am not a pure raw foodist, interacting with David led me to thinking about, "just what did humans eat a couple thousand years ago and why might that be important?" Eventually, that kind of thinking led me to write my book, "I'm Too Lazy to be a Vegan: But Why I Should Be."

The next few years were filled with hula, kids school plays, birthdays, holidays. We took a couple of cruises to the Caribbean and the Bahamas. I did a few pieces of art and was in the newspaper a few times. At some point I became the president of our homeowner's association for a couple of years. We still managed to have our annual Christmas party inviting all our family, friends and neighbors. Looking back, I don't know how we jammed so much into so little time.

In 2012 Tami's twins graduated Kindergarten. I went to their graduation ceremony and thoroughly enjoyed myself.

In December, Tom's brother, Dennis, died. He and Tom were very close and it was a tough time for Tom. He had probably been closer to Dennis that any other sibling.

The next several years were good years with loads to do and see. I was lucky enough to get instruction from a very famous Kumu Hula, by the name of Keli'I Frank Chang and I studied with him for a couple of years. We had a ceremony and we were awarded certificates. On the certificate I received it reads: “The above recipient has been found worthy of the title of "Olapa" under the hula genealogy of the Kumu Hula - Frank Keli’I Chang on this day of April 22, 2015. After more than twelve years in hula I was awarded the title of "Olapa," which means I am, at last, a real "hula dancer."

Kumu Frank had a lot of very serious medical problems. When I last spoke to him, he was in the hospital and was very frightened and depressed. I worked with him on keeping good thoughts. "Don’t live what might happen tomorrow, today. There is enough bad that happens in life without borrowing what 'might' happen tomorrow." I told him that we will all die sometime but there is no sense experiencing it until we get to it.

On November 22, 2017 he wrote me what would be the last message he would write to me. It said: “What a pleasure it was to speak with you today! My heart and my mind are rejuvenated with hope! I’m going to put print outs of positive affirmations in my room! Thank you so much for your wisdom and knowledge - it’s priceless!"

Kumu died on November 26th just four days later. I hope he went with peace and without fear. Kumu Frank was such a kind, loving man and I will always cherish all that I learned from him.

Left: My first hula performance 2010.

Claudia age 63

Bottom: Claudia with Writer and health expert, David Wolfe 2010.

Claudia age 63

Claudia performing at a friend's birthday party. March 2011
Claudia age 64

Chapter 45
Change, Change, Change

May 16, 2013 saw the birth of our first great-grandson. My granddaughter, Shailyn gave birth to Elliot Dean Lewis. I was 64 years old and a great-grandmother. Wow! Life seems to fly by.

I received a Certificate of Completion to certify that I was an "Eating Healthy Professional" by Genesis Healing Educations. Not really a big deal, but it says that I continue to investigate food. I thought that it is something we put in our bodies at least three times a day so we ought to know as much about the subject as we can. I had, long ago, decided that we should be eating organic when possible. We should eat lots of greens. And, it isn't the carbohydrates that are bad; It is the "new" oils that they mix with the carbs, that are taking us down. And of course, we should go very sparingly with dairy.

In April of 2014, I was getting something out of a large cabinet that was over the toilet in my bathroom when it detached from the wall and started falling. I did my best to get out of its way, but it landed on my right shoulder and back. Man, I thought I broke every bone in my body. I could barely move. Luckily, I had my cell phone on me and I called my daughter. Her husband, Dave, came and took me to the hospital. The doctor at the hospital couldn't believe how bruised up I already was and yet had no broken bones. He also couldn't believe that at sixty-seven years old, and I took no medicine. My poor little paralyzed daughter came up to the hospital so I wouldn't be alone.

I recovered and Dave bolted the cabinet in the wall and hung on it himself to show me that it could never fall again.

I decided that the HHH house was too much maintenance for me. It didn't look like Tom would be home for another few years and with over an acre of property, a pool and pool house and a huge house to care for along with Tami's family and all my other activities; I had to choose to eliminate something. We were over a half million in debt on the house by then so it seemed that it was right to let it go. I put the house on the market. Being such a unique house, I thought it might take a minute to find the right buyer but I had a bit of time before I would just have to sell.

Tami had gotten a bed sore from sitting in her wheel chair for too long at a time and it just wouldn't heal. She didn't feel like her doctors were doing anything about them either. There were some treatments that they just weren't willing to give her. One of her bed sores kept getting worse and was nearly two inches long, over an inch deep and almost to the bone. She and Dave decided that they should move to Fresno, California close to his parents. They felt that the medical in California was a lot better because the state insurance paid for more things.

By then, we had about gone through all our savings, had borrowed heavily on our house and were down to whatever income we brought in. Even when they left, we would still have the payments on both houses until we sold something. We told them we could buy them a travel trailer that would get them to California, and give them gas and expense money, but that was about all we could do. Tom was able to find a large travel trailer that cost about $7,000 and we gave them a couple thousand for gas. So, in August of 2015 they packed up all four of my grandkids and headed for California.

In talking to my son, I explained that we were down to it and I was very worried about Tami. My sweet son told me not to worry, that Tom and I had shouldered the expense long enough and from there on he would help with what Tami and Dave needed if Dave's parents weren't able to help. That was such a relief. I was so proud of the man my son had become. He was and is such a generous man. Not just to me, but he often helps family or friends in need. He is a giver, not a taker.

The Hickory Head Hammock (HHH) house sold just before Tami moved so we had to find a place to live very quickly. As it turned out, we were able to rent a neighbor's house for a bit. It would give us a chance to remodel the house Tami had been living in.

Because of her wheel chair all the doorways were trashed. The kitchen had no cabinet doors and everything was in disrepair. I had cleaned the house when Tami first became paralyzed, but when the girls got old enough to clean, I stopped. It was just too much for me to keep up with their house and mine. They had all lived in the house for about ten years so it was time for a complete makeover. I told Tom that if we remodeled the house the way I wanted it, instead of just to sell it, I would live in it until he retired which would be in about 2017. He agreed it would be the best plan.

So, we remodeled the mobile home and I moved into it. It seemed kind of funny that I had worked my whole life to wind up in a trailer, but that was the case at the time.

After moving back to California, both Claudia and Brandi had a hard time getting re-established in school. I know it was a hard struggle for them and to encourage them to stick it out, I offered that when they got their High School diploma, I would take them on a cruise. Thankfully, they both did get their diploma and then went on to college.

In March of 2017, I took Claudia to the Bahamas on the Carnival ship, "Liberty," It was a great trip and we had a delightful time swimming with the stingrays on Nassau!

In July, Brandi and I sailed on the same ship and again, we got to swim with the stingray on Nassau. We also went to a "Bahamian House," where we got to eat authentic Bahamian food.

I cherish the time I spent with each of my granddaughters on those cruises. They had had a tough time in life with everything that happened and yet they made it through. I had a photo book made up for each of them to commemorate our cruise time together.

In 2017 I entered the Hoike Hawaii Competition in Orlando, Florida as a Solo Performer in two categories. One was Auana (modern hula) and the other was Oli (Chanting in Hawaiian). I did not place in the Auana, but I won 2nd Place in Oli which surprised me no end. I was up against three native Hawaiian-speaking people and I took second for chanting in Hawaiian! My Kumu (teacher) was so proud and so was I. I was awarded a big trophy that is proudly displayed with my Karate trophies in my bedroom.

The next few years saw grandkids going out on their own and more great-grandkids being born.

For Tom and my 28th Anniversary, I surprised him with a "Day of Travel." We started out with a boat ride touring the Harris Chain of Lakes, then we got in a “Seaplane” and toured in that, and lastly, we went on a train ride, stopping for a great lunch at a little restaurant along the way. It was something different and believe me; when you have been married that long it becomes difficult to come up with something new. The seaplane didn’t just go up and fly around, he did several takeoffs and landings so that we got the full experience. The seaplane was kind of a bucket list item for us, although Tom was not in great shape to squeeze himself into the back of the plane, it was quite an experience and we checked that one off our list.

In December of 2017, Tom finally retired from the Motion Picture and Television Industry. He had worked for 40 years in it and it was showing. Having been on his own in California for about 10 years, he was eighty pounds overweight, his knees were shot and he walked stooped over like a very old man.

"Look what the years have done?" I thought. We both looked and felt like we were at the end of life. I couldn't let this be our end.

If I have learned anything in my years, I have learned about the laws of attraction and about nutrition. I knew I couldn't keep these dark thoughts in my mind for us to have any chance of happiness that we deserve.

Tom had gone to doctors who said, there was nothing to do but to have his knees replaced. Looking at him, I knew he was not in good enough condition to undergo surgery of any kind. I sat him down and explained it to him. I offered him a better way. If he would eat only the food I prepared he would lose weight.

My diet has been mostly vegan and starch-based for many years, except when Tom would come home from California for a visit and then it was whatever he ate, which was seldom nutritious. I had taken almost no medications since taking myself off of it in 2005 and still, my heart remained good. I still had a bad hip and back, but other than that, I was in pretty good shape.

Tom agreed to try my diet. At first, I wouldn't let him go anywhere by himself. I knew he would be sneaking a hotdog, hamburger or a bear claw and I wanted him to really see what a good diet could do. To make this short, Tom lost 80 pounds in about 7 months. With every pound, his knees got better.

At one point, Tom called the doctor who was supposed to do the knee surgery. He explained that he had lost weight and his knees were better. He wanted to try some injections before he decided to replace the knees. They politely told him "they didn’t do that" and abruptly brushed him off. In other words, if you aren’t having a high-priced knee surgery … shut up and go away!

Losing the weight, Tom straightened up and began to look like his old self …. Well, except for the gray, thinning hair.

When Tom retired, he was given a lump sum retirement, plus his monthly pension. The lump sum and selling the trailer afforded us to buy a house in the Orlando area closer to the theme parks that we love to visit. We used to take the grandkids to the parks, but now we go by ourselves for the exercise.

In December of 2017, I got a good look at myself in the mirror and was appalled at what I saw. I guess I hadn’t taken a good look in the mirror much in the last few years because all of a sudden, I looked my age and a bit more. So, for my 70th birthday, I got a facelift. Trust me when I tell you that having your face “lifted” is no easy procedure and not for the faint of heart, but when it was healed, I was very pleased with the results. I didn’t look 28, but I no longer looked 80 either.

You may find this strange, but the Law of Attraction is part of why I had the lift done. When you look in the mirror, you make judgments about yourself. Maybe you think, "Dang, I'm old." I think what you attract with that is what "old people" have. More aches and pains and disease. I now look in the mirror and do not think "old." I think young, and so that is what I attract. Things that young people do. I walk more upright and move faster. At least, that is the way I perceive it.

In March of 2018, we went to Bullhead City, Arizona to visit my brother, Pat. He hadn't sounded good on the phone and was having a hard time getting to the doctors. While he said he was fine, I needed to see him for myself to find out what was going on with him and what I could do to help.

When we got there, Pat himself looked horrendous. The doctor had put him on steroids and he had that "moon face," that people on steroids get. He was tethered to an oxygen generator and was just sitting at his kitchen table with a mess of papers before him. He was also somewhat drunk. He was only 68 years old, but looked much older.

I was aghast at how he was living. His house was filthy and in disrepair. The faucet in his kitchen sink was falling out and had rusted. Dirty dishes were piled high. His back door had been knocked off its hinges and rainwater had buckled the floor. He had no clean clothes that I could find and the sheets on his bed were filthy.

My brother had always been a very clean person. He was also a contractor and could literally fix anything. There was something terribly wrong here.

In talking with him he told me that he had messed up and missed a doctor's appointment and so the doctor refused to refill his pain medicine, and he could not get another appointment for three weeks. The only thing he could do was drink because of the back pain. I had a couple of pain pills on me and told him, I would give them to him if he would stop drinking. He agreed to it and put the bottle away.

I wasn't sure where to start, but knew we had to start somewhere. I put Tom to work fixing the door and anything else he could repair. I started by finding a local cleaning service to get his house cleaned. The girl would be out the next day. I started on the laundry and don't even know how many loads I did, but pretty soon the house was taking shape. The lady who cleaned the house was a fabulous person. She was kind and understanding and was a miracle worker. I paid her extra because she was so amazing.

Next, I contacted the local Vietnam Veteran's Association and talked to a man who worked with Vietnam Veterans. Tom and I went to talk to him. He said there were resources that Pat would be entitled to if he only applied. I got all the paperwork and went back to Pat's trailer.

I explained to Pat what needed to be done. He said he didn't think he could fill out the paperwork, so I filled it out. All he needed to do was to go see the man. He would have to make the contact; a family member was not allowed to.

I offered for Pat to come and live with us, but it wasn't his first choice. I said OK we could try to see what happened if he got hooked up with the Veteran's Association and leave any other decisions for another day.

I arranged for the cleaning lady to come in every two weeks. All Pat had to do was make contact with the Veterans Association.

I hugged my brother and kissed him and asked him one more time if he would move in with us, but he declined. Tom and I went back to Florida. I had done what I could and could only hope that things worked out.

I talked to Pat on the phone several times and he was a bit fuzzy about whether he had contacted the Veterans Association or not which means, of course, he did not. He eventually confirmed that he had not contacted them in an email to me.

I'm going to write a bit more about Pat here because even though this is my story, I don't live in a vacuum. The things around me affect how I live and react to the world. My brother was a big, important part of my life and so it is appropriate to share some of his life with you. A part that you might never hear about him if I don't write it now. I will do this through some emails we have shared.

12-07-2013 My brother sent me this poem which it appears he had just written. It is about coming home from Vietnam.

Back to the World

J.P.Gilligan 12-07-2013

Back to the world, in one fell swoop
Back to the world, with a bunch of the troops
Strangers each other, yet brothers together,
Just old young men, harder than leather

"Fill out this form - stand in that line"
We're anxious to finish and quit marking time.
Go with the flow, don't cause a commotion,
Don't need any medals, don't want a promotion.

"If you have any problems, write 'em down here.
We'll take care of you all!" Was it said with a leer?
So, we write down the stuff about lumps and scars.
It ain't no big thing, it happened on Mars.

We expected our lives would just start again.
We'd celebrate well with some toke and some gin.

Claudia Gilligan

This place seems strange now, no longer ours
Yet it's the same buildings and streets and cars

As hard as we try, we never fit in
In this new old place, so far from the sin
We'd lived here once, of that we're certain
Before all the killin' and dyin' and hurtin'

Friends, not strangers, tell us we're odd.
We sit in the corner and don't give them a nod.
They talk of something with conviction and poise.
We pretend to listen, but for us it's just noise.

Our minds are engulfed with friends left behind.
Feeling we deserted them is pushed from the mind
Will we see them again? We hope, yet hope not,
Would only remind us of the hell where we fought.

By any device, be it sex, drugs or brew
We manage somehow to attack life anew
But the thoughts keep on nagging of our friends far away
Still busting their humps in that sickening fray.

Our battle's more futile than theirs, it would seem
They just have to survive, but we have a dream,
A dream of the life we thought we would gain
Once back in the world, far from the pain.

But pain is still ours, is it mixed in our blood?
We stuff our emotions, least a tear bring a flood
This pain is etched so deeply inside,
That if you ain't been there, we just can't confide.

For sanity's sake, to protect us from all,
We hide what's inside us behind a high wall
A wall that's so strong emotions can't rend
It keeps us safe, though we're dead to the end.

But the wall is for you as much as for us
Just leave us alone and we won't make a fuss
For the tiger inside is safe in his cage
Prod him unwanted and he'll lash out in rage

The rage is so great, a shit-hook it'd fill
Lacking reason and devoid of will
A rage that is forged from guilt and fear
From doing our jobs and still being here.

The dreams we once had that kept us afloat
Were of lives full of promise and joy and hope
But the dreams have all lingered and died, at last
Killed by the ghosts who delight in the past.

In vain we wait for the promises not kept
From those for whose honor we dutifully leapt
We're now middle aged, yet ancient we feel

And still we refuse to bend, bow or kneel.

What do they mean, the promises they gave?
Will they keep them now or when we're all in a grave?
Can they give us back pieces of life lost in hell?
Can they turn back the clock, can they un-ring the bell?

There is no solution, I'm loathe to remember
To undo three decades of life in a blender
So, on we all go, one day at a time
Hoping to find some reason or rhyme

Yet the spawn of the leaders who led that endeavor
Would still do it again, from now 'til forever
Puffed up with pride, they would send even faster
More eager young men off to certain disaster

I would forgive all and call off the debt,
If they would learn this hard lesson and never forget:
"War isn't a game played with pawns on a board.
If you must give the order you should carry the sword."

Email from Pat dated: January 2014

I know, for a lot of people, the Vietnam War is ancient history, but for those of us who were there, it sometimes seems like just a few years ago. I suppose the current state of relations between our countries might be less irritating if it were simply a page in the history books to me.

No matter what your opinion of the war, right, wrong or no comment, we lost over 58,000 Americans and maimed a few hundred thousand more, while the dimwits in charge diddled around. Eventually, they decided to give up and shortly thereafter the communist in the north steamrolled over the south, slaughtering who knows how many people in the process. At last, they had peace, but in the end, the situation was the same as it would have been if we had stayed home and not spilled all that blood to begin with.

I, for one, felt like my government played me for a schmuck, first insisting it was important enough for me to risk my life and then saying, “Well maybe it was an ill-conceived idea and mistakes were made.” [sic] Or worse, blaming the people who were risking their lives on a daily basis for the failure - a failure which rightly belongs to the idiots in charge who were safe at home in D.C.

I know it’s pointless crying over spilled milk, but to this day, our government continues to insult those who gave their lives or limbs in that god-forsaken patch of tropical hell with policies that are nothing short of insane.

Sometime after Vietnam became a unified communist country, we “normalized relations” with them and removed travel restrictions, etc. Next, we negotiated trade agreements, even gave this former enemy nation "favored-nation status" and entered into free trade agreements with them. I know we should forget the past and move on. Free trade is a good thing, I’m told by people who must be far wiser than I, regarding such matters.

I question their wisdom because, with the trade deals we’ve agreed to, Vietnam becomes one more nation with which we have a large trade deficit. They buy some goods from us, but we buy a lot more from them. According to the government, “The U.S. goods trade deficit with Vietnam was $19.6 billion in 2013, a 25.5% increase ($4.0 billion) over 2012." As you can see, the trade gap grew over 25% last year and will no doubt continue to widen, while our national debt moves north of 18 trillion Dollars.

Now in spite of a communist country --a former enemy, getting a juicy trade deal with us, we also lavish foreign aid dollars on them! I'm sure some intellectual in the state department would carefully explain they need the financial assistance for land mine removal and for Agent Orange related health problems and to improve roads and all the other issues. Frankly, my dear, I don't give a damn!

I might point out that instead of giving free money to Vietnam we could use some of it for our own veterans who were blown up by Vietcong mines and booby traps and satchel charges and mortars. I might suggest we use some of the money to help our own vets who suffer from the toxic effects of Agent Orange, especially since our government is no longer denying it was harmful. I could suggest a lot of uses for the money, but none of it should be given to a communist country that is already conquering us with a trade deal we agreed to without even having a gun to our heads.

Is this what "peace with honor" looks like? More importantly, does anyone not understand why I have utter disgust and contempt for what our government and by extension our nation has become?

J.P. Gilligan

Email dated December 12, 2016, from Pat to my sister in response to her letting him know she had sent him a Christmas present:

I wish you hadn't done that. I've been trying to get the energy and ambition to at least buy some presents for my grandkids and it doesn't look like I'll be able to even do that. I know it's crass and crude but I'll probably send their mothers some cash to buy them something.

Daughter "A" (initial only) says her kids have enough toys and suggested I buy them clothes and even gave me their sizes, but what do I know about children's clothes? I'm sure anything I chose will be geeky or unstylish so I'd prefer to send money and best wishes.

As for everyone else, all they'll get are my best wishes for happiness and goodwill, since even shopping for groceries these days is a strenuous chore that I put off until I'm eating catsup on crackers.

Love and Merry Christmas

Pat

Email from Pat dated: July 17, 2016, RE: Memories
(I am using initials only for people he refers to.)

I hate contemplating the past because, in retrospect, I realize I've made some really idiotic decisions! After moving back to Los Angeles from Big Bear and could no longer work, I tried to get help from the VA. They sent me to a shrink who wanted to give me a psychological test called the Minnesota multi-phasic personality assessment. Since they wouldn't claim responsibility for my back problems, I thought I could get them to give me disability for post-traumatic stress disorder but when I researched the test I learned it had built-in lie detectors to determine if anyone was faking it. Since I knew I wasn't slick enough to fool it, I decided to answer the questions honestly and the result was a DX of clinical depression and PTSD.

I didn't think it meant much at the time, but when I look back at the past, I see where it's had a dramatic impact on the decisions I've made. In short, for serious life-threatening situations, I function like a well-oiled machine, but when it comes to normal everyday stress, I suffer brain lock and can't think my way out of a paper bag.

It happened when I finished the last construction project I did in Hawthorne, after M and I moved to Big Bear. I was running out of money and trying to keep the money flowing, waiting for R to find a buyer for the property but she never even brought a single lookie Lou to see it. I know if it was her property she would have found a buyer. I should have known something was amiss, but I didn't. In retrospect, I think R was hoping I'd get desperate enough to sell her the property at a discount. Instead, I just gave it to her. What can I say, brain freeze? When I offered to give it to her, I still had some money due on the construction loan and she wanted me to give her that as well. I should have said "forget it" at that point but I couldn't think straight. I did say no to giving her the balance of the construction loan. I regret not simply letting the bank take the property because after giving them a property with $140K in equity, R's husband bitched about having to pay $1600 in closing costs.

If I had been able to think straight at that point, I would have given the property to you. At the very least you would have said "Thank you."

It would have been nice if M had stood by me on some occasions but she never did. Why do I hook up with bitches who work against me? Too late in the game to ask I suppose.

J.P. Gilligan

My reply to Pat was:

Being who we are, Pat, I would have taken the property, found some way to turn a profit on it and given you all the proceeds. Tom has given me everything he could and even though we have our differences, I always know he is on my side. That's why he's a keeper! LOL, Awe yes, MEMORIES!

Email July 14, 2017, Re: his experience after discharge from the army.

Yes, I will forward this email but with some comments of my own, as a Vietnam Vet: I love it that members of the military are proud to wear their uniform in public. My generation - the Vietnam Vets, were made to feel ashamed of our uniforms, thus we shed them whenever possible. We wore them to get discounts on public transportation but that was about it. When I first returned from Nam and was discharged from the army I decided to go first class, so I checked into the Seattle Hilton. The snotty little clerk, looked my uniform up and down as if inspecting some disgusting bug and announced "military personnel has to pay in advance." I was sorely tempted to drag his sorry ass over the counter and carefully explain what all the do-dads on my uniform meant, but I decided to take the high road. I had the room fee in spades since I had a bunch of back pay I had never spent. So, I pulled out a wad big enough to choke a horse and said, "I think I can cover it."

When I checked out of the Seattle Hilton, I left most of my military gear in the room. I was so aggravated and ashamed at having been in the army that I didn't want anyone to know. If you know a Vietnam Veteran, tell him you're sorry. Don't say, "Welcome Home." For me, it's decades too late to mean anything.

J.P.Gilligan

On May 15, 2018, I received an email in response to my inquiry as to if he had contacted the Vietnam Veterans Association:

Sister Dear,

I know it must be frustrating for you to try to help me and I don't seem to do anything to help myself but I don't know what to tell you. I have trouble talking to anyone on the phone - partly because of hearing problems and partly due to psychological issues. Right now, I have an Rx from my pain management doctor that I'm supposed to hand-deliver to the VA clinic in Kingman, to get it filled for free, but driving to Kingman is such a chore I will probably pay $78 to get it filled here, at Walgreens.

I will really try to contact the people you recommended, although I don't even know what I'm supposed to ask them.

J.P.Gilligan

On several occasions, one of Pat's children, who was about thirty years old, took to Facebook and wrote scathing things about Pat. Many people chimed in, in support of her. After a time, I could no longer hold my tongue and replied.

"Just for your edification, my brother, A's father, is a Veteran of the Vietnam War. He served his country and came back DIFFERENT than he went. He didn't get shot or blown up. He was sprayed with Agent Orange. It damaged his whole system. None of you have a clue about him or his life and therefore really have no right to an opinion. While "A" (initials only) has a need to hate him, the rest of you do not serve her with your vitriolic endorsements of her self-pitting diatribe."

"A" - stop focusing on what your father can or cannot do for you. Acknowledge what he has already done - even though it was before you were born. Even if it is a small amount. Focus on that with gratitude and it will expand. You are the source of your feelings, not your father. You get to choose if you want to live a life focused on lack or a life focused on abundance. You don't have to go looking for love when love is where you come from!"

"I am proud of my brother! I know that he has done the best with what he has been given. He lives in pain every day of his life and it is

NOT something he can choose to change with perspective."

"You however have a choice. Choose wisely because what you sew is what you reap! My brother and thousands like him served their country because they BELIEVE IT WOULD MAKE A BETTER WORLD FOR THEIR FUTURE CHILDREN!"

"Before any of you run your mouth, spend a day researching what it is like to be a veteran. Go spend some time with veterans in hospitals and psych wards. Go spend a day talking with men and women at VFWs. Earn your opinion - the way VETERANS EARNED YOUR RIGHT TO HAVE ONE!" I'm telling you this for your own good, no one else's.

The last message I got from my brother, was on July 21, 2018. It was on my cell phone. It was a garbled message that I could not understand. I messaged back and told him I couldn't understand and when I got no response, I called. He did not answer. That didn't seem that unusual. Sometimes he would ghost me for a time because he just wasn't up to answering.

By August 3rd, I hadn't heard from him and I became concerned. I called the Bullhead police department and asked them to do a welfare check on him. They called me back to let me know that Pat had passed away. They found him on the floor. He had been dead for some time because bodily fluids ran down the floor from the kitchen table to his bedroom. I believe he died just after the last message I received but his death certificate states the day he was found. He had died alone in a trailer in Bullhead, Arizona. Such a sad ending to what was, at one time, a brilliant and industrious young man. RIP Brother RIP.

One of my most treasured possessions from my brother is a little framed certificate he gave to me on my 50th birthday. It is a Certificate of Recognition which reads:

Certificate of Recognition

Be it known to all that Claudia M. Gilligan on this twenty-first day of March 1997 having demonstrated exemplary skills in the area of "Love and Understanding" and having performed above and beyond the call of duty is hereby awarded the Certificate of Recognition as SISTER OF THE CENTURY. It was signed by "Authorizing Sibling - Pat."

What more could a sister ask for?

Some of my brother's ashes in a memorial urn. He loved Dobies!

2014
Pat 65
Claudia 67
Teri 69

Tom and Claudia on Christmas Cruise 2013. Claudia age 66

Claudia Gilligan

Claudia and Kumu Hula Frank Chang at our Uniki April 4, 2015

Claudia age 68

I am now a real "Hula Dancer!"

ʻŌlapa

Claudia Kamālamalama Gilligan

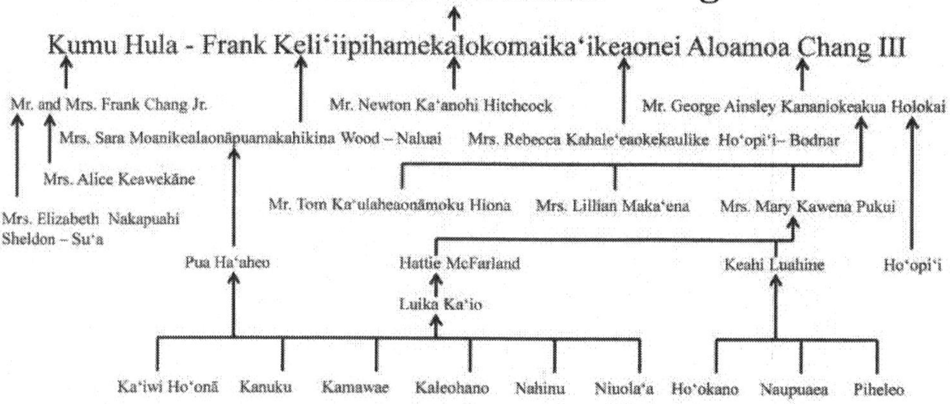

The above recipient has been found worthy of the title of **ʻŌlapa** *under the hula genealogy of Kumu Hula - Frank Keliʻi Chang on this day of:*

Apelila 22, 2015

E hoʻomau i ka hula o ko kākou mau Tupuna mau loa.

Grantor of Title

March 21, 2017, I celebrated my 70th birthday with others who had a birthday around the same time. Only family are in this picture, though others were included in the celebration.
From Left: My son Andy age 48, Husband Tom age 65, Me age 70, Granddaughter Claudia 21, and granddaughter Brandi age 19.
It was a great celebration and as you can see, we ate a lot of cake.

Granddaughter Claudia's Graduation cruise to Nassau March 26, 2017. Big Claudia 70 - Li'l Claudia 21

Left:
Claudia and BFF Lorraine 2017

Claudia age 70

Right:
BFF Lorraine and her husband Maurice on one of their jaunts.

They have often been the support that I needed in times of trial.

Claudia Gilligan

My last hula competition for which I won a trophy of Oli (chanting in Hawaiian). This is the dress I made for my 'Auana (modern hula) performance. Unfortunately, I did not win in that category. My beautiful granddaughters, Claudia and Brandi were my attendants.

I am age 70

My Kumu Kawehi Punahele and my trophy for chanting in Hawaiian.

I am still 70 years old.

Beautiful people! Kamai Punahele and Kumu Kawehi Punahele With me in my chanting costume for competition.

Still age 70!

Granddaughter Brandi's Graduation
Cruise to Nassau August 1, 2017
Claudia 70 - Brandi 19

Chapter 46
The Bucket List

In 2019, Tom and I decided that it was time to really look at the things we still wanted to do before we got too old to do them. One of the things I had always wanted to do was to see every state in the United States.

Early in the year, we busied ourselves with things to see around Florida and a nice cruise with Tom's sister, Jan. It was just a small cruise to Nassau and a few other places but as always it was a load of fun. We have gone on many cruises and I think I have been to nearly every island in the Caribbean and the Bahamas except for Cuba. I just love to go because of the great weather. One of my favorite places is Jamaica. Nassau has a spectacular aquarium that I love to visit.

We planned a trip to the east coast for late in the year so that we could see the changing of the leaves in Vermont. We took off on the 1st of October for our trip. The one problem we faced was how to maintain our vegan diet, for the most part, on the trip. We solved that problem by buying a portable freezer that we could hook to the "lighter" in the car to keep it running. I cooked a lot of our beans and rice, spaghetti, bean burgers, cauliflower, and rice, etc. I also made a bunch of what I call spoon salad. It is salad chopped small so that more can fit in a two-cup container. For the most part, we were able to maintain a good diet for the whole trip, stopping occasionally to make a new batch of salad in a hotel room.

Right off, I got the sense that Tom was on a mission. I had not planned on a rigid itinerary, but Tom apparently had. His "I'm in charge" personality came out and we had to have a "discussion" about that. In the end, he let go of those expectations and just went where the wind blew us. If we saw a sign about something that sounded interesting, we just diverted our route to see it. One of those places was "Wall Drug Store" in South Dakota. We had been seeing signs for this place for, I'm sure, more than a hundred miles. We speculated on the enormous amount of money that they were putting out for highway billboards and finally just had to go there. It might have started out as a drug store, but has just been added onto to where it is like a shopping mall inside with many different stores for anything imaginable. If you can‘t find it at Wall's, you don‘t need it!

We went to ghost towns and Indian museums, wax museums and dinosaur digs. We saw so many famous monuments. Some places we visited were Mount Vernon the home of George Washington, Mount Rushmore with the carving of four presidents, the Crazy Horse monument which is an ongoing sculpture of the famous Indian featured on horseback in the Black Hills of South Dakota, Carl Sandburg's State Historic House, Lincoln Museum complete with a replica of the log cabin he was raised in, Monument Circle, a Soldiers and Sailors monument in Indianapolis, Indiana which when I was a kid seemed so much bigger. We toured both the Canadian side and the U.S. side of Niagara Falls. We toured the Baseball Hall of Fame, Covered bridges and the turning of the leaves, Boston and the home of Paul Revere, Statue of Liberty and Ellis Island, Central Park and the "Alice in Wonderland Statue", Liberty Bell, Lincoln Memorial, Washington Monument, The White House in Washington D.C., The Smithsonian Institute, Monticello the home of Thomas Jefferson, Golf Hall of Fame, and one of my favorites was Walden Pond the famous home of Henry David Thoreau. And so much more.

Walden Pond is beautiful and serene. The little cabin that Thoreau had built and describes in his book is a reconstruction, but the woods he walked through and the pond itself are original. It gave me a thrill knowing I was walking where Thoreau had walked just as it had thrilled me to walk through the homes of Presidents Washington and Jefferson and walk where they had walked.

We also visited "cranberry farms." Having gone to a cranberry festival in Warrens, Wisconsin, I wanted to visit some cranberry farms. We found several that "float" the cranberries for harvest and found one that was harvesting as we showed up. But, I also wanted to see a “dry” harvest farm. Tom thought I was nuts because he had never heard of a dry harvest. I explained that only cranberries that are “dry” harvested can be sold as "fresh" cranberries. The "float" harvest is for juice. We had a bit of testy discussion before I said, look, just go to where I tell you and be quiet. (Maybe I did not say it as gentle as that sounds).

I directed him to the "Flax Pond" a dry Cranberry farm. It was an amazing experience and, in the end, Tom was very happy that I had been so insistent (intractable).

At the farm, we met Dot Angley who, along with her husband Jack, has been running the farm since 1967. From their little shop we learned so much about cranberry harvesting from ancient times to the present.

We also were able to stop for a visit with our granddaughter, Shailyn, and our great-grandkids. We worked in a visit with my, sister Peggy Lee, who I hadn’t seen for several years.

Along the way, we diverted from our normal vegan fair to indulge in all the famous food we could find like: Philly Cheesesteak in Philadelphia, Boston Cream pie in Boston, New York Pizza, Maine Lobster, etcetera,

etcetera, etcetera. I especially loved the Philly cheesesteak made by an old black man who said his secret ingredient was love and I could taste it!

We arrived back home tired but exhilarated from all the wondrous things we had seen. It was truly a great adventure.

On Thanksgiving we went for a 10-day cruise with Tom's sister, Jan. We went to Costa Maya, Mexico; Belize City, Belize; Island of Roatan, Honduras all in the Caribbean, and Ocean Cay, MSC Marine Reserve in the Bahamas. We arrived home on December 23rd just in time for Christmas.

The first part of 2020 was another trip to California. Tom always had a colonoscopy every year because of having colon cancer, but we managed to visit "The Regan Library" which, oddly enough, is in Simi Valley where we used to live. When we were living there we were too busy with work and everything else to visit it. Odd how that works out.

Just laying around on the Resolute desk with Presidents Trump and Obama. Tom, of course, is in the Presidents seat!2019 Claudia age 72

Chapter 47
The Covid-19 Pandemic

Early in February 2020, I began hearing disturbing reports about a "Coronavirus" that supposedly came from a wet market in Wuhan, China in December of 2019. On February 11, 2020, the CDC (Center for Disease Control) a federal agency, named the virus; Covid-19.

I looked up Wuhan, China, and found that there was also a research facility in Wuhan that could have developed this virus and I suspected that this was germ warfare and not a simple animal-to-human jump of a virus. I didn't think we were being given the straight information. I just didn't buy it and I don't buy it now.

The first reported Covid-19 death in the United States was on February 6, 2020.

I went to Tom and told him I thought that this virus was going to spread and it would take at least a year before it would peter out and I told him that just in case, I wanted to supply our house with everything we would need to stay inside for a year. He gave me that "look." And, I gave him another "look." I explained to him that if I was wrong, we would just have a year's worth of "everything" which we would eventually use. When all is said and done, Tom trusts my judgment. We set about buying what we might need which included the biggest upright freezer we could find. By February 28, 2020, we were done and had everything needed.

I contacted all my family and let them know what my suspicions were. Some of them laughed and thought I was losing it. A few prepared as best as their finances would allow.

On March 11, The World Health Organization declared Covid-19 a pandemic and on March 13th, President Trump declared a nationwide emergency, and soon afterward, the whole world shut down.

While the pandemic was horrendously stressful for many because they had to work and live in the world, Tom and I did not have to leave our safe little space. "We had no food worries and we were in need of nothing. Every ten days Tom would go to the store to buy fresh salad makings and when he brought them home I gave them a quick dunk in water with a tiny bit of bleach. We used wipes to sanitize our mail and every package we received. We were comfortable and made it through without fear other than what we had for our family and friends which I refused to think about. Just another one of those things that thinking about would not help anyone and, knowing the law of attraction, could only hurt us all.

I watched what happened in New York City and told Tom, "They are killing people with ventilators!" There were a lot of "wonky" things going on it seemed. How do you keep your mind from noticing things when doing so only adds to their manifestation?

I busied myself with making a bunch of clothes for me and Tom. I had a lot of material in my craft room that had been waiting for some free time to make it into something. I made dresses and pantsuits and a matching shirt for Tom.

Fortunately for us, I have always been Tom's barber. I have cut his hair since we met, so he didn't need to go out for that. I know many people were really desperate to get out and get a haircut, but we didn't have that problem. I also did my own hair and hair color so no problem there. The only thing I could not do myself was my acrylic nails, so I let them go natural. We could catch up on that kind of thing when the pandemic was over.

My sister Teri sent me a picture of a rooster that she wanted me to paint for her, plus, I decided to do a set of paintings for my great-grandkids and my son and daughter, like the ones that I had painted for Tami and Andy when they were little. It was a set of four pictures of cute little dogs in different clothes. I think I made six sets of four pictures each. That took a bit of time. I sent them out as Christmas gifts.

I had not cut my hair for many years because of dancing the Hula and it was way-down past my butt. So, in November of 2020, I finally cut it. My hair had started to thin a bit and I wasn't liking the texture of it. I kind of thought it had been dyed a time or two too many. I had never allowed my hair to go gray and I probably never will because for most women, I think it just makes them look washed out and old. No, I will not go, silently, into that dark night, but hats off to those who don't mine their grey.

I had thought about cutting it many times, but at the last minute I would always chicken out. Since I wasn't dancing the Hula anymore, I decided it was time. I put my hair in a ponytail, took a pair of scissors and quickly cut it off before I could change my mind. I hacked off about 27 inches of hair. Everyone was shocked that I had done it when I posted it on social media, (Facebook and the like). What was done was done!

Early in 2021 my old cat "Fluffy" died. I have always had cats. Fluffy had been with me for more than 16 years. He had been a faithful friend. I love it when a cat lays on your chest and purrs. I think it is healing. I would certainly miss my healing with fluffy.

I had another cat named "Dinky" that had been given to me by my friend, Mac. Her gardener had found the cat in the wheel well of his truck and they needed to find a home for him. Mac called me to see if I would take the cat and I had agreed on the condition that it had to get along with Fluffy. She and her husband, Dave brought the cat over and it ran and hid under my bed and didn't come out for days. I don't know if it was because of being in the wheel well of the truck or something else, but the poor cat was just terrified of everything. After Fluffy died I thought Dinky might get better, but instead, he got worse. He would no longer go outside or go in his cat box. After a few months we decided to find him another home where, hopefully, he wouldn't be so traumatized.

We went through the pandemic for a year without much discomfort. It was more of a "staycation" than anything. Tom did a lot in the yard and I always have loads of stuff to do. I find that if you are prepared, you just don't experience as much trauma.

I started making Christmas presents for my kids and grandkids. When my granddaughters were little, I used to have a plastic goose that sat on the doorstep. The goose had outfits for all the holidays. The girls would all spend hours dressing that goose. It had always been a favorite thing at grandma's house. I thought I would get a goose for each of the girls and make outfits for each goose. Six geese times twelve outfits each makes seventy-two outfits. What was I thinking of? I jumped in and started.

In February of 2021, we had purchased a travel trailer and planned to go wandering for about three months. We didn't think it would be good for Dinky to stay home by himself or to take him in the trailer with us. So, we found a family who wanted him and surprisingly enough, it seemed to work out. If I'd have known he would do better somewhere else, I would have given him away sooner.

We didn't get another cat because we had planned yet another big trip around the country.

Tom got the Moderna vaccination in January, but I wasn't going to get it because it was too new and too different. I'm not big on vaccinations, but in May, I finally got the one-shot, Johnson & Johnson vaccine. We would be traveling and seeing our great-grandchildren. Tom finally badgered me into it and I finally acquiesced saying, "OK, but if it kills me, it's YOUR fault." Yes, I am a bit evil!

June 2, 2021, we set out on another adventure to see the remainder of the states that we hadn't yet seen. Of course, we started out by visiting our kids, grandkids and great-grandkids. We went to Gibbs Gardens in Georgia which is an absolutely beautiful place with ponds that reminded me of a Degas painting. We went to "Dollywood," in Tennessee. Having worked with Dolly Parton years ago, it was a definite must. Of course, we went to the "Grand Ole Opry." We spent a day in the Belmont Mansion which was owned by Adelicia Acklen Hayes, who at one time was the wealthiest woman in Tennessee. Then on to Andrew Jackson's "Hermitage," the home of the people's President. It was again, another opportunity to walk in the home and gardens of a "distant in history" President. Then on to "Parker Crossing," a civil war battleground, The James K. Polk Home, A doll museum that looked to have every doll ever manufactured, Loretta Lynn's Ranch with a replica coal mine like the one her father worked in. Her "Mansion" was fabulous on the outside but quaint on the inside. On to the "First Home of William Jefferson Clinton." Then we went to "Texarkana" and stood on the state line separating Texas and Arkansas. We had worked on a TV show with the same name and in it, the whole town was divided by a line right through stores and homes. It was interesting just to be in the place that inspired the story. Next, we visited with two granddaughters in Texas. Then on to Waco, Texas, and The Magnolia Table for breakfast. We also visited the Chip & Joanna

Gains “Fixer Upper” Silos. We had a great dinner and show at Dolly Parton’s “Stampede” and the next day on to see four more great-grandkids in Missouri. Next was the home of President Truman and then on to a Fabulous National Museum of Toys & Miniatures in Kansas City, Missouri which was a surprisingly fabulous place. A quick stop at a “Frontier Fort” with live buffalo and then on to the biggest Buffalo Statue. We visited the Memorial graves of “Custer’s Last Stand.” More museums and on to Yellowstone National Park. Of course, we saw "Old Faithful" and “Grand Prismatic Springs.” The Grand Teton Mountains were spectacular and of special interest to me because I had done a painting of the mountains from a magazine picture, years ago. We fished here and there and went to a huge dinosaur dig. We panned for gold and found a “bit of color.” Had a nice stop at the Idaho Potato Museum where we stopped to eat some “Tater Tots.” The Museum of Clean was our next stop where we were thoroughly entertained by Don Aslett, the museum’s owner who has a wonderful sense of humor and every vacuum ever made. We made it to a museum of "Gas Pumps and Signs," and then a stop to spend a few days with my daughter, Tami in Fresno, California. We spent a day at the Nixon Library. Then a nice visit with my son, Andy in southern California. More fishing and a “Car Museum” on old Route 66. A visit to “Meteor Crater” which is HUGE. Next, we followed Route 66 to Winslow, Arizona to the “Standing on the Corner” park inspired by the “Take it Easy” sung by the Eagles. A drive through “The Petrified Forrest” and “The Painted Desert.” Nashville’s “The Parthenon" is a replica of the one in Athens, Greece - well, that saved us a trip!

Three months later we arrived back home. They say you will love or hate a travel trailer. We loved it. We had made all the changes to it that ensured that we would. In a 33-foot trailer, we had two bedrooms and three TVs. What's not to love with that?

As soon as we got home, we jumped on an airplane and flew to Seattle Washington to board a cruise ship to Alaska. Tom had been there before, but it was my 50th state. Alaska was .... COLD. Nonetheless, we got to ride on a dog sled and saw the glaciers. We were both done with that item on our bucket list. It was a fabulous adventure and one I will never forget.

Several years ago, my sister Teri and I started buying a "Christmas Ornament" at each of the places we had traveled to. I had a load of them from this trip.

Having the trailer had made it possible to pretty much stay away from people and keep us safe and on a good diet. We did put on about ten pounds extra which I had lost in a couple of weeks being back home and eating just my cooking.

When we got back in September, I shared all my adventures with my sister, Teri. She wasn't doing very well. She was on oxygen all the time now and the doctor put her on steroids and just like my brother, Pat, she had that "moon face." I was surprised to see how much she had changed since the pandemic had hit.

Since she had moved to Florida, we had enjoyed outings together. We often took my grandkids to amusement parks and the like and often just she and I would sneak off to go to one of the Disney parks. We even, finally, got those Mickey Mouse ears we had always wanted. There we were, ladies in their seventies standing in line to have our ears embroidered with our names.... At last!

On November 21, 2021, Teri's husband, Jerry, called and told me that Teri was in the hospital and he didn't think she was going to make it. He said she was unconscious when they took her to the hospital in an ambulance. I asked if she was awake now and could I talk to her and he said he wasn't at the hospital. I was a bit alarmed by that because I don't believe in leaving anyone at the hospital by themselves. I remember what happened to my mother. I told him I would go right to the hospital which was about an hour's drive away.

When I got to the hospital and was taken to her bed in the ER, she was alert and talking. She said she was very uncomfortable and wanted out of there. I went to talk to the nurse in charge. She wasn't at her station, so I read Teri's chart. Teri had pneumonia and was given antibiotics, but was negative for Covid-19.

I went back to Teri and told her what the report said. Teri was trying to take the oxygen off. I tried to get her to keep it on. Then she said she wanted Jerry. I called Jerry and told him he should come down, that Teri wanted him.

They wouldn't let both of us stay in the room, so I went out telling Jerry that Tom and I would go get breakfast and then be back.

We went to a local restaurant, but barely got seated when Jerry called. He said Teri wanted out of the hospital and was going to sign herself out. Jerry needed Tom to help him get her in the car. We left right away and went back to the hospital.

When we got to the hospital they were wheeling Teri out in a wheelchair. Tom and Jerry got her in the car with her oxygen bottle and we drove the fifteen minutes to Teri and Jerry's house. Jerry parked on the lawn so he could get Teri right up to the steps and then Tom and Jerry were able to get her in the house. She was very unsteady on her legs. She went right to her office and got on the computer. I don't know if she called her son or if he called her, but they talked for a bit. He was upset that she had left the hospital and wanted her to go back. Teri was firm, saying she had been an EMT and knew what was best for her. I guess we are both a bit stubborn.

Pretty soon Teri said she wanted to lie down, so Tom helped her into her room and into bed. It was tough. I don't know how much Teri weighed, but it looked to be over two hundred pounds. She was gasping for air by the time we got her settled. By that time, the woman who helped her clean house and such came and helped get her oxygen on right.

Teri looked very tired and very spent. She held my hand and at one point she looked up at me, squeezed my hand and said, "Thank you for everything you have done for me." I kissed her on the forehead and left for her to rest. We both said, "I love you" and I told her I would be back the next day.

The next morning, I called Jerry to see how she was doing. Jerry said she was fine and had slept through the night. He said she was cold so he had put a heating pad on her. Well, of course you know I was alerted. First off, my sister hadn't slept the night through in years. I hung up and called Teri's house friend, Dawn and asked if she would "go over and put her eyes on Teri?" A few minutes later, Jerry called to tell me that Teri had died in the night. My beautiful sister was gone. Of us three little urchins who had survived the farm, I was now the only one left.

My sister had six kids all together and they had planned to come out for Thanksgiving. When Teri died, they came out anyway because they had already paid for their condominium. The original plan was that they, including Teri, were going to take the grandkids to Disney World. I think that was why Teri wanted out of the hospital. She didn't want to miss out.

In some way, I think Teri died, not from Covid-19 but from the Covid-19 pandemic. Being locked up and alone for two years had taken a toll on her. Of course, we talked on the phone nearly every day, but it wasn't a celebration of life that she talked about. It was how terrible everything was and how bitter and neglected she felt. I think she had been through so much, that she had not dealt with, that in the end, that was all that was left for her. Her life seemed just a tragedy.

In January of 2022, they had a memorial service for my sister in California because most of her family lived there. It was for Teri's children and grandchildren to say their last goodbye and find some closure. I did not go to the service. Teri and I had said our goodbye the day before she passed. I can't help but think Teri knew she was dying and took that opportunity to thank me and for us to say one last "I love You, I love you more." I prefer to keep that memory. I did write a poem to be read at her service. I will put it here as a memorial to my sister.

A Sister's Goodbye

By Claudia Gilligan 1921

Sister, my sister, what can I say
You have left me, left me and now gone away.

So many memories, throughout the years
So many memories and so many tears.

Life wasn't easy, nor was it kind.
But we held it together, most of the time.

Big sister, little sister never apart
Big sister, little, a part of my heart.

Our teen years not fancy but still had some fun
Laughing and dancing, out on the run.

Then we had babies and a whole 'nother life.
We were now mamas and some young man's wife.

That didn't work well, back out on our own.
Struggling, struggling to make us a home.

No one had taught us because no one was there
We just held to each other for most of our care.

We cherished our children and just did our best.
There was no practice, we went right to the test.

Like a little old tub in an all mighty sea,
We were tossed all about, you, Pat and me.

Life goes by quickly, overnight we are old.
And life missed the promise the old movies told.

It's the good times I cherish, the fun that we had,
Christmas and Easter, July 4th for dad.

I miss you my sister, so hard to say bye.
Somehow, I can't think but what I just cry.

Sister, my sister, what can I say
How sad, very sad that you've now gone away.

Claudia Gilligan

Sister Teri's memorial

November 21, 2021

Tom and I at Dollywood for our 33 Wedding Anniversary.
And they all said it wouldn't last!
Claudia age 74

Chapter 48

Seventy-Five and Counting

March 21, 2022, was my 75th birthday. But my mind still says I'm 28. I don't feel old and I'm looking forward to the future and more great-grandbabies, more parties, more learning and more adventures.

As I have taken this look back at my life, I have seen patterns. I can see the "law of attraction" winding in and out of my life. You may scoff, but I see it as clear as day. The law of attraction is a belief that, "What you think and feel attracts like energy into your experience." It is a bit more complicated than that, but not much. The law of attraction does not care if you are rich or poor, black or white, educated or ignorant. It is just like gravity. What you sew, is what you reap. A thought held is a thing created. It's not about being good or bad. As Warner Erhard used to say, "What's so is what's so!" Or as Bob Procter is known to say, "The Law of Attraction doesn't care if you are thinking, get into debt or get out of debt, if you are thinking 'debt,' debt is what you are attracting!"

I have read and studied much on this subject and have spent so much of my life attempting to master the principles. I have presented my life story as I lived it. These were my true perceptions at the time, but I have come to a much more profound understanding of what is true and that I am only a victim in my own mind and decisions. I don't mean that the things I have written are not accurate. All the things written here happened as told. Nor do I mean that the characters involved are absolved of their deeds. Nor do I mean that I am "at fault" for the bad that has happened in my life. I only mean that I am "responsible" for what has occurred in my life. I am "able to respond" to what has happened in my life and my choice of response will determine what will happen next in my life. There is a profound difference.

One of my teachers, Dr. Sue Morter, is a great teacher, not because she knew it all or because she got it all right, but because she was willing to share her struggle with good and evil (positive and negative energy) right in front of me. In her struggle, she taught me to resist the temptation of the negative and aspire to hold love in my heart in the face of adversity. That is not an easy thing to do and perhaps, at least for me, it takes a lifetime to master.

I think it started with "flopping down in that hospital crib," when I was but two years old. My mother wrote in my baby book that in July of 1949, I had Measles, Whooping Cough Pneumonia and dehydration. I don't know how I attracted that or if it was a function of my mother's fear, having lost her first child, which would have been a powerful creator. My mother would have been 29 years old with two other kids at home, including my seven-month-old brother, Pat. She left me in the hospital and I was so distraught that I flopped down in that bed feeling totally "abandoned." And that one act set the tone for so much of my life. How many times have I experienced "abandonment?" Most of my husbands abandoned me in one way or another. I think I carried that little fit, I had, just a little bit too far and when I put the emotions of judgment with that, I created a powerful spell over my life. I continued to create further by re-living my tragic story in my head.

At 15 years old, I wrote in my baby book that my ambitions were to be an actress, dancer, poet, writer, housewife, and millionaire. I later added, "working in some field of entertainment." Looking back, I have accomplished all of that. When I worked on the movie E.T. I was put in as one of the kids, in the Halloween scene, to toilet paper the camera. I have also written and played in many plays and productions which I have put on throughout my life. I have studied tap, ballet, belly, modern and hula dancing. That and my hula dancing for 12 years and all our performances at Disney certain qualifies me as a dancer. I might not have kept the money long, but we certainly reached the goal of millionaires. Poet, writer and housewife….. Check! And, working in "some field of entertainment?" I was a set painter, sign-writer and scenic artist in the Motion Picture and Television Industry for 30 years.

I had a heart attack, when, with all the desire in my body, I wanted to retire from the studios. I just didn't want to do it anymore and I didn't want to fight with Tom about it either. Be careful what you pray for, you might not like HOW it comes to you.

The time I spent reading my, "Stoddard's Lectures," set me up for my globe-trotting adventures. And yes, even my daughter's paralysis comes from my deep desire to rescue her from drug addiction, and her desire as well. Today, she is paralyzed but safe! Be careful and specific about what you pray for, because it might come true. Not bad or good, it's just what's so!

In 1947, the year I was born, the "Dead Sea Scrolls" were found in the Qumran Caves near the Dead Sea. They were written in many languages, dating back to the 3rd century BCE, by a mystical Jewish sect known as the Essenes. I won't go much further to explain them other than to say that I believe our understanding of the "Law of Attraction," as we know it today, came from some of those writings.

From these esoteric teachings, I have come to believe in what is known as, "The Seven Essene Mirrors." These mirrors "reflect" the lessons we need to learn in this life. As I have said, we live in a world dominated by the Law of Attraction. The true explanation of the Essene Mirrors is much bigger than what I can put here as it would take a book in itself to fully explain. I will only offer a brief glimpse of my understanding of their meaning. If interested, there are many books of study that will serve you.

The Seven Essene Mirrors

1. The 1st mirror reflects the moment of now: What we are right now. When negative shows up in our life, we have an opportunity to look back and see where we created it with our negative thinking and judgments. It gives us an opportunity to correct that thinking so that the situation will clear up in the matter of living. "To thine own self be true" and "the truth will set you free." You cannot change something you cannot acknowledge. Do you tell yourself the truth or make excuses for your behavior?

2. The 2nd mirror reflects everything that we judge, decide, feel, or know and has a profound effect on what will show up next in our life. It might not be right away, but if you think, believe or feel it, you create it, to a lesser or greater extent. To me, emotion is: Thought faster than the speed of words! Whatever you create is out there, in the world, waiting….. waiting for you. I never want to create a rule for someone else to live by, that I am not willing and able to live by myself. You don't need to be conscious of your judgments for them to reflect on you. They will just show up as to how you feel about yourself. Do you just feel unworthy?

3. The 3rd mirror reflects things we have lost. This is often about noticing things in other people that we admire or are jealous of. These are things we have lost or they have never been a quality in ourselves. If we notice this, we can begin to become who we want to be; eventually becoming whole and perfect. "You don't have to go looking for love when love is where you come from." Are you jealous of others?

4. The 4th mirror reflects our compulsions. At times we blind ourselves to our true path by taking a divergent path. This can lead to addiction or compulsions. It gives us something "else" to do besides what we should be doing. You may be stuck in this reflection for a few days or a lifetime. It is always for you to notice and correct your path. "What you resist will persist." Are you indulging in a compulsion?

5. The 5th mirror reflects our image of our mother and father. It originates with the image we have of our parents but is about our relationship with the "divine" in ourselves. Our self-nurturing. Beyond a few years at the beginning of our life, we are responsible for our own nurturing. We are the parent and the child and switch places, many times in life. Love yourself as you would your child.

6. The 6th mirror reflects the "Dark Night of the Soul." This is the opportunity to become either an inspired person of love or a victim. Letting go of hurts or offenses gives us power. "Forgive us our trespasses as we forgive those who have trespassed against us." Dr. Sue Morter is a master of this one. Remember, no one comes into this life saying, "Oh boy, I hope I get to be an asshole when I grow up!"

7. The 7th mirror reflects ourselves. How we perceive ourselves is how the world will perceive us, as well. Learning to be kind to oneself is not a function of selfishness, but a function of the divine in us all. Judging ourselves is still judgment. Recognizing this and learning to truly love myself was one of the most difficult things for me to do.

You can spend a lifetime in these reflections, and it is a journey. At times I have been at full actualization of these principles and I feel strong and resilient and loving and generous. At other times, I get lost in the everyday world and forget all about them. I read a great book once called, "Chop Wood, Carry Water," which is about living in our everyday world while maintaining a sense of the divine. It is easy to be very spiritual when you can sit under the Yum Yum tree and contemplate your navel, but it is quite another thing, all together, when the kids are crying, the boss is yelling at you or your husband is drunk and obnoxious. But, then, this is the challenge of life.

I have several times "awoke" to find that years have passed while I was in a blind state of passing time without any awareness of the divinity of life. I just want to stay in a state of compassion, understanding, forgiveness and love but sometimes find myself unkind, angry, resentful, and unforgiving. Perhaps that is just the "wheel of life." Perhaps it is necessary for some reason. I just don’t like it.... Oops, what I mean is "it is just another learning opportunity!" I don't want to attract things that I don’t like!

A simple misinterpreted word can lead us into the blind unknown. You can walk by a TV and be programmed by something your mind hears, that you are completely unaware of. That is, I think, why I love Hawaiian music. It is, for the most part, about beauty and love. I mute or turn off most ads when watching TV because so many of them suggest one is depressed, anxious, has restless leg syndrome, constipation or worse. I don't want any of that, so I don't listen to it. You might not think it affects you, but some of those commercials play over and over and over. For this same reason, I don't indulge in watching "horror" movies. I don't think the mind can, at times, distinguish between "real" and "portrayed" events. In some way, our minds believe we are actually experiencing the events. I know this because of the times when I have watched something only to have adrenalin shoot right down to my hands to ready me for flight or fight. I don't think that is good for us. I think there is enough tragedy that we manifest in life without borrowing more. I guess it is there because someone needs it to work out their stuff in life, but I don't.

Because of my understanding of the "Law of Attraction," and resolving so much in my life, I, for the most part, have lived a charmed life and I truly live better than most queens throughout history. You might laugh, but I am quite serious. What queen has ever had all the luxuries and conveniences that we have today? When I think of all the great things I have been witness to, in my lifetime, I am in awe. The first man walking on the moon, computers, the internet, cell phones and so much more. Coming from living on a farm that had no plumbing, and only an outhouse, to now I have a $400 toilet seat that washes my derrière, and blows it dry with warm air. One just has to laugh. I am privileged!

I have seen so much of this world that it is kind of mind-boggling. Just the fact that I have visited every state in the United States is beyond what most people will ever experience, and certainly more than most people who came before me. I have met so many famous people including The President of the United States. I have taken more courses and learned more things than most people can even imagine. At one point I put certificates on the wall, but then there just wasn't enough wall so I took them all down.

I remember one person saying to me once, and not in kindness, "do you ever make a mistake or are you just good at everything?" I told them that it is all an illusion. If you attempt enough things, it will create the illusion that you can do anything. I just try more things than most people, and I fail at a few. I remember once I was making peanut brittle and didn't cook it long enough. It turned out more like "peanut taffy." I laughed and thought I wanted to share it with people who thought I didn't make mistakes. I actually called a company that made "bronzed baby shoes," and asked them if they could bronze my failed peanut brittle. The guy laughed and said no, the bronze would melt the peanut brittle and just make a mess. I was disappointed but later thought, "I bet I could bronze that peanut brittle if I put my mind to it!" Laugh-Out-Loud, that is just how my brain works.

I wish I could say that I am able to forgive all the people that have hurt me in life, but I am no saint yet. I try, I really do and sometimes I feel like I succeed. But, then something happens and I'm right back where I started. Some lessons must be learned over and over before we get it. Pray for me.

In truth, this isn't just a book about me, no book could be. It is about the interactions and reactions I have to the world and people around me. We all live in a cohesive world, we are all stuck together. What affects one in some way affects us all.

I like to focus on healthy people in my life. I have some friends, Kaua and John, who are just such healthy and happy people. They focus their life on their four children and on helping others. They are always available to lend a hand. I didn't have positive role models growing up, so when I find them, I really admire, respect and appreciate them.

Another couple I admire is Shirdawn and JJ. They have adopted, I don't know, a dozen children. Whenever I look at their Facebook pages, their focus is on these children. All these children are in sports and healthy activities. I know JJ works long, hard days because he works in the same industry that I worked in. That leaves the day to day care to Shirdawn. She is truly a mother worthy of emulating. They have opened their hearts to so many. They are truly great role models. If you don't feel you have good role models in your life, look for one outside your family circle.

Both my son and daughter are people I look up to and am very proud of. They have endured the "back-story" of their lives and are compassionate and loving people. The kind of people I truly admire.

So, what of the future? I have been studying stem cell therapy and other things that might extend life beyond our "life expectancy" of eighty-three years. I have always maintained that I will live to the age of 125 or better, so of course, this type of thing comes to my attention. And, I'm sure the "Law of Attraction" will see that I get there. One of my grandmothers lived to be well into her ninety's and much has changed in medicine since then.

Today I am grateful for everything in my life. The good the bad and the ugly. If it weren't for the negative, I would not be who I am today. I am very grateful for my children who have taught me as much as I have taught them. I am grateful for all the opportunities I have been given throughout my life. I am even, somewhat, grateful to all the men who dominated or abused me because they are why I am the strong, independent, and self-assured woman that I am today. I am not a victim, nor am I merely a survivor. I am a victor!

I am grateful for all the teachers I have found in my life including my best friends, Nova, Paula and Marlene who have passed on but will never be forgotten. I am so truly grateful for all the friends who are in my life now. I am grateful for all the teachers who have shared their wisdom with me in person or through all those books I have been privileged to read.

Most of all, I am grateful for my wonderful husband, Tom, who has walked beside me for over 35 years. We have had some issues, but I always know that, aside from the male ego stuff that runs most men, he is truly there for me. The man who has stood beside me in the darkest of times, laughed with me in the lightest of times and who I really FEEL loves me.

Ah, if only I knew back then what I know now. Probably the only regret I have in life is that there are so many people that I haven't been able to help with all that I have learned. Even though I have presented all the information I have acquired to others, sometimes repeatedly, and yet they can't hear. But maybe it is just because they have their own path and I have mine. What is left to say except …. What a journey!

A Path Well Traveled

All souls suffer and all souls know
Yet each to the other denies it so.
Denial’s game in play each day
Sad eyes turn and walk away.

Each one looking for passion's truth
Horrendous childhood and tragic youth.
All born gentle of soul and mind,
Learns to leave it all behind.

Where did our world go so astray,
That dreams of love in words decay?
Passing shadows of its demise
Is seen in sad and lonely eyes.

Wandering down my path in time
A crooked path without design.
Yet seers of a by-gone past
Awakes to light the way at last.

Salvation's nod to clear the haze
Renews the dream of other days.
And reveals the mysteries unraveled
While traveling down a path well-traveled.

Claudia Gilligan 2022

Well, that's my story. I guess all that is left to do is to adjust my crown and continue on my journey down "A Path Well Traveled."

Filmography

2004 - Torque - Movie

2003 - Alias - TV Series

2002 - 2003 - Hotel - TV Movie

2001 - Stop at Nothing - TV Movie

2000 - 2001 - Titans - TV Series

2000 - Cruel Intentions 2 - Video

1999 - The 13th Warrior - Movie

1998 - Texarkana - TV Movie

1998 - Phycho - TV Movie

1995 -1997 - Deadly Games - TV Series

1997 - Gone Fishn' - Movie

1997 - Beautician and the Beast - Movie

1995 - Angus - Movie

1995 - The Four Diamonds - TV Movie

1993 - The Firm - Movie

1992 - Buffy the Vampire Slayer - Movie

1991 - Doc Hollywood - Movie

1990 - Three Men and a Little Lady - Movie

1987 - 1989 - Matlock - TV Series

1987 - Max Headroom - TV Series

1987 - Prince of Darkness - Movie

1986 - American Anthem - Movie

1985 - Prizzi's Honor - Movie

1985 - Solomon's Universe - Movie

1984 - 2010 - Movie

1984 - Hard to Hold - Movie

1984 - A Streetcar Named Desire - TV Movie

1983 - Cracking up - Movie

1982 - E.T. the Extra-terrestrial - Movie

1981 - Fire on the Mountain - TV Movie

1980 - 9 to 5 - Movie

1975 - 1979 - Starsky and Hutch - TV Series

1979 - Friends - TV Series

1979 - Hart to Hart - TV Series

1979 - Charlie's Angels - TV Series

1978 - Fantasy Island - TV Series

1978 - Six Million Dollar Man -TV Series

1978 - Coming Home - Movie

1978 - The Love Boat - TV Series

1977 - High Anxiety - Movie

1977 - The San Pedro Bums - TV Series

1977 - Family - TV Series

1977 - The Rockford Files - TV Series

1976 - Captain and the Kings - TV Mini Series

1976 - Gray Lady Down - Movie

1976 - Columbo - TV Series

1976 - Emergency - TV Series